Scottish Independence and the Idea of Britain

From the Picts to Alexander III

Dauvit Broun

EDINBURGH
University Press

© Dauvit Broun, 2007, 2013

First published in hardback in 2007 by
Edinburgh University Press Ltd
22 George Square, Edinburgh EH8 9LF
www.euppublishing.com

This paperback edition 2013

Typeset in 10.5/13 Sabon
by Servis Filmsetting Ltd, Manchester, and
printed and bound in Great Britain by
CPI Group (UK) Ltd, Croydon CR0 4YY

A CIP record for this book is available from the British Library

ISBN 978 0 7486 2360 0 (hardback)
ISBN 978 0 7486 8519 6 (paperback)
ISBN 978 0 7486 3011 0 (webready PDF)
ISBN 978 0 7486 8520 2 (epub)

The right of Dauvit Broun to be identified as author of this work has been
asserted in accordance with the Copyright, Designs and Patents Act 1988.

Contents

Preface and Acknowledgements

Most books by academics these days owe at least their date of publication to the Research Assessment Exercise. This one, however, would not have existed without it. Since the last RAE I have pursued the theme of this book in a number of articles, but without giving any thought to bringing them together. They could not easily be made into a collection of essays because there is too much overlap between a few of them and in others only some parts were relevant to this particular theme. The RAE requires each member of staff to submit four pieces of work, and it dawned on me that this would allow little scope to indicate that I have been working on the subject of this book, especially if berths were to be found for the fruits of other projects. It is difficult to exaggerate the importance of a successful outcome in the RAE for our institutions and for the continuing viability of our disciplines, so there was nothing else for it but to draw the material together so they could find a home together when it came to identifying four items for assessment. In the end, about half of the book consists of repeats of material that has been published since the last RAE. The opportunity has been taken to expand or contract some sections, correct errors, update references and reduce the number of collateral footnotes, so there is no item that has been reproduced exactly as it first appeared. That is not to say that what follows supersedes the originals. In all but two cases (chapters 4 and 7) the original articles have sections on matters beyond the scope of this book: if you want to find out why I have argued that Cinaed mac Ailpín was a Pict, for example, you will need to look up the article from which most of chapter 3 has been derived; or if you wish to read about the kingdom of Strathclyde, you will need to look at the article from which much of chapter 5 has been extracted. I am very grateful to the editors and publishers of the articles reproduced in chapters 3, 4, 5 and 7 for their very ready cooperation in this, particularly Professor Thomas Owen Clancy, Professor John Gillingham, Professor James Kirk, Dr Pamela O'Neill, Caroline Palmer and Professor David Wright. I am particularly grateful to John Davey of EUP for his encouragement of this project from the outset.

The full list of material extracted from previously published articles in this book is:

For chapters 3, 4, 5 and 7:

'Alba: Pictish homeland or Irish offshoot?', in Pamela O'Neill (ed.), *Exile and Homecoming. Papers from the 5th Australian Conference of Celtic Studies, University of Sydney* (University of Sydney, 2005), 234–75: pp. 236–64 have been incorporated into chapter 3.

'The Church and the origins of Scottish independence in the twelfth century', *Records of the Scottish Church History Society* 31 (2002) 1–35: pp. 3–35 have been incorporated into chapter 4.

'The Welsh identity of the kingdom of Strathclyde, *ca* 900–*ca* 1200', *Innes Review* 55 (2004) 111–80: pp. 122–3, 141–70 and a passage at 117 have been incorporated into chapter 5.

'The absence of regnal years from the dating clause of charters of kings of Scots, 1195–1222', John Gillingham (ed.), *Anglo-Norman Studies XXV* (Woodbridge, 2003), 47–63: pp. 48–63 have been incorporated into chapter 7.

Parts of chapter 6 have been derived from:

'The origin of the Stone of Scone as a national icon', in David Breeze, T. O. Clancy and Richard Welander (eds), *The Stone of Destiny: Artefact and Icon*, Society of Antiquaries Monograph Series no. 22 (Edinburgh, 2003), 183–97: pp. 186–90, a passage in 191, and 192 (also a passage in 185 in chapter 8).

'The Welsh identity of the kingdom of Strathclyde, *ca* 900–*ca* 1200', *Innes Review* 55 (2004) 111–80: pp. 171–80.

Occasional passages have also been re-used from:

'The Picts' place in the kingship's past before John of Fordun', in Edward J. Cowan and Richard J. Finlay (eds), *Scottish History: the Power of the Past* (Edinburgh, 2002), 11–28: a passage at 17, and another at 26–7.

'The Declaration of Arbroath: pedigree of a nation?', in G. W. S. Barrow (ed.), *The Declaration of Arbroath: History, Significance, Setting*, Society of Antiquaries (Edinburgh, 2003), 1–12: a passage at 2–3 and another at 7.

It is a great pleasure to thank those who have helped me in writing this book, and to thank again those who read and commented on the original versions of the material reproduced here. First in importance has been Nerys Ann Jones, whose constant support and encouragement is deeply appreciated, especially as this book neared completion. I must also thank her for helping to improve the prose of chapter 10. Alex Woolf very kindly read over chapter 1 for me, and also earlier versions of chapters 3, 4 and 5, providing me with many invaluable comments and criticisms. I also owe him specific thanks for making me realise the meagre evidential base for Stainmore as Strathclyde's southern limit. Similar generosity and kindness have been shown me by Thomas Clancy in early versions of chapters 3–6, and by Simon Taylor in previous versions of chapters 3 and 5. Without the friendship and help of this formidable trio my work would be very much poorer. I am also grateful to Archie Duncan for his friendship and support, and for reading a version of chapter 5 and sharing his work on Alexander III's inauguration before publication. Geoffrey Barrow and Rees Davies kindly read an earlier version of chapter 4, to my great benefit, and Norman Shead read chapter 5 and saved it from error, for which I am extremely grateful. I am also enormously grateful to Huw Pryce for reading over and helping substantially with an earlier version of chapter 7, and to Keith Stringer for very generously sharing his unrivalled knowledge of the charters of Alexander II and saving me from grievous error. I am also grateful to John Hudson for discussion of some key points. The chapter where I was most dependent on help and support was the previous version of chapter 5. I am particularly grateful to Emilia Jamroziak and Raymond McCluskey for reading and commenting so promptly and helpfully on the sections relating to Pomerania and Spain, and I am especially grateful to Betty Knott and Greta-Mary Hair for allowing me to use their forthcoming edition of the Office of Kentigern, and to Greta-Mary Hair for her willingness to talk me through it and answer questions. I am also grateful for stimulating discussion with my fellow workers in the field of medieval Scottish historiography, particularly to Alice Taylor and Nicola Royan who each work at either end of the tradition of writing on the kingship's history begun in the twelfth century and culminating in Boece. The person in this small field who I would like to thank most of all is Steve Boardman, who has suffered unflinchingly from listening to my half-formed notions and who has given so much friendship and inspiration in return. The whole thrust of this book as an exploration of the mental landscapes inhabited by our medieval forbears – of their 'being-in-the-world' – with an appreciation of their horizons and celebration of their capacity to innovate within established frameworks, originates in the inspiration and enthusiasm of my teacher, Walter Ullmann, who supervised my first investigation of the Scottish royal inauguration ritual. I dedicate this book to his memory in everlasting gratitude.

Dauvit Broun
The Feast of Gilbert of Caithness 2006

Abbreviations

APS, i.	Thomas Thomson and Cosmo Innes (eds), *Acts of the Parliament of Scotland*, vol. i, AD *MCXXIV*–AD *MCCCCXXIII* (Edinburgh, 1844)
AT	Whitley Stokes, 'The Annals of Tigernach. Third fragment AD 489–766'. *Revue celtique* 17 (1896) 119–263; 'The Annals of Tigernach. The fourth fragment AD 973–AD 1088', *Revue celtique* 17 (1896) 337–420; 'The Annals of Tigernach. The continuation AD 1088–1178', *Revue celtique* 18 (1897) 9–59, 150–97, 268–303.
AU	S. Mac Airt and G. Mac Niocaill (eds), *The Annals of Ulster (to AD 1131). Part I: Text and Translation* (Dublin, 1983)
BBCS	*Bulletin of the Board of Celtic Studies*
ByS	Thomas Jones (ed.), *Brenhinedd y Saesson or The Kings of the Saxons* (Cardiff, 1971)
ByT (Pen. 20, gol.)	Thomas Jones (gol.), *Brut y Tywysogion Peniarth MS. 20* (Caerdydd, 1941)
ByT (Pen. 20, trans.)	Thomas Jones (trans.), *Brut y Tywysogion or The Chronicle of the Princes. Peniarth MS. 20 Version* (Cardiff, 1952)
ByT (RB)	Thomas Jones (ed.), *Brut y Tywysogion or The Chronicle of the Princes. Red Book of Hergest Version* (Cardiff, 1955)
Chron Fordun i.	W. F. Skene (ed.), *Johannis de Fordun Chronica Gentis Scotorum* (Edinburgh, 1871)
Chron Fordun ii.	Felix J. H. Skene (trans.), *John of Fordun's Chronicle of the Scottish Nation*, ed. W. F. Skene (Edinburgh, 1872)
CMCS	*Cambridge/Cambrian Medieval Celtic Studies*
CS	W. M. Hennessey (ed.), *Chronicum Scotorum. A Chronicle of Irish Affairs from the Earliest Times to AD 1135, with a supplement, containing the events*

	from 1141 to 1150 (London, 1866)
EHR	*English Historical Review*
ES	Alan Orr Anderson, *Early Sources of Scottish History*, AD *500–1286*, 2 vols (Edinburgh, 1922)
Glas. Reg.	Cosmo Innes (ed.), *Registrum Episcopatus Glasguensis*, Maitland and Bannatyne Clubs, 2 vols (Glasgow and Edinburgh, 1843)
IR	*Innes Review*
JL	Ph. Jaffé, rev. Samuel Löwenfeld and others, *Regesta Pontificum Romanorum*, 2 vols (Leipzig, 1885–8)
LG	R. A. S. Macalister (ed.), *Lebor Gabála Érenn, The Book of the Taking of Ireland*, 5 vols, Irish Texts Society (London, 1938–56)
PBA	*Proceedings of the British Academy*
PL	J.-P. Migne, *Patrologiæ cursus completes . . . series Latina*, 221 vols (Paris).
Potthast	Augustus Potthast, *Regesta Pontificum Romanorum*, 2 vols (Berlin, 1874–5)
RCAHMS	The Royal Commission on the Ancient and Historical Monuments of Scotland
RRS, i.	G. W. S. Barrow (ed.), *Regesta Regum Scottorum*, vol. i, *The Acts of Malcolm IV King of Scots 1153–1165, together with Scottish Royal Acts prior to 1153 not included in Sir Archibald Lawrie's 'Early Scottish Charters'* (Edinburgh, 1960)
RRS, ii.	G. W. S. Barrow (ed.), with the collaboration of W. W. Scott, *Regesta Regum Scottorum*, vol. ii, *The Acts of William I, King of Scots 1165–1214* (Edinburgh, 1971)
RSCHS	*Records of the Scottish Church History Society*
S	http://www.trin.cam.ac.uk/charterwww/eSawyer.99/eSawyer2.html: The Electronic Sawyer: an on-line version of the revised edition of Sawyer's *Anglo-Saxon Charters* section one [S 1–1602] prepared under the auspices of the British Academy / Royal Historical Society Joint Committee on Anglo-Saxon Charters by S. E. Kelly and adapted for the WWW by S. M. Miller
SAEC	Alan Orr Anderson, *Scottish Annals from English Chroniclers*, AD *500 to 1286* (London, 1908)
SGS	*Scottish Gaelic Studies*

SHR	*Scottish Historical Review*
TCWAAS	*Transactions of the Cumberland and Westmorland Antiquarian and Archaeological Society*
TDGNHAS	*Transactions of the Dumfriesshire and Galloway Natural History and Antiquarian Society*
TGSI	*Transaction of the Gaelic Society of Inverness*
THSC	*Transactions of the Honourable Society of Cymmrodorion*
TRHS	*Transactions of the Royal Historical Society*

Sees of exempt dioceses beyond Italy, c. 1250

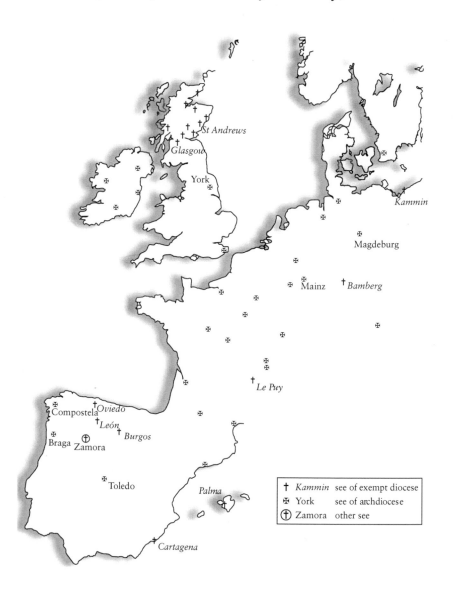

St Andrews
Glasgow
York
Kammin
Magdeburg
Mainz   Bamberg
Le Puy
Compostela Oviedo
León
Braga Burgos
Zamora
Toledo
Palma
Cartagena

† Kammin	see of exempt diocese
✠ York	see of archdiocese
✛ Zamora	other see

Kings of Scots, 1005–1286

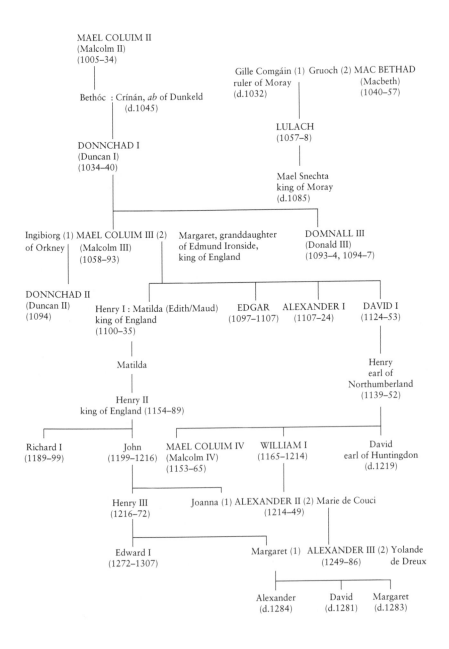

MAEL COLUIM II
(Malcolm II)
(1005–34)

Bethóc : Crínán, *ab* of Dunkeld
(d.1045)

Gille Comgáin (1) Gruoch (2) MAC BETHAD
ruler of Moray   (Macbeth)
(d.1032)   (1040–57)

DONNCHAD I
(Duncan I)
(1034–40)

LULACH
(1057–8)

Mael Snechta
king of Moray
(d.1085)

Ingibiorg (1) MAEL COLUIM III (2)   Margaret, granddaughter   DOMNALL III
of Orkney   (Malcolm III)   of Edmund Ironside,   (Donald III)
             (1058–93)   king of England   (1093–4, 1094–7)

DONNCHAD II
(Duncan II)   Henry I : Matilda (Edith/Maud)   EDGAR   ALEXANDER I   DAVID I
(1094)   king of England   (1097–1107) (1107–24)   (1124–53)
                (1100–35)

Matilda

Henry
earl of
Northumberland
(1139–52)

Henry II
king of England (1154–89)

Richard I   John   MAEL COLUIM IV   WILLIAM I   David
(1189–99)   (1199–1216)   (Malcolm IV)   (1165–1214)   earl of Huntingdon
                                 (1153–65)   (d.1219)

Henry III   Joanna (1) ALEXANDER II (2) Marie de Couci
(1216–72)   (1214–49)

Edward I   Margaret (1) ALEXANDER III (2) Yolande
(1272–1307)   (1249–86)   de Dreux

Alexander   David   Margaret
(d.1284)   (d.1281)   (d.1283)

1

Introduction

Writing about Scottish Aspirations to Independence before the Age of Robert Bruce and William Wallace

Hákon IV, king of Norway (1217–63), left nothing to chance in securing an orderly succession to the throne on his death. According to the saga of his life, the elderly king arranged for his son, Magnús, to be crowned on 14 September 1261, taking care that the ceremony was a replica of Hákon's own coronation and anointment in 1247 by the papal legate William of Sabina.[1] But there was one person standing up in the choir of the church whose presence in Norway at this time had not been planned. A Scottish knight (called 'Missel' in the saga), along with a 'certain archdeacon', had been sent by Alexander III as envoys to the king of Norway; their attempt in July to escape back to Scotland without Hákon's permission had been foiled, and Hákon had ordered them to be detained over the winter.[2] From his vantage-point the Scottish knight was able to see Magnús's consecration at the altar, and was deeply moved. 'He wondered greatly', we are told, 'because it was not the custom to crown kings in Scotland'; and, according to the fullest account of the saga, 'he was so greatly pleased with the consecration that he wept'.[3] The mention of the knight's tears is, of course, first and foremost testimony to the saga-teller's art. If it was part of the original *Saga of Hákon Hákonarson* it would have been a poignant touch that a Norwegian audience shortly after King Hákon's death might have particularly appreciated: Hákon had died in Kirkwall returning from an expedition to assert his sovereignty over the Hebrides against Alexander III's claims, so a vivid reminder that the king of Scots lacked the symbols of coronation and anointment which signified kingship in its fullest sense would not have gone unnoticed.[4] The knight's emotional response to the ceremony would not, however, have been out of place. As someone close enough to Alexander III to be entrusted with royal business abroad, he must have known that hopes of gaining coronation and anointment from the pope for the king of Scots had been consistently frustrated by opposition from the king of England.[5] As recently as May 1259 an embassy had been sent to Henry III without success to ask (among other things) that he lift his objections,[6] presumably so that Alexander III could be anointed and crowned to mark a formal end to his minority. If the knight wept at Magnús's consecration, he would doubtless have been moved not simply by wonder, but by bitter regret that this was unattainable for his own king.

The requests for coronation and anointment is important evidence of a Scottish desire that their kingdom be recognised as of equal status with any other in Latin Christendom. Equally, their frustration indicates their inability to break loose for ever from the king of England's view of himself as overlord of Britain. The request for papal recognition of Scottish independence was not simply about negating the king of England's claim, however, but was part of a coherent vision of the Scottish kingdom as a sovereign territory in which the king of Scots was the ultimate secular authority. A prime occasion for articulating this was in the Treaty of Perth, ratified on 2 July 1266 by Alexander III and representatives of Magnús VI, when the king of Norway ceded Mann and the Hebrides to the king of Scots. There it was explained what it meant to be part of the Scottish realm: 'all the men of the said islands . . . as well lesser as greater, shall be subject to the laws and customs of the kingdom of Scotland and be judged and dealt with according to them from now on'.[7] As Hector MacQueen has observed, this statement in the treaty 'reinforces for Scotland an important point on the link between law and national identity in the medieval period: that the connection was not simply a matter of feudal authority over vassals but of kingship extending over territory and the people within it'.[8]

This book is not about Scottish law and custom in the twelfth and thirteenth centuries. This has already been expertly discussed in a number of fundamental studies by Hector MacQueen and David Sellar. Neither is it about the institutions and practice of royal government, a subject which has been a central concern of generations of historians, and which has been put on a new and firmer footing by the edition of the charters of David I (1124–53), Mael Coluim IV (1153–65) and William I (1165–1214) by G. W. S. Barrow, each accompanied by a discussion of the workings of the royal household and of the documents produced in the king's name.[9] Similar editions of the acts of Alexander II (1214–49) and Alexander III (1249–86) are due to be published in the near future. This book, rather, is concerned with how the kingship of the Scots was regarded by those who had a stake in the Scottish kingdom, especially those who were closely associated with the king through ties of lordship and service, or through his patronage of their church. In particular, this book is about how they envisaged their king as the ultimate secular authority within his realm, a concept whose key components changed in a way which had a fundamental effect on how the king of Scots was seen in relation to other kings, and particularly the king of England. This change will be examined from the beginning, as it were, with a fresh attempt to explain the first appearance of *Alba* (the Gaelic for 'Scotland') in Irish chronicles under the year 900, and will finish on the eve of Edward I's challenge to Scotland's status as a sovereign kingdom nearly four centuries later. The expectations and aspirations of those close to the king (and presumably of the king himself), and an appreciation that what may seem natural today (or may have seemed natural in the 1290s) would at an earlier stage have been unthinkable, are obviously important to an understanding of what were regarded as legitimate objectives of royal policy, and thereby of Scotland's development as a kingdom.

Territorial sovereignty and the equal status of independent countries are interlocking concepts which are readily understood today. It was not always so, even if 'territorial sovereignty' is interpreted less strictly than in the age of nation states, and is taken to mean a supreme jurisdiction within geographical limits over secular affairs alone. As far as Scottish (and British) history is concerned, it is important to ask when the idea of a sovereign kingdom was first articulated and what its antecedents were. The answer to both parts of the question will lead to what is meant by the origins of Scottish independence in the title of this book. An early inkling of what we would recognise as a sense of Scotland's territorial sovereignty was the embassies sent by kings of Scots to Hákon IV to gain Mann and the Isles. The ill-starred expedition of the knight and the unnamed archdeacon in 1261 was the latest in a number of such missions, although it was evidently the first to be sent by Alexander III after he had taken personal control of government after his minority: his father, Alexander II, had died on 8 July 1249 on the island of Kerrera while mounting an invasion of the Hebrides. When Scottish envoys were first despatched to Hákon's court in 1244, it is said in the *Saga of Hákon Hákonarson* that they argued that the original acquisition of the Isles by Magnús III (king of Norway 1093–1103) had been unfair, and they offered to pay for their recovery.[10] As it stands this would suggest that Alexander II regarded his claim to the Isles as justified by the notion that they had once been within the Scottish realm. It is perfectly possible, indeed, that Alexander had been advised that the Hebrides and Argyll constituted the original kingdom of the Scots: this claim appeared in a version of the Scottish king-list written early in the reign of William I (1165–1214) which became, in Alexander II's time, part of the standard Scottish account of the kingship's past.[11] This would have cut no ice with

Hákon IV. Unfortunately for the Scots Hákon also seems to have aspired to establish Norway as a sovereign kingdom. Not only did he gain papal recognition in 1247 of his status as king in the fullest sense (in the secular sphere), but he also made a concerted effort to establish his authority over all putative Norwegian territory.[12] Greenland was first approached in the 1240s, and recognised Hákon's overlordship in 1261. The following year Iceland finally became part of Hákon's kingdom after decades of struggle: one of Hákon's opponents had been none other than Sturla þórðarsson, who composed Hákon's saga in the two years following Hákon's death.[13]

Hebridean leaders, in contrast, had been more willing to acknowledge dependence on Hákon, even though, as Alex Woolf has argued compellingly, Norwegian suzerainty over the Isles was a recent phenomenon, and not the political reality which (it has generally been supposed) was bequeathed to kings of Norway by Magnús III.[14] According to this view, the Hebrides were Hákon's most significant early success in promoting the sovereignty of his kingship over whatever could be construed as Norwegian territory. King Haraldr of Mann responded swiftly to Hákon's summons to attend the coronation at Bergen in 1247,[15] and was joined the following year at Hákon's court by two descendants of Somairle (Somerled), one of whom Hákon made king of the Isles.[16] In 1253 the same two descendants of Somairle served in Hákon's expedition against the king of Denmark,[17] and the following year (according to the Chronicle of Mann) Haraldr's brother, Magnús, was 'appointed king over all the islands' by Hákon, who 'by the authority of his seal' confirmed this to Magnús and his heirs.[18] We are told that Magnús's opponents were devastated by this news, and by Hákon's charter granting the kingdom to Magnús and his heirs: 'dismayed in mind, they melted away, their hopes dead', an awesome testimony to Hákon's power and authority in the eyes of the chronicler. The determination of both Alexander III and Hákon IV to vindicate what they saw as their territorial sovereignty led inevitably to war. The first move was a raid into Skye in 1262 which (according to the saga of Hákon's life) was reported to the Norwegian king along with news that 'the Scottish king intended to lay under himself all the Hebrides'.[19] Hákon's response was the impressive expedition which departed from Bergen on 11 July the following year and reached the Firth of Clyde, encountering local forces at Largs on 2 October and ravaging Loch Lomond. Hákon's death in Kirkwall on 16 December 1263 on his way back to Norway, and the failure to secure Norwegian sovereignty over the Isles, set the scene for the final acceptance of what, in essence, the Scots had proposed in 1244: the purchase of the Isles from the king of Norway.[20]

STUDYING THE CONCEPTUALISATION OF ROYAL AUTHORITY

The attempt to infer from such events any fundamental ideas about the status and nature of kingship is bound to be imprecise and debatable. It has been suggested by Ted Cowan, for example, that in their policy towards the Isles 'the two Alexanders were as intent as was Hakon upon the creation of a strong central monarchy'.[21] According to this view, Alexander III and Hákon IV would have both been attempting to 'tame the Hebrides' as part of a more general model of 'crown versus kin'.[22] Although a desire to impose strong central monarchy and an aspiration to implement territorial sovereignty are not, of course, mutually exclusive, there is (at the very least) a significant difference of emphasis between these positions as explanations of the actions of the Alexanders and Hákon IV in relation to the Isles. If the idea of territorial sovereignty lay at the heart of the dispute, then the issue was not control of the inner workings of Hebridean society as such, but simply whether the Isles 'belonged' to either the Scottish or the Norwegian kingdom.

If the interpretation of events is uncertain evidence for ideas about kingdoms, there is also a broader anxiety about the viability of identifying and discussing any concepts of this kind apart from what is written in carefully worded official pronouncements such as the Treaty of Perth. Maybe all that can be claimed is what Rees Davies stated at the end of a discussion of 'the concept of a people': 'hopelessly elusive and possibly illusory as it is, and lacking that documentary and archival solidity which are the prerequisites of modern academic historiography', it is 'not . . . altogether unworthy of our attention as historians'.[23] But this would be too minimalist a position. No-one (and certainly not Rees Davies)[24] would deny Susan Reynolds's achievement in her book, *Kingdoms and Communities in Western Europe 900–1300* (1984, second edition 1997) of showing the importance of the mental landscape of norms and assumptions about the nature of kingdoms and peoples as a contribution to our understanding of medieval society and politics. To this end evidence such as origin-legends, king-lists, genealogies and inauguration rituals has been used as a way into the minds of those who created, read or performed such celebrations of individual kingships.[25] But, as Reynolds acknowledged, a book on such a large canvas as *Kingdoms and Communities* did not offer her much scope for engaging with primary sources as much as she would have liked.[26] Focusing a book on a single kingship, by contrast, allows a deeper and more detailed treatment to be attempted.

A study of the conceptualisation rather than the practice of royal authority may seem to invite historians beyond the bounds of 'documentary and archival solidity', but the approach to key primary material adopted in this book is rooted in tried and tested techniques of textual criticism and diplomatic (that is, the study of documents, particularly their formal elements). The use made of these methodologies, however, goes beyond traditional and familiar concerns. Instead of taking a classical approach to textual criticism, where the emphasis is on establishing original texts, the objective here is to use the same basic techniques to locate stages in a text's development, and to focus on what this reveals about new ideas as well as inherited assumptions. Likewise, in the case of diplomatic, rather than explaining the detail of a document's prose chiefly in terms of bureaucratic practice, attention will be given to how some routine features, or small variations in established forms, may reflect the ideas rather than the day-to-day reality of government. Subjecting texts relating to the same kingdom to close scrutiny, moreover, makes it easier to place them in their textual and historical context, and so be more open and sensitive to the unexpected. A capacity to yield new perspectives, and even to surprise, exists even in sources which are well known to historians. In this book these include chronicles and king-lists, royal charters, papal bulls, Jocelin's *Life of Kentigern*, John of Fordun's chronicle and the material associated with it known as *Gesta Annalia*, 'Yearly Deeds', as well as texts that are less well known or have recently been discovered, such as the Offices of the Feast of St Kentigern and the full text of version 'A' of the legend of St Andrews' foundation. A particular premium will be placed on the construction of a continuous history of Scottish kingship from ancient origins, if only because this is on a scale that allows for a more detailed exploration of underlying assumptions and aspirations, and offers the opportunity (in chapter 2) to draw significant comparisons with similar material relating to the English, Irish and Welsh. It has long been thought that such a complete account of the kingdom's past was the peculiar achievement of John of Fordun, whose *Chronica Gentis Scottorum* ('Chronicle of the Scottish People') may be dated to sometime between early 1384 and August 1387 – long after the period discussed in this book. It has recently become apparent, however, that Fordun had access to a lost work about a century older than *Chronica Gentis Scottorum*, and that much of his scheme of Scottish history from the origin of the Scots in Greece and Egypt was moulded at this earlier stage, rather than by Fordun himself. In chapter 8 the nature of this lost work will be explored further than has hitherto been attempted, leading in chapter 9 to a fresh assessment of the elusive and controversial question of the existence of a history of Scotland attributed to 'Veremundus'.

The creation of a fully-fledged narrative of Scottish history at least a century earlier than Fordun's celebrated history can be recognised as an important landmark in the development of the idea of Scotland as a sovereign kingdom. It provided the concept of a sovereign realm with the authenticity of a distant and continuous past. When combined with the sense of Scotland's particular laws and customs articulated in the Treaty of Perth, it also gave the idea of Scotland's independence an infrastructure which could help to perpetuate it in people's minds in the future. Scotland was finally equipped with the essential elements of its modern identity as a nation, elements which have sustained its claim to be regarded as a nation despite the loss of independence three hundred years ago. A century before Alexander III's reign (1249–86), however, even the most basic aspects of the modern idea of Scotland, both as a country and as England's equal in status (although not in power), would have been unthinkable.

BECOMING A SOVEREIGN KINGDOM: THE CONCEPT OF TERRITORIAL SOVEREIGNTY

It has long been recognised (although not necessarily given sufficient emphasis) that, for Scots themselves, it was not until the early thirteenth century that 'Scotland' acquired its modern meaning as the name of a country stretching from the Pentland Firth in the north to the Tweed in the south.[27] The earliest appearance in a contemporary Scottish source of 'Scotland' in this sense – simple and matter-of-fact as anyone might use the term today – is in the Chronicle of Melrose, in the annal for 1216 (entered into the original manuscript of the chronicle in 1218 or shortly thereafter): the burning of Berwick, Roxburgh, Dunbar and Haddington by King John of England is described as happening 'in the southern part of Scotland', and a miraculous vision of the moon is said to have occurred 'in the western part of Scotland, which is called Galloway'.[28] Previously 'Scotland' (either Gaelic *Alba* or Latin *Scotia* or *Albania*) had only been used to denote the country north of the Forth and south of Moray, or the mainland from Fife to Caithness.[29] There is also place-name evidence which shows that inhabitants of Argyll did not regard themselves as part of *Alba*, 'Scotland', or even as *Albanaig*, 'Scots'.[30]

The unambiguous status of the Forth as the southern limit of 'Scotland' until the thirteenth century is particularly striking. By 1200 it had ceased to be the kingdom's border for nearly two-and-a-half centuries. Kings of Scots had ruled south of the Forth more or less continuously since the mid-tenth century when, in the material on the reign of

Illuilb mac Causantín (954–62) in the *Chronicle of the Kings of Alba*, we are told 'Edinburgh was evacuated, and abandoned to the Scots to the present day'.[31] There is some uncertainty, given the complex history of this text, about what is meant here by 'the present day'.[32] The extent of the annexation of old Northumbria is also debatable, even after the battle of Carham on the Tweed was won by Mael Coluim II (1005–34) in 1018.[33] There is no doubt, however, that Mael Coluim III (1058–93) and the descendants of his marriage with Margaret of England had ruled most of what is now southern Scotland since the winter of 1069–70.[34] Overlordship over Galloway was enforced in 1160, and finally put on a formal footing following the acceptance of Lachlan (known more often as Roland) as ruler of Galloway by Henry II of England in 1186.[35] On the face of it, therefore, the enduring significance of the Forth as 'Scotland''s southern boundary seems decidedly odd.[36] This has never been accounted for satisfactorily, and will be revisited in the next chapter. The explanation which will emerge will form a cornerstone to an understanding of the concept of secular authority proposed in this book. The point to emphasise at this stage is that it shows that the realm of the king of Scots was regarded as consisting of more than one country: not only 'Scotland', but Lothian, 'Cumbria' (the old kingdom of Strathclyde, not the modern region) and Galloway in the south. Galloway (at least) remained separate to the extent of being recognised as having its own laws, even in relation to the prosecution of the most serious crimes that were elsewhere reserved to the crown: for example, it was stated to be exempt from the provisions enacted by Alexander II with a large assembly of prelates, earls and barons on 13 February 1245 concerning the apprehension and conviction of criminals (including murderers and violent robbers) because it 'has special laws within it'.[37] Galloway was also in a unique position because the bishopric of Whithorn from 1128 had embraced the authority of the archbishop of York,[38] and so remained apart from the Scottish Church when this was recognised as an independent province by the pope (either in 1189 or 1192).

In the north Moray had a special significance for Scottish kingship. Mac Bethad mac Findláich (1040–57), ruler of Moray, and his stepson Lulach (1057–8) had been kings of Scots, and Lulach's son (Mael Snechta, d.1085) and grandson (Oengus, killed in 1130), were rivals to Mael Coluim III and David I for the throne. Moray was not, however, regarded routinely as part of Scotland, and there is place-name evidence which suggests that the people of Moray in turn did not regard themselves as 'Scots'.[39] Both Lulach's son and grandson, moreover, are referred to as king of Moray in the *Annals of Ulster*.[40] This separation of

Moray from 'Scotland' may have been a legacy of the bitter contest for the Scottish throne that could have been as old as a century before Oengus, son of Lulach's daughter, was killed leading an army into the heart of 'Scotland' at the Battle of Stracathro in 1130.[41] His death left Moray at the mercy of David I who, over the following decades, established an infrastructure of control including burghs, monasteries and a few incoming lords.[42] The king's authority in the north was, nonetheless, repeatedly challenged from the late 1170s by risings in support of another lineage claiming the throne, the descendants of Donnchad mac Maíl Choluim (Duncan II), who had reigned briefly in 1094: this threat was finally extinguished in 1230 by an act of breathtaking savagery.[43] The intensity of feeling can also be gauged by references to Moravians as 'apostate' and 'treacherous' in a versified king-list written during the reign of Alexander II (1214–49).[44] Soon after Moray was finally brought securely under royal control, the far north of mainland Scotland fell fortuitously into the hands of an earl loyal to the king. In the aftermath of the killing of John, earl of Orkney and Caithness, in 1231, leading Orkneymen decided to go to King Hákon of Norway the following year in a bid to resolve the dispute between Earl John's family and his killers. On their way back disaster struck, and 'the best men in the islands' were drowned.[45] Caithness was acquired (through some relationship with previous earls of Orkney) by a member of the family of the earls of Angus, and soon after was shorn of Sutherland and was itself divided among heiresses.[46]

The underlying explanation of this change from a realm consisting of a number of countries to a single country, 'Scotland', can be traced through a distinctive feature in the drafting of charters. It was not uncommon for it to be said that the subject of a donation by the king (be it land or a church) was to be held as freely, peacefully (and so on) as any other similar property was held. John Hudson has observed that, 'unlike English or, for example, Breton charters, Scottish charters quite often add a geographical or regnal element to such clauses'.[47] For example, the church of Forteviot was granted by Mael Coluim IV to Richard of Stirling, his chaplain, to be held 'as freely and quietly as any church in my demesnes in Scotland' (meaning, presumably, Scotland north of the Forth).[48] Of particular interest, however, is how, in non-royal charters, the kingdom more commonly became the point of reference in this clause. One example cited by Professor Hudson is a charter of Roland, lord of Galloway (1185–1200), in which a grant in alms to Kelso abbey is to be held as well as Kelso's other grants in alms 'in the kingdom of Scotland'.[49] The earliest instance known to Geoffrey Barrow is in a charter of Bishop Robert of St Andrews (1127–59), where reference was made to 'the kingdom of the king of Scots'.[50] Professor Barrow commented that

> from the last years of the twelfth century the phrase becomes such a commonplace that it is impossible to glance through any corpus of Scottish private charters without encountering it again and again, usually in the form 'within the kingdom of Scots' (or 'of Scotland').[51]

As Keith Stringer has pointed out, the statement that the subject of a grant was to be held as freely as any other was held in the kingdom shows an acceptance of standard legal customs throughout the realm.[52] It is not difficult to see how an expectation that law and custom in relation to property should be the same throughout the king's territory could engender a sense of the kingdom as a single country.[53] This would increasingly have had practical effect with the creation of a judicial system across most of the kingdom: by the end of William I's reign (1165–1214) a kingdom-wide framework had almost certainly taken shape consisting of at least two justiciarships as well as sheriff courts in all regions securely under royal control.[54] Early in the reign of Alexander II there is evidence not only that perambulations (a judicial process for establishing the bounds of an estate) conformed to a standard procedure according to an 'assize of King David', but that a central record of these was kept 'in the roll of the justiciar'.[55]

There was, however, some notable variation in how the kingdom was referred to in the charter-clause stating that the subject was to be held 'as freely as . . .' The more cumbersome 'kingdom [or land] of the king of Scots' is still found about half a century after the earliest known use of the straightforward 'kingdom of Scotland' in 1161 or 1162,[56] which suggests that the idea of a 'kingdom of Scotland' rather than simply the king's lands may only have become a routine feature of the mental landscape of those who drafted documents in the beginning of the thirteenth century. Once this stage had been reached, it was but a short step from *regnum Scocie* to using *Scocia* on its own to refer to the kingdom's territory, a step that may have been easier to take in the freer prose of a chronicle than in the formulaic habitat of charters. Ambiguity can, nonetheless, still be traced in the genre of chronicles in the early thirteenth century, making it possible that, at the very least, 'Scotland' in both its 'new' and 'old' guises existed together as late as the reign of Alexander II. In *Gesta Annalia* we are told how in 1214 William I made peace with the earl of Caithness in the autumn, and then 'returned from Moray to Scotland, and progressed from Scotland into Lothian', and how on his way back his health deteriorated, and he died shortly there-after at Stirling on 4 December.[57] Not enough is known about this part of *Gesta Annalia* to determine where and when this passage was written; it is obvious enough, though, that these words must originally have been penned no more than a few years earlier than the first mention of 'Scotland' in its modern sense in the Chronicle of Melrose.

As far as the notion of Scotland as a sovereign territory is concerned, and how this developed, this book will serve to complement rather than challenge the scholarly consensus. The restricted sense of 'Scotland' as the name of the country north of the Forth, south of Moray and east of Argyll has been acknowledged by historians since at least W. F. Skene dis-cussed it in the first volume of *Celtic Scotland* (1876);[58] the gradual adop-tion of the phrase 'kingdom of Scotland' in charters has also been known since Geoffrey Barrow first drew attention to it in the last of his Ford Lectures in 1977.[59] There is still scope, however, for adding to our under-standing of the significance of this idea as it developed from 'kingdom [or 'land'] of the king of Scots' and 'kingdom of the Scots', beginning around 1160 and gathering momentum by 1200, through the use of 'Scotland' in the Chronicle of Melrose in referring to both Galloway and the Merse, until the unambiguous articulation of territorial sovereignty in the Treaty of Perth. A fresh perspective will be advanced in chapters 5 and 6 both on the fragility of the notion of the kingdom as a unified entity in the late twelfth century, and also on how compelling this idea of the kingdom as a single country had become by the mid-thirteenth century. Particular attention will also be paid in chapter 2 to the Forth's signifi-cance as a border, not simply between sheriffdoms or more local units, but as the limit of 'Scotland', and also of the 'Scots', long after the kingdom of 'Scotland' and the 'Scots' had stretched far beyond it.

BECOMING A SOVEREIGN KINGDOM: THE KING OF SCOTS IN RELATION TO THE KING OF ENGLAND

The other dimension of being a sovereign kingdom was the idea that the king of Scots was or should be equal in status with the king of England. There seems to be a general assumption (among scholars on both sides of the border) that, although political realities often dictated otherwise, kings of Scots at least 'aimed to treat with English kings on equal terms'.[60] A diametrically different conclusion is offered in this book. The springboard is Rees Davies's nuanced discussion of submission and dom-ination across Britain and Ireland in this period;[61] the substance is an examination of how royal authority was conceptualised, using the approach outlined above. The result in chapter 7 is a new perspective on this issue whose most radical element is the proposition that, until the thirteenth century, equality of status with the king of England – far from being a natural aspiration – was inconceivable for a king of Scots whose realm embraced most of what is Scotland today. The discussion, however, will follow the path laid down by Rees Davies in seeking to move beyond a rather two-dimensional argument about who owed homage to whom for what: unlike Professor Davies, however, the quest for ecclesiastical independence will be placed in the foreground in chapter 4, and detailed consideration will also be given in chapters 2 and 3 to earlier conceptualisations of the basis of royal authority. The unthinkability of kings of Scots as naturally on a par with kings of England will emerge as an essential element in a mental landscape which (however alien and paradoxical this may seem today) also had at its core a concept of Scottish independence. This will provide essential background for a fresh discussion in chapter 6 of the beginnings of the idea that Scotland was a sovereign kingdom in the fullest sense that was possible in the thirteenth century: namely, that its king was regarded as the highest secular authority within the kingdom's bounds, and was thereby the equal of any other king.

A preliminary inspection of the current tendency to regard parity with England as a natural goal for Scottish kings suggests that this is not, in any event, as compelling as might be supposed. This is not to deny how attractively neat and tidy it is to discuss this issue in terms of homage versus independence, or that it can be reassuring (from a Scottish point of view) to see Scots opt for independence (as we might understand this) whenever the opportunity arose. A particularly clear-cut example, it might be thought, is David I. Geoffrey Barrow has commented persuasively that[62]

> David's dealings with Stephen and the Empress Maud . . . are especially important as evidence of how the Scots saw their kingship during the first of three medieval periods (1136–53, 1266–86, and 1314–29) in which it was at the height of its power and authority. In particular David's assertion of independence against any claims that Stephen might put forward shows that he had repudiated the status of client king.

There is nothing ostensibly wrong with this, of course. David's successes following the death of Henry I of England on 1 December 1135 and the coronation of Stephen on 22 December were certainly impressive. He met Stephen at Durham on 5 February 1136, and came to an agreement that he would be left in possession of Carlisle (which he had taken), and that the honour of Huntingdon would be granted to his son and heir, Henry.[63] Despite military failure at the Battle of the Standard (22 August 1138) even more favourable terms were agreed with Stephen at Durham on 9 April 1139 in which the earldom of Northumberland was added to Henry's possessions.[64] In the aftermath of Stephen's capture at the Battle of Lincoln (2 February 1141) David I and his son Earl Henry extended their control deeper into England, as far as the Ribble in the west and the Tees in the east. It has been pointed out by Keith Stringer that David and his son ruled northern England 'in complete independence of Stephen' and that they 'acknowledged no other superior'.[65] Professor Barrow (followed by Professor Stringer) has described David's achievement as 'the creation of a new political entity, a Scoto-Northumbrian kingdom . . ',[66] a designation which neatly captures its conglomerate nature:[67] as king of a number of countries – 'Scotland', Lothian and 'Cumbria' (i.e., Strathclyde), as well as Moray – it would have been simple enough conceptually to extend this framework to include northern England, and recall the Northumbria of living memory, whose last earl of the old line (Waltheof, executed by William the Conqueror in 1076) was Earl Henry's maternal grandfather.[68] It is true that David had other reasons to deny homage to Stephen: at least one contemporary thought that he avoided becoming Stephen's man because he had been the first layman on 1 January 1127 to take the oath recognising Henry I's daughter, Maud/Matilda, as the king of England's heir.[69] Be this as it may, it would be difficult to deny that David became as much a king as Stephen, and that after 1141 he functioned as if he meant this to continue, regardless of who might be king of England, extracting a promise to this effect from the sixteen-year-old future Henry II when he knighted him at Carlisle in May 1149.[70]

A problem arises only if it is supposed that David's desire to avoid submission to the king of England was a long-held aspiration shared by his predecessors and inherited by his successors. Insofar as this was not motivated by a desire to preserve the purity of his oath to Henry I, should it not be seen simply as a function of his policy of expansion into northern England? He appears, clearly enough, to have wished to engineer a fundamental realignment of power in Britain, so that the king of England would no longer have been dominant. His principal objective was the creation of a new Scoto-Northumbrian realm, however, not the independence of the Scottish kingdom as such. That this was recognised by contemporaries can be gauged by the attempts of Irish chroniclers to give him an appropriate title at his death: for them he was not simply 'king of Scotland' (*rí Alban*), but king of Scotland and either *Saxan*, 'English', or *Bretan*, 'Britons'.[71] This being so, we should probably imagine that contemporaries regarded equality of status with the king of England as only as new as this new realm. The corollary would be that, when Mael Coluim IV surrendered northern England to Henry II in exchange for the restoration of Huntingdon in 1157, this would have killed off the idea that the king of Scots had parity of status with the king of England. Mael Coluim IV's acceptance of Huntingdon, binding himself and his successors to performing homage to the king of England, can be seen as perfectly logical if the loss of northern England in any case implied a restoration of the kingship's subordination. If the political realities in 1157 meant that Mael Coluim IV had little choice but to agree to the dismemberment of his grandfather's legacy, the fact that his gaining of Huntingdon was at the expense of an earldom which he did not hold directly himself (his brother, William, had been installed in Northumberland by David I) would no doubt have helped to make the settlement with Henry II acceptable.

On this reading of the events of 1136–53, it follows that they can tell us nothing about the expectations of earlier kings of Scots in relation to kings of England. As far as the aspirations of subsequent kings are concerned, the claim to the northern counties did not die until 1237, but there was no longer any suggestion of an independent Scoto-Northumbrian realm. Homage to the king of England, either for land in the north or for Huntingdon, was the reality; and, with the extinction of David's expanded kingdom, it is not immediately obvious that homage of itself would have been regarded as irksome before the idea of sovereign kingship was espoused. It is noteworthy that in 1216, when Alexander II, like David I, took advantage of civil strife in England and made himself master of Carlisle, he lost no time in leading a force to Dover to meet Louis of France and do homage to Louis as putative king of England.[72] It is also noteworthy that, although Alexander was treated as an equal with Henry III when it came to swearing his oath by proxy to abide by the provisions of the Treaty of York (on the principle that direct oath-taking was for lesser mortals than kings), part of the agreement was that Alexander would be invested by Henry III with £200 worth of lands in Northumberland, for which Alexander did homage and fealty before the treaty was concluded:[73] in fact, Alexander had to wait until 1242 before he was given sasine of these estates.[74] To return again to Geoffrey Barrow's assessment of the significance of David I's 'assertion of independence', the difference between 1136–53 and 1266–86 is that in the later period parity of status with the king of England was based on the mere fact of being king of Scots; in the former it was a function of David's creation of a new Scoto-Northumbrian realm. In the end, the most natural aspirations evidenced by David's conspicuous success were the ancient desire of all kings to expand their territory, and the primal concern of families to vindicate inherited claims to lordship. If David's policy in northern England is to be explained chiefly in terms of political ambition rather than personal conscience, there is nothing to say that his freedom from ties of homage was not simply a consequence of these more basic aspirations, rather than itself forming the principal objective of his dealings with Stephen.[75]

BECOMING A SOVEREIGN KINGDOM: CORONATION AND ANOINTMENT

This is not the end of the matter, however. Archie Duncan, in a brilliant study of the political history of the period culminating in a detailed discussion of Edward I's dealings with the Scots before the outbreak of war in 1296, has provided a sustained argument that Scottish kings from Alexander I to Mael Coluim IV aspired to parity of status with kings of England.[76] In doing so, he has taken as his touchstone not the periods of strength listed by Professor Barrow but the attempts by Scottish kings in the twelfth century to gain metropolitan status for St Andrews from the pope. There is little doubt that the bishop of St Andrews was regarded in Scotland as the premier bishop of the realm: the problem was that he lacked the official sanction of the pope that was required if he was to be an archbishop. Professor Duncan argued that the objective was not simply to negate the rival claims of archbishops of Canterbury and York to authority over the Scottish church, but specifically that kings of Scots wished to be crowned and anointed, for which (according to this line of argument) an archbishop would have been seen as an essential prerequisite. He suggested that this initiative should be traced back to Alexander I (1107–24), who desired the 'rites of Christian kingship' so that his 'position would then be that of other kings, and not dependent upon the gift or assent of the English king'.[77] According to Professor Duncan this policy was continued by David I (1124–53) and Mael Coluim IV (1153–65), dropped by William I (1165–1214), and then resumed in the reigns of Alexander II (1214–49) and Alexander III (1249–86).

Professor Duncan is the first to admit that there is no direct evidence that Alexander I made any request for promoting the bishop of St Andrews to an archbishop. His argument is self-confessedly circumstantial, focusing on Alexander's plans for upgrading both the time-honoured royal inaugural site of Scone (where an Augustinian priory was founded by him) and the ecclesiastical establishment at St Andrews.[78] He is also completely frank that the proposition that David I and Mael Coluim IV sought coronation and anointment is hypothetical.[79] There is, in fact, no direct evidence that any king of Scots in the twelfth century aspired to coronation and anointment, or that any request was made in the thirteenth century for the bishop of St Andrews' elevation to the rank of archbishop. This naturally makes it difficult to posit a necessary link between the two. On the one hand, the metropolitan status for St Andrews can readily be seen as an end in itself which was resolved when the independence of the Scottish church was finally recognised in the bull *Cum universi* (either in 1189 or 1192). On the other hand, requests for coronation and anointment could readily have been made in the thirteenth century as a separate issue (presumably on the basis that the bishop of St Andrews could perform the rite, as indeed occurred when coronation and anointment was finally conceded by the pope in 1329).[80] This would coincide with the period when coronation and anointment generally began to be regarded as increasingly essential. As Professor Duncan observed, these rites were not essential in the twelfth century.[81]

Why, then, did Professor Duncan argue that the quest for an archbishop and the desire for coronation and anointment ran in tandem? He cited two key pieces of evidence. One is a papal instruction of May 1225 that Scottish bishops were to hold a provincial council, which Professor Duncan argued could have been prompted by a request for metropolitan status for St Andrews: the Scottish church was unique in being a province without an archbishop, which meant that there was no-one in Scotland with the authority to call the annual councils which were required by the terms of the Fourth Lateran Council of 1215.[82] On the face of it this suggestion is perfectly plausible, but it is not necessary. Professor Watt has provided an alternative account in which the instruction of 1225 is the final stage in a process of making the Scottish church 'fit for purpose'.[83] This began with the reissue in November 1218 of *Cum universi*,[84] and was followed by the visit of a papal legate, who held a council of 'the prelates of the whole realm' at Perth in February 1221.[85] Professor Watt argued that the legate's report to Pope Honorius III (1216–27) must have been instrumental in persuading the pope that it would be impracticable if councils of the Scottish church could only be called when a papal legate was present, and that an alternative arrangement was required, resulting in the instruction dated 19 May 1225.[86]

The other piece of evidence cited by Professor Duncan relates potentially to the issue of coronation and anointment in the twelfth century. In a passage in Aelred of Rievaulx's eulogy of David I written shortly after the king's death,[87] Aelred declares that he knew that David 'did not strive after kingship', so that when he succeeded to the throne 'he so dreaded the *obsequia* which are offered by the people of the Scots according to the custom of the country at the inaugural raising up of their kings that he was only with difficulty compelled by the bishops to accept them'.[88] The role played by the bishops has persuaded commentators that there was something about the inauguration ceremony which 'offended David's religious principles',[89] 'doubtless because he correctly saw them as fundamentally pagan'.[90] This being so, it would seem fair to assume that David wanted this changed. It is but a small step from this to supposing that he wished it to be replaced with coronation and anointment.

The passage, however, belongs to a lengthy account of David I's 'meekness' (*mansuetudo*), revolving on the biblical quotation: 'the meek shall inherit the earth, and shall delight themselves in the abundance of peace'.[91] Aelred presents this as a key element in David's success, linking the king's lack of 'haughtiness' (*superbum*) to his ability to 'tame' (*mansuefacta*) the 'total barbarity' of his people. David's reluctance to become king and dread of the inauguration ceremony should therefore be read in the same light as another passage in Aelred's account of the king's meekness. There Aelred declares that he saw David often, 'when he was punishing robbers or traitors, beating his breast [and] shedding tears, to make it clear that he was obeying justice as an administrator of the laws in punishing the guilty, not practicing cruelty'.[92] Whichever way you look at it, what is being presented is an idealised (if not highly contrived) image of Christian kingship. It is impossible to know how much of this is simply Aelred, and how much of this was really David. Although there is a formal possibility that there was something pagan about the ceremony of inauguration which Aelred has omitted to mention because it was irrelevant to his theme, this does not need to be inferred in order to make sense of Aelred's account. All that is required is a ceremony that would justify Aelred's use of the word *obsequia*, 'submissions', which would, of course, be appropriate in a general way for any royal inauguration. The rest of the passage could have been generated in the same way as David's breast-beating and weeping when handing down punishments: that is, either by Aelred's heightened portrayal of David as an ideal king, or by David's own awareness of this ideal and his commitment to be its embodiment. If David was self-consciously trying to draw attention to how kingship and piety could be combined, he certainly had a powerful role-model in his elder sister, Matilda, Henry I's queen, who was a key figure in his upbringing.[93] She is reputed to have taken the role of a pious queen to extremes, not only by wearing haircloth under her royal robes and going barefoot in church during Lent, but 'washing the feet of the diseased and handling their foul discharging sores, after which she would kiss their hands'.[94] Aelred, in the same work that includes his eulogy of David, tells how the young David was shocked to find his sister washing and kissing the feet of lepers.[95] In Robert Bartlett's penetrating assessment, this was 'a step further in the calculus of self-abnegation' than the washing of the feet of poor men during Lent which Matilda would have learned of in the *Life of Margaret* as one of her mother's activities.[96] It is not inconceivable, then, that David might indeed have made some show of his reluctance to be inaugurated as king. The point, however, would have been to highlight piety as a radical element of king-ship, not (of course) to avoid being king at all (any more than his the-atrical behaviour in ordering punishments should be taken as a desire to avoid condemning the guilty).

If the papal mandate of 1225 is not accepted as compelling evidence that St Andrews' promotion to an archbishopric was being pursued shortly after Alexander II requested coronation by the legate in 1221, and if Aelred's account of David's reluctance to be inaugurated is dis-counted as evidence that David wished to change the ritual the year before he attempted to gain metropolitan status for St Andrews in 1125, then the link between archbishopric and coronation is left only as a general proposition. There is, it is true, the example of Roger of Sicily, who persuaded Pope Anecletus II in 1130 to permit Roger to choose one of his bishops to become archbishop (Palermo was selected) so that he and his successors would be crowned by that archbishop.[97] The circum-stances were unusual, however: there was a schism between Anecletus and Innocent II, and Roger was Anecletus's most prominent supporter. When Innocent became sole pontiff following Anecletus's death, the need for good relations with someone as close and powerful as Roger of Sicily made it possible for Roger to have Anecletus's grant of coronation and metropolitan status confirmed (in due course), although this was con-ceded only grudgingly.[98] Archie Duncan has suggested that David had hopes of gaining something similar from Anecletus, although, of course, there was much less need for popes to be on good terms with the king of Scots than with someone who was ruler of Sicily and much of southern Italy.[99] All in all, the most natural reading of the evidence would be one in which the quest for metropolitan status for St Andrews was on its own an objective of kings of Scots in the twelfth century, and the attempts to gain coronation and anointment only arose in the thirteenth century. A convincing account of these as separate issues of concern at different points in the kingship's history must also, however, make it possible to understand the lack of interest in either of them during the reign of William I (1165–1214). This will be attempted in the course of chapters 4 and 5 on ecclesiastical independence and in the discussion of aspirations to sovereign kingship in chapter 7.

INDEPENDENCE AND SUBMISSION BEFORE DAVID I

Looking before David I, there is no doubt that Donnchad (1094), Edgar (1097–1107) and Alexander I (1107–24) were client kings of William Rufus and Henry I of England, and that their father, Mael Coluim III (1058–93), made explicit submissions to William the Conqueror and William Rufus. If there were grievances, they could have been about whether the terms of submissions had been kept, rather than a desire to renounce them on principle.[100] Nevertheless, there is one event which has been presented as hinging on the issue of homage. Even if it did not, it can shed light on how Mael Coluim III viewed his relationship with the king of England because it is from a near contemporary source that is (on the face of it) likely to represent Mael Coluim's position accurately (although not necessarily in full).[101] The event is Mael Coluim III's abortive meeting with William Rufus at Gloucester on 24 August 1093: William had asked Mael Coluim to come to meet him, but changed his mind after Mael Coluim had made the long journey south. This remarkable incident is reported most fully by John of Worcester, writing in the early 1120s using earlier material. Turning to the most recent edition and translation, we are told that before the kings came face to face William had insisted that Mael Coluim should 'do him homage' according to the judgement of his (William's) court; Mael Coluim had refused, stating that he would only accept the judgement of the leading men of both kingdoms and 'do homage' to William on the frontier of their kingdoms, as was customary.[102] This provoked William into calling off the meeting. John of Worcester's actual words are more ambiguous, however. Taken literally, William insisted that Mael Coluim should 'do right to him' (*rectitudinem ei faceret*), and Mael Coluim retorted that he would only 'do right' (*rectitudinem facere*) to William on the border. It is not immediately apparent, however, that *rectitudinem facere* should be translated here as 'to do homage', rather than simply 'to do right' in the sense of settling a dispute.[103] There is, indeed, no shortage of possibilities about what such a dispute might have been about. The most plausible suggestion is that William objected to Mael Coluim's plans for the marriage of his daughter, Edith (then housed in Wilton nunnery) to Alan of Brittany and Richmond, or that William had plans to marry her himself.[104] (Edith married Henry I in 1100 and is conventionally referred to thereafter as Matilda.) Another suggestion is that William had reneged on an agreement (1091) to restore property and revenue in England to Mael Coluim.[105] Another less likely possibility is that William's seizure of Carlisle in 1092 was the cause of the dispute.[106] An attractive solution is to explain the disagreement in terms of a combination of these factors.[107] The reason for particularly preferring marriage plans for Edith as the point at issue, however, is that, according to the Anglo-Saxon Chronicle (MS E), the meeting was at William's insistence, sending hostages to Mael Coluim so that he might come.[108] This suggests that it was William, not Mael Coluim, who felt wronged.[109] Perhaps the dispute hinged on who ultimately had authority over Edith, which could readily have developed into a difference over procedure. Be this as it may, Mael Coluim's insistence that the matter be resolved on the border shows that he refused to accept that 'his status was simply that of an English baron'.[110] It also shows (as W. W. Scott has pointed out) that there were procedures for settling disputes in place since the eleventh century on the principle that the border was a boundary between kingdoms.[111] But if *rectitudinem facere* is interpreted as referring to the resolution of a dispute, then it must follow that homage on the border was not on Mael Coluim's mind. Indeed, there is no reason to suppose that Mael Coluim regarded submission of itself as an affront, as long as the terms were honourable: he was prepared to negotiate submission in 1091 and, significantly, ensure that he had not only an annual pension but also twelve vills from the king of England restored to him, presumably so that he could travel south more readily at the king of England's behest.[112] Nonetheless, despite this willingness to acknowledge the king of England's superiority, Mael Coluim's insistence on doing right on the border has been described (not unreasonably) as 'a declaration that Scotland was a separate and independent kingdom'.[113] Making sense of this apparent paradox has already been touched on as a question to be pursued further, and will feature in chapters 4 and 7. It looks particularly ripe for consideration within Rees Davies's broader discussion of submissions to the king of England,[114] and is obviously important for understanding the subsequent history of Scottish aspirations and how these related to English overlordship.

THE IDEA OF BRITAIN

The general shortage of evidence relating to Scotland before the reign of Mael Coluim III makes it especially difficult to offer any useful comment about how those close to the king may have seen their kingdom in relation to the king of England. The most obvious indication of how they conceptualised their kingship is the name of the kingdom itself in the Gaelic language spoken habitually by the king and his entourage as well as by those who offered him hospitality or spiritual guidance: *Alba*, which remains the Gaelic word for Scotland to this day. It has long been known that *Alba* first appears as the kingdom's name in a contemporary source in the notice of Domnall mac Causantín's death in 900. During the reign of his successor, Causantín mac Aeda (d.952, reigned probably 900–43) *fir Alban*, 'men of Alba', is found in the same source for the first time.[115] The evidence for the adoption of *Alba* will be discussed in chapter 3, as will the various explanations that have been offered in the past decade for why it became the kingdom's name. All that need be noted at this stage is that *Alba* before the tenth century was the regular Gaelic term for 'Britain'. On the face of it, it seems bizarre that a word for 'Britain' should be coined for a kingdom based only on (part of) the area north of the Forth. 'The riddle of its meaning', as one recent commentator put it,[116] has particularly perplexed and puzzled historians of late, especially since confidence began to ebb away from the traditional explanation just over a decade ago.[117] The standard account was that the Scottish kingdom was created simply as a union between Pictland and the pre-viking realm of Dál Riata (equated roughly with Argyll), whose kings were claimed as ancestors by kings of Scots from the late tenth century (if not earlier).[118] It seemed appropriate that this new kingdom should have been given a new name, and this, it was thought, was how *Alba* came to mean 'Scotland' rather than 'Britain'. The architect of this 'union' was for centuries regarded as Cinaed mac Ailpín (d.858), putative king of Dál Riata, but this has been challenged (and Cinaed even identified as a Pict).[119] In any event, the coining of *Alba* occurred (on the face of it) two generations after Cinaed mac Ailpín. It will be recalled that there is also place-name evidence which points clearly to the fact that the inhabitants of Argyll at some stage did not regard themselves as part of *Alba*:[120] although it is difficult to pin this down chronologically, it would seem most readily to represent an early state of affairs (and certainly pre-thirteenth century).

The most challenging question to answer is how *Alba* meaning 'Britain' came to be applied at all to the kingdom, and specifically to Scotland north of the Forth. An answer will be attempted in chapter 3. Suffice to say at this stage that only Michael Davidson has made the radical but perfectly logical proposition that, when *Alba* was adopted as the kingdom's name, the term still meant 'Britain' without any qualification. Michael Davidson was aware of how extraordinary the implications of this would be: 'We are faced, then', he said, 'with the rather outlandish prospect . . . that from the 910s onwards Constantín's title was an implicit claim to rulership over all of Britain'.[121] He drew attention to a further implication: that the descendants of Cinaed mac Ailpín were making a claim to rule over the whole island at the same time as an identical claim was being made by kings of England.[122] It could readily be inferred from this that kings of *Alba* (in the tenth century, at least) regarded themselves as on a par with their English counterparts. Logical though this may seem at first sight, it is very difficult to sustain in political reality. There is no evidence that any king of *Alba* even tried to prosecute a claim to supremacy, whereas such a claim was placed firmly on the agenda of English kingship by Athelstan after his invasion of Scotland in 934. Also, the lack of any charters as such in the kingdom of *Alba* before the twelfth century or a Scottish coinage before David I's conquest of Carlisle suggests a profound difference in scale and substance between the power of Scottish and English kings.[123] It is also striking that the authority which was advertised by English kings in their pennies and documents in the tenth century was often self-consciously British.[124] Soon after 'king of the English' was established from 973 as the appropriate title on English coins, 'England' and 'Britain' were referred to as synonymous in Æthelweard's chronicle:[125] certainly, the use of English terminology did not imply an abandonment of British pretensions.[126] The solution to the conundrum of the title 'king of *Alba*' that will be proposed in chapter 3 will at least offer the prospect (however paradoxical this may seem) of showing how *Alba* meaning 'Britain' need not be incompatible with a readiness, when necessary, to acknowledge the superior power of the king of England as overking of Britain.

The idea of an overkingship of Britain as 'a potent element of political mythology' bequeathed to kings of England by Athelstan and his successors in the tenth century plays a central role in Rees Davies's recent monograph, *The First English Empire: Power and Identities in the British Isles 1093–1343* (2000).[127] Professor Davies argued that it was conceivable that England could have developed into the core of an all-embracing British kingdom in which lesser rulers retained their local power under English overlordship, and cultural differences were tolerated. Had this been the course of British history, then the leaders of localities across the islands of Britain and Ireland could all have become accustomed to enjoying the protection of the king and the opportunity to participate in the highest political and social circles, limited only by their fortune and ambition. But this is not what happened. As far as Rees Davies was concerned,

. . . as the Angevin power contracted mainly into the confines of an English state and its annexes, and as the ideology and institutions of that state became more stridently and defiantly English, so the prospect of the kingship of the English converting itself into the monarchy of the British Isles other than on its own terms largely disappeared . . .[128]

This increasing self-awareness in the twelfth century of being English in contrast to what were seen as barbaric Celtic neighbours has been brought vividly to life by John Gillingham.[129] In Professor Davies's view this involved a deliberate turning away from the legacy of an overking-ship of Britain: 'The triumph of this English definition of self-identity . . . marked, in effect, the abandonment of a British ideology, and with it the concept of a monarchy of the whole of Britain'. As a result, 'the ide-ological and mythological basis of the claim of the English to control over, and overlordship of, the rest of Britain . . . was left unexplained and unresolved', leaving 'the question of the disjunction between the terms "Britain" and "England" hanging in the air',[130] a situation which has left a legacy of confusion and embarrassment to this day as people south of the border struggle (and often fail) to maintain a distinction between England and Britain.

There is, however, an unexpected Scottish perspective on this issue. Rees Davies assumed that 'the Scots had elaborated their own self-contained and exclusive mythology', which was evident even if the focus was limited to the period between the reading aloud of the royal pedi-gree at Alexander III's inauguration in 1249 and the Declaration of Arbroath of 1320, with its claim that Robert I was the latest in a suc-cession of 113 kings unbroken by a single foreigner.[131] But what emerges from a fresh consideration of how the kingship's ancient history was por-trayed is that the Scots singularly lacked a self-contained and exclusive mythology until this was briefly sketched during the wars of independ-ence.[132] It will be argued that one of the elements in the legitimation of Scottish kingship through its past was to identify it with the idea of a kingdom of Britain, not in a proprietory sense (as did kings of England), but as a way of adding lustre to their position as the leading king in northern Britain. One conclusion which emerges from this is that the identification of Britain as their domain by English kings can be placed in a context which makes it perfectly understandable. As a result, the dis-junction between 'Britain' and 'England' emerges as more apparent than real, and the cross-over between them can be seen as quite natural (however irritating the failure to distinguish Britain from England may be from a Scottish point of view). Another conclusion is that what finally killed off the possibility of a kingdom of Britain was not only the strident exclusivity of English self-identification described so compellingly by Professor Davies, but also the emergence of the idea that the king of Scots was a sovereign ruler of equal status with any other king (and especially the king of England).

READING THIS BOOK

The meat of the book is organised under four headings ('The Idea of Britain', 'Independence', 'Sovereign Kingship' and 'National History'), which brings out a sense of chronological as well as thematic development. The chapters within each section are arranged in pairs so that the second chapter investigates a key question arising from the first. Chapters 8 and 9, additionally, relate not only to the general question of sovereign kingship, but follow on from the main theme pursued in chapter 2. The book has at its core an argument about the conceptualisation of the highest secular authority before the age of the nation state, at least insofar as this can be seen in medieval Britain and Ireland in the period discussed by Susan Reynolds in her *Kingdoms and Communities in Western Europe, 900–1300*. Instead of approaching the question of national identity in the Middle Ages by drawing attention to those elements of the modernist discourse which can be identified before the fourteenth century,[133] the aim on this occasion is to place medieval ideas themselves in the foreground. What emerges is a way of understanding the history of national identity in Britain and Ireland which in some key respects chimes both with perennialist and constructivist perspectives (that is, both with those who hold that national identity is founded on long-established elements and is based on something 'real', and with those who regard it as 'imagined' and essentially created by a particular group in a particular situation to fulfil a specific social or political objective). This book, more obviously, is also a discussion from a Scottish perspective of Rees Davies's outstanding work on British history, developing some of the key issues he raised about political identities and aspirations. The book has also benefited greatly from recent groundbreaking work on English, Irish and Welsh identity in this period (thinking particularly of John Gillingham, Máire Herbert and Huw Pryce), which provides some vital points of reference and comparison.[134] Most obvious of all, of course, this is a book on Scottish history, dealing with a matter of major concern for those who seek a perspective on Scotland's current constitutional position. Special mention must be made of Archie Duncan's *The Kingship of the Scots, 842–1292* (2002), whose compelling account of the political history of Scottish independence and royal succession should be read alongside this book's focus on the aspirations and assumptions of those associated with Scottish kingship. The concern for the political ideas of those who were close to the kingship also means that this book can be read as the chronological forerunner of the doyen of Scottish historical books with a political idea at its core: G. W. S. Barrow's *Robert Bruce and the Community of the Realm of Scotland* (4th edition, 2005). Where it differs from all these books, however, is in its concentration on particular kinds of texts. The most prominent are those concerned with the kingship's past, and it is to these that we will turn in the next chapter.

NOTES

1. Gudbrand Vigfusson (ed.), *Icelandic Sagas*, vol. ii, *Hakonar Saga and a fragment of Magnus Saga, with appendices* (London, 1887), 318–19; *ES*, ii. 602–4.

2. Vigfusson (ed.), *Icelandic Sagas*, ii. 315; *ES*, ii. 601–2. For the possible identity of 'Missel', see E. J. Cowan, 'Norwegian sunset, Scottish dawn', in Norman H. Reid (ed.), *Scotland in the Reign of Alexander III, 1249–1286* (Edinburgh, 1990), 103–31, at 117 (suggesting Mael Ísu laird of Rossie, son of the earl of Strathearn), and A. A. M. Duncan, *Scotland: the Making of the Kingdom* (Edinburgh, 1975), 588 n. 40 (suggesting Simon Fraser).

3. Vigfusson (ed.), *Icelandic Sagas*, ii. 319; *ES*, ii. 604 n. 1.

4. The author of the saga (the Icelander, Sturla Þórðarsson), the circumstances of its composition and its outlook on the Hebrides are discussed in Cowan, 'Norwegian sunset, Scottish dawn', 104–9. See also Sverre Bagge, *From Gang Leader to the Lord's Anointed: Kingship in* Sverris saga *and* Hákonar saga Hákonarsonar (Odense, 1996), 91. I am grateful to Alex Woolf for bringing this book to my attention.

5. See below, 180, 203.

6. *Close Rolls of the Reign of Henry III, A.D. 1256–1259* [ed. K. H. Ledward] (London, 1932), 477; Joseph Bain (ed.), *Calendar of Documents relating to Scotland*, vol. i, *1108–1272* (London, 1881), no. 2157; Duncan, *Scotland: the Making of the Kingdom*, 576.

7. *APS*, i. 420 col. b; Gordon Donaldson, *Scottish Historical Documents* (Edinburgh, 1974), 35; *ES*, ii. 655 n. 4.

8. Hector L. MacQueen, '*Regiam Majestatem*, Scots law and national identity', *SHR* 74 (1995) 1–25, at 10. On this aspect of the treaty see also R. I. Lustig, 'The Treaty of Perth: a re-examination', *SHR* 58 (1979) 35–57.

9. G. W. S. Barrow (ed.), *The Charters of King David I. The Written Acts of David I King of Scots, 1124–53 and of his son Henry Earl of Northumberland, 1139–52* (Woodbridge, 1999); *RRS*, i; *RRS*, ii.

10. Vigfusson (ed.), *Icelandic Sagas*, ii. 238–9; *ES*, ii. 539–40.

11. Dauvit Broun, *The Irish Identity of the Kingdom of the Scots in the Twelfth and Thirteenth Centuries* (Woodbridge, 1999), 146–53. For the text, see M. O. Anderson, *King and Kingship in Early Scotland*, 2nd edn (Edinburgh, 1980), 253, 270, 281, and below, 168.

12. Knut Helle, 'The Norwegian kingdom: succession disputes and consolidation', in Knut Helle (ed.), *The Cambridge History of Scandinavia*, vol. i, *Prehistory to 1520* (Cambridge, 2003), 369–91, at 386–7.

13. Cowan, 'Norwegian sunset, Scottish dawn', 105–6; Bagge, *From Gang Leader to the Lord's Anointed*, 91 (and 122 for attempts to incorporate Iceland into the kingdom, beginning in 1219, and becoming a concerted effort from 1240).

14. Alex Woolf, 'History or propaganda? Norway's claim to the Isles', unpublished lecture delivered at the Largs Viking festival in 2005. I am very grateful to Alex Woolf for sending me a copy of this paper and allowing me to refer to it.

15. P. A. Munch (ed.), *Chronica Regvm Manniæ et Insvlarvm* (Christiana, 1860), 23; Joseph Stevenson (ed.), *Chronicon de Lanercost. MCCI-MCC-CXLVI*, Bannatyne Club (Edinburgh, 1839), 54; *ES*, ii. 546 and n. 2.

16. Vigfusson (ed.), *Icelandic Sagas*, ii. 255; *ES*, ii. 548.

17. Vigfusson (ed.), *Icelandic Sagas*, ii. 275; *ES*, ii. 577. Their appearances with Hákon in 1248 and 1253 are placed in context in W. D. H. Sellar, 'Hebridean sea kings: the successors of Somerled, 1164–1316', in Edward J. Cowan and R. Andrew McDonald (eds), *Alba: Celtic Scotland in the Middle Ages* (East Linton, 2000), 187–218, at 204–5.

18. Munch (ed.), *Chronica Regvm Manniæ*, 26; *ES*, ii. 578.

19. Vigfusson (ed.), *Icelandic Sagas*, ii. 327; *ES*, ii. 605.

20. The final sum agreed in the Treaty of Perth in July 1266 was 4,000 merks over four years, followed by an annual payment of 100 merks. *ES*, ii. 655 n. 4; Donaldson, *Scottish Historical Documents*, 34–6; *APS*, i. 420–1.

21. Cowan, 'Norwegian sunset, Scottish dawn', 124.

22. *Ibid.*, 125–6.

23. R. R. Davies, 'The peoples of Britain and Ireland 1100–1400. 4. Language and historical mythology', *TRHS* 6th series 7 (1997) 1–24, at 24.

24. For example, he describes himself as 'deeply indebted' to her work on origin-legends and the community of the realm (see next note) in R. R. Davies, 'The peoples of Britain and Ireland 1100–1400. 1. Identities', *TRHS* 6th series 4 (1994) 1–20, at 4 n. 5.

25. See in general Broun, *Irish Identity*, 3–7. Important studies include Susan Reynolds, 'Medieval *origines gentium* and the community of the realm', *History* 68 (1983) 375–90; Donnchadh Ó Corráin, 'Irish origin-legends and genealogy: recurrent aetiologies', in Tore Nyberg and others (eds), *History and Heroic Tale: a Symposium* (Odense, 1985), 51–96; D. N. Dumville, 'Kingship, genealogies and regnal lists', in P. H. Sawyer and I. N. Wood (eds), *Early Medieval Kingship* (Leeds, 1977), 72–104; T. O. Clancy,

'Kingmaking and images of kingship in medieval Gaelic literature', in Richard Welander, David J. Breeze and Thomas Owen Clancy (eds), *The Stone of Destiny: Artefact and Icon* (Edinburgh, 2003), 85–105, and Janet L. Nelson, *Politics and Ritual in Early Medieval Europe* (London, 1986).

26. Susan Reynolds, *Kingdoms and Communities in Western Europe 900–1300*, 2nd edn (Oxford, 1997), xi.

27. W. F. Skene, *Celtic Scotland*, vol. i, *History and Ethnology* (Edinburgh, 1876), 2–3 and 3 n. 4 (where references in foreign as well as Scottish sources are extracted).

28. A. O. and M. O. Anderson (eds), *The Chronicle of Melrose from the Cottonian Manuscript, Faustina B. IX in the British Museum*, with an index by W. Croft Dickinson (London, 1936), 62, 64 (Joseph Stevenson (ed.), *Chronica de Mailros* (Edinburgh, 1835), 122, 125). For the dating of the annal's entry into the chronicle, see Dauvit Broun and Julian Harrison (eds), *The Chronicle of Melrose Abbey*, vol. i (forthcoming).

29. Dauvit Broun, 'Defining Scotland and the Scots before the wars of independence', in Dauvit Broun, Richard J. Finlay and Michael Lynch (eds), *Image and Identity: the Making and Remaking of Scotland through the Ages* (Edinburgh, 1998), 4–17, at 6–7.

30. *Ibid.*, 12; W. J. Watson, *The History of the Celtic Place-Names of Scotland* (Edinburgh, 1926), 12; Ian A. Fraser, 'The place-names of Argyll: an historical perspective', *TGSI* 54 (1984–6), at 188. Note also Penalbanach (NGR NM469579) in Mishnish on Mull, which presumably means 'Scotsman's pennyland' (*peighinn*).

31. Benjamin T. Hudson, 'The Scottish Chronicle', *SHR* 77 (1998) 129–61; Anderson, *Kings and Kingship*, 249–53, at 252; *ES*, i. 468.

32. See David N. Dumville, 'The Chronicle of the Kings of Alba', in Simon Taylor (ed.), *Kings, Clerics and Chronicles in Scotland, 500–1297* (Dublin, 2000), 73–86, at 79.

33. Dauvit Broun, 'The Welsh identity of the kingdom of Strathclyde, *ca* 900–*ca* 1200', *Innes Review* 85 (2004) 111–80, at 139 n. 117.

34. *Ibid.*, 138–40.

35. Richard Oram, *The Lordship of Galloway* (Edinburgh, 2000), 79–104; also esp. Duncan, *Scotland: the Making of the Kingdom*, 183–6, where it is argued that a decision about enforcing the king's peace in the context of judicial combat was enacted at Dumfries in 1186 and that the arrangements for collecting tribute agreed at Lanark should be dated to 1187.

36. It continued to be regarded to some extent as the limit of 'Scotland' as late as the fourteenth century (if not beyond): see below, 54.

37. *APS*, i. 403; Hector L. MacQueen, 'Canon law, custom, and legislation', in Richard D. Oram (ed.), *The Reign of Alexander II, 1214–49* (Leiden, 2005), 221–51, at 233.

38. See below, 153 n. 82.

39. Watson, *History of the Celtic Place-Names*, 12–13, 349.

40. AU 1085.1, 1130.4; *ES*, ii. 46, 173.

41. Mac Bethad's father is referred to as 'king of Alba' in AU, and his cousin likewise in AT: *ES*, i. 551 n. 4, 571. Although rulers of Moray sometimes appear as *mormaer* or earl, no other *mormaer* or earl is ever referred to as 'king'. See Alex Woolf, 'The "Moray Question" and the kingship of Alba', *SHR* 79 (2000) 145–64, at 149–50; Seán Duffy, 'Ireland and the Irish Sea Region, 1014–1318', unpublished Ph.D. dissertation (Trinity College Dublin, 1993), 21–2. I am grateful for discussions with Alex Woolf on this point.

42. R. D. Oram, 'David I and the conquest and colonisation of Moray', *Northern Scotland* 19 (1999) 1–19; Richard Oram, *David I: the King who made Scotland* (Stroud, 2004), 91–3, 102–10. Urquhart's role as a 'victory church' is asserted despite indications that it may have been founded after Kinloss (21 May 1150): certainly Penick, a possession of Urquhart in its foundation-charter, was listed as belonging to Dunfermline on its elevation to an abbey (probably 11 June 1150): Barrow (ed.), *Charters of David I*, 137, 144–5.

43. Stevenson (ed.), *Chronicon de Lanercost*, 41; *ES*, ii. 471. On this lineage, Meic Uilleim (the MacWilliams), see most recently R. Andrew McDonald, *Outlaws of Medieval Scotland: Challenges to the Canmore Kings 1058–1266* (East Linton, 2003), 61–75.

44. See Dauvit Broun, 'Contemporary perspectives on Alexander II's succession: the evidence of king-lists', in Richard D. Oram (ed.), *The Reign of Alexander II, 1214–49* (Leiden, 2005), 79–98, where it is suggested that the text was composed soon after William I's death.

45. Vigfusson (ed.), *Icelandic Sagas*, ii. 152 (ch. 173); *ES*, ii. 484.

46. Barbara E. Crawford, 'The earldom of Caithness and the kingdom of Scotland, 1150–1266', in K. J. Stringer (ed.), *Essays on the Nobility of Medieval Scotland* (Edinburgh, 1985), 25–43; Oram, 'Introduction: an overview of the reign of Alexander II', in Oram (ed.), *The Reign of Alexander II*, 1–47, at 40.

47. John Hudson, 'Legal aspects of Scottish charter diplomatic in the twelfth century: a comparative approach', in John Gillingham (ed.), *Anglo-Norman Studies XXV, Proceedings of the Battle Conference, 2002* (Woodbridge, 2003), 121–38, at 131.

48. *RRS*, i. no. 257.

49. Hudson, 'Legal aspects', 131; Keith J. Stringer, 'Acts of lordship: the records of the lords of Galloway to 1234', in T. Brotherstone and David Ditchburn (eds), *Freedom and Authority: Scotland c.1050–c.1650: Historical and Historiographical Essays presented to Grant G. Simpson* (East Linton, 2000), 203–34, no. 25 (date *ca* 1193?×1196) (contrasted with no. 12, 1164 ×*ca* May 1174, where Lothian is the point of reference).

50. G. W. S. Barrow, *The Anglo-Norman Era in Scottish History* (Oxford, 1980), 153; Thomas Thomson (ed.), *Liber Cartarum Prioratus Sancti*

Andree in Scotia. E registro ipso in archivis baronum de Panmure hodie asservato (Edinburgh, 1841), 124.

51. Barrow, *Anglo-Norman Era*, 154.
52. Keith J. Stringer, 'The charters of David, earl of Huntingdon and lord of Garioch: a study of Anglo-Scottish diplomatic', in K. J. Stringer (ed.), *Essays on the Nobility of Medieval Scotland* (Edinburgh, 1985), 72–101, at 90.
53. This, indeed, may be reflected in the gradual preference in this clause for 'kingdom of Scotland' (or 'of Scots'), with the emphasis on Scotland and Scots, rather than 'kingdom [or land] of the king of Scots', where the emphasis is on the king himself. A systematic investigation of the evidence would be highly desirable.
54. G. W. S. Barrow, *The Kingdom of the Scots*, 2nd edn (Edinburgh, 2003), 68–111, at 81–8, 110–11; Hector L. MacQueen, 'Sheriffdoms', in *Atlas of Scottish History to 1707*, ed. Peter G. B. McNeill and Hector L. MacQueen (Edinburgh, 1996), 192–4.
55. Cosmo Innes (ed.), *Liber S. Thome de Aberbrothoc*, 2 vols (Edinburgh, 1848–56), i. 162–3.
56. Barrow, *Anglo-Norman Era*, 153–4, citing a charter of Mael Coluim, earl of Fife (1204–30) for North Berwick (datable 1204x21 April 1214: J. M. Todd, *Syllabus of Scottish Cartularies: North Berwick* [1996]), and a charter recording the grant by Mael Coluim IV of lands in the South-East to Walter the Steward (*RRS*, i. no. 183, 'probably 24 June 1161'). Both survive as original single sheets.
57. W. F. Skene (ed.), *Johannis de Fordun Chronica Gentis Scottorum* (Edinburgh, 1871), 279; *ES*, ii. 399 (note).
58. See n. 27.
59. Barrow, *Anglo-Norman Era*, 153–4.
60. Richard Mortimer, *Angevin England 1154–1258* (Oxford, 1994), 140. Among Scottish historians, see e.g., A. A. M. Duncan, *The Kingship of the Scots, 842–1292: Succession and Independence* (Edinburgh, 2002), 81, and G. W. S. Barrow, *Kingship and Unity: Scotland 1000–1306*, 2nd edn (Edinburgh, 2003), 43; 1st edn (London, 1981), 37. (All subsequent references are to the first edition.)
61. R. R. Davies, *Domination and Conquest: the Experience of Ireland, Scotland and Wales 1100–1300* (Cambridge, 1990), chs 1, 3 and 4; see also his *The First English Empire: Power and Identities in the British Isles, 1093–1343* (Oxford, 2000), chs 1 and 3, and his '"Keeping the natives in order": the English king and the "Celtic" rulers 1066–1216', *Peritia* 10 (1996) 212–24.
62. Barrow, *Kingship and Unity*, 37.
63. Thomas Arnold (ed.), *Symeonis Monachi Opera Omnia*, vol. ii (London, 1885), 287; Richard Howlett (ed.), *Chronicles of the Reigns of Stephen, Henry II, and Richard I*, vol. iii (London, 1886), 146; *SAEC*, 171–3.
64. Howlett (ed.), *Chronicles of the Reigns of Stephen*, 177–8; *SAEC*, 214–15.

Although it was stipulated that the key castles of Bamburgh and Newcastle would be retained by King Stephen, they were in fact controlled by Henry: Barrow, *Kingdom of the Scots*, 2nd edn, 142–3.

65. Keith J. Stringer, *The Reign of Stephen: Kingship, Warfare and Government in Twelfth-Century England* (London, 1993), 35.

66. G. W. S. Barrow, *David I of Scotland (1124–1153). The Balance of New and Old*. The Stenton Lecture 1984 (Reading, 1985), 18; Stringer, *Reign of Stephen*, 36. The title of Oram, *David I*, ch. 10, is 'The "Scoto-Northumbrian" Realm'.

67. Although this is not emphasised by Barrow or Stringer (or Oram), it is given attention in David Carpenter, *The Struggle for Mastery: Britain 1066–1284* (London, 2003), 185.

68. See, for example, the table at Kapelle, *The Norman Conquest of the North*, 30.

69. Diana Greenway (ed.), *Henry, Archdeacon of Huntingdon, Historia Anglorum, The History of the English People* (Oxford, 1996), 706–7.

70. William Stubbs (ed.), *Chronica Magistri Rogeri de Houedene*, vol. i (London, 1868), 211; P. G. Walsh and M. J. Kennedy (eds), *William of Newburgh, The History of English Affairs*, book I (Warminster, 1988), 98–101. *SAEC*, 221 and 222 n. 1.

71. The evidence is summarised in *ES*, ii. 219 n. 6, and discussed in Duffy, 'Ireland and the Irish Sea Region', 29. The one which comes closest to reflecting the reality of this new realm is the seventeenth-century translation of an Irish chronicle into English, Denis Murphy (ed.), *The Annals of Clonmacnoise* (Dublin, 1896), 204, where David is called 'king of Scotland, Wales, and the borders of England' (where Wales is presumably *Bretan*, which in this context would probably have referred to the kingdom of Strathclyde/Cumbria).

72. Anderson (eds), *The Chronicle of Melrose*, 63 (Stevenson (ed.), *Chronica de Mailros*, 123); *ES*, ii. 409–12. See Keith J. Stringer, 'Kingship, conflict and state-making in the reign of Alexander II: the war of 1215–17 and its context', in Richard D. Oram (ed.), *The Reign of Alexander II, 1214–49* (Leiden, 2005), 99–156.

73. E. L. G. Stones (ed.), *Anglo-Scottish Relations 1174–1328: Some Selected Documents*, 2nd edn (Oxford, 1970), no. 7: see 48 n. 3 for an explanation of vicarious swearing of oaths.

74. Stones (ed.), *Anglo-Scottish Relations*, 40 n. 2; Duncan, *The Kingship of the Scots*, 121, where the point that Alexander II became Henry III's *fidelis* for these lands is emphasised.

75. Carpenter, *The Struggle for Mastery*, 178–85, is a perceptive account of the wider relationship between David's expansion into England and the transformation of Scotland.

76. Duncan, *The Kingship of the Scots*, chs 4 and 5.

77. *Ibid.*, 88; see also 81.

78. *Ibid.*, ch. 5, esp. 88.

79. *Ibid.*, 115.
80. Michael Penman, *David II, 1329–71* (East Linton, 2004), 45. Pope John XXII's bull is published in facsimile, transcribed and translated in Cosmo Innes (ed.), *Facsimiles of the National Manuscripts of Scotland*, 3 parts (Southampton, 1867–71), ii. no. xxx. For another translation see James Cooper, *Four Scottish Coronations*, special issue of the Aberdeen Ecclesiological Society and the Glasgow Ecclesiological Society (Aberdeen, 1902), 47–9. It is stipulated that the bishop of St Andrews (whom failing, the bishop of Glasgow) should perform the rite.
81. Duncan, *The Kingship of the Scots*, 115.
82. *Ibid.*, 119. The document is translated in Watt, *Medieval Church Councils in Scotland*, 44.
83. D. E. R. Watt, *Medieval Church Councils in Scotland* (Edinburgh, 2000), 41–4.
84. Stones (ed.), *Anglo-Scottish Relations*, no. 5.
85. Watt, *Medieval Church Councils in Scotland*, 40–1.
86. *Ibid.*, 41–2.
87. This forms an integral part of the (unpublished) full text of the work known to scholarship as *Genealogia Regum Anglorum*. (The text printed in Migne, *Patrologia Latina*, cxcv. cols 711–38 is a shortened version.) It is possible to imagine, though, that some of the prose of the eulogy of David could have been written originally as a funeral address. The eulogy, as it is found in the full text, was incorporated into Fordun's chronicle and, thereby, Bower's *Scotichronicon*, which means that the only translation of part of the full text to have been published is in John and Winifred MacQueen and D. E. R. Watt (eds), *Scotichronicon by Walter Bower in Latin and English*, vol. iii (Edinburgh, 1995), 139–69.
88. MacQueen and Watt (eds), *Scotichronicon*, iii. 144–5 (translation adapted significantly).
89. Oram, *David I*, 74; see also Bruce Webster, *Medieval Scotland. The Making of an Identity* (Basingstoke, 1997), 46.
90. G. W. S. Barrow, *Scotland and its Neighbours in the Middle Ages* (London, 1992), 37.
91. Psalm 36:11 (Vulgate); MacQueen and Watt (eds), *Scotichronicon*, iii. 262.
92. MacQueen and Watt (eds), *Scotichronicon*, iii. 144–5.
93. Oram, *David I*, ch. 3; see also Luis Huneycutt, *Matilda of Scotland* (Woodbridge, 2003).
94. R. A. B. Mynors, with R. M. Thomson and M. Winterbottom (eds), *William of Malmesbury, Gesta Regvm Anglorvm*, vol. i (Oxford, 1998), 756–7. See Robert Bartlett, *England under the Norman and Angevin Kings 1075–1225* (Oxford, 2000), 38.
95. *PL*, xcxv. col. 735.
96. Bartlett, *England under the Norman and Angevin Kings 1075–1225*, 38. On Matilda and the Life of Margaret, see Lois L. Huneycutt, 'The idea of

the perfect princess: the Life of St Margaret in the reign of Matilda II (1100–1118)', in Marjorie Chibnall (ed.), *Anglo-Norman Studies XII Proceedings of the Battle Conference 1989* (Woodbridge, 1990), 81–97.

97. Duncan, *The Kingship of the Scots*, 90.

98. Donald Matthew, *The Norman Kingdom of Sicily* (Cambridge, 1992), 33–53. Palermo's metropolitan status was not finally confirmed until 1156 (*ibid.*, 192).

99. Duncan, *The Kingship of the Scots*, 90.

100. For example *ibid.*, 46–7.

101. As pointed out in W. W. Scott, 'The March Laws reconsidered', in Alexander Grant and Keith Stringer (eds), *Medieval Scotland. Crown, Lordship and Community: Essays Presented to G. W. S. Barrow* (Edinburgh, 1993), 114–30, at 121.

102. P. McGurk (ed.), *The Chronicle of John of Worcester*, vol. iii (Oxford, 1998), 64–5.

103. Alan Anderson translated this 'to do him [William] justice' and 'to do right': *SAEC*, 110 and n. 3.

104. Frank Barlow, *William Rufus* (London, 1983), 310–16; Oram, *David I*, 52–5. There may also have been a question about whether Edith had taken the veil, although it has been observed by Christopher Brooke that the idea she had been a nun 'had a certain vogue in the reign of Stephen' because it implied that Stephen's rival, Henry I's daughter, Matilda, would have been illegitimate: M. R. James (ed.), revised C. N. L. Brooke and R. A. B. Mynors, *Walter Map, De Nugis Curialium: Courtiers' Trifles* (Oxford, 1983), 474 n. 1.

105. A. O. Anderson, 'Anglo-Scottish relations from Constantine II to William', *SHR* 42 (1963) 1–20, at 12; Duncan, *Scotland: the Making of the Kingdom*, 121 (whence Oram, *David I*, 52); and most recently Duncan, *The Kingship of the Scots*, 46–7.

106. W. M. Aird, 'Northern England or Southern Scotland? The Anglo-Scottish border in the eleventh and twelfth centuries and the problem of perspective', in John C. Appleby and Paul Dalton (eds), *Government, Religion and Society in Northern England 1000–1700* (Stroud, 1997), 27–39, at 28; see also J. G. Scott, 'The partition of a kingdom: Strathclyde 1092–1153', *TDGNHAS* 3rd series 72 (1997) 11–40, at 16.

107. Judith Green, 'Anglo-Scottish relations, 1066–1174', in Michael Jones and Malcolm Vale (eds), *England and her Neighbours 1066–1453. Essays in Honour of Pierre Chaplais* (London, 1989), 53–72, at 57–8. William E. Kapelle, *The Norman Conquest of the North. The Region and its Transformation 1000–1135* (London, 1979), 149–52, brings together the 1091 agreement and the issue of Carlisle, partly by suggesting that the twelve vills promised to Mael Coluim may have been in Cumberland.

108. Susan Irvine (ed.), *The Anglo-Saxon Chronicle. A Collaborative Edition*, gen. eds David Dumville and Simon Keynes, vol. vii, *MS E* (Cambridge, 2004), 103; *SAEC*, 109.

109. As Barlow suggested: see n. 104.
110. Carpenter, *The Struggle for Mastery*, 121; note also Oram, *David I*, 36.
111. W. W. Scott, 'The March Laws reconsidered', in Alexander Grant and Keith Stringer (eds), *Medieval Scotland. Crown, Lordship and Community* (Edinburgh, 1993), 114–30, 121–2, 127–8. See also Barrow, *The Kingdom*, 2nd edn, 126–8.
112. Duncan, *The Kingship of the Scots*, 46. See also Scott, 'The March Laws', 126–7.
113. Scott, 'The March Laws', 121. The discussion seems to assume that homage was the issue, but the description of Mael Coluim's position is apposite given its emphasis on the distinction between his kingdom and William II's.
114. See n. 61.
115. For *rí Alban* ('king of *Alba*') and *fir Alban* see AU 900.6 (also CS 900.5) and AU 918.4.
116. Michael Raymond Davidson, 'Submission and Imperium in the Early Medieval Insular World', unpublished Ph.D. dissertation (Edinburgh, 2003), 128.
117. See below, 72–4.
118. Broun, *Irish Identity*, 174, 188–9; Dauvit Broun, '*Alba*: Pictish homeland or Irish offshoot?', in Pamela O'Neill (ed.), *Exile and Homecoming. Papers from the Fifth Australian Conference of Celtic Studies, University of Sydney, July 2004* (Sydney, 2005), 234–75, at 264–5; but see also David N. Dumville, '*Cethri Prímchenéla Dáil Riata*', *Scottish Gaelic Studies* 20 (2000) 170–91.
119. Broun, '*Alba*: Pictish homeland or Irish offshoot?', 265–74; David N. Dumville, *The Churches of North Britain in the First Viking-Age. The Fifth Whithorn Lecture, 14th September 1996* (Whithorn, 1997), 35–6.
120. See above, 7 and 27 n. 30.
121. Davidson, 'Submission and Imperium', 129.
122. Citing, for example, how Eadred, who was king 951–5, showed a preference in his documents for the title *rex et primicerius tocius Albionis*, 'king and chief of all Albion': *ibid.*, 159.
123. On the absence of charters, see most recently Dauvit Broun, 'The adoption of brieves in Scotland', in Marie-Thérèse Flanagan and Judith A. Green (eds), *Charters and Charter Scholarship in Britain and Ireland* (London, 2005), 164–83. For a discussion of the significance of having a coinage, see Ian Blanchard, 'Lothian and beyond: the economy of the "English empire" of David I', in Richard Britnell and John Hatcher (eds), *Progress and Problems in Medieval England. Essays in Honour of Edward Miller* (Cambridge, 1996), 23–43, esp. 33–7.
124. David N. Dumville, *Wessex and England from Alfred to Edgar* (Woodbridge, 1992), 146–54; Eric John, *Orbis Britannie and Other Studies* (Leicester, 1966), 52–6.
125. A. Campbell (ed.), *Chronicle of Æthelweard* (London, 1962), 9. It has been suggested that Æthelweard may have been the first to use the term

Anglia for England, in which case it would be striking that, for him, it was equated with *Britannia*: see Nicholas Banton, 'Monastic reform and the unification of tenth-century England', in Stuart Mews (ed.), *Religion and National Identity*, Studies in Church History, no. 18 (Oxford, 1982), 71–85, at 85 n. 74.

126. Davies, *The First English Empire*, 9–10, 51. Note, for example, the discussion in Frank Barlow, *Edward the Confessor* (London, 1970), 136–7, of the idea of Edward's realm as Britain in the Life of Edward the Confessor.

127. Davies, *The First English Empire*, 36–7.

128. *Ibid.*, 140; see also 93, 112.

129. John Gillingham, 'The beginning of English imperialism', *Journal of Historical Sociology*, 5 (1992) 392–409; John Gillingham, 'The English invasion of Ireland', in Brendan Bradshaw and other (eds), *Representing Ireland: Literature and the Origins of Conflict, 1534–1600* (Cambridge, 1993), 24–42; John Gillingham, 'The foundations of a disunited kingdom', in Alexander Grant and Keith J. Stringer (eds), *Uniting the Kingdom? The Making of British History* (London, 1995), 48–64. The first and third of these articles are reprinted in John Gillingham, *The English in the Twelfth Centure: Imperialism, National Identity and Political Values* (Woodbridge, 2000), chs 1 and 6.

130. Davies, *The First English Empire*, 52.

131. *Ibid.*, 47.

132. Dauvit Broun, 'The Picts' place in the kingship's past before John of Fordun', in Edward J. Cowan and Richard J. Finlay (eds), *Scottish History: the Power of the Past* (Edinburgh, 2002), 11–28.

133. In a Scottish context, see Broun, *The Irish Identity*, 8–10.

134. For example, John Gillingham, *The English in the Twelfth Century: Imperialism, National Identity and Political Values* (Woodbridge, 2000), esp. on Gaimar's influence on centuries of English national history, and Geoffrey of Monmouth's Welsh agenda; Máire Herbert, 'Sea-divided Gaels? Constructing relationships between Irish and Scots *c.* 800–1169', in Brendan Smith (ed.), *Britain and Ireland 900–1300* (Cambridge, 1999), 87–97, and Máire Herbert, 'Rí Éirenn, Rí Alban: kingship and identity in the ninth and tenth centuries', in Simon Taylor (ed.), *Kings, Clerics and Chroniclers in Scotland 500–1297* (Dublin, 2000), 62–72, on the Irish emphasis on Ireland and Alba as separate, rather than forming a single Gaelic world; and Huw Pryce, 'British or Welsh? National identity in twelfth-century Wales', *English Historical Review* 116 (2001) 775–801, on the Welsh identification of Wales as Britain, and on their switch from 'Britons' to 'Welsh'.

PART I

The Idea of Britain

2

Ancient Kingdoms and Island Histories

The Historiographical Portrayal of Ultimate Secular Authority
from the Eleventh to the Thirteenth Centuries

By the end of the thirteenth century it was the firm conviction of Scottish leaders that their kingdom could boast as long a history of freedom as any other kingdom. It was assumed that if a kingdom was independent within the memory of most people this automatically meant that it must have been an independent kingdom in the deep past. This was explained with striking candour by Scottish procurators at the papal Curia in 1301 while engaged in a war of words with Edward I's representatives:[1]

> It is certain that, just as the kingdom of Scotland has recently been shown to have been free when its last king died [Alexander III in 1286], so it is presumed to have been free from antiquity if we make an assumption from the recent past and apply it to the more remote past before then, just as the laws dictate.

This principle was given substance not only in the statement in the Declaration of Arbroath (1320) that Robert I was the 113th in an unbroken succession of Scottish kings without a single foreigner intervening, but by a similar claim to institutional longevity in an account of the kingship's history written during King John's reign (1292–1304). There John appeared as the latest in a list of more than 110 kings, and it was calculated that the kingdom was 1,976 years, 9 months and 8 days old on the day of John's inauguration on 30 November 1292.[2] Another account, datable to sometime between 1296 and 1306, was less ambitious, making John merely the fifty-second king of Scots, but it shared the Declaration of Arbroath's insistence that every king had been a Scot.[3]

There are other examples of kingdoms at this time which sported a long history. The Irish Remonstrance of 1317 proclaimed that Ireland had an even more impressive record of freedom, stretching back for 197 kings until, it was stated, the English Pope Hadrian IV (1154–9) 'improperly conferred *de facto* lordship' on Henry II of England in 1170.[4] The English themselves regarded Geoffrey of Monmouth's vivid account of over 100 British kings spanning about 1,800 years up to the seventh century AD as the ancient history of their monarchy.[5] Further afield, we may note the amazing coincidence that Eirikr VI of Denmark (1286–1319), who was Robert Bruce's contemporary (both were born in 1274), was, like Robert in the Declaration of Arbroath, advertised as the 113th king of his country.[6] There are also instances, like the Declaration of Arbroath, in which a claim to ancient independence was elaborated precisely because the kingdom's sovereignty was at issue. The impressive account of Danish history by Saxo Grammaticus, written sometime between 1208 and 1218, for example, was produced (so Saxo tells us) at the behest of Absalon, archbishop of Lund (1178–1201), in what has been seen as a deliberate attempt to give substance to Denmark's independent status which Absalon was keen to advance.[7]

Given that the claim of the Scottish kingdom to an ancient history was far from unusual, a logical place to start in order to gain a deeper understanding of this phenomenon in its wider context would be Susan Reynolds's pioneering work on the political ideas which underpinned such statements of ancient origins.[8] She observed that, during the early and central Middle Ages, 'communities of common descent, law and language' came, with the development of government, to be thought of increasingly as kingdoms so that 'kingdoms and peoples came to seem identical – not invariably, but sufficiently often for the coincidence of the two to seem the norm to contemporaries'.[9] Britain and Ireland are awkward, however. She noted that 'despite the common association of language, people, and descent, English writers of the thirteenth century do not seem to have expressed any sense of regnal solidarity through a regnal descent myth' focused on England itself (as opposed to Britain);[10] the Scots, on the other hand, 'produced [in the Declaration of Arbroath] one of the most eloquent statements of regnal solidarity to come out of the middle ages', although 'its subjects did not even have a common language'.[11] The Irish, for their part, had already in the 'Irish Remonstrance' of 1317 'used some of the same arguments [as the Declaration of Arbroath] about their difference from the English', even though they were 'not united in a kingdom'.[12] In all these cases the kingdom's profile in the past is a key part of the puzzle: a potent element in the Scottish and Irish statements to which Reynolds referred is the idea that Scotland and Ireland were ancient kingdoms; the lack of a regnal descent myth specifically for England speaks for itself.

A crucial ingredient in explaining this puzzle has been pinpointed by Rees Davies: 'The idea of Britain', he observed, 'exercised a powerful hold over the medieval mind. It had a depth, a resonance, a precision, and an incontestability which did not belong to the imprecise, contestable, and

Johnny-come-lately competitors – England, Scotland, Wales'.[13] He described how the most powerful kings of England were hailed as rulers of all Britain; how Canterbury regarded its archbishop as primate of Britain; and how Welsh churchmen, poets and leaders looked forward to a time when the island would once again be theirs, and the English destroyed. He observed that at the heart of these aspirations was the vision of a kingdom of Britain which was articulated with a markedly different emphasis by Welsh and English historians: the former by invoking the ancient island realm that had once been theirs, the latter by insisting that 'Britain' had become 'England'.[14] The magnetic force of the island of Britain in shaping the way that ultimate secular power was imagined was sufficiently strong that, even in the case of a precociously unified polity such as England, the sense of a kingdom of the English could not avoid being merged with the idea of Britain. Anything less would have seemed to diminish the authority of the king of England.

If the idea of Britain was so compelling, however, then how was a sense of Scottish regnal solidarity achieved? The statements of an ancient Scottish kingship referred to earlier all seem to show that for Scotland there was a clearer sense that kingdom and people were identical than was the case for Wales and England. This is all the more remarkable given that the Scots had less cultural homogeneity than the Welsh or English, and a less well developed royal government than England. Rees Davies, understandably, was unable to engage in any depth with the fairly intractable Scottish material, but he suspected that 'the Scottish situation . . . was not dissimilar' to the Irish and Welsh, whose historical myths 'were already age-old when the twelfth century opened'.[15] It remains to be seen once the Scottish material has been examined more fully, how far the idea of Scotland as a distinct and ancient kingdom can be traced before the 1290s. To what extent was the Scots' sense of regnal solidarity untroubled by the reality of geography which was defied by its borders? The answer is important for a proper assessment of the power of the island of Britain in influencing how the highest secular authority was imagined.

In order to explore this further it will be useful to focus on a form of articulating regnal solidarity that was developed not only in Scotland but also in England and Wales so that significant parallels and contrasts might be drawn. It will also be important to include Ireland, for if the conception of political authority was influenced by the fact that Britain is an island, then it is obviously relevant to investigate this in relation to the island of Ireland, too. An expression of regnal solidarity which meets these criteria is the continuous narrative of a kingship's history. This was a new historiographical phenomenon of the eleventh and twelfth centuries in Britain and Ireland, and represents one of the most significant examples of the increasing prominence of kingdoms in the mental landscape. It was not the rise of a new genre: indeed, it could take markedly different literary forms. What all have in common is that they made it possible to tell the story, not just of a few famous kings and heroic battles, but of a kingship over many centuries, typically (but not invariably) stretching from the deep past to the present day. This was not only an expression of the central place of a kingdom in a society's perception of itself, but was a crucial element in the mental infrastructure which enabled a heightened sense of regnal solidarity to be sustained. The more cogently the narrative was constructed, the more readily it could enter the political and cultural bloodstream. So powerful was this phenomenon that it remained a central feature of the writing and reading of History for centuries. Indeed, it would not be too much to say that, although much of the detail, emphasis and method, as well as the language and literary style, have of course changed fundamentally, the national histories which enjoyed unquestioned supremacy until recently can be recognised as the direct descendants of the continuous regnal narratives that were created for the first time in this period.

The main business of this chapter is an examination of this phenomenon and what it reveals about the development of regnal identity in this period. England, Ireland, Scotland and Wales were each endowed with impressive accounts of long successions of kings, enabling a meaningful comparison to be made between them in what they reveal about the aspirations and assumptions which underpinned them. Despite the questions raised by the example of Scottish regnal solidarity, the result goes significantly further than Rees Davies in suggesting the hold which the island of Britain exercised over ideas of kingship and the past, and offers an additional dimension to Susan Reynolds's observation of the way that kingdoms and peoples came to seem identical in this period.

THE CREATION OF CONTINUOUS REGNAL HISTORIES: ENGLAND, WALES AND IRELAND

The intimate relationship between the earliest English continuous regnal narratives and more modern accounts of English History was first remarked upon by Rees Davies. He described the English History taught in schools and universities until a generation ago as a 'wonderfully self-confident and intellectually deeply satisfying construct' whose 'academic apotheosis' was the achievement of a generation of Oxford scholars in the late nineteenth century, including Bishop William Stubbs, author of *The Constitutional History of England* (1874–8), and J. R. Green, author of *A Short History of the English People* (1874).[16] Institutional and constitutional development was its rationale, a deep appreciation of England's continuity lay at its heart, and it embodied a powerful sense of England's superiority within Britain. It is a view of History, moreover, which remains alive into the twenty-first century: as the general editor of *The New Oxford History of England* explains,

> the institutional core of the story which runs from Anglo-Saxon times to our own is the story of a state-structure built round the English monarchy and its effective successor, the Crown in Parliament, and that provides the only continuous articulation of the history of peoples we today call British.[17]

Professor Davies argued compellingly that this construct 'was arguably first shaped in the early twelfth century' by William of Malmesbury and Henry of Huntingdon, who 'in effect laid down some of the basic guidelines for its historiography: it should be regnal, political, continuous, developmental, and self-containedly English'.[18] Both William and Henry started work independently at much the same time: the earliest drafts of William of Malmesbury's *Gesta Regum Anglorum*, 'Deeds of Kings of the English', it has been argued, 'were written over a number of years up to about 1126';[19] the first version of Henry of Huntingdon's *Historia Anglorum*, 'History of the English', can be dated to sometime between 1123 and 1131.[20] These works were followed in the next decade by an account of English history in the vernacular, Geffrei Gaimar's *Estoire des Engleis*, the earliest surviving history in French.[21] The extant text consists of 6,526 verses of Anglo-French poetry covering the period from the arrival of Cerdic in 495 to the death of William Rufus in 1100. The poem has been seen as rather tedious, although it has been emphasised that it comes into its own as a narrative towards the end as Gaimar's dependence on the Anglo-Saxon Chronicle ceased.[22]

Professor Davies pointed out that the construct of a continuous English past was almost immediately challenged by an altogether more ambitious statement of regnal history: Geoffrey of Monmouth's brilliant *Historia Regum Britannie* ('History of Kings of Britain'), begun by 1135 and completed by 1138, created a vivid account of an ancient British kingdom ruled by a succession of kings spanning almost two millennia up to the seventh century AD, including the mighty figure of Arthur.[23] Geoffrey's portrayal of a kingship encompassing the island of Britain from ancient times until the onset of English hegemony was constructed as a history of and for the Welsh, identified as the remnants of Geoffrey's

Britons: although Geoffrey stopped his narrative centuries before his own day (announcing that he was leaving the task of writing Welsh history beyond the 680s to his contemporary Caradog of Llancarfan), he stole a glance at the future, and prophesied that the Welsh would one day be restored as rulers of Britain.[24] Geoffrey also saw his work as having an Anglo-Norman audience, dedicating it first and foremost to Robert, earl of Gloucester.[25] The astonishing number of extant manuscripts, however, shows that it captured the imagination not only of English readers, but also of readers on the Continent.[26]

It was not long before this Welsh past was adopted and adapted by English historians and repackaged as England's ancient history.[27] Within five years of its publication Geoffrey's vision had been incorporated by Alfred of Beverley into his impressive survey of English history.[28] Alfred's work may itself have been of limited influence, but it was an important taste of better things to come. A little more than ten years later Geoffrey's own text was revised from an English perspective, and a vernacular version, Wace's *Roman de Brut*, made it accessible to England's French-speaking elite.[29] Wace's *Brut* had, in fact, been anticipated, at least in principle, by Geffrei Gaimar, who considered in his *Estoire des Engleis* that English history embraced the Trojan War and the history of kings of Britain. It is possible that he may have covered these subjects in a lost part of his work.[30]

Such appropriation of Geoffrey's vision of a British past for English purposes should come as no surprise. English writers had since (at least) the late tenth century seen England and Britain as synonymous.[31] It was inevitable, therefore, that Geoffrey of Monmouth's glorious British past should be identified by English historians as part of England's history.[32] This is also reflected in how Gaimar's *Estoire des Engleis* was read. Gaimar's *Estoire* is preceded by Wace's *Brut* in all four manuscripts of Gaimar's work; in two of these it is followed by Jordan Fantosme's chronicle of the Anglo-Scottish war of 1173–4, which has led Peter Damian-Grint to suggest that all three texts were seen in the early thirteenth century as 'forming a complete composite history of Britain'.[33] On a more general level, the number of extant manuscripts of the various vernacular accounts of kings from Brutus to the Plantagenets suggests that this vision of English regnal antiquity soon reached deep into the nervous system of English historical consciousness. As far as French prose versions are concerned, for example, Diana Tyson has counted thirteen manuscripts which end with Henry III (1216–72), John (1199–1216) or Richard I (1189–99).[34] The existence of Wace's *Brut* and similar works in the vernacular also meant that this narrative was accessible to many in the Anglo-Norman realm, including the king himself: Wace was made a canon of Bayeux by Henry II (1154–89) on the strength of his *Roman de Brut*,[35] and King John is documented as enjoying 'a romance of the history of England' while at Windsor.[36]

This does not mean that Geoffrey's history was surrendered by the Welsh. *Historia Regum Britannie* itself was translated into Welsh three times in the thirteenth century.[37] Geoffrey's suggestion that Welsh history could be continued from where he left off was taken up in Strata Florida by the end of the thirteenth century (certainly after 1282, the last year in the chronicle, and possibly after 1286). Thomas Jones suggested that this seminal text, now lost, was 'possibly called *Cronica* (or *Historia*) *Principum Walliae* (or *Britanniae*)'.[38] It survives only because it was translated on more than one occasion: these Welsh versions are known under the title *Brut y Tywysogion*, 'Chronicle of the Princes', and may be dated originally to the early fourteenth century.[39] In a manner reminiscent of Henry of Huntingdon's *Historia Anglorum*, the annalistic structure of the original text behind *Brut y Tywysogion* was adapted into a 'stepping stone' chronology: in one version events are described as occurring 'a year after that' (or 'X years after that'); in another version the simple formula 'and then' is used. Unlike Henry of Huntingdon, though, the chronological *terra firma* is intermittent *Anno Domini* dates rather than the beginning of a reign, and the material has been selected rather than repackaged.

The Latin original of these works was not the first attempt to give an account of Welsh history using *Historia Regum Britannie* as a springboard. The earliest is a text known to scholarship as version C of *Annales Cambriae*: this finishes with events in 1288 in its only extant manuscript, although the archetype has been dated to sometime after 1202.[40] Caroline Brett has shown that not only does this include a preface containing material on kings of Britain derived from Geoffrey of Monmouth, but the text of *Annales Cambriae* itself has been rewritten in line with Geoffrey's narrative.[41] Version C of *Annales Cambriae* may therefore represent the first sustained attempt to produce a single work in which Geoffrey of Monmouth's history of a British kingdom was married with a rudimentary account of events in Wales. The apotheosis of this process of creating a chronologically complete vision of the Welsh past was when *Brut y Brenhinedd* (the translation of *Historia Regum Britannie*) was prefaced by *Ystoria Dared* (a translation of *De Excidio Troiae Historia*) and followed by *Brut y Tywysogion*, a combination which is found in two groups of manuscripts and dates back to the fourteenth century.[42] This trilogy has been described by Brynley Roberts as 'a "majestic compilation" of some two or three thousand years of Welsh history' from Trojan origins to the loss of sovereignty in 1282. [43] This bears comparison with the 'complete composite history of Britain' inhabited by Gaimar's *Estoire des Engleis* in two of its manuscripts, and shows that, for all the obvious limitations of *Brut y Tywysogion* and Gaimar's *Estoire* as continuous regnal narratives, they were nonetheless capable of fulfilling this role.

The construction of Ireland's regnal, continuous and self-contained past was achieved earlier than those of the English and the Welsh, and with some exceptional scholarly *élan*. Irish historians in the mid-eleventh century created a complete vision of Ireland's history by integrating the account of Gaelic origins into a comprehensive exposition of Ireland's legendary settlers, from the first to arrive on the island before the time of Noah up to the Gaelic colonisation led by the sons of Míl. This immensely impressive text, known to scholarship as *Lebor Gabála Érenn* ('The Book of the Taking of Ireland'), was the subject of much revision and elaboration – almost as soon as it had been written. [44] The outstanding historian at this time was Gilla Coemáin mac Gilla Shamthainne (who was alive in 1072). [45] It has been pointed out that one of his works seems to have been used as a source of *Lebor Gabála*, while another, in contrast, appears to have drawn on *Lebor Gabála* itself, which suggests not only that *Lebor Gabála* was first composed in his lifetime, but that he belonged to the same scholarly circles as its creator(s). [46] The work which betrays a particular awareness of *Lebor Gabála* is his celebrated poem on kings of Ireland, *Ériu árd, inis na ríg*, 'Noble Ireland, island of the kings'. [47] In its earliest manuscript this work consists of 149 stanzas, of which the first 32 give an account of each taking of Ireland from the first settler before the Flood to Éremón son of Míl, first of the Gaels to rule Ireland, before listing over a hundred pre-Christian kings of Ireland, with reigns-lengths and explanations of how each of them died. This formed a pair with a poem giving a plainer account of kings of Ireland in the Christian era up to the early eleventh century. [48] Together these poems provided, in a memorable form, the first continuous account of Ireland's history from its first settlers and primeval, pre-Gaelic, kings all the way to the recent past. [49] They were themselves based on two poems by Flann Mainistrech (d.1056) on pre-Christian and Christian kings of Ireland written for Mael Sechnaill mac Domnaill (980–1002, 1014–22), the last of the southern Uí Néill to be king of Tara and acknowledged ruler of Ireland. [50] Flann provided details of the kings' deaths, but only a very occasional reign-length. [51]

A compelling case has been made by Peter Smith for seeing *Lebor Gabála*, Gilla Coemáin and Flann as the culmination of a larger project begun in the early eleventh century to produce 'a compendium of the historical knowledge of the entire Irish nation and its leaders'.[52] The most remarkable scholarly achievement of this 'school' was Gilla Coemáin's poem of fifty-eight stanzas, *Annálad anall uile*, a chronological tour de force in which key events of Ireland's past from its first settlement after the Flood to 1072 are synchronised with the history of the world from its very beginning.[53] This was a one-off masterpiece. The legacy of Flann and Gilla Coemáin was not only in providing an authoritative and full vision of an ancient and enduring kingdom of Ireland, but in developing a particular sub-genre of regnal history: what Francis John Byrne has aptly described as a series of summarised *aideda* or death-tales.[54] This was particularly suited to emphasising the institutional longevity of a kingship in contrast to the mortality of kings, and was deployed (on a smaller chronological scale than Gilla Coemáin's *Ériu árd, inis na ríg*) for 'provincial' kingships (such as Ulster, Connacht and Leinster).[55]

Scholars of this rank not only shaped the historical imagination of their compatriots for six centuries and more, but could be men of power and influence in their own time. A major early figure in articulating a vision of a primordial kingdom of Ireland was Eochaid ua Flainn, who has been identified with Eochaid ua Flannacáin, a leading member of the ecclesiastical establishment of Armagh.[56] In one poem Eochaid gave an account of Ireland's history ending with a succession of kings before and after the first Gaelic settlers.[57] In his death-notice in 1004 he is referred to as *suí senchasa*, 'sage of history': John Carey has pointed out that he is the first (and Flann Mainistrech the second) in a succession of seven scholars accorded this title in Irish chronicles in the following century and a half.[58] He has also drawn attention to Eochaid's 'massive influence' in Armagh (all abbots from 1001 to 1134 were his descendants), a pattern also discernible at Monasterboice (where Flann Mainistrech was *fer légind*, the head of the scriptorium): Flann's son and two grandsons all held the office of superior.[59]

It was not only the 'basic guidelines' for English historiography as regnal, political and continuous that were laid down as early as the mid-twelfth century, therefore; the same conception of a regnal and continuous past – and with conspicuous chronological depth – was given narrative expression for Ireland by the mid-eleventh century, and for the Welsh in the mid-twelfth century (albeit confined to the remote past, and with a more deliberate focus on Wales itself only being produced by the late thirteenth century). They all perpetuated the same essential idea: that there was such a thing as a continuous narrative of English, Irish and Welsh history, and that this narrative had as its central thread the existence of, or development towards, a kingdom relating to each people. There are, however, striking differences between historians of the eleventh and twelfth centuries in their approach to History and in the form of their work. Geoffrey of Monmouth's flamboyant attitude to the reconstruction of the past contrasts with the concern of English historians for veracity and impartiality, or the careful dependence on tradition shown by their Irish counterparts. On the other hand, the king-list poems of Flann Mainstrech and Gilla Coemáin seem sparse and dull compared with the vivid narrative of Geoffrey's prose. Each, however, was designed for a different purpose. It has been suggested, for example, that Irish scholars composed poetry as a way of packaging an array of detailed information so that it could be more easily learned and retained by Gaelic men of learning as part of their training.[60] The substantial variety in form exhibited by these literary enterprises, moreover, was to a large extent dictated by the nature of their sources. The deepest chronological reaches of the Irish king-list material was constructed on the basis of an alternating succession between different branches of the descendants of the first Gaelic settlers, making best use of the detailed genealogical framework articulated by scholars of an earlier era; the catalogue of deaths which this inspired set the tone of the work as a whole. Henry of Huntingdon and William of Malmesbury were heavily dependent on Bede and the Anglo-Saxon Chronicle, which gave them the material with which to weave their narrative line; it did not, however, afford them the chronological substance achieved by their Irish counterparts in a way which could be sustained throughout: that was only achieved by their successors who had the benefit of Geoffrey of Monmouth's work. Geoffrey of Monmouth himself, although it has been argued that he made clever use of Welsh material that suited his purpose,[61] had nothing to go on comparable in scale with what was available to Irish and English scholars;[62] but this merely allowed his creative genius the freedom to conjure up a vision of a long and ancient line of kings punctuated by vivid portrayals of strong and weak rulers which captured the imagination not only of English and Welsh writers but of Continental audiences, too. To some extent, then, the very different results of these similar endeavours could be seen as a consequence of the pioneering nature of each enterprise. In each case there was no continuous regnal narrative on this scale which could be the foundations of their work. In each case, including Geoffrey of Monmouth, their creations were built on existing structures which were designed for a different purpose. And in each case the nature of the existing literary landscape played an important part in determining the character of the continuous regnal history they erected upon it.

The different intellectual environments they inhabited also contributed to how these seminal works were conceived and the ways in which they subsequently flourished.

The authors of these pioneering works, however, did not themselves invent the image of a kingdom of Ireland, a Welsh kingdom of Britain, or a kingdom of England. These already had a literary life, for example, in tales of kings of Tara and the Welsh triads. It has been argued that, in the case of England, King Alfred's literary legacy reveals a 'vision of one people united through a shared history, common faith and opposition to the Danes under a single rulership'.[63] In the case of Wales, Rachel Bromwich, editor of the Welsh triads, has argued that the earliest material in the corpus represents 'the oldest stratum in medieval Welsh literature as a whole', and that the title given to this material, *Trioedd Ynys Prydein* (literally, 'Triads of the Island of Britain'), is significant because 'they commemorate the traditions of the Island of Britain as a whole; they look back upon the essential and still ideal sovereign unity of the country'.[64] Tara, for its part, is regularly equated explicitly with the kingship of Ireland. In *Togail Bruidne Da Derga*, for example, the identification of the king of Tara as ruler of Ireland was probably in the earliest version of the tale, which has been dated to the ninth century.[65] What makes all the regnal histories of the eleventh and twelfth centuries different, and what they all have in common, is that the central figure was not an individual king or dynasty, but a kingship.

No ideological or cultural impulse as such could be said to have been shared by these early historians. Geoffrey of Monmouth may have been moved to write in response to the achievements of his English contemporaries, and inhabited much the same cultural climate, but the significantly earlier Irish works were unknown to him. Gilla Coemáin and Flann Mainistrech, for their part, were working within a centuries-old tradition of historical verse.[66] Out of these very different backgrounds a significantly similar result was achieved: each kingdom was portrayed as an enduring institution of ancient origin. Moreover, these texts were more than just a bare listing of a succession of kings or a loosely related account of events year by year; they had some consistent narrative detail, even if (as in the case of the poems of Flann Mainstrech and Gilla Coemáin) this amounted to little more than summarised death-tales. Each kingdom now had a coherent and chronologically fulfilling story of its past. This was the essential conception which was retold and later reshaped up to the twentieth century in Wales and Ireland as much as in England.

SCOTLAND AS AN EXCEPTIONAL CASE

There can be no doubt that these major historical works were known in Scotland. Geoffrey of Monmouth's history inspired an alternative name for Edinburgh Castle, which appears occasionally as 'Castle of the Maidens' in the place-date of royal charters from around 1140.[67] The first edition of William of Malmesbury's *History* was presented to David I as soon as it was finished (probably in late 1126 or early 1127 when he was in England);[68] Henry of Huntingdon's *History* was a source for the Declaration of Arbroath.[69] If French literature was known and composed in William I's household, then it is not fanciful to assume that a work like Wace's *Brut* would have been known there.[70] A knowledge of Irish regnal historiography, on the other hand, is specifically suggested by a list beginning with Cinaed mac Ailpín (d.858), probably written in 1124, which, in common with Irish 'provincial' king-lists composed in this period, adopted the characteristic form used by Flann Mainistrech and Gilla Coemáin of a series of summarised death-tales.[71] All in all, it might seem natural, therefore, to expect that Scottish scholars in the twelfth century would also have been inspired to equip their kingdom with a vision of a continuous regnal history stretching into the deep past. It is often claimed, indeed, that the Scottish kingdom had already achieved a precocious degree of cohesion before the twelfth century,[72] which it might be supposed would have made it easier for Scots to conceive of their kingdom as an ancient and enduring entity.

The truth about Scottish history-writing, however, would seem to have been very different. It was not until at least a century after Geoffrey of Monmouth and his English counterparts that anything like a comparable narrative of Scottish kingship was produced: indeed, little was made of the opportunities that existed to portray the king of Scots, even in a simple catalogue, as the latest in a long line of predecessors on his throne. The king-list text of probably 1124 which has just been referred to, for example, contained only two dozen kings and reached back a mere 275 years or so, a significantly less impressive structure than that expounded in similar texts for kings of Ulster or their like, and barely visible when set alongside the mighty monument erected for the kingdom of Ireland. In a world where antiquity and legitimacy went hand in hand, the Scottish effort can hardly be regarded as claiming the same status for its kingship as its supposed Irish counterpart. This lack of ambition is even more striking if a late-eleventh-century poem, known to scholarship as *Duan Albanach*, is regarded as Scottish in origin.[73] It boasted a succession of over fifty kings (assuming that a couple of verses have been lost), from Loarn and Fergus, sons of Erc mac Echdach, through Cinaed mac Ailpín (without any hint of a break), and up to Mael Coluim III (1058–93), as well as a brief summary of earlier settlements in Scotland. Not only is it devoid of the limited narrative detail of Irish king-list poems, but it had no influence on any extant Scottish history-writing. The text itself survives only in modern Irish manuscripts, the earliest from the mid-seventeenth century.[74] When an attempt was made during the reign of William I (1165–1214) to extend the succession back before Cinaed mac Ailpín, neither *Duan Albanach* nor its source was used.[75] Instead, considerable ingenuity had to be deployed in order to join a different list of kings of Dál Riata ending with Fergus mac Echdach (d.781) to the list beginning with Cinaed mac Ailpín in such a way that the whole succession would be consistent with the account of Cinaed's ancestry in the royal genealogy.[76] There seems otherwise to have been little desire in the twelfth century to proclaim the reigning king as the latest in a long succession. It is not until the next century that even the barest outline of a regnal history focused on Scotland can be detected taking shape. The first flicker of the flame of Scottish History was the gradual assemblage in the thirteenth century of the most obvious materials relating to the kingship's past and Scottish origins.[77] The two clearest options were to present the king of Scots as the successor of kings of the Picts or successor of kings of 'Scots' of Dál Riata. Sometime during the reign of Alexander II (1214–49) a king-list was written which, for the first time, included both Dál Riatan and Pictish antecedents.[78]

A simple list of kings and their reign-lengths is the most minimal form of regnal history possible. It can only have had a very limited audience, probably even among men of letters. The lists of kings of Ireland by Flann Mainstrech and Gilla Coemáin were at least designed to be memorable, and their conception as a series of summarised death-tales gave their work some narrative substance. When did Scottish History acquire some flesh on its bare bones? The earliest extant full-scale history is John of Fordun's *Chronicle of the Scottish People* (written sometime between 1384 and 1387). It can be shown, however, that much of its structure has been derived from an earlier work that may be dated to 1285. This will be discussed in chapter 8, along with the possibility that there may have been an earlier narrative attributed to 'Veremundus' (identified as Richard Vairement, a *céle Dé* of St Andrews, who is first mentioned in 1239 and appears for the last time on record in 1267).[79]

Why did it take so long to produce a regnal narrative? It might be objected that this is an unreasonable question: acts of creativity on this scale are not done to order. This, nevertheless, would be too easy a response. It would not have required the genius of a Geoffrey of Monmouth to fashion a continuous regnal history for Scotland if that had been needed. Geoffrey of Monmouth seems to have had very little material to hand which could have met his needs.[80] Scottish historians, in contrast, were blessed with the Pictish king-list, which, in the form in which it was finally constructed – known to scholarship as *Series Longior* or the longer list – gave nearly a hundred kings reigning for a total of nearly 2,000 years.[81] Mael Coluim III (1058–93) was presented in a list at the end of *Lebor Bretnach* as the direct successor of these kings, a text which Thomas Clancy has shown is of Scottish origin.[82] Instead of this splendid king-list becoming the basis of a full-bodied narrative, however, it was largely ignored and was not incorporated into a coherent account of the kingship's past until Thomas Innes's celebrated *Critical Essay* published in 1729.[83] The shorter list, which still boasted about sixty kings, was saved from obscurity by its inclusion alongside a Dál Riata list in the aforementioned king-list of Alexander II's reign (1214–49). There is no indication that any king in the twelfth century was presented specifically as a successor of Pictish kings.[84]

This belated recognition of the kingship's Pictish antecedents calls for some comment. Superficially the most obvious point is that the kingdom's immediate origin was described in terms of a destruction of the Picts by Cinaed mac Ailpín, descendant of Irish kings. Taken literally, this would hardly allow for the portrayal of any meaningful continuity. This cannot be a sufficient explanation, however. At the very least the accession of Cinaed could have been recast in less dramatic terms (as modern historians have attempted to do in a misguided attempt to endow this legend with more plausibility than it deserves).[85] A superficial comparison may be made with the ability of English historians in the twelfth century and later to present their kings as the successors not only of Anglo-Saxon kings but also of Geoffrey of Monmouth's British kings.

The most direct explanation is that a self-contained and exclusively Scottish regnal past, such as the Pictish king-list could have offered, was not needed in the twelfth century. The established way of expressing the kingship's claim to an authenticating antiquity was *not* by presenting the reigning monarch as the latest in a long line of kings who ruled all, or even part, of what was then Scotland. Instead, the Scottish kingship obtained its authenticating antiquity from pre-Christian Irish kings. A vivid illustration of this is the reading aloud of the king's Irish ancestry at the inauguration of Alexander III in 1249.[86] In the royal genealogy, indeed, there were more kings of Ireland than there were successors of Fergus Mór, and nearly as many kings of Ireland as there were kings from

Cinaed mac Ailpín.[87] This was not all. Irish royal ancestry was complemented from the twelfth century by descent through St Margaret from English kings. This possibility was exploited, for example, in an unpublished history of the Scottish kingship written at Dunfermline during the reign of Alexander III (possibly *ca* 1250).[88] This text gives an account of each king of England from Edmund Ironside to William Rufus before switching to Mael Coluim III and his successors, with a particular interest in St Margaret.[89] This approach was given more elaborate treatment by Aelred of Rievaulx in his eulogy of David I written in 1153 or 1154.[90] Dunfermline was St Margaret's own foundation, and was the burial place of kings during the twelfth century.[91] This aspect of Scottish royal ancestry may well, therefore, have been encouraged by the kings themselves. Aelred himself, moreover, had close ties with the Scottish royal court, where he had once been a household official, and he doubtless represented an important current of opinion in the Scottish kingdom.[92]

The most obvious way in which these genealogical links displayed the Scottish kingship's credentials was by providing a claim to ancient royal roots. There was another, more fundamental, aspect to this than mere antiquity, however. Both the king's Irish and English pedigrees affirmed his status in terms of the God-given fact that Ireland and Britain were islands. Scottish kings were proclaimed as descended from kings of Ireland. Their English roots led even more directly to kings in the tenth century who were portrayed unambiguously as kings of Britain. Aelred, for example, in his account of David I's English ancestors, spoke of how all the island had been given through God's agency to Edgar without bloodshed, and how 'Scotland, Cumbria and Wales hastened enthusiastically to subject themselves to him'.[93] This could also have pointed to the potential of a kingship of Britain in the future insofar as they, as Margaret's descendants, were regarded as the true heirs of the English kingship whose right had been usurped by William the Conqueror. This point of view was forcibly expressed by Adam of Dryburgh, writing in 1180, and was also alluded to by William of Malmesbury in the covering-letter to the first edition of his *Gesta Regum Anglorum*, 'Deeds of Kings of the English', in which he described David I as 'sole heir to such a line of kings and princes'.[94] The claim that Scottish monarchs were the true heirs to the English crown was to be repeated into the late middle ages.[95]

Looking again at the pioneers of English, Irish and Welsh regnal history, the island of Ireland and the island of Britain can be seen to have been equally fundamental in shaping their historical imagination. The portrayal of a continuous and ancient kingdom of Ireland was only part of a much larger scheme of the island's history which Eochaid ua Flannacáin, Flann Mainistrech and Gilla Coemáin themselves elaborated. It will also be recalled that English and Welsh historians both defined their kingships in relation to Britain. Not only did English writers regard England as a more up-to-date name for Britain, but kings of England were, from the mid-twelfth century, presented as successors of the kings of Britain who Geoffrey of Monmouth had so vividly brought to life. The Welsh, for their part, saw themselves as Britain's original inhabitants (and still do).[96] It was this claim which sustained their identification with the kingdom of Britain which in Merlin's prophecy (again by Geoffrey of Monmouth) they were destined one day to recover.[97] The conception of the past which all these have in common is that when it came to presenting a kingship as an institution of awesome antiquity, the chief point of reference was not a concept of the English, Welsh or Irish as peoples, but an aspect of God's creation whose permanence was instantly perceptible: the geographical reality of Britain and Ireland. This is particularly stark in the case of the Scottish kingship in the twelfth century, where descent from kings of Ireland and from kings of England/ Britain, rather than from ancient kings of Scotland, was what was emphasised.

For the English, Irish and Welsh the association of kingdom and country continued thereafter to be satisfied by referring to the islands of Britain and Ireland. The way this was constructed allowed both English and Welsh to be presented as distinct peoples each with their own claim on Britain. Rees Davies has portrayed the designation of Britain as England by medieval Englishmen as a denial of Welsh claims to the island: 'the final solution to the British problem', as he called it.[98] That may be so; but the English were no different from anyone else in defining their kingdom in terms of their island, and may simply have been inspired by this, rather than by a specific desire to counter the Welsh. It may be noted, also, that the Welsh for 'island', *ynys*, was used to translate the Latin *regnum*, 'kingdom':[99] in *Brenhinedd y Saesson*, for example, it appears twice in that sense (and, from the context, seems to mean 'England' on both occasions).[100] It is true that the semantic growth of *ynys* to mean 'realm' may have been incubated in the special conditions of a literary formula (the 'island of Britain with its three adjacent islands'),[101] but the fact that *ynys* as 'realm' took hold outside this context is nonetheless striking. A crucial stage, it appears, was when the formula mutated into *tair ynys Prydain*, 'the three realms of Britain', which lies behind Geoffrey of Monmouth's primordial division of the island between the three sons of Brutus, with one receiving England, another Wales and the third

Scotland.[102] If the phrase *tair ynys Prydain* was originally inspired by the fact that Britain was inhabited chiefly by English, Welsh and Scots[103] (rather than because triplication represented an 'original mythical concept of the sovereign unity of the Island of Britain'),[104] then it would be notable how the geographical term *ynys* could be used in this way even when kingdoms were notionally equated with peoples.

In one fundamental respect the Scottish situation in the twelfth century and into the thirteenth was quite unlike that of the English, Irish or Welsh: no claim of exclusive right to Britain or Ireland was entertained by Scottish historians for the Scots.[105] Their kingship was legitimised by jumping piggyback onto the achievements of Irish and English historians, rather than by developing a vision of it as constituting a kingdom and country on a par with the English, Irish and Welsh. It would be too simple, however, to conclude that, before the mid- to late thirteenth century, the overpowering sense of geography as the appropriate framework for political legitimacy at the highest level meant of itself that a self-contained exclusive regnal history for Scotland was inconceivable. A continuous narrative may not have been developed, but the simple idea of a kingdom with an impressively long past is amply attested by Pictish king-lists. What, if anything, was the connection between geography and this clear (if basic) portrayal of an ancient Pictish kingdom?

It will be recalled that in general usage (as witnessed in placenames and incidental references in charters and in *Gesta Annalia*) 'Scotland' was regarded as the area north of the Forth, east of Drumalban (that is, the range of mountains running north from Ben Lomond) and south of Moray.[106] It is not difficult to see how Moray and the area west of Drumalban could have been regarded as distinct from the kingdom's core region as late as the reign of Alexander II (1214–49).[107] The Forth, however, made no sense in terms of the political realities in this period. Yet it was, if anything, deemed to be the most significant boundary of 'Scotland'. At the same time as 'Scotland' was referred to almost casually as the region between the Forth, Drumalban and Moray, it was also imagined self-consciously by the author of *De Situ Albanie* ('Concerning the Location of *Alba*'), writing during the reign of William I (1165–1214), as stretching from the Forth to the northern shore of the mainland.[108] For him the Firth of Forth was not simply the southern limit of *Alba* of old, moreover: he also referred to it in passing as the sea that 'divides the kingdoms of the Scots and the English'.[109] In the imagination of those associated with Scottish kingship, could Scotland north of the Forth have made sufficient sense as a geographical unit to sustain the notion of a self-contained ancient kingdom?

THE FORTH AND THE IDEA OF AN ANCIENT KINGDOM IN NORTHERN BRITAIN

The Firth of Forth and the boggy ground to the north of the River Forth inland from Stirling towards the mountains above Loch Lomond formed a formidable physical barrier that before the modern era would have nearly divided the island of Britain in two. This was vividly represented in medieval maps by depicting Scotland north of the Forth–Clyde isthmus as practically an island. As the editor of the 'Gough Map' (produced about 1360) observed, this was 'one of the most persistent features of the early cartography of Scotland'.[110] In the map of Britain by Matthew Paris (d.1259), Scotland north of the Forth is completely severed from the south but for the bridge at Stirling.[111] None of the map-makers had enough detailed knowledge of Scottish geography to challenge this cartographical habit. Although it says more about how Scotland was seen by educated Englishmen than anything else, the habit itself may reflect a more widely-held assumption about the significance of this geographical divide. This is suggested by the way Stirling itself was sometimes referred to by late medieval Scots. The Battle of Bannockburn, for example, was described in one place in Bower's *Scotichronicon* of the 1440s as 'beside the royal burgh of Stirling in Scotland, lying on the boundary of Britain'.[112] The legend on the seal of the burgh of Stirling itself in the late thirteenth century declared it to be on the frontier between Scots and Britons.[113]

Apart from Stirling itself, where before Wallace and Murray's famous victory in 1297 a bridge had been constructed over the Forth which joined with a causeway leading to firmer ground near the Abbey Craig,[114] the River Forth itself was passable only at a few points:[115] the fords at Drip close to Stirling;[116] the Fords of Frew about eight miles upstream, and a ford at Cardross about four miles further on.[117] No doubt those with local knowledge, once they had crossed from the south, would have been able to pick their way safely through the wetlands north of the river. For anyone else, the only obvious route linking north and south that did not involve passing by Stirling was the road from Kippen to Doune via the Fords of Frew. The ford here remains to this day a striking site: for a stretch of some eighty yards in summer the river's depth becomes no more than that of a paddling pool, but for a small channel near the north bank where the water courses up to an adult's knees. Not for nothing has it been mentioned as one of the seven wonders of Scotland.[118] Here, presumably, are the 'fords of the Forth' that were fortified by Cinaed mac Maíl Choluim (971–95).[119]

Was this, however, regarded as the southern border of an age-old kingdom? An immediate answer is offered by the longer Pictish king-list, which begins with an account of the legend of Cruithne and his seven sons who, together, signify Pictland's primordial territory stretching from Fife to Caithness. Clearly what the author had in mind was the landmass between the Forth and the Pentland Firth. But there is a problem. If the Pictish king-list originated in Pictish times, then (according to the standard view of the extent of Pictish settlement) its vision of the Forth as the limit of the Pictish kingdom could simply reflect cultural and political realities, rather than being an example of the power of this geographical feature in shaping expectations of what would constitute an ancient realm. It remains to be seen, therefore, if the logic of geography was in this case sufficiently compelling on its own, after the expansion of the power of kings of Scots south of the Forth in the mid-tenth century, to maintain this image of an ancient Pictish kingdom from Fife to Caithness.

Help is at hand in three texts datable to the mid- to late eleventh century. Two of these texts have been met already: *Lebor Bretnach*, consisting chiefly of a Gaelic translation and adaptation of *Historia Brittonum*, which has been shown by Thomas Clancy to have been written in Scotland (probably in Abernethy) during the reign of Mael Coluim III mac Donnchada (1058–93); and *Duan Albanach*, 'Scottish poem', which is largely a versified list of kings from the sons of Erc mac Echdach to Cinaed mac Ailpín and beyond to Mael Coluim.[120] Its reference to Mael Coluim III as still living shows that it, too, belongs to his reign. The third text is an account of Pictish origins composed in the reign of Mac Bethad mac Findlaích (Macbeth) (1040–57) which was printed as §§6 and 7 in Van Hamel's edition of *Lebor Bretnach*.[121] It survives in the Book of Ballymote and the Book of Lecan,[122] but only the Book of Ballymote has the last two verses in which the reference to Mac Bethad is found.[123] Although it cannot be demonstrated that this poem and *Duan Albanach* were written in Scotland, their subject-matter could readily be explained by supposing a Scottish origin; certainly, the evidence hitherto adduced for an Irish authorship for *Duan Albanach* is not compelling.[124] In any event, all these texts belong to a Gaelic scholarly milieu which operated across Gaelic Scotland and Ireland in this period, so that too strict a concern for distinguishing between Irish and Scottish texts devoted to the history of the Scottish kingdom may not only be fruitless, but might also encourage the dubious proposition that Scottish leaders could be insulated from works originating in Ireland on a key Scottish subject.

The Pictish antecedents of Scottish kingship are most obviously proclaimed in *Lebor Bretnach*. Thomas Clancy has argued that this was much more than simply a translation of *Historia Brittonum*.[125] Not only was material trimmed or rewritten, but there were also significant additions which reflected a Scottish interest. A particularly telling expansion of the earlier Latin text is in the treatment of the brief section on settlements in western Britain. This is enlarged and rewritten to become chiefly about Pictish origins, including a statement of the legend of Cruithne and his seven sons who took 'the north of the island of Britain', and how Oenbecán son of Cait son of Cruithne in the next generation took the 'highkingship' over all seven divisions.[126] This is plainly an elaboration of the same idea of an ancient kingdom stretching from Fife to Caithness found at the beginning of the longer Pictish king-list. Such an addition of Pictish material would not have done any violence to the conception of *Historia Brittonum*. As David Dumville has pointed out, it was not so much a 'history of Britons' as a 'history of the inhabitants of Britain', and includes accounts of Gaelic and English settlements in Britain as well as material on the Britons themselves and their experience of Roman rule.[127] The only inhabitants of Britain about whom no detail was offered in *Historia Brittonum* were the Picts, so to some extent it would have been natural for this to have been made good by the Scottish scholars engaged in *Lebor Bretnach*. What is striking is that the Gaelic settlement of Scotland, in contrast, has been reduced to a single mention: this, moreover, is in a passage where the original Latin has been expanded to include a comparison between Dál Riata, who we are told took the Picts' share of the island, and the English, who took the Britons' share.[128] The most potent indication that the Picts in *Lebor Bretnach* were regarded as the kingdom's antecedents, however, is the likely inclusion of the longer Pictish king-list ending with Mael Coluim III himself. This is found only in one branch of the text's stemma, which naturally raises questions about its status as part of the original *Lebor Bretnach*.[129] As Thomas Clancy has pointed out, however, there is strong circumstantial evidence that it was there from the beginning: the dating of *Lebor Bretnach* to Mael Coluim's reign and its Scottish origin can be established without reference to the king-list, so the most economical explanation of how a Pictish king-list of Mael Coluim's reign became part of the text would be to regard it as another Scottish element added to *Historia Brittonum* by the creators of *Lebor Bretnach*.[130]

The distinctive message of *Lebor Bretnach* in defining the Scottish past was that the island of Britain was from ancient times divided into two realms, and that the king of Scots was the heir to the northern Pictish part. It was not necessary to look only to Pictish history in order to make much the same point, however. A very similar sentiment evidently informed the author of *Duan Albanach*, even though his focus was chiefly on Gaelic, not Pictish, kings, and his matrix was Irish historiography, in contrast to the British material which formed the core of *Lebor Bretnach*. Its king-list begins not with Cinaed mac Ailpín, but with Fergus and his brothers, the sons of Erc mac Echdach, who in the previous century were portrayed in *Míniugud Senchasa fher nAlban* as the progenitors of the leading kindreds of Dál Riata and as the conquerors of *Alba*.[131] In *Duan Albanach* Mael Coluim III is numbered as the fifty-second king of the seed of Conaire, legendary king of Ireland, rather than the latest in a longer series of successors of Cruithne, first king of the Picts. There is an obvious parallel here, if this is considered alongside *Lebor Bretnach* and its Pictish king-list, with the twin Irish and British dimensions of the Scottish kingship's past which have been observed in the twelfth and thirteenth centuries. But *Duan Albanach* is not exclusively a statement of the kingship's Gaelic forbears. The scene is set by providing a brief account of successive settlements: Albanus, brother of Briutus, from whom the land was named *Alba*, but who was expelled by his brother across the English Channel; Briutus himself then held *Alba* 'as far as the conspicuous peak of Fodudhan' (which has been convincingly identified as North Berwick Law);[132] next was Erglán of Clann Nemid; then the Picts with seventy kings from Cathluan to Causantín; and finally the sons of Erc mac Echdach. This catalogue was surely designed on the model of *Gabála Érenn*, the takings of Ireland, the complete account of Ireland's past that Irish scholars were working on to such lasting effect in the eleventh and early twelfth centuries. The message is clear: '*Alba* as far as the peak of Fodudhan' had existed since ancient times, and was as distinct an entity as the island of Ireland itself.

The account of Pictish origins published as §6 (prose) and §7 (verse) in Van Hamel's edition of *Lebor Bretnach* stands in between these two poles. The final two stanzas of the poem present a summary of the kingdom's history which, like *Duan Albanach*, represents the reigning king as the last in a succession of fifty kings beginning with the sons of Erc mac Echdach, who (a-historically) are regarded as the successors of a longer series of Pictish kings. Unlike *Duan Albanach*, however, the fifty kings are not the chief subject of the poem, which is devoted instead to describing how the Pictish kingdom of *Alba*, 'from the bounds of Cait to the Forth', came into being. They are merely mentioned in the penultimate stanza (without any reference to a conquest of the Picts), before the poem returns in its final verse to the sixty-six kings 'who possessed the Pictish kingship'. As a result, Mac Bethad appears straightforwardly as the heir of this Pictish kingdom. Instead of placing the Picts in the context of British history, however, the legend is largely concerned with their sojourn in Ireland. They are described as landing in the territory of Uí Chennselaig where they helped Crimthann king of Leinster to defeat and exterminate his enemies, but became so powerful that Éremón son of Míl feared that they might take possession of Tara and expelled them from Ireland;[133] their leader, Cathluan, took them to *Alba*, which they conquered from the Britons. Before leaving Ireland, however, Éremón agreed to give them Irish wives on condition that they swore an oath that the mother's nobility would determine possession of the kingship. Little of this outline was original, except the association with Leinster. For the author of this poem, however, the depiction of the Picts, from the beginning (as it were), as intermarried with Gaels clearly remained relevant. Again, the desire for an authenticating antiquity in both an Irish and a Pictish context comes to mind.

Our understanding of these texts must, however, be limited by an inability to say with any precision when and where they were written. We can guess at the political context of each work, and of the specific agendas that may have been operating in each case, but for *Lebor Bretnach* and *Duan Albanach* especially there is little to hold onto securely. There is a little more scope in the case of the legend of the Picts acquiring Irish wives in Leinster. The key here is its reference (in the prose) to Uí Chennselaig. This suggests a desire to bring to mind a link between Mac Bethad and Domnall mac Maíl na mBó. Domnall was the first Uí Chennselaig king of Leinster for many centuries; he fought successfully for mastery of the province between 1046 and 1054, and went on to establish himself as the dominant force in the south of Ireland.[134] The kingship of Leinster had up to this point been dominated by the Uí Dúnlainge based in the north of the kingdom around the Liffey. Benjamin Hudson has pointed to a passage in the intractable quasi-prophetic king-list poem known as the 'Prophecy of Berchán' in which the mother of Mael Coluim II (1005–34) is referred to as a cow from the Liffey, pointing to family ties between Uí Dúnlainge and Mael Coluim's branch of the royal dynasty.[135] It is not inconceivable, then, if Mael Coluim's branch and Uí Dúnlainge were a 'team', for Mac Bethad and Domnall mac Maíl na mBó to have found common cause. It is also possible that the emphasis on entitlement to kingship through the mother was particularly topical at this time. The evidence that Mac Bethad's mother was a daughter of Mael Coluim II mac Cinaeda is too late to be accepted without qualification: whatever Mac Bethad's claim by blood may have been, however, it cannot have been simply through patrilinear descent.[136] His stepson and successor, Lulach, who could have been designated as next in line during Mac Bethad's reign, more certainly based his claim to the kingship on the fact that his mother, Gruoch, was the granddaughter of a king. Any emphasis on the mother's transmission of a right to kingship, however, would not have had the political edge of legitimising one dynasty against another in this period. Donnchad ua Maíl Choluim (1034–40), who Mac Bethad killed to become king, evidently had no claim through his father, Crínán (d.1045); his royal blood came via his mother, Bethóc, daughter of Mael Coluim II mac Cinaeda. As far as *Duan Albanach* and *Lebor Bretnach* are concerned, it is tempting to associate them with the pressure experienced by Mael Coluim III mac Donnchada from Norman kings of England, beginning with the submission of Mael Coluim to William I of England at Abernethy in 1072 (all the more so if *Lebor Bretnach* was actually written at Abernethy). If the earliest manuscript of *Lebor Bretnach*, however, is as early as the mid-eleventh century (as has been argued),[137] then that would make it unlikely that *Lebor Bretnach* itself was written as late as 1072, which would mean that the portrayal of *Alba* as an ancient entity in both texts need not have been inspired by English aggression. The picture is complicated further by the likelihood that behind all three texts lies a compendium of material on Pictish origins which would mean, at the very least, that the interest in *Alba's* ancient past was not simply a hurried response to an immediate political situation.

If the political context is uncertain, however, the intellectual and historiographical milieu is much clearer. In fact, the timing of these texts could be explained chiefly as a response to scholarly stimuli. In the case of *Lebor Bretnach* this would depend on the proposition that it followed the production (possibly at Abernethy) of a new recension of *Historia Brittonum* itself (the 'Nennian' recension), and may have been inspired by that achievement.[138] The immediate intellectual springboard for *Duan Albanach*, for its part, is betrayed by its character as a Scottish version in miniature of one of the earliest recensions of *Gabála Érenn* (Scowcroft's *a* and Macalister's first redaction).[139] This could also have supplied much of the detail: Albanus's expulsion across the English Channel, the destruction of the tower of Conann after which Erglán came to Scotland and Erglán's particular association with northern Britain.[140] In fact, *Duan Albanach* may be regarded as a precious witness to one of the earliest stages in the development of this Irish historiographical monument. It may be inferred that the version of *Gabála Érenn* which was its direct source consisted of the sequence of the 'taking' of Ireland coupled with Flann Mainistrech's poem listing the Christian kings of Ireland, which is now visible only in a later recension

(Scowcroft's *b*, where Flann's listing of pre-Christian kings of Ireland in two other poems is also found, possibly as an interpolation).[141] Be this as it may, *Duan Albanach* has certainly been inspired by the school of historical scholarship represented by Flann Mainstrech and Gilla Coemáin, and can be recognised as an attempt to reproduce its achievement on a much smaller scale for *Alba*. In some manuscripts of *Duan Albanach* and *Lebor Bretnach* these works are, in fact, attributed to Gilla Coemáin himself. Although these ascriptions of authorship are problematic, Thomas Clancy has argued judiciously that they cannot simply be ignored, and may possibly be explained as a result of a link between Gilla Coemáin and a Scottish centre (such as Abernethy) in which material (such as *Lebor Bretnach* and the Pictish king-list) was transmitted to Gilla Coemáin and distributed through him in Ireland.[142]

Even though we lack the means to interpret these texts fully, they can nevertheless show some of the ways in which it was possible to conceive of *Alba* in the mid- to late eleventh century. What all share is a sense of *Alba* as an enduring geographical reality corresponding to the British mainland north of the fissure of the Forth, which continued to be regarded as the southern limit of 'Scotland' long after the eleventh century. The fact that it had lost whatever political or cultural significance it might once have had as the notional southern limit of Pictland does not, however, explain why Pictish history, and particularly the impressively long list of Pictish kings, failed to become the basis of a continuous narrative that could have stood alongside similar achievements on behalf of the English, Irish and Welsh past. When this narrative was eventually written (as will be discussed in chapters 8 and 9), the barrier of the Forth continued to loom large in identifying the ancient kingdom of Scotland. The reason why the Pictish past was no longer emphasised in the twelfth century was that the descent of Margaret's sons and their successors afforded an opportunity to present the kingship with a more impressive British profile. After 1097 the kingship's sense of its innate superiority in the north of Britain could now be claimed on a larger and more exclusive stage. Until Geoffrey of Monmouth's work was repackaged as English regnal history, however, the appeal to an Anglo-Saxon heritage would not have permitted the same impressive chronological depth afforded by the Pictish past to be retained. The lustre of an authenticating antiquity would still have been available to Scottish kings, however, through their claimed descent from pre-historic kings of Ireland, an aspect of their imagined past that would have been boosted by the school of historiography represented by Flann Mainstrech and Gilla Coemáin in the mid- to late eleventh century.

When the kings of Scots in the twelfth century found legitimacy in their pedigree from kings of Ireland and Britain it was not, therefore, because there was no alternative. It was because Pictland could not compete. It is apparent, from those texts on Scottish origins which can be recovered, that Ireland was regarded as the Scottish homeland even in the thirteenth century – potent testimony to the importance of Irish ancestry in defining the kingship's status.[143] What may have made the Pictish past particularly expendable, however, was that the English royal ancestry enjoyed by St Margaret's descendants offered an intimate connection to a much more impressive island kingship: the British realm of Athelstan and Edgar. It is unlikely to be a coincidence that the last king to appear heading the longer Pictish king-list was Mael Coluim III, whose sons by Margaret were the first kings to boast English royal ancestry.

NOTES

1. Norman F. Shead, Wendy B. Stevenson and D. E. R. Watt and others (eds), *Scotichronicon by Walter Bower in Latin and English*, vol. vi (Aberdeen, 1991), 151.
2. Anderson, *Kings and Kingship*, 286–9. Most lists would have dated the advent of the Scottish kingdom to 443 BC (give or take a few years): *ibid.*, 221 and n. 11. See also Broun, *Irish Identity*, 197–9.
3. Dauvit Broun with A. B. Scott (eds), '*Liber Extravagans*', in D. E. R. Watt (ed.), *Scotichronicon by Walter Bower in Latin and English*, vol. ix (Edinburgh, 1998), 54–127, at 78–9.
4. Shead, Stevenson and Watt (eds), *Scotichronicon*, vi. 384–403, at 386–7.
5. The process by which Geoffrey's *Historia Regum Britannie* came to be regarded as English History is discussed in R. William Leckie jnr, *The Passage of Dominion: Geoffrey of Monmouth and the Periodization of Insular History in the Twelfth Century* (Toronto, 1981). See also Davies, *The First English Empire*, 41–3.
6. *Annales Ryenses*, *s.a.* 1287 (Eirikr's coronation): E. Kroman (ed.), *Danmarks Middelalderlige Annaler* (Copenhagen, 1980), 150–76. See Dauvit Broun, 'The Declaration of Arbroath: pedigree of a nation?', in Geoffrey Barrow (ed.), *The Declaration of Arbroath: History, Significance, Setting* (Edinburgh, 2003), 1–12, at 10 n. 12.
7. Hilda Ellis Davidson (ed.) and Peter Fisher (trans.), Saxo Grammaticus, *The History of the Danes*, vol. i (Cambridge, 1979), 4 (and 1 for date of Saxo's work). For Archbishop Absalom, see Hilda Ellis Davidson and Peter Fisher, Saxo Grammaticus, *The History of the Danes*, vol. ii, commentary (Cambridge, 1980), 19. Absalom advised Knud IV (1182–1202) that he should refuse to repeat the homage which Danish kings in the twelfth century had hitherto made to the German emperor.

8. Susan Reynolds, *Kingdoms and Communities in Western Europe*, 2nd edn (Oxford, 1997), ch. 8; Susan Reynolds, 'Medieval *origines gentium* and the community of the realm', *History* 68 (1983) 375–90.
9. Reynolds, *Kingdoms and Communities*, 260.
10. *Ibid.*, 272.
11. *Ibid.*, 274, 276.
12. *Ibid.*, 276.
13. Davies, *The First English Empire*, 35. For what follows, see 35–53.
14. *Ibid.*, 44–9.
15. Davies, 'The peoples of Britain and Ireland, IV', 16–18. See also Davies, *The First English Empire*, 47.
16. Rees Davies, *The Matter of Britain and the Matter of England. An Inaugural Lecture delivered before the University of Oxford on 29 February 1996* (Oxford, 1996), 17–23. The quotation is at 22.
17. J. M. Roberts, 'General editor's preface', in Bartlett, *England under the Norman and Angevin Kings*, viii.
18. Davies, *Matter of Britain*, 22, 16; see generally 12–17.
19. Mynors (ed.), *William of Malmesbury*, i. xxii.
20. Diana Greenway (ed.), Henry, Archdeacon of Huntingdon, *Historia Anglorum, The History of the English People* (Oxford, 1996), lxvi–lxvii.
21. Alexander Bell (ed.), *L'Estoire des Engleis by Geffrei Gaimar*, Anglo-Norman Text Society (Oxford, 1960) (at li–lii for dating 'towards the close of the five-year period 1135–40'); Antonia Gransden, *Historical Writing in England*, vol. i, *c.500–c.1307* (London, 1974), 209.
22. Peter Damian-Grint, *The New Historians of the Twelfth-Century Renaissance: Inventing Vernacular Authority* (Woodbridge, 1999), 49–52.
23. Neil Wright (ed.), *The Historia Regum Britannie of Geoffrey of Monmouth*, vol. i, *Bern, Burgerbibliothek, MS. 568* (Cambridge, 1985), xii–xvi.
24. John Gillingham, 'The context and purposes of Geoffrey of Monmouth's History of the Kings of Britain', in Marjorie Chibnall (ed.), *Anglo-Norman Studies XIII. Proceedings of the Battle Conference 1991* (Woodbridge, 1990) 99–118, is of fundamental importance in showing that Geoffrey's work was written on behalf of the Welsh: it is reprinted in John Gillingham, *The English in the Twelfth Century: Imperialism, National Identity and Political Values* (Woodbridge, 2000), 19–39: see esp. 20–31. He notes G. W. S. Barrow, 'Wales and Scotland in the middle ages', *Welsh Historical Review*, 10 (1980–1), 302–19, at 305, as a precursor. See also Davies, *Matter of Britain*, 9–11.
25. Wright (ed.), *Historia Regum Britannie*, i. xii–xv. This should not, of course, be seen as compromising the Welsh intention of his work: indeed (as Gillingham, *English in the Twelfth Century*, 36–7, shows) it must be read in the light of Robert of Gloucester's use of Welsh allies.
26. Julia C. Crick, *The Historia Regum Britannie of Geoffrey of Monmouth*, vol. iii, *Summary Catalogue of Manuscripts* (Cambridge, 1989); Julia C.

Crick, *The Historia Regum Britannie of Geoffrey of Monmouth*, vol. iv, *Dissemination and Reception in the Later Middle Ages* (Cambridge, 1991).

27. Davies, *Matter of Britain*, 16–17.

28. Leckie, *Passage of Dominion*, 86–92; Thomas Hearne (ed.), Alfred of Beverley, *Annales, siue Historia de Gestis Regum Britannie* (Oxford, 1716).

29. Leckie, *Passage of Dominion*, 102–17; Neil Wright (ed.), *The Historia Regum Britannie of Geoffrey of Monmouth*, vol. ii, *The First Variant Version* (Cambridge, 1989); and Ivor Arnold (ed.), Wace, *Le Roman de Brut*, La Société des Anciens Textes Français, 2 vols (Paris, 1938–40). For other 'vernacularisations' (albeit fragmentary) in French, note the six items discussed in Damian-Grint, *New Historians*, 61–5, dated by him to the second half of the twelfth century.

30. Damian-Grint, *New Historians*, 50–1; P. Damian-Grint, 'A 12th-century Anglo-Norman Brut fragment (MS BL Harley 4733, f.128)', in Ian Short (ed.), *Anglo-Norman Anniversary Essays*, Anglo-Norman Text Society (London, 1993), 87–104.

31. See above, 22.

32. I draw a distinction between this and its subsequent use as political 'propaganda' which Professor Gillingham has shown was a development of the late twelfth century: Gillingham, *English in the Twelfth Century*, 22–3.

33. Damian-Grint, *New Historians*, 51. The English histories of Henry of Huntingdon and William of Malmesbury are occasionally found combined with Geoffrey's *Historia Regum Britannie* in MSS: see Crick, *Historia Regum Britannie*, iv. 48–9, 72–3. There are also three MSS in which Geoffrey's work is followed by a genealogy of dukes of Normandy (as far as Henry I in the earliest MS): the connection, obviously, is that Henry I was also king of England. See Julia Crick, 'Two newly located manuscripts of Geoffrey of Monmouth's *Historia Regum Britannie*', in James P. Carley and Felicity Riddy (eds), *Arthurian Literature XIII* (Cambridge, 1995), 151–6, esp. 155–6.

34. Diana B. Tyson, 'Handlist of manuscripts containing the French prose Brut chronicle', *Scriptorium* 48 (1994) 333–44.

35. Damian-Grint, *New Historians*, 54.

36. Bartlett, *England under the Norman and Angevin Kings*, 633.

37. Brynley F. Roberts (ed.), *Brut y Brenhinedd Llanstephan MS. 1 Version* (Dublin, 1971), xxviii–xxx; Henry Lewis (gol.), *Brut Dingestow* (Llandysul, 1942), xviii–xx.

38. Thomas Jones (trans.), *Brut y Tywysogyon or The Chronicle of the Princes, Peniarth MS 20 Version* (Cardiff, 1952), xiii, xxxvii–xxxix (see xxxix n. 3 for *terminus post quem* of 1286).

39. Thomas Jones (ed.), *Brut y Tywysogyon, Peniarth MS 20* (Caerdydd, 1941); Thomas Jones (ed.), *Brut y Tywysogyon or The Chronicle of the Princes, Red Book of Hergest Version* (Cardiff, 1955). For a third version, in which the account of Welsh events was combined with material on English history,

see Thomas Jones (ed.), *Brenhinedd y Saesson or The Kings of the Saxons, BM Cotton MS. Cleopatra B v and The Black Book of Basingwerk NLW MS. 7006* (Cardiff, 1971). In general, see Thomas Jones, 'Historical writing in medieval Welsh', *Scottish Studies* 12 (1968) 15–27 (note at 24–5 the possibility of 1282 as the date of composition for the original Latin chronicle).

40. Caroline Brett, 'The prefaces of two late thirteenth-century Welsh Latin chronicles', *BBCS* 35 (1988) 63–72.

41. *Ibid.*, 70.

42. Brynley F. Roberts, 'Testunau hanes Cymraeg canol', in Geraint Bowen (gol.), *Y Traddodiad Rhyddiaith yn yr Oesau Canol* (Llandysul, 1974), 274–302, at 294–9; Brynley F. Roberts, 'The Red Book of Hergest version of *Brut y Brenhinedd*', *Studia Celtica* 12/13 (1977/8) 147–86, at 157–8 and 172.

43. Roberts (ed.), *Brut y Brenhinedd*, 59.

44. Essential discussions are John Carey, *The Irish National Origin-Legend: Synthetic Pseudohistory*, Quiggin pamphlet no. 1 (Cambridge, 1994), and R. Mark Scowcroft, '*Leabhar Gabhála*, part I: the growth of the text', *Ériu* 38 (1987) 79–140. For the text see R. A. S. Macalister (ed.), *Lebor Gabála Érenn, The Book of the Taking of Ireland*, 5 vols, Irish Texts Society (London, 1938–56), although this has to be read alongside Scowcroft's article and John Carey, *A New Introduction to Lebor Gabála Érenn. The Book of the Taking of Ireland* (London, 1993). The only accessible translation of a discrete version is John Carey's of the first recension in John T. Koch (ed.), *The Celtic Heroic Age: Literary Sources for Ancient Celtic Europe and Early Medieval Ireland and Wales* (Malden, Mass., 1995), 213–66.

45. Recent discussions are Peter J. Smith, 'Early Irish historical verse: the evolution of a genre', in Próinséas Ní Chatháin and Michael Richter (eds), *Ireland and Europe in the Early Middle Ages: Texts and Transmission* (Dublin, 2002), 326–41, at 337–41, and John Carey, '*Lebor Gabála* and the legendary history of Ireland', in Helen Fulton (ed.), *Medieval Celtic Literature and Society* (Dublin, 2005), 32–48, at 44–5.

46. Carey, '*Lebor Gabála*', 44–5.

47. Published as poem CXV in *LG*, v. 486–531.

48. R. I. Best and M. A. O'Brien (eds), *The Book of Leinster, formerly known as Lebar na Núachongbála*, vol. iii (Dublin, 1957), 471–90 and 491–5.

49. This may, however, have been anticipated by Flann Mainistrech, if the first of his two poems on the kings of Ireland was originally preceded by a third poem on an earlier era: it survives only in mangled form, and is not certainly Flann's work (see Scowcroft, '*Leabhar Gabhála*. part I', 131–2).

50. Carey, '*Lebor Gabála*', 43; Smith, 'Early Irish historical verse', 340–1. Best and O'Brien (eds), *Book of Leinster*, iii. 504–8, 509–1. See Scowcroft, '*Leabhar Gabhála*. part I', 96–7, 118–19, 130, 132–3, for the king-list scheme in general and the related prose *Réim Rígraide*.

51. Smith, 'Early Irish historical verse', 340 and n. 91
52. *Ibid.*, 340.
53. Smith argues compellingly for the significance of this work (*ibid.*, 338–40). The most accessible edition is Whitley Stokes (ed.), *The Tripartite Life of Patrick with Other Documents Relating to that Saint*, vol. ii (London, 1887), 530–41. In the Book of Leinster it is sandwiched between his two poems on kings of Ireland and the poems on the same subject by Flann Mainistrech: Best and O'Brien (eds), *Book of Leinster*, iii. 496–503.
54. F. J. Byrne, '*Clann Ollaman Uaisle Emna*', *Studia Hibernica* 4 (1964) 54–94, at 60–1.
55. Broun, *Irish Identity*, 192.
56. Carey, '*Lebor Gabála*', 41 and n. 31; Smith, 'Early Irish historical verse', 336 n. 66 (noting John Carney's doubts).
57. Poem LXV in *LG*. His work is listed in Scowcroft, '*Leabhar Gabhála*. part I', 120 n.114. See also Carey, '*Lebor Gabála*', 41–2.
58. Carey, '*Lebor Gabála*', 42 and n. 34.
59. *Ibid.*, 41–3; Tomás Ó Fiaich, 'The church of Armagh under lay control', *Seanchas Ardmhacha* 5 (1969) 75–127; M. E. Dobbs, 'The pedigree of the family of Flann Mainistrech', *Journal of the County of Louth Archaeological Society* 5 (1923) 149–53.
60. Carey, *Irish National Origin-Legend*, 20. See also Smith, 'Early Irish historical verse', 326–7.
61. Roberts (ed.), *Brut y Brenhinedd*, xv–xx; Brinley F. Roberts, 'Geoffrey of Monmouth and Welsh historical tradition', *Nottingham Mediaeval Studies* 20 (1976) 29–40.
62. He may well have had a brief list of early kings correlated with Eli and his successors as kings of Judea (from Jerome): Molly Miller, 'Geoffrey's early royal synchronisms', *BBCS* 28 (1978–80) 373–89 (who suggests, at 389, that it is likely that only one copy of the original list existed). For a suggestion that a simple poem, with king-list, genealogy and pieces of narrative detail, may have been available, see Peter C. Bartrum, 'Was there a British "Book of Conquests"?', *BBCS* 23 (1968–70) 1–6.
63. Sarah Foot, 'The making of *Angelcynn*: English identity before the Norman Conquest', *TRHS* 6th series 6 (1996) 25–49, at 45.
64. Rachel Bromwich (ed.), *Trioedd Ynys Prydein. The Welsh Triads*, 2nd edn (Cardiff, 1978), lxviii.
65. See Broun, *Irish Identity*, 190 and n. 228 for references.
66. An impressive recent analysis is Smith, 'Early Irish historical verse'.
67. Barrow, *Charters of David I*, nos 70, 97–8, 125, 130 and 212 (that is, half of those datable to 1140–53 which have an Edinburgh place-date). The earliest are no.70 (1138×47, possibly 1140 or 1141) and no. 97 (1140×1).
68. R. M. Thomson, with collaboration of Michael Winterbottom, *William of Malmesbury Gesta Regvm Anglorvm, the History of the English Kings,*

vol. ii, General Introduction and Commentary (Oxford, 1999), 7–8; see Barrow, *Charters of David I*, 39, for David's whereabouts.

69. Broun, 'The Declaration of Arbroath', 4.

70. D. R. R. Owen, *William the Lion 1143–1214: Kingship and Culture* (East Linton, 1997), esp. 114–57.

71. See above, 45; Broun, *Irish Identity*, 159, 192.

72. For example, Stephen T. Driscoll, 'The archaeology of state formation in Scotland', in W. S. Hanson and E. A. Slater (eds), *Scottish Archaeology: New Perceptions* (Aberdeen, 1991), 81–111, at 81; Duncan, *Scotland: the Making of the Kingdom*, 111; Alan Macquarrie, *Medieval Scotland: Kingship and Nation* (Stroud, 2004), 91.

73. K. H. Jackson, 'The poem *A eolcha Alban uile*', *Celtica* 3 (1955) 149–67; K. H. Jackson, 'The Duan Albanach', *SHR* 36 (1957) 125–37. See below, 55, for its place of origin.

74. See Jackson, 'The poem', 149 for stemma: the earliest MS is Dualtach Mac Fir Bisigh, *Book of Genealogies*, 414–16.

75. It shared a king-list source with an Irish text of *ca* 1120, *Comaimsera Ríg nÉrenn ocus Ríg na Cóiced iar Creitim*, a synchronism of Christian kings of Ireland and of the provinces: Broun, *Irish Identity*, 170–1.

76. *Ibid.*, 146–53.

77. *Ibid.*, ch. 5, 109.

78. *Ibid.*, 154–7, 160–4. This is the archetype of Marjorie Anderson's 'X' group of lists: Anderson, *Kings and Kingship*, 52–67.

79. Barrow, *Kingdom of the Scots*, 2nd edn, 192–3.

80. See above, nn. 61–2.

81. This is also known as 'P' (Anderson, *Kings and Kingship*, 77–84: two witnesses are edited at 245–9, 261–3). For classification of all MSS, see Molly Miller, 'Matriliny by treaty: the Pictish foundation-legend', in Dorothy Whitelock and others (eds), *Ireland in Early Mediaeval Europe. Studies in Memory of Kathleen Hughes* (Cambridge, 1982), 133–61, at 159–61.

82. A. G. Van Hamel (ed.), *Lebor Bretnach: The Irish Version of the Historia Britonum ascribed to Nennius* (Dublin, [1932]), 82–7. Thomas Owen Clancy, 'Scotland, the "Nennian" recension of the *Historia Brittonum*, and the *Lebor Bretnach*', in Simon Taylor (ed.), *Kings, Clerics and Chronicles in Scotland, 500–1297* (Dublin, 2000), 87–107, at 92–102.

83. Thomas Innes, *A Critical Essay on the Ancient Inhabitants of the Northern Parts of Britain, or Scotland* (1729; repr. Edinburgh, 1879), 414–16.

84. The 'Poppleton collection' (Anderson, *Kings and Kingship*, 240–60), datable to the reign of William I (1165–1214), includes a copy of the longer Pictish king-list, but this was placed before the *Chronicle of the Kings of Alba*, which runs no further than the reign of Cinaed mac Maíl Choluim (971–95). William himself is presented as the latest in a succession beginning with Fergus son of Erc and running through Cinaed mac Ailpín, who is described as *primus rex Scottorum*.

85. See 72, below.
86. See 177–8, and 220 for the text added in 1285.
87. Those between Conaire and Éremón are listed in Broun, *Irish Identity*, 191 n. 232.
88. See *ibid.*, 196. The text is closely related to Aelred's *Genealogia Regum Anglorum* and is currently being investigated by Alice Taylor. I am very grateful to Alice Taylor for discussing this with me.
89. It may not be complete: see 231 n. 9.
90. On the full text, see 31 n. 87.
91. Stephen Boardman, 'Dunfermline as a royal mausoleum', in Richard Fawcett (ed.), *Royal Dunfermline* (Edinburgh, 2005), 139–53.
92. He was probably *rannaire*: *RRS*, i. 32. Aelred's continuing influence may be gauged from the fact that Rievaulx, which Aelred entered *ca* 1134 and ruled as abbot, 1147–67, was the mother house of Melrose (founded 1136), which was, in turn, the mother house of Newbattle (1140), Kinloss (1150) and Coupar Angus (1164) (and others founded after Aelred's death). Rievaulx was also the mother house of Dundrennan (1142) in Galloway.
93. *PL*, xcxv. col. 726: *et ad subdendum se ei Scotia Cumbria Wallia libens accurreret.* See also Davies, *The First English Empire*, 10; and note also Anderson (eds), *The Chronicle of Melrose*, 15 (Stevenson (ed.), *Chronica de Mailros*, 34–5), derived from the northern English chronicle used as the chief source of the Chronicle of Melrose when it was first written in 1173/4.
94. Adam of Dryburgh, *De tripartito tabernaculo* (*PL*, cxcviii. cols. 609–792, at 722–3); Mynors, Thomson and Winterbottom (eds), *William of Malmesbury, Gesta Regvm Anglorvm*, i. 3–4: *solus . . . tantorum regum et principum heres.*
95. For example, in the tract (combined with a brief chronicle) following a manuscript of Wyntoun's *Original Chronicle* (London, British Library MS Royal 17 D xx), printed in W. F. Skene (ed.), *Chronicles of the Picts, Chronicles of the Scots* (Edinburgh, 1867), 378–90, at 383–4.
96. A particularly insightful discussion is Dafydd Glyn Jones, *Gwlad y Brutiau, Darlith Goffa Henry Lewis 1990* (Abertawe, 1991), republished in his collection *Agoriad yr Oes* (Tal-y-bont, 2002). A passionate discussion of the future potential of this British identity is R. R. Davies, *Beth Yw'r Ots Gennyf i am – Brydain? Darlith Goffa Syr Thomas Parry-Williams 1998* (Aberystwyth, 1998).
97. *Prophetie Merlini* was published separately by Geoffrey before the completion of *Historia Regum Britannie*, and in due course appeared in §§109–117 of the great work: Wright (ed.), *Historia Regum Britannie of Geoffrey of Monmouth*, i. x-xi; Roberts (ed.), *Brut y Brenhinedd*, 55, 59. It was translated independently into Welsh: see Roberts, 'The Red Book of Hergest version', 158–9, 166–72, and the observation at 172 that 'this section of the text usually has more marginal notes in the manuscripts than any other'.

98. Davies, *First English Empire*, 49 (and 48 for the 'Welsh challenge'). Note also Rees Davies's concluding remarks at 202–3.

99. Thomas Jones, 'Teir ynys Prydein a'e their rac ynys', *BBCS* 17 (1958) 268–9; Bromwich (ed.), *Trioedd Ynys Prydein*, 235–6.

100. Thomas Jones (ed.), *Brenhinedd y Saesson, or the Kings of the Saxons* (Cardiff, 1971), 10 (under the year 773 = 774) and 64 (under the year 1044 = 1046).

101. See Rachel Bromwich and D. Simon Evans (eds), *Culhwch and Olwen. An Edition and Study of the Oldest Arthurian Tale* (Cardiff, 1992), 94–5, where it is noted that the three adjacent islands were identified in *Historia Brittonum* (829/30) as the Isle of Wight, Mann and Orkney: David N. Dumville (ed.), *The Historia Brittonum*, vol. iii, The 'Vatican' Recension (Cambridge, 1985), 63.

102. *Historia Regum Britannie*, Bk II, ch. 1: see Bromwich and Evans (eds), *Culhwch and Olwen*, 95. This is also reflected in additions to the tract, *Enweu Ynys Prydein* ('The Names of the Island of Britain'): Bromwich (ed.), *Trioedd Ynys Prydein*, 228 §6 and cxxii–cxxvii, esp. cxxv.

103. Note also that Jones, 'Teir ynys Prydein', 269, suggested a link with *tria regna Britannie* in the *Life of Gildas* by Caradog of Llancarfan, and argued that Caradog's 'three kingdoms of Britain' were England, Wales and Scotland.

104. The explanation favoured in Bromwich and Evans (eds), *Culhwch and Olwen*, 95.

105. Unless the title *rí Alban* is taken literally to have meant 'king of Britain', denoting a claim to rule the entire island: see above, 21–2. See the next chapter for an alternative explanation of *Alba* as 'Britain' in this context.

106. See above, 7, 9–10.

107. See above, 8–9.

108. In two accounts of an original sevenfold division of the kingdom: Dauvit Broun, 'The seven kingdoms in *De situ Albanie*: a record of Pictish political geography or an imaginary map of Alba?', in E. J. Cowan and R. Andrew McDonald (eds), *Alba: Celtic Scotland in the Middle Ages* (East Linton), 24–42. It is edited in Anderson, *Kings and Kingship*, 240–4. See also David Howlett, 'The structure of *De Situ Albanie*', in Simon Taylor (ed.), *Kings, Clerics and Chronicles in Scotland, 500–1297* (Dublin, 2000), 124–45.

109. *regna Scottorum et Anglorum diuidit*: Anderson, *Kings and Kingship*, 242. This occurs in a passage attributed to Andrew, monk of Dunfermline and bishop of Caithness (d.1184).

110. E. J. S. Parsons, *The Map of Great Britain circa* A.D. *1360 known as the Gough Map* (Oxford, 1958), 11.

111. This map is reproduced on the cover of this book. For this and other medieval maps of Britain see G. R. Crone, *Early Maps of the British Isles* A.D. *1000–*A.D. *1579* (London, 1961), plates 2–8.

112. Shead, Stevenson and Watt (eds), *Scotichronicon*, vi. 354–5.

113. This, at any rate, is how the words *Hic armis Bruti hic stant Scoti cruce tuti* were interpreted by Bower: *ibid.*, vi. 354–7. See J. H. Stevenson and M. Wood, *Scottish Heraldic Seals* (Glasgow, 1940), i. 80, and Duncan, *Kingship of the Scots*, 5, for alternative interpretations of the Latin (which is in a slightly different order on the seal: HIC ARMIS BRVTI SCOTI STANT HIC CRVCE TVTI).

114. The causeway existed by *ca* 1218: see Barrow, *Robert Bruce*, 4th edn, n. 107.

115. RCAHMS *Stirlingshire*, vol. i (Edinburgh, 1963), 4.

116. Its exact location is disputed: see *ibid.*, i. 114–15.

117. Barrow, *Scotland and its Neighbours*, 212–13, where he suggests that this was *pons Aghmore* on Gough's map.

118. Watson, *History of the Celtic Place-Names*, 350.

119. Mentioned in the *Chronicle of the Kings of Alba*: Anderson, *Kings and Kingship*, 252–3.

120. See above, 48–9, 50.

121. Van Hamel (ed.), *Lebor Bretnach*, 8–14. See also Skene (ed.), *Chronicles*, 32–44. It is identified as 'version 4f' of the origin-legend in Gearóid Mac Eoin, 'On the Irish legend of the origin of the Picts', *Studia Hibernica* 4 (1964) 138–54.

122. And also an eighteenth-century copy: the MSS are listed (under P#E) in J. M. P. Calise, *Pictish Sourcebook: Documents of Medieval Legend and Dark Age History* (Westport, Conn., 2002), 15; 256–79 gives the text of each witness. The first lines alone of the poem appear in recension *m* of *Lebor Gabála* in Rawl. B. 512 (R*m* in Scowcroft's scheme: see Scowcroft, 'Leabhar Gabhála. part I', 118–19; Calise, *Pictish Sourcebook*, 71), where the poem is attributed to Flann Mainistrech.

123. These verses must be original because the last line is followed by the required closure of repeating the beginning of the poem.

124. Máire Herbert, '*Rí Éirenn, Rí Alban*: kingship and identity in the ninth and tenth centuries', in Simon Taylor (ed.), *Kings, Clerics and Chroniclers in Scotland 500–1297* (Dublin, 2000), 62–72, at 71 n. 11.

125. Clancy, 'Scotland, the "Nennian" recension', at 93–7.

126. Van Hamel (ed.), *Lebor Bretnach*, 25–6 (§14).

127. David N. Dumville, '*Historia Britonum*: an insular history from the Carolingian age', in A. Scharer and G. Scheibelreiter (eds), *Historiographie im frühen Mittelalter* (Munich, 1994), 406–34.

128. Van Hamel (ed.), *Lebor Bretnach*, 28.

129. D. N. Dumville, 'The textual history of "Lebor Bretnach": a preliminary study', *Éigse* 16 (1975–6) 255–73, at 266.

130. Clancy, 'Scotland, the "Nennian" recension', 99–102.

131. John Bannerman, *Studies in the History of Dal Riata* (Edinburgh, 1974), 41, 118–19. On this text see now David N. Dumville, 'Ireland and North Britain in the Earlier Middle Ages: contexts for *Míniugud Senchusa Fher nAlban*', in Colm Ó Baoill and Nancy R. McGuire (eds), *Rannsachadh na Gàidhlig 2000* (Aberdeen, 2002), 185–212.

132. Watson, *History of the Celtic Place-Names*, 28; Jackson, 'The Duan Albanach', *SHR* 36 (1957) 125–37, at 134.
133. The name Crimthann would have called to mind a pivotal figure, Crimthann son of the eponym of Uí Chennselaig and ancestor of all Uí Chennselaig kings bar one. Éremón is the legendary leader of the first Gaels to settle in Ireland (many generations before the proto-historical Crimthann was understood to have flourished).
134. Donncha Ó Corráin, *Ireland before the Normans* (Dublin, 1972), 133–7.
135. Benjamin T. Hudson, *The Prophecy of Berchán: Irish and Scottish High-Kings of the Early Middle Ages* (Westport, Conn., 1996), 52, 90, 220.
136. Alex Woolf, 'The "Moray Question" and the kingship of Alba', *SHR* 79 (2000) 145–64, at 154–6.
137. See Clancy, 'Scotland, the "Nennian" recension', 101.
138. *Ibid.*, 87–92.
139. Translated by John Carey in Koch (ed.), *The Celtic Heroic Age*, 213–66.
140. For Erglán's ending up in northern Britain, see Carey in Koch (ed.), *The Celtic Heroic Age*, 232, at §50. It could also have supplied the seventy kings from Cathluan to Causantín.
141. Scowcroft, '*Leabhar Gabhála*. part I', 131–2. See also 119–20 for an instance of *b*'s retention of a crucial early structural feature. Flann's poem here may have been superseded in other recensions by the development of a continuation of *Réim Rígraide* ('Roll of Kingship') into the Christian era (*ibid.*, 129–30), which may have taken *Réim Rígraide* itself as its springboard (that is, an account of the succession of kings of Ireland from the first of the *Gaedil* up to the Christian era in recensions other than Scowcroft's *b*): for *Réim Rígraide* see *ibid.*, 118–19: notice that *b* differs here from the other recensions (and may therefore preserve an earlier arrangement).
142. Clancy, 'Scotland, the "Nennian" recension', 103–7.
143. Broun, *Irish Identity*, esp.129–32.

3

Alba *as 'Britain' after 900 and the Pictish Antecedents of the Kingdom of the Scots*

It has long been known that *Alba* was originally a Gaelic word for 'Britain',[1] and that it acquired its modern meaning of 'Scotland' through its use as the Gaelic term for the kingdom of the Scots since the tenth century. Some pressing questions remain unanswered, however. In chapter 1 it was asked whether *rí Alban*, if it literally meant 'king of Britain', was originally a claim to be paramount ruler of Britain, as Michael Davidson has suggested. It finds no corroboration in any text of historical fiction (such as the early sections of a king-list), however, and would have been completely divorced from political reality. In the light of this it is little wonder that other explanations of *Alba* in this context have been favoured. All modern discussions have as their starting point the fact that, in those sources with the best claim to preserve contemporary record, the appearance of *Alba* as the kingdom's name coincides with the disappearance of any further reference to the Picts. The Pictish kingdom was ostensibly replaced by Gaelic *Alba*, as if *Alba* represented a deliberate break with Pictish identity, or at least a fundamental refashioning of Pictish kingship. How is this to be squared, however, with the indications in the previous chapter that the kingship's Pictish past continued to play a pivotal role in defining the kingdom as late as the reign of Mael Coluim III (1058–93)? It appears, in short, that the kingship of *Alba* after 900 cannot be explained straightforwardly either as a kingship of Britain or as a self-consciously Gaelic renaming designed to mark a break with Pictish kingship. In this chapter it is argued that another explanation is available: one in which the Britishness of *Alba* is fully acknowledged without supposing that this meant a claim to be the predominant king of the whole island, and in which continuity with the Picts is seen not as a historiographical device, but as a fundamental facet of the kingship's identity. What lies at the heart of both is the compelling logic of the landmass between the Forth and the north coast as a concept that could legitimise the kingship's claim to be the highest secular authority in northern Britain.

EXPLAINING *ALBA*

Until recently it was generally held that the kingdom of Scotland, *Alba*, first came into being when Cinaed (Kenneth) mac Ailpín, who most scholars have regarded as king of the Gaelic or 'Scottish' realm of Dál Riata (usually equated with Argyll), created a united 'Scoto-Pictish' realm around the year 843. It was typically maintained that he achieved this by force, and that his takeover of Pictland may also have involved claims to the kingship through his mother (in the belief that succession to Pictish kingship was matrilineal rather than patrilineal).[2] More recent statements of this view have emphasised the military rather than the dynastic aspects of Cinaed's conquest of the Picts.[3] Seen in this light, it has seemed natural that a new name in the language of the conquerors, *Alba*, should have been coined for the new kingdom that had been created.

The only part of this narrative, however, which can be found in a source capable of passing the basic test of acceptability as a witness to what may or may not have happened in this period, is that there was a king of Picts who was called Cinaed son of Ailpín at his death in 858. For a source to pass this test there needs to be good cause to regard it as written by someone in Scotland or with links to Scotland at or near the time the recorded events occurred; also, there needs to be some reason to assume that it was not written in a conscious attempt to fictionalise the past. Only the common source of extant Irish chronicles can be said to meet these requirements at all readily (although even this is not an entirely straightforward matter).[4] The particular problem with the oft-repeated view of Cinaed as 'uniting Picts and Scots' is not simply that it is unsupported by any compelling evidence, but that it runs counter to what is found in Irish chronicles. In the *Annals of Ulster* (AU) and *Cronicum Scotorum* (CS), the two principal Irish chronicles relating to this period,[5] the kingdom of the Picts and the Picts themselves continue to be very much in evidence a generation after Cinaed mac Ailpín (most notably in the title 'king of the Picts' given to Cinaed mac Ailpín and his successors until his son, Aed, who was killed in 878). It is not until the next generation that any change is apparent, when Latin *Picti* is replaced from 900 by a Gaelic term, *Alba*. For example, the designation *rex Pictorum*, 'king of Picts', applied to Cinaed and his sons becomes *rí Alban*, 'king of *Alba*', for his grandsons; and instead of referring to *Picti*, the kingdom's inhabitants are *fir Alban*, 'people of *Alba*'.[6] It has also been pointed out not only that 'Scotland' before the thirteenth century was regarded generally as not including Argyll, but that Cinaed's realm is referred to simply as *Pictavia*, not *Albania*, in the earliest extant text where he appears as the first in a succession of kings of Scots.[7] This text is the *Chronicle of the Kings of Alba*, whose earliest core was probably composed during the reign of Illulb son of Causantín (954–62), Cinaed's great-grandson.[8] By then the descendants of Cinaed's sons, Causantín and Aed, monopolised the kingship, so it should not be too surprising that Cinaed was regarded as founding the kingdom. It is doubtful, however, that the passage on Cinaed's annihilation of the Picts was an original part of the chronicle, which may (at most) have described Cinaed as a king of Dál Riata who came to Pictland and ruled there for sixteen years. The idea of a unification of Scottish and Pictish kingdoms was not, in fact, made explicit until an expanded version of the Scottish king-list datable to the reign of Alexander II (1214–49).[9] This was given more narrative substance in Fordun's chronicle, and has been repeated for generations thereafter: until very recently it was still the norm to number Scottish kings from Cinaed mac Ailpín, who thus became 'Kenneth I'.[10]

The extreme weakness of the evidential basis for Cinaed's 'Scottish' takeover of Pictland is today widely recognised by scholars, and as a result there has been a significant shift of emphasis in recent scholarship. Cinaed's pivotal role has been qualified and even challenged, either by positing an earlier dynasty of Gaelic kings who ruled both Picts and Dál Riata, and whose legacy Cinaed therefore continued to develop,[11] or (more commonly) by concentrating attention on the change from Pictish to *Alba*-based terminology visible by 900.[12] Most would now regard the decades before and after 900 rather than the 840s as the crucial turning point,[13] moving the focus away from Cinaed mac Ailpín and onto his grandsons Domnall (who died in 900) and Causantín (who died in 952).[14] Nonetheless, the fundamental idea that the origins of the Scottish kingdom signified the end of Pictish identity remains unchallenged, in part sustained by the fact that, at some point, Gaelic replaced the Pictish language as the mother tongue of the kingdom's inhabitants. Some formulations of the switch from Pictish to *Alba*-based terminology, however, look beyond the Gaelicisation of the Picts for an explanation. Máire Herbert has compared the adoption of *Alba* as the designation of kings and their people with the appearance from the 850s of *fir Érenn* 'men of Ireland' as 'an omnibus term for a diverse royal following' led by the 'king of Ireland', *rí Érenn*.[15] She envisaged the coining of *Alba* in this context as a 'change of name for both [Gaels and Picts which] marked a departure from the past'.[16] The end of a distinctive Pictish identity is therefore seen in terms of the emergence of 'a politically-defined grouping which transcended other affiliations'.[17] David Dumville has articulated something similar, but with a crucial difference: the grand-sons of Cinaed mac Ailpín are presented as Pictish rulers who took the name *Alba*, 'the kingdom of Britain', because it was acceptable to both Gaelic and Pictish traditions.[18] The suggestion is refreshingly bold: previous scholars (with the exception of Pinkerton nearly two centuries ago) have regarded Cinaed mac Ailpín and his descendants as Gaels.[19] In Dumville's eyes, though, the adoption of *Alba* is a datable 'name-change',[20] and, as such, seems to be regarded as a conscious break with 'Pictland'. Other recent accounts of this period are more explicit in seeing the adoption of *Alba* as the kingdom's name as marking the end of Pictish identity. It has been described in one place as 'a very significant change in terminology' which manifests (among other things) 'a strong indication of the demise of the Pictish element'.[21] Another scholar has written that, 'when [after Viking attacks] it [the Pictish kingdom] finally emerged from political chaos following a victory in 904 won by Cinaed's grand-son, Constantine [Causantín], the kingdom had survived but its identity had been transformed' so that it was now the kingdom of *Alba*, which meant 'that region of Britain that was Gaelic in speech and character'.[22] The prize for the most heightened prose, however, must go to my own statement that the coining of *Alba* as the kingdom's name in 900 was 'a dramatic, not to say outrageous change of meaning', on the grounds that this word, hitherto denoting 'Britain', was now applied to a kingdom which, on one interpretation of the evidence, occupied only the east of Scotland north of the Forth.[23] The obvious weakness with this statement, however, is that it is surely impossible, on the basis of mere chronicle-references, to know enough about how *Alba* was understood by con-temporaries to permit such a confident assertion that its meaning changed so radically in 900.

A salutary warning against too simplistic an interpretation of name-change is to be found in a recent study by Huw Pryce of the Latin names used by Welsh writers for their own country and people in a wide range of literate contexts in the twelfth century.[24] Initially *Britannia* and *Britones* or *Britanni*, literally 'Britain' and 'Britons', was the usual des-ignation; in the 1120s and 1130s, however, these were supplanted by *Wallia* and *Walenses*, Latinisations of the English words for Wales and the Welsh. It is striking that this change is visible at roughly the same time in a number of sources: the Book of Llandaff, letters sent by bishops and princes, and to some extent also in chronicle-texts.[25] It would be a mistake, however, to suggest that the Welsh in the 1120s and 1130s abandoned their identity as the original inhabitants of Britain, and had subserviently adopted the English idea of who they were. The British dimension of Welsh identity continued unabated, expressed in various literary forms.[26] The decision to adopt *Wallia* for Wales when writing in Latin certainly represented a change, but, as Huw Pryce has perceptively argued, the change was in the situation of Wales within the wider world.[27] The growth of cultural, social and institutional links across Latin Christendom and the presence of a hostile Anglo-Norman realm made it necessary for the Welsh when writing Latin to find a way of identifying Wales as a distinct part of Britain, something that could not, of course, be achieved by using the word *Britannia*. At most, therefore, Welsh identity was adapting to new surroundings; the disuse of the term *Britannia* in this context did not signify a rejection of Britishness. Returning to the case of *Alba* in 900, there must be some anxiety that the notion that it represented a radical change owes as much, if not more, to an inherited assumption that Pictish identity was abandoned in favour of something decisively different. This is so deeply embedded in historiographical consciousness that any repetition or reformulation is bound to be attractive, especially if it is linked in our minds to the death of the Pictish language. It is not clear, however, that any of this is justified. Could the adoption of *Alba* as the kingdom's name signify continuity, rather than a break with Pictish identity? The bulk of this chapter is chiefly an attempt to answer this question. The prize at the end of what is a long journey over the rugged terrain of the longer Pictish king-list, Irish chronicles and the *Chronicle of the Kings of Alba* is an explanation of the use of the Gaelic term for 'Britain' in this context which does not require that *Alba* suffered an outrageous or particularly novel change of meaning.

ALBA AND THE LONGER PICTISH KING-LIST

The longer Pictish king-list contains within it the mortal remains of the only extant parchment text that can claim to be partially in the Pictish language.[28] The dominant language of the text is Latin, but Kenneth Jackson argued that the name-forms of most of the sixty to seventy kings in the section from 'Gilgidi' or 'Gede' to the Bredei who immediately precedes Cinaed mac Ailpín are probably Pictish.[29] For example, there is 'Uurguist' rather than Gaelic 'Fergus'; 'Onuist' rather than Gaelic 'Oengus'; 'Drest' rather than Gaelic 'Drust'; 'Bredei' rather than Gaelic 'Bruide' and 'Ciniod' rather than 'Cinaed'. This section must have existed soon after 840, although some of it is probably older.[30] What makes the longer king-list longer than the other extant archetypal Pictish list is the appearance of additional material both at the beginning and at the end. These additional sections stand out from the rest of the text because of their use of Gaelic name-forms. The section added at the beginning is a very considerable extension of the Pictish royal succession deep into antiquity. More than forty kings have been added, beginning with the eponymous Cruithne (whose name is simply a Gaelic collective noun for 'Picts') and his seven sons, who each rule the kingdom in turn, followed by a further six kings and then a curious series of nearly thirty kings called Bruide. We will return to Cruithne and his seven sons in a moment, for they hold the key to what is probably the earliest extant appearance of *Alba* as the name of the kingdom ruled by Cinaed mac Ailpín's descendants.

First we need to date this section, and in order to do that we need to turn our attention to the material added at the end. As it stands in its fullest form, the list concludes with Cinaed mac Ailpín and his successors up to Mael Coluim III mac Donnchada, king of Scots 1058–93. Mael Coluim is not given a reign-length, so the list as we have it can be dated to his reign. There is, however, good evidence for an intermediate stage between Bredei,[31] Cinaed mac Ailpín's immediate predecessor, and Mael Coluim III. A careful examination of the list as a whole reveals two appearances of the word 'and' before a king's name: once before Bredei, Cinaed mac Ailpín's predecessor, and the second time before Causantín, Cinaed mac Ailpín's son. Marjorie Anderson has pointed out that 'and', when it appears so rarely in a list in this way, is likely to signify where the list once came to an end: in a nutshell, it is like saying 'A, B, C, D, E, F and G', and later adding 'H, I and J'.[32] According to this line of argument, it seems that the king-list once ended with 'Bredei' (which, it will be recalled, coincides with the end of the Pictish name-forms) and was subsequently extended only as far as Cinaed mac Ailpín's son, Causantín, who reigned as king of Picts from 862 to 876. Comparison with copies of the king-list belonging to a recension which began only with Cinaed mac Ailpín suggests that the portion from Causantín mac Cinaeda was added in a single block at least as far as Donnchad ua Maíl Choluim (1034–40), if not to Donnchad's son, Mael Coluim III.[33] The stages in the list's development, as revealed by the way it ends, may be summarised:

(i)   A list of Pictish kings using Pictish orthography ends with Bredei, who was king early in the 840s.

(ii) This is subsequently updated, using Gaelic name-forms, by adding Cinaed mac Ailpín (d.858), his brother Domnall (d.862) and Cinaed's son, Causantín (whose reign-length is left blank).

(iii) This is continued by using a list ending no later than Donnchad ua Maíl Choluim (1034–40). Causantín mac Cinaeda's reign-length is supplied from this source. The most economical scenario is that, if the source of this final section did not already extend as far as Mael Coluim III, then the list was updated to Mael Coluim when it was extended from Causantín mac Cinaeda onwards.

Now, let us look again at the section added to the beginning, extending from Cruithne and his seven sons as far as the (nearly) thirty Bruides. It cannot be proved, but it would seem natural that whoever added this would on the same occasion have updated the historical list, as it were, as far as the reigning king. According to this assumption, therefore, the section from Cruithne to the (nearly) thirty Bruides was added either in the reign of Mael Coluim III (1058–93), or during the reign of Causantín son of Cinaed (862–76). In making a decision about this we need to bear in mind that all the fullest witnesses of this king-list, that is, those continued up to Mael Coluim III, appear to belong to *Lebor Bretnach*, the Gaelic translation and adaptation of *Historia Brittonum*, which on other evidence can be dated to the early part of Mael Coluim's reign[34] and, moreover, has been shown by Thomas Clancy, again on other evidence, to be a Scottish text.[35] It is easy to envisage how the Scottish scholar responsible for *Lebor Bretnach* might, when including the Pictish king-list in his work, have continued it to Mael Coluim III by adding the successors of Causantín mac Cinaeda in a batch from another king-list. It is less easy to see why at that point he might also have added the section beginning with Cruithne and his seven sons. Certainly he could not be regarded as having invented the material from Cruithne to the (nearly) thirty Bruides on that occasion. There are clear indications in §13 of *Lebor Bretnach* that a different recension of the section from Cruithne to the Bruides was already in existence (which was probably derived from a 'detached' portion published in the apparatus of §4 of Van Hamel's edition of *Lebor Bretnach*).[36]

For other evidence that the king-list already began with Cruithne and his seven sons before it was included in *Lebor Bretnach* it is necessary to bring into view the recension of the longer list incorporated into a collection of Scottish historical pieces which survives only in a manuscript produced in York *ca* 1360.[37] In Molly Miller's very helpful classification this is *Series Longior* 1 ('SL1' for short); the list included in *Lebor Bretnach* is 'SL2'.[38] There is an obvious difference between SL1 and SL2 of particular significance here: the intrusion in SL2 of a passage in Gaelic on the claims of 'Gud' and 'Cathluan' to be the first king.[39] This appears directly after the section from Cruithne to the (nearly) thirty Bruides, which might make one wonder whether the passage on Gud and

Cathluan could not have been added before the king-list sported the section beginning with Cruithne. The answer to this is found by turning to SL1, which has the section from Cruithne to the (nearly) thirty Bruides but does *not* include the passage on Gud and Cathluan. The possibility that this passage may have been removed at some stage from an ancestor of SL1 can be ruled out by a close examination of the text: it is very difficult to see how SL2 could evolve into SL1 at this point. It is quite straightforward, however, to envisage how SL2 could develop from SL1 by the addition of the passage on Gud and Cathluan. The significance of this detail is that it is stated in *Duan Albanach* (and in a related account of Pictish origins found in two manuscripts of *Lebor Bretnach*, discussed below) that there were seventy Pictish kings from Cathluan to Causantín who (we are told) was the last Pictish king.[40] As Marjorie Anderson has pointed out, in SL2 seventy kings can be counted from Cathluan to Causantín son of Cinaed.[41] There is little doubt, therefore, that a list very like SL2 (i.e., the Pictish king-list in *Lebor Bretnach*) already existed when *Duan Albanach* was composed during the reign of Mael Coluim III (1058–93), and that, at that stage, it already included both the section with Cruithne and the Bruides and also the passage on Gud and Cathluan. It may also be inferred from the fact that Causantín son of Cinaed was regarded as the seventieth and last Pictish king that this prototype of SL2 finished with Causantín. Putting this all together, then, it appears that the statement that there were seventy kings from Cathluan to Causantín affords a glimpse of the longer king-list beginning with Cruithne and his sons at a point before it was attached to *Lebor Bretnach* and (probably at the same time) extended from Causantín son of Cinaed to Mael Coluim III. This would mean that the section with Cruithne's seven sons was not added to the king-list during the reign of Mael Coluim, but during the reign of Causantín son of Cinaed mac Ailpín, that is, sometime between 862 and 876.

Looking now in more detail at Cruithne's seven sons, we are immediately aware of two curious features.[42] One is that they are (insofar as they can be recognised at all) the names of Pictish regions: for example, *Fíb* is now Fife; *Fotlaig* presumably refers to the people of Fotla (which can be identified with Atholl); *Fortrenn* is the genitive of *Fortriu*, the most prominent Pictish kingdom and *Cait* is the nominative plural of *Cataibh*, a dative plural form which has become the modern Gaelic name for the north of Scotland.[43] The other curious feature is that they fall very neatly into two alliterative groups: four names beginning with 'F' and three beginning with 'C'. Clearly, they would fit perfectly into a poetic stanza. It is most unlikely, on the face of it, that all Pictish regions, when rendered into Gaelic, began with either 'F' or 'C', and doubly unlikely that they would fall into two groups that could each fit so readily into a line of verse. There are, moreover, some signs of contrivance in order to meet poetic requirements. If *Fotlaig* refers to Atholl (which seems a reasonable deduction because Atholl is probably *Ath Fhotla*, 'new Fotla', i.e., 'new Ireland'[44]), then why has *ath* been dropped unless to make this begin with 'F' and so alliterate with *Fíb* and *Fortrenn*? Also, at least one of the unidentifiable names, *Fidach*, looks a little artificial: it literally means 'woody', which could accurately have described an extensive area of woodland, but need not have been a proper noun as such. The clinching evidence that Cruithne's seven sons originated in verse is that a stanza actually exists. It is a quatrain in Gaelic with seven syllables to the line and the lines paired by end-rhyme.[45]

Mórseiser do Chruithne claind
Raindset Albain i seacht raind
Cait Ce Círig cetach clann
Fíb Fidach Fotla Fortrenn[46]

'Seven of Cruithne's offspring
Divided *Alba* into seven shares
Cait, Ce, Círig, children with hundreds,
Fife, *Fidach, Fotla, Fortriu*.'[47]

The poem in its written form originates in the 'detached' portion of the king-list that I have referred to already, printed by Van Hamel as section 4 of his edition of *Lebor Bretnach*.[48] This goes under the title *Do Bunad Cruithnech*, 'Concerning Pictish Origins', and has yet to have its status determined.[49] It has a claim, in fact, to be the original version of the section with Cruithne's seven sons and the (nearly) thirty Bruides added to the beginning of the king-list. Be this as it may, it would appear that the earliest statement of Cruithne's seven sons is the quatrain, and that this was the source of the material on Cruithne's sons included in the king-list during the reign of Causantín son of Cinaed mac Ailpín (862–76).

ALBA: 'PICTLAND' AND 'BRITAIN'?

Having climbed so high up this mountain of textual analysis, what do we see when we admire the view? The point of the quatrain is to project the Picts as composed of regions which form a single territory stretching from Caithness in the north to Fife in the south. What catches our eye in particular is that this territory, 'Pictland', is referred to as *Alba*. From the vantage-point of the textual criticism we have just followed it would appear that *Alba* in this sense was known, used and approved by learned men in Pictland in the 860s or 870s, and that it could be earlier still.[50] It hardly needs to be added that there is no suggestion here that *Alba* is inimical in any way to Pictish identity. If anything the reverse is true. Moreover, the appearance of *Alba* in this context, far from heralding the demise of Pictishness, was the source of the longer king-list's vivid vision of Pictland as a unified kingdom in which each of Cruithne's seven sons was in turn king of the Picts.

But, it might be asked, what about the plentiful evidence that *Alba* meant Britain?[51] For example, in Irish chronicles there is a reference to Vikings returning from *Alba* in 871 with English, Britons and Picts as slaves.[52] *Alba* must mean Britain here. Also, in 866 a Gaelic phrase is used, *Gaill Érenn ocus Alban*, 'the foreigners of Ireland and Alba',[53] which is given a Latin parallel in the obit of a *rex Nordmanorum totius Hibernie et Britannie* in 873:[54] clearly *Alba* in 866 is the same as *Britannia* in 873.[55] If the stanza on Cruithne's sons is dated no later than the reign of Causantín son of Cinaed (862–76), which is when it was used by the author of the longer king-list, then it must be conceded that *Alba* in this period could mean both Pictland and Britain. How is this to be explained?

A direct parallel to this has already been met in the Welsh use of *Britannia* before the 1120s and 1130s. As well as referring to the whole island, there are a number of cases where it plainly meant what we would now call 'Wales':[56] for example, Asser described Offa's dyke as 'a great vallum between *Britannia* and Mercia',[57] and referred to King Alfred's dominion over south Wales by saying that 'all the districts of the south-ern region of *Britannia*' belonged to him,[58] while in the *Life of Cadog*, written in the late eleventh century, a tale is told which involves swim-ming from England across the Bristol Channel *versus Britanniam*, 'to Wales'.[59] Huw Pryce has commented that, 'at one level, *Britannia* may simply have meant "land of Britons" . . . ', and yet, 'underlying this use of a "British" vocabulary to describe Wales and the Welsh was surely an assumption that the country and the people *were* in a sense Britain and Britons . . .'[60] In other words, we are not dealing here with 'Britain' simply as a geographical term, but as an emblem defining a people who claimed a particular association with the island. It would appear, then, that something very similar was behind the application of *Alba*, the Gaelic word for Britain, as a designation for Pictland. The simplest inter-pretation of this otherwise extraordinary use of the term *Alba* is that the Picts also regarded themselves as peculiarly the people of Britain, so that it was appropriate to call their country 'Britain': in Gaelic, *Alba*.

If this is accepted then it offers a new perspective on the switch from Pictish to *Alba*-based terminology visible from 900 in Irish chronicles. Instead of representing the abandonment of Pictishness for something outrageously new, it would suggest that *Alba* was simply a continuation of a core element of Pictish identity, albeit in Gaelic. Before looking in more detail at the chronicle-evidence to see what light it may shed on the appearance of *Alba* for 'Pictland' in 900, and indeed whether this interpretation is sustainable, there is another more twisting route towards the Pictish word for their country that must be explored. This route takes us through the wider pool of names in Welsh for the Welsh themselves, for Britain and for Picts. This is pretty terrifying terrain where nothing is straightforward and some of it is genuinely confused; but if the eye is fixed firmly on the idea that the Picts as well as the Welsh seem to have regarded themselves as quintessentially British, then it is possible to come out at the other end of this terminological safari in one piece.

Let us start with Latin and Gaelic. It will be recalled that Latin *Britannia* can be used for a Brythonic territory, such as 'Wales',[61] and that, as we have seen, Gaelic *Alba* is likewise used particularly for 'Pictland'. There is, however, no clear cut example of Latin *Britannia* being used for 'Pictland' or Gaelic *Alba* for 'Wales'. On the face of it the answer is simple: there was no need. There were well-established Latin words for 'Picts' and 'Pictland', *Picti* and *Pictavia*, and a regular Gaelic term *Bretain* for the Welsh (of Strathclyde as well as of Wales), borrowed from Latin.[62] But the situation is not quite so neat and tidy. When *Alba* appeared on the scene there was already a Gaelic vocabulary for 'Picts': as well as *Cruithne* which has been met already, there was *Cruithen*, 'a Pict', *Cruithni*, 'Picts', and *Cruithentúath*, literally 'Pict-folk' or 'Pictland'. *Cruithentúath* is especially significant here because it could, it might be thought, function instead of *Alba*. This overlap is striking, and will need to be pigeon-holed for further consideration.

Moving on to Welsh itself, it is noticeable, as Huw Pryce points out, that the standard Welsh word for 'Britain', *Prydain* (usually spelt *Prydein* before the later Middle Ages), is nowhere attested as referring only to Wales.[63] The preferred vernacular term was *Cymru*.[64] This difference between the semantic range of Cambro-Latin *Britannia* and Welsh *Prydain* seems odd. If the Welsh were perfectly happy to refer to Wales as 'Britain' when speaking Latin, why not do the same when speaking their own language?

There is ample evidence in Welsh literature that they regarded themselves as British. There was, however, a peculiar difficulty with the term *Prydain*. The waters were muddied by the existence of a closely related word, *Pryden*, or more commonly *Prydyn*, which is found, for example, in the early sequence of elegies known as the *Gododdin*.[65] There it refers to 'Picts' or 'Pictland', not 'Britain'. Now, according to Kenneth Jackson *Prydyn* (*Pryden*) derives from **Priteni*, while *Prydain* (*Prydein*) derives from **Pritani*.[66] **Priteni* and **Pritani* were simply different forms of a pre-Roman Celtic word for 'Britain'. This can be represented in a chart:

Prydain (*Prydein*)	< **Pritani*	'Britain'
Pryden/Prydyn	< **Priteni*	'Pictland'
NB Gaelic *Cruithni*, 'Picts'	< **Priteni*	

Such a tidy differentiation between these terms is not, however, what is found in Old Welsh material.[67] Given the close kinship and similar sound of these words, it is no surprise that, as Ifor Williams observed, '*Pryden* and *Prydain* . . . are perpetually confused in texts, and also in pronunciation'.[68] This is particularly noticeable in *Armes Prydein Vawr*, 'The Great Prophecy of Britain', written in the mid-tenth century,[69] the earliest Welsh text to refer on a number of occasions to both 'Picts' and 'Britain'. The two words, *Prydyn* and *Prydain* (spelt *Prydein* in the poem), counting both together, appear five times. There are two cases in which the rhyme confirms that *Prydyn* was used not for 'Picts' but for 'Britain'.[70] The only other appearance of *Prydyn* is in the line *Gwydyl Iwerdon Mon a Phrydyn*, 'the Irish of Ireland, Mann (or Anglesey) and Pictland', referring to the principal regions inhabited by Gaels.[71] *Prydein* appears twice, and on both occasions means 'Britain'.[72] In another early text, *Culhwch ac Olwen* (which has been dated to around 1100), the confusion works the other way, with *Prydein* (i.e., *Prydain*, 'Britain') appearing as 'Pictland' on both occasions where *Prydyn* would be expected.[73] Again, this can be represented in a chart:

Prydain (*Prydein*)	< **Pritani*	'Britain', also 'Pictland'
Pryden/Prydyn	< **Priteni*	'Pictland', also 'Britain'
NB Gaelic *Cruithni*, 'Picts'	< **Priteni*	

It is clear from this that, although *Prydain* and *Prydyn* should be regarded as separate words, they overlapped or were readily confused. *Prydyn*, although it could mean 'Pictland', could also be used for 'Britain'; equally, *Prydain*, although it might often mean 'Britain', was also applied to 'Pictland'. Here is a possible answer to why *Prydain* was not used to mean Wales. It was not simply that a completely different Welsh word, *Cymru*, was available. It may also have been because it was impossible to sustain a separation of *Prydain* in a narrower sense meaning 'Wales' from *Prydyn* meaning 'Pictland'. It was as if the potential for this bifurcated word for 'Britain' to be applied to only a small part of the island was all spent on the Picts, from whom the Welsh wished to be distinguished (because Brythonic people were successors of Roman Britain, while the Picts were not).[74]

Let us pause briefly for breath in this arduous discussion of names and quickly recap on where we have reached. The Welsh word *Prydyn* is derived from a word for 'Britain', and could still be used to mean 'Britain' in the tenth century. It was also the word for 'Picts', and as such seems to have smothered the potential of this word or the closely related *Prydain* to be used for 'Wales' itself (given that the Welsh regarded themselves as distinct from the Picts). The next part of this journey must therefore start with the question: how could *Prydyn* meaning 'Picts' have been so strong? Here we are getting further and further into the realm of speculation. It is worth remembering two points, though. One is that the Pictish language (as revealed, for example, by place-names) was P-Celtic and therefore akin to Welsh.[75] *Prydyn* as 'Picts' may, therefore, reflect Welsh awareness that this version of the word for 'Britain' was a term used by the Picts for themselves. Secondly, it has long been recognised that the Gaelic word for Picts, *Cruithni*, is a Q-Celtic version of *Prydyn* (because both are derived from **Priteni*).[76] It seems likely, therefore, that the Gaelic word was taken from the P-Celtic word for Britain current in north Britain. This, again, would point to *Prydyn* as ultimately a Pictish word. Like *Prydyn* itself, *Cruithne* originally meant 'British' (hence its application to the *Cruithni* in northern Ireland, who presumably were once particularly associated with Britain). All these distant and winding lines of argument seem therefore to point to one conclusion: that *Prydyn* is ultimately a Pictish word for 'Britain', and that it was used for their own country in the same way as *Britannia* was used in Cambro-Latin to denote both 'Britain' and 'Wales'.[77]

With this in mind it is possible to return to the question of why *Alba*, the Gaelic word for 'Britain', was used for 'Pictland' when there were perfectly serviceable Gaelic words: *Cruithentúath* and the collective noun *Cruithne*. The most immediate answer would be that *Alba* was a direct Gaelic equivalent of the Pictish word underlying Welsh *Prydyn*, which meant 'Britain' and was used specifically for Pictland. In other words, *Alba* may have been a translation-loan into Gaelic of the Pictish word for their country. This kind of thing, of course, is done quite commonly in an acquired language (as in Highland English idioms translated directly from Gaelic usage), or where two languages are in close contact (as in English idioms imported literally into Gaelic). The two ways of referring to 'Pictland' in Gaelic would therefore be the result of two different processes: one a recent Picto-Gaelic word, *Alba*, derived from *Prydyn* (or something very like it), and the other the long-established terms *Cruithentúath* or *Cruithne*.

ALBA IN CONTEMPORARY CHRONICLES

The quatrain on Cruithne's seven sons is at best evidence only of the existence of *Alba* as a term for Pictland no later than 876. Stylistic and metrical considerations, rather than anything else, may have dictated the choice of *Alba* rather than *Cruithentúath* on that occasion. Yet it was *Alba* that became predominant in the tenth century. In order to shed light on this we need now to turn to the chronicles.[78]

It has been shown repeatedly that all extant Irish chronicles are derived ultimately from an earlier chronicle as far as the year 911. Nicholas Evans has recently shown that it was continued in Armagh's stewartry in the area of Brega and Conaille, and noted evidence to suggest that this was where the common source was kept in the ninth century as well.[79] The suggestion, then, is that the appearance of *Picti* and *rex Pictorum* up to the 870s, and the switch to *fir Alban* and *rí Alban* from 900, reflects how those associated with Armagh described the people and kingdom based in the east of Scotland. Where did they get this from?

A crucial factor in assessing the adoption of *Alba* for Pictland in Irish chronicles is that something very similar is detectable in the *Chronicle of the Kings of Alba*, a king-list covering the period from the 840s to the 970s with notes of events during each reign. We have met it briefly already,[80] where it was noted that an analysis of the way each item is introduced and other stylistic features points to the reign of Illulb mac Causantín (954–62) as the probable time of its original composition. Its subsequent text history is complicated, and has not yet been fully elucidated.[81] Unfortunately the references to the kingdom's inhabitants have been updated throughout to *Scoti* at some later stage in the text's development. Thankfully there was evidently no attempt to update the name of their country as well. It is called *Pictavia* during the reign of Cinaed mac Ailpín, and is mentioned four times thereafter. The first three times it is still called *Pictavia*: in the mid-860s when the Vikings devastated *Pictavia*; in the mid-870s, when Vikings stayed a year in *Pictavia* following their victory at Dollar in 875 and in another Viking devastation of *Pictavia* during the reign of Domnall, grandson of Cinaed mac Ailpín, who died in 900 after a reign of more than a decade. The last time the country is mentioned, however, it is *Pictavia* no more: in an event datable to 903 we are told that 'the Northmen plundered Dunkeld, and all *Albania*'. *Albania* is, of course, simply *Alba* in a Latin guise. Here, then, we have a switch from Pictish to *Alba*-based terminology that coincides remarkably well with what is found in Irish chronicles.

A key question arises: are the Irish chronicles and the *Chronicle of the Kings of Alba* independent witnesses of this change? If so, then this would suggest that the change relates to a development that was so significant that it could be noticed by two separate contemporary commentators. If they are not independent, however, then the coincidence need only reflect a change within a single text or centre of recording. To make any progress on this it is necessary to consider more closely the sources of the *Chronicle of the Kings of Alba*.

Needless to say none of these sources survives, so any attempt to identify them is fraught with difficulty. There is one strain of material, however, that is readily recognisable. From 849 until 952 there are fifteen items which are said to have occurred in a specific regnal year. This is one of the features that point to Illulb's reign as the time when the text was first composed. The most obvious kind of source that would have allowed events to be assigned to years like this is a year-by-year chronicle (like the Irish chronicles). Now, three of the references to *Pictavia* and *Albania* are found in items which appear to have been derived from a year-by-year chronicle. This strain of annalistic material, therefore, contains the same switch from *Pictavia* to *Albania* that we have seen in Irish chronicles. Where was this chronicle-source written? Could there be a connection between it and the core Irish chronicle to 911?

Fortunately the crucial item in which *Albania* is mentioned is something of a giveaway. Notice how Dunkeld is emphasised when we are told that 'the Northmen plundered Dunkeld, and all *Albania*'. Presumably there were other important churches plundered in 'all *Alba*' apart from Dunkeld, yet Dunkeld is the only one mentioned. The most natural explanation would be that this was written by someone in Dunkeld, or closely associated with Dunkeld. If so, when we read *Albania* here in the *Chronicle of the Kings of Alba*, we may actually be hearing the word *Alba* used by members of the church at Dunkeld. Dunkeld is particularly significant because it was, at least since 849, the centre of the cult of St Columba in Scotland: the founding of a church for St Columba's relics in 849 is, in fact, the first chronicle-based item that can be identified in the *Chronicle of the Kings of Alba*. Now, if the first traceable use of *Alba* in Scotland was in Dunkeld, then this opens up a potential link with the core Irish chronicle to 911. It will be recalled that it seems to have been associated with a stewartry of Armagh in this period. The head of the church in Armagh was the *comarba* or 'heir' of St Patrick, just as the head of the Columban family of churches (which in Ireland was based in this period at Kells) was known as the *comarba Coluim Chille*, the 'heir of St Columba'. As it happens, the period around 900 was witness to a remarkable development: so close had Armagh and the Columban family of churches become that Mael Brigte mac Tornáin, *comarba* of St Patrick since 888, became also the *comarba* of St Columba in 891, and held the two headships together until his death in 927.[82] If it is asked where a chronicle in Armagh's ambit in this period might have got its Scottish information from, the most likely answer would be Dunkeld, the chief Columban church in mainland Scotland. It is noticeable that the only Scottish church (apart from Iona) mentioned in Irish chronicles in this period is Dunkeld, when the deaths of abbots are recorded in 865 and 873.[83] It is also noticeable that three of the fifteen items in the *Chronicle of the Kings of Alba* attributable to a putative Dunkeld chronicle relate to the deaths of Irish kings.[84]

A good case can be made, therefore, that Scottish items in the Irish core chronicle were based on information acquired from Dunkeld.[85] They are the nearest we can get to a Scottish witness in this period. It is possible, therefore, that the preference for *Alba*-based terminology in Irish chronicles in the tenth century reflects the usage ultimately of only one major church (Dunkeld).[86] The minimal interpretation of the change from *rex Pictorum*, *Picti* and *Pictavia* to *rí Alban*, *fir Alban* and *Alba* (Latinised to *Albania*) therefore remains in play: that all we see about 900 is a move from Latin to Gaelic; a trend that is visible more generally in the Irish chronicles and may legitimately be conjectured in Dunkeld, too.[87] Seen in this light, the apparent translation of *Pictavia* as *Alba* rather than *Cruithentúath* may simply reflect the contemporary perspective of Picts who spoke Gaelic.[88]

If Dunkeld and Armagh and churches associated with them monopolise our information from tenth-century Scotland then it is difficult to say to what extent their terminology reflected widespread use.[89] Could *Alba*, indeed, have gradually become the norm chiefly because of Dunkeld and Armagh's influence? Also, if *Alba* was a translation-loan from the Pictish word for 'Britain' used to denote their country, this does not preclude the possibility that it may have also acquired a wider significance as a term used by Picts and Gaels, along the lines suggested by Máire Herbert and David Dumville.[90] Indeed, within a few generations *Alba* could be used to refer to the kingdom as a self-consciously Gaelic entity whose origins lay in Dál Riata, as in the statement that Fergus Mór and his brothers, progenitors of Scottish Dál Riata, 'took *Alba*'.[91] This is found in *Míniugud Senchasa fher nAlban*, the 'Explanation of the History of the people of *Alba*', which is generally accepted as a tenth-century text based on earlier material. If it was composed in Scotland, it would be the earliest extant Scottish statement of the idea that the Scottish kingship had Irish origins – an idea articulated more fully in relation to the kingdom's history in *Duan Albanach*.[92]

ALBA AFTER THE PICTS

It will be recalled that the adoption of *Alba* has hitherto been seen as evidence for the deliberate setting aside of a distinct Pictish identity, and maybe even of a determined rejection of Pictishness. If, however, the appearance of *Alba* is viewed as simply a change in language rather than identity (Latin *Pictavia* > Gaelic *Alba*), then this would be true not only of our chronicle sources but also of the population at large. When they turned from Pictish to Gaelic, they would also have referred to their country as *Alba* rather than by its name in Pictish (which would, it is suggested, have been a Pictish derivative of **Priteni*, akin to Welsh *Prydyn*). This would be no different from Gaelic speakers who, when speaking English, call themselves 'Scots' rather than *Albannaig* (or *Albannaich* in modern Gaelic). When the mother tongue of Picts ceased to be Pictish and became Gaelic, *Alba* and *Albannaig* would naturally have been the words used by them routinely for their country and for themselves, in exactly the same way as, in the thirteenth century, many of their descendants, who no longer spoke Gaelic, referred to their country as 'Scotland' and to themselves as 'Scots', using the English (or Inglis) equivalent words for *Alba* and *Albannaig*. In this way it becomes possible to detect a basic strain of continuity from being Pictish through to being Scottish today. The words may have altered with the passing of languages, but the name itself is essentially the same: a vessel whose cargo and appearance may have been altered over centuries, but which can still, under its numerous coats of paint and repeated refitting to keep it 'fit for purpose', be recognised as having once been the Pictish derivative of **Priteni*, a pre-historic Celtic word for Britain.

The use of *Alba* as the Gaelic term for their own country, and specifically for the landmass north of the Forth, testifies to the abiding power of geography in shaping political identity. The ancient succession of Pictish kings, for its part, at least as it was constructed during the reign of Causantín mac Cinaeda, represented a claim to sole rule over this particular inflection of Britishness. It was this emblematic identification with the idea of 'Britain', as well as the delineation of the imagined southern limit of the original Pictish kingdom by the geographical barrier of the Forth as far as its headwaters, that may have made it seem appropriate for Pictish kings and their 'Scottish' successors to sport such an impressively deep (albeit skeletal) regnal past. It allowed Scottish kingship to articulate a sense of being a cut above other kingships in the north without actually claiming to be paramount king of the whole island: to occupy an enduring position of superiority without aspiring to the impossible goal of 'king of all Britain', the title brandished so effectively by kings of England from Athelstan to Edward the Confessor.[93]

It has been argued that the Picts, by regarding themselves as indigenous to Britain, were analogous to the Welsh, and that this intimate identification with Britain was continued in the Gaelic designation of their kingdom as *Alba*. There was, however, also a significant difference between the Picts and the Welsh. A dominant aspect of the Welsh idea of their past was a sense of loss and oppression. The roots of their kingships lay either in the 'Old North', Roman Britain, or a figure like Beli Mawr, the British king who faced Caesar.[94] They had suffered conquest by the English, and could now only look forward, with the certainty of prophecy, to the destruction of the invaders and re-establishment of the kingdom of Britain. In contrast, it was possible to present *Alba* as an ancient entity that continued to thrive in the present under Mac Bethad and Mael Coluim III.[95] In part this must have reflected the fact that the kingdom was defined geographically by the barrier of the Forth. It must also, in part, have reflected the difference between the Scottish and Welsh interaction with the English. No territory north of the Forth had fallen under the power of an English king since Ecgfrith and his host had been cut down at the battle of Dún Nechtáin in 685. No English army is known to have engaged a Pictish force in Pictland or near its borders since Berhtfrith's victory at the plain of Manaw at the head of the Firth of Forth in 711.[96]

But this changed with the advent of an English kingdom stretching from Wessex to Northumbria under Athelstan (924/5–39), and Athelstan's dedication to the task of being 'king of all Britain'. The king of Scots soon discovered where he stood in this new political landscape. In 934, after Athelstan had led an army nearly ninety miles north of the Forth, and sent his ships even further north, Causantín mac Aeda was to be found on 13 September in Athelstan's entourage, appearing as a *sub-regulus*, an 'under-kinglet', among the witnesses of a charter.[97] A little later, in another of Athelstan's charters, he is named in a group of five *subreguli* in the list of witnesses.[98] This arrangement did not survive beyond Athelstan's death. Indeed, no king of England, until William I in 1072, is known to have taken an army north of the Forth; and no subsequent king of Scots appears in any context with this lowest of royal designations. But a precedent had been established for what a kingship of all Britain could mean for the relationship between the king of England and the king of Scots. The next chapter will examine the impact of this relationship on the independence of the Scottish kingdom, looking particularly at the period between the late eleventh and late twelfth centuries. It will be argued that it was in this period, not the tenth century, that Scotland's independence faced its first fundamental challenge, and was first articulated in terms of the kingdom's freedom.

NOTES

1. An essential discussion of *Alba* meaning Britain is David N. Dumville, 'Britain and Ireland in *Táin Bó Fraích*', *Études Celtiques* 32 (1996) 175–87. The chronicle material is discussed at 182–3 and nn. 36–8.
2. For literature on this, see Broun, *'Alba*: Pictish colony or Irish offshoot?', 236 n. 6.
3. Macquarrie, *Medieval Scotland: Kingship and Nation*, 72; Edward James, *Britain in the First Millennium* (London, 2001), 138, 230; A. D. M. Barrell, *Medieval Scotland* (Cambridge, 2000), 3. In fairness, neither Barrell nor James would claim to have first-hand experience in researching this period of Scottish history.
4. See below, 84–6. The only other source which yields some material which might meet these criteria is the *Chronicle of the Kings of Alba*. The discussion of the *Chronicle's* genesis in B. T. Hudson, 'The Scottish Chronicle', *SHR* 77 (1998) 129–61, at 133–6, fails to distinguish between the text and its sources. For discussion of the text see M. Miller, 'The last century of Pictish succession', *Scottish Studies* 23 (1979) 39–67, at 58–60; David N. Dumville, 'The Chronicle of the Kings of Alba', in S. Taylor (ed.), *Kings, Clerics and Chroniclers in Scotland 500–1297* (Dublin, 2000) 73–86.
5. The other major witness, dubbed the Annals of Tigernach (AT), has a lacuna from 767 to 973. AU survives in two manuscripts of the late fifteenth and early sixteenth centuries; CS is a seventeenth-century manuscript, and AT fourteenth-century.
6. For *rex Pictorum* and *Picti* see AU 858.2, 862.1 (also CS 862.1), 865.2 (*regio Pictorum*), 871.2, 875.3, 876.1 (also CS 876.1), 878.2; for *rí Alban* and *fir Alban* see AU 900.6 (also CS 900.5) and AU 918.4. *Cruithentúath* is also used in AU 866.1 and CS 904.6: on this term, see below, 81.
7. Dauvit Broun, 'The birth of Scottish History', *SHR* 76 (1997) 4–22, at 6.

8. The evidence for this (e.g. the way each item is introduced) has not been published. (It was explained in a paper on the chronicle I gave at the Celtic Department, University of Aberdeen, on 12 December 2005.) The most recent edition is Hudson, 'The Scottish Chronicle'.

9. Dauvit Broun, 'The Picts' place in the kingship's past before John of Fordun', in Edward J. Cowan and Richard J. Finlay (eds), *Scottish History. The Power of the Past* (Edinburgh, 2002), 11–28, at 21–3.

10. There was a Pictish king with the same name who died in 775. Also, Cinaed's brother and successor, Domnall, was known as 'Donald I', although there were two kings of Dál Riata called Domnall in the seventh century: Domnall Brecc (d.642) and Domnall Donn (d.695).

11. M. O. Anderson, 'Dalriada and the creation of the kingdom of the Scots', in D. Whitelock, R. McKitterick and D. Dumville (eds), *Ireland in Early Mediaeval Europe: Studies in Memory of Kathleen Hughes* (Cambridge, 1982), 106–32; Benjamin T. Hudson, *Kings of Celtic Scotland* (Westport Conn., 1994), 34–6; John Bannerman, 'The Scottish takeover of Pictland and the relics of Columba', in D. Broun and T. O. Clancy (eds), *Spes Scotorum, Hope of Scots. Saint Columba, Iona and Scotland* (Edinburgh, 1999), 71–94.

12. See below. For an important and original account of this period in which Cinaed's role is reasserted, see Patrick Wormald, 'The emergence of the *regnum Scottorum*: a Carolingian hegemony?', in B. E. Crawford (ed.), *Scotland in Dark Age Britain* (St Andrews, 1996), 131–60. He argued (at 144) that 'just because we know so little about him is no excuse for denying Kenneth mac Alpin the role of conquest': see also 138–9.

13. Note, however, that Giric's reign in the 880s has been proposed as the critical period in Duncan, *Kingship of the Scots*, 15.

14. As far as I am aware Edward J. Cowan, 'Destruction of a Celtic people: the Viking impact upon Pictland', *Celtic Collections, Acta* 16 (1989) 99–112, is the earliest discussion of this period that promotes Causantín rather than Cinaed as the crucial figure for the founding of Scotland.

15. Máire Herbert, '*Rí Éirenn, Rí Alban*: kingship and identity in the ninth and tenth centuries', in Simon Taylor (ed.), *Kings, Clerics and Chroniclers in Scotland 500–1297* (Dublin, 2000), 62–72, at 69.

16. *Ibid.*, 70.

17. *Ibid.*, 69.

18. David N. Dumville, *The Churches of North Britain in the First Viking-Age. The Fifth Whithorn Lecture, 14th September 1996* (Whithorn, 1997), 35–6 (without the scope on that occasion to explain why he regarded Cinaed as a Pict).

19. Chiefly on the basis of the genealogies of kings of Scots extant from the 990s. On these texts, see Broun, '*Alba*: Pictish colony or Irish offshoot?', 264–5.

20. Dumville, *The Churches of North Britain*, 36 n. 106.

21. T. O. Clancy and B. E. Crawford, 'The formation of the Scottish kingdom', in R. A. Houston and W. W. J. Knox (eds), *The New Penguin History of Scotland from the Earliest Times to the Present Day* (London, 2001), 28–95, at 64. For a similar statement, see Sally M. Foster, *Picts, Gaels and Scots*, 2nd edn (London, 2004), 109; 1st edn (London, 1996), 112. See also n. 23, below.

22. Alex Woolf, 'Birth of a nation', in Gordon Menzies (ed.), *In Search of Scotland* (Edinburgh, 2001), 24–45, at 42.

23. Dauvit Broun, 'The origin of Scottish identity in its European context', in B. E. Crawford (ed.), *Scotland in Dark Age Europe* (St Andrews, 1994), 21–31, at 21. This evidently lies behind the statements of Clancy and Crawford and Foster referred to above: see Clancy and Crawford, 'The formation', 93, and Foster, *Picts, Gaels and Scots*, 1st edn, 112; 2nd edn, 109. In light of this, I owe these authors a profound apology for changing my view so fundamentally on this issue.

24. Huw Pryce, 'British or Welsh? National identity in twelfth-century Wales', *English Historical Review* 116 (2001) 775–801. This topic was also discussed more briefly in Kaele Stokes, 'The delineation of a medieval "nation": *Brittones*, *Cymru* and *Wealas* before the Norman conquest', in Pamela O'Neill (ed.), *Nation and Federation in the Celtic World: Papers from the Fourth Australian Conference of Celtic Studies* (Sydney, 2003), 304–16.

25. Pryce, 'British or Welsh?', 777–84.

26. For an excellent summary, see R. R. Davies, *The Age of Conquest: Wales 1063–1415* (Oxford, 1991), 77–80.

27. Pryce, 'British or Welsh?', 784–96.

28. Editions: Anderson, *Kings and Kingship*, 245–9, 261–3; Van Hamel (ed.), *Lebor Bretnach*, 82–7. The recensions and MSS are classified in M. Miller, 'Matriliny by Treaty', in D. Whitelock, R. McKitterick and D. Dumville (eds), *Ireland in Early Mediaeval Europe: Studies in Memory of Kathleen Hughes* (Cambridge, 1982), 133–61, at 159–60. Work by Nicholas Evans on the development of Pictish king-lists is in progress, and promises to put our understanding of these texts onto a new scholarly footing.

29. See K. H. Jackson, 'The Pictish language', in F. T. Wainwright (ed.), *The Problem of the Picts* (Edinburgh, 1955), 129–66, at 144–5; also J. T. Koch, 'The loss of final syllables and loss of declension in Brittonic', *BBCS* 30 (1983) 201–30, at 219. Note also the discussion of 'Onuist' in Katherine Forsyth, 'Evidence of a lost Pictish source in the *Historia Regum Anglorum* of Simeon of Durham', in Taylor (ed.), *Kings, Clerics and Chronicles*, 19–32, at 23–5. As it stands the list may reflect Pictish orthography to some extent, but cannot be regarded automatically as an accurate record of Pictish forms (especially given the likelihood of copying errors).

30. What follows on the king-list and the quatrain on Cruithne's sons has grown out of David E. Brown, 'The Scottish Origin-legend before Fordun',

unpublished Ph.D. dissertation (Edinburgh University 1988), 410 n. 80; Dauvit Broun, 'The origin of Scottish identity', in C. Bjørn, A. Grant and K. J. Stringer (eds), *Nations, Nationalism and Patriotism in the European Past* (Copenhagen, 1994), 35–55, at 48–50; and Broun, 'The origin of Scottish identity in its European context', 24–5.

31. The MSS of the longer Pictish king-list read 'Bred', which I take to be a mis-copying of 'Bredei'.

32. Anderson, *Kings and Kingship*, 79.

33. Broun, *The Irish Identity*, 168. The archetype of the section from Causantín's reign-length to Mael Coluim mac Cinaeda's reign-length (list θ) can be dated to the reign of Donnchad ua Maíl Choluim (1034–40): *ibid.*, 166. This suggests that the updating of the longer king-list beyond Causantín mac Cinaeda (who would not have had a reign-length given if the continuation after 'Bredei' occurred during his reign) would have occurred no earlier than 1034.

34. See D. N. Dumville, 'The textual history of "Lebor Bretnach": a preliminary study', *Éigse* 16 (1975–6) 255–73, at 269–70; T. O. Clancy, 'Scotland, the "Nennian" recension of the *Historia Britonum*, and the *Lebor Bretnach*', in Simon Taylor (ed.), *Kings, Clerics and Chroniclers in Scotland 500–1297* (Dublin, 2000), 87–107, at 88 and n. 1.

35. Clancy, 'Scotland, the "Nennian" Recension of the *Historia Britonum*, and the *Lebor Bretnach*'.

36. Van Hamel (ed.), *Lebor Bretnach*, 23–4. For §4 see below.

37. Edited in Anderson, *Kings and Kingship*, 240–60 (the king-list is at 245–9). It concludes with the king, Bredei, who precedes Cinaed mac Ailpín in the other recension: any material from Cinaed onwards has doubtless been omitted in order to avoid overlap with the *Chronicle of the Kings of Alba*, which begins with Cinaed mac Ailpín. For the manuscript, see Julia C. Crick, *The Historia Regum Britannie of Geoffrey of Monmouth*, vol. iii, *Summary Catalogue of the Manuscripts* (Cambridge, 1989), 256–61.

38. Miller, 'Matriliny by treaty', 159–60.

39. Anderson, *Kings and Kingship*, 84 and n. 32, and 261 for edition of a witness. For an account of Pictish origins featuring Cathluan see Van Hamel (ed.), *Lebor Bretnach*, 12–14 (§7). See also Skene (ed.), *Chronicles*, 27, 398 (for lists) and 32–44 (for the account featuring Cathluan), and also Calise, *Pictish Sourcebook*, 197, for a list of references to Cathluan.

40. Van Hamel (ed.), *Lebor Bretnach*, 9; see Broun, *The Irish Identity*, 168 n. 18 (and references cited there, esp. Scowcroft, 'Leabhar Gabhála. part I', 116–18).

41. Anderson, *Kings and Kingship*, 78.

42. What follows supersedes the similar discussion in Broun, 'The origin of Scottish identity', 48–50 and Broun, 'The origin of Scottish identity in its European context', 24–6.

43. For a discussion of the location of these regions, and previous literature on this, see Broun, 'The seven kingdoms'. Alex Woolf, 'Dún Nechtain, Fortriu

and the geography of the Picts', *SHR* 85 (2006) (forthcoming), shows that Fortriu was in the north of Scotland (probably in the area round the Moray Firth).

44. Watson, *History of the Celtic Place-Names*, 28–9. I am grateful to Alex Woolf for warning me, however, that the interpretation of *Ath Fotla* as 'New Ireland' is not certain.

45. Van Hamel (ed.), *Lebor Bretnach*, 5 (with minor orthographical amendments); see also *ibid.*, 23 n. 52. The quatrain is also found in MSS of *Lebor Gabála* along with the mangled rendering of the (nearly) thirty Bruides found in §4 of *Lebor Bretnach*. For discussion, see Scowcroft, '*Leabhar Gabhála*. part I', 116–18.

46. Analysis: $7^1 \; 7^1 \; 7^1 \; 7^2$, with rhyme between *a* and *b*, *c* and *d* (*deibide*), and the two pairs linked by consonance: cf. Gerard Murphy, *Early Irish Metrics* (Dublin, 1961), 35: '*cetharchubaid*, "four-harmonied", used in the ninth century to describe a *rannaigecht* quatrain in which each of the four end-words either rimes or consonates with another word'. The quatrain appears to be a *deibide* example of this phenomenon.

47. I take the names to be either nom. plural (for people): *Cait* ('the Cats'), *Círig* ('the crested people': cf. *Círcinn*, 'crest-heads', in the longer king-list); or nom. sing (*Fidach*, 'woody'); or indeclinable: *Cé*, *Fíb*. For *Fotla* note the form *Fotlaig* (reconstructed from 'Floclaid'/'Foltlaid'/'Fodlid' in the MSS) in the longer king-list (i.e., 'people of *Fotla*'). *Fortrenn* is gen. sing., so perhaps *fir* is understood ('[people] of Fortriu').

48. Van Hamel (ed.), *Lebor Bretnach*, 5–6. Note that his main text is an abbreviated version, and that the full text continues at 6 n. 51.

49. Anderson, *Kings and Kingship*, 83 proposed that the longer king-list was the source of the 'detached' portion printed by Van Hamel as §4 of *Lebor Bretnach*, but her identification of an error shared by §4 (Van Hamel (ed.), *Lebor Bretnach*, 6 n. 51) and the version of the longer list attached to *Lebor Bretnach* (§48 in Van Hamel's edition), which is the most compelling part of her argument, is contradicted in Van Hamel (ed.), *Lebor Bretnach*, 83 (§48) n. 4, where *Urfexir* is the reported reading, not *Fet(h)*.

50. Note also the quatrain ostensibly celebrating the taking of *Alba* by Unust son of Uurgust, the most powerful Pictish king on record, who reigned 729–61: see T. O. Clancy (ed.), *The Triumph Tree. Scotland's Earliest Poetry AD 550–1350* (Edinburgh, 1998), 144. Unfortunately the likely genre (it was probably part of a panegyric poem) and the possibility that Unust was, at one stage, regarded as exercising overlordship in Britain, mean that this cannot with any confidence be regarded as an example of *Alba* being used for 'Pictland'.

51. The evidence is best presented in Dumville, 'Ireland and Britain', 177–80.

52. AU 871.2; CS 871.2 (but without mentioning Picts).

53. AU 866.1.

54. AU 873.3.

55. Dumville, 'Ireland and Britain', 182 n. 36.
56. A.W. Wade-Evans (ed.), *Vitae Sanctorum Britanniae et Genelogiae* (Cardiff, 1944), vii and nn. 1–4; Pryce, 'British or Welsh?', 777–8.
57. W. H. Stevenson (ed.), *Asser's Life of King Alfred*, with article by Dorothy Whitelock (Oxford, 1959), 12 (ch. 14); Wade-Evans (ed.), *Vitae Sanctorum Britanniae*, vii n. 3.
58. Stevenson (ed.), *Asser's Life of King Alfred*, 66 (ch. 80); Pryce, 'British or Welsh?', 777.
59. Wade-Evans (ed.), *Vitae Sanctorum Britanniae*, 92–3; Pryce, 'British or Welsh?', 777–8.
60. *Ibid.*, 778.
61. Note also areas of Brythonic settlement on the Continent: not only Brittany, but also the diocese of *Britonia* in Galicia, north-west Spain (and note also the place-name Bretoña in the same region): see, for example, N. Chadwick, 'The colonisation of Brittany from Celtic Britain', *PBA* 51 (1965) 235–99, and more recently S. Young, 'The bishops of the early medieval diocese of Britonia', *Cambrian Medieval Celtic Studies* 45 (Summer 2003) 1–19.
62. Note, for example, AU 865.3, 913.8, 950.2, 971.1, 975.2, 997.5 (*rí Bretan Tuaiscirt*, 'king of northern Britons').
63. Pryce, 'British or Welsh?', 780.
64. *Ibid.*, 780.
65. John T. Koch (ed.), *The Gododdin of Aneirin. Text and Context from Dark-Age North Britain* (Cardiff, 1997), 32 (line 475|492); Ifor Williams (ed.), *Canu Aneirin*, 2nd edn (Caerdydd, 1961), 19 (line 475) and 20 (line 492). See further Broun, '*Alba*: Pictish colony or Irish offshoot?', 255 n. 75.
66. K. H. Jackson, 'Two early Scottish names', *SHR* 33 (1954) 14–18.
67. This is true also of the *Gododdin*, where the MS reading of line 475 has *Prydein* rather than *Pryden*: it is generally agreed that rhyme shows this to be an error (Williams (ed.), *Canu Aneirin*, 190; Koch (ed.), *The Gododdin*, 161).
68. Ifor Williams (ed.), *Armes Prydein. The Prophecy of Britain from the Book of Taliesin*, trans. R. Bromwich (Dublin, 1972), 21–2 (note on *Prydyn*). This comment is a discrete sentence, without ellipsis, in the original: Ifor Williams (gol.), *Armes Prydein o Lyfr Taliesin* (Caerdydd, 1955), 14.
69. Various dates have been mentioned as possible, ranging from *ca* 930 to *ca* 980. The literature is reviewed in Helen Fulton, 'Tenth-century Wales and *Armes Prydein*', *THSC* n.s. 7 (2001) 5–18.
70. Williams (ed.), *Armes Prydein*, trans. Bromwich, lines 67, 105 (and 49, note on line 105).
71. *Ibid.*, line 10. It has to be said, however, that *Prydyn* for 'Britain' cannot be ruled out here either, especially perhaps if *Mon* is translated 'Mann'.
72. *Ibid.*, lines 152, 167.

73. Bromwich and Evans (eds), *Culhwch and Olwen*, 92, 128–9. For the dating, see lxxxi–lxxxiii, where it is pointed out that, although both extant MSS are fourteenth-century, the language is 'archaic and belongs to the end of the O[ld] W[elsh] period'. For another example of *Prydein* for *Prydyn* see Bromwich (ed.), *Trioedd Ynys Prydein*, 228, 233 (probably second quarter of the twelfth century: see *ibid.*, cxxiv). *Prydein* (i.e., *Prydain*) meaning Scotland also appears in *ByT* (RB), 166, 242; *ByT* (Pen. 20, gol.), 59 (twice), 208; *ByS*, 76 n. 17, and 262, 264. Presumably this was a translation of *Scotia*, which would explain how the account of the death of Magnus Barelegs has been placed in *Prydein* rather than Ireland (which could have been *Scotia* in the lost Latin chronicle) in one version (*ByT* (RB), 46), and *yr Alban* in another version (*ByT* (Pen. 20, gol.), 36). Note also an instance where *Prydein* for 'Wales' (rather than 'Britain') occurs where the Latin original read *Britannia*: *ByT* (Pen. 20, trans.), 149 (discussion of 12 line 30). Note also *Prydain* for 'Scotland' in Dafydd Johnston (ed.), *Iolo Goch, Poems* (Llandysul, 1993), 33 (and 164 for comment), although *Prydyn* for 'Scotland' is normal in this corpus (*ibid.*, 3, 37, 43, 77, 79). I am grateful to Thomas Clancy for this reference.

74. Note that, in what is probably the earliest attested appearance of *Prydyn* (in the *Gododdin*), it is coupled with 'pagans and Gaels': see above, n. 65. Note also that, when medieval Welsh writers thought in detail of Britain as an island, the information they gave betrays a southerly focus (suggesting a particular association with Roman Britain), which has led Dafydd Glyn Jones to ask if Scotland/*Prydyn* was considered as part of the island of Britain (his answer is 'yes and no'): Jones, *Gwlad y Brutiau*, 24 (followed by a useful summary of the evidence).

75. The best discussion of this question is Katherine Forsyth, *Language in Pictland. The Case against 'non-Indo-European Pictish'* (Utrecht, 1997).

76. Jackson, 'Two early Scottish names', 17–18.

77. Dumville, 'The Chronicle of the Kings of Alba', 85 (see also Dumville, 'Ireland and Britain', 77 n. 13) has suggested that *Albidosi*, mentioned uniquely in the *Chronicle of the Kings of Alba*, may be a reference to the inhabitants of *Alba*. For discussion and an alternative interpretation, see Broun, '*Alba*: Pictish colony or Irish offshoot?', 258 n. 85.

78. What follows supersedes Broun, 'The origin of Scottish identity', 40–5, and updates Dauvit Broun, 'Dunkeld and the origin of Scottish identity', in Broun and Clancy (eds), *Spes Scotorum*, 95–111.

79. Nicholas J. Evans, 'The Textual Development of the Principal Irish Chronicles in the Tenth and Eleventh Centuries', unpublished Ph.D. dissertation (University of Glasgow, 2003) 145–78.

80. See above, 73.

81. See Dumville, 'The Chronicle of the Kings of Alba'.

82. Máire Herbert, *Iona, Kells and Derry: the History and Historiography of the Monastic* familia *of Columba* (Oxford; repr. Dublin, 1996), 74–6.

83. AU 865.6 (*Tuathal mac Artgusso prímepscop Fortrenn 7 abbas Duin Caillenn*), 873.8 (*Flaithbertach mac Muirchertaigh princeps Duin Chaillden*).

84. Mael Sechnaill mac Maíle Ruanaid in 862, Aed mac Néill in 879 and Cormac mac Cuilennáin in 908. Clearly there was information coming from Ireland to Dunkeld as well. The links need not have been purely ecclesiastical: Cinaed mac Alpin's daughter, Mael Muire, was wife of both Aed and Aed's successor, Flann Sinna (who died in 916). Mael Muire herself died in 913. See Herbert, '*Rí Éirenn, rí Alban*', 68–9.

85. This probably remained the case in AU for some time after 900. Certainly Dunkeld is almost the only Scottish ecclesiastical centre mentioned (apart from Iona): the killing of abbots of Dunkeld is noted in two battles (AU 965.4, 1045.6), and the burning of Dunkeld is mentioned in AU 1027.7.

86. The information to hand is, of course, far too meagre to establish how this material was transmitted. For some idea of the mechanics of this process, see Evans, 'The Textual Development of the Principal Irish Chronicles', 179–261.

87. David N. Dumville, 'Latin and Irish in the Annals of Ulster, AD 431–1050', in Whitelock, McKitterick and Dumville (eds), *Ireland in Early Mediaeval Europe*, 320–41 (although note that this trend is more prominent from 939 in AU and later in the *Annals of Inisfallen*: see *ibid.*, 331–2).

88. Perhaps the ascription of the quatrain on Cruithne's seven sons to Colum Cille (Van Hamel (ed.), *Lebor Bretnach*, 5 n. 40 and 23 n. 52), if original, might also indicate that it was regarded as particularly associated with Dunkeld.

89. It cannot be assumed, on the strength of its putative use of an annalistic source from Dunkeld, that the *Chronicle of the Kings of Alba* itself was originally composed in Dunkeld (*pace* Hudson, 'The Scottish Chronicle', 135–6). It may be inferred, however, that it was probably composed in a church which at least had links to Dunkeld. The material relating to the 960s and 970s shows an interest both in St Andrews and in Brechin/Angus (hence the suggestion by Hudson that it was continued in St Andrews, *ibid.*, 136, and the suggestion that the chronicle was composed in Brechin: Edward J. Cowan, 'The Scottish chronicle in the Poppleton manuscript', *IR* 32 (1981) 3–21, at 12).

90. See above, 73–4.

91. John Bannerman, *Studies in the History of Dalriada* (Edinburgh, 1974), 41 lines 2–4, 47 and 118–19 for discussion. On this text see now David N. Dumville, 'Ireland and North Britain in the earlier Middle Ages: contexts for *Míniugud Senchasa fher nAlban*', in Colm Ó Baoill and Nancy R. McGuire (eds), *Rannsachadh na Gàidhlig 2000* (Aberdeen, 2002), 185–211.

92. See Broun, *Irish Identity*, 188–9, for the genealogical significance of Fergus.

93. Davies, *The First English Empire*, 37, and above, 22.

94. P. C. Bartrum (ed.), *Early Welsh Genealogical Tracts* (Cardiff, 1966), 9–13; *Historia Brittonum* §19.

95. See above, 55–8.

96. AU 711.3 (and in equivalent annal in AT); Colgrave and Mynors (eds), *Bede's Ecclesiastical History of the English People*, 566–7; *ES*, i. 213; *SAEC*, 49–50.

97. S426.

98. S1792.

PART II

Independence

4

The Church and the Beginning of Scottish Independence

From the Council of Windsor and the Submission of Abernethy (1072) to Cum universi and the Quitclaim of Canterbury (1189)

It is impossible to say whether there were many meetings between kings of England and kings of Scots prior to the submission of Mael Coluim III to William the Conqueror at Abernethy in 1072. Of course, the general shortage of sources for this period, particularly from Scotland, means that it cannot be demonstrated conclusively that a particular event or series of events did *not* happen, just because there is no reference to it in what survives. After 1072, however, it is known that every king of Scots before the conquest of Scotland in 1296, with the exception of Domnall Bán, met and formed some kind of relationship with the king of England. This relationship has often been seen in 'feudal' terms: in other words, to assume that what was at issue was whether the king of Scots was a vassal owing service in return not only for land held of the king of England, but for Scotland itself. According to this view, Mael Coluim's submission at Abernethy would have been seen by William as an act of 'feudal subjection'.[1] Likewise, it has been taken as read that the manifest subordination of Edgar and Alexander I to William Rufus and Henry I meant that they acknowledged the king of England to be their lord for Scotland.[2] Indeed, a charter of Edgar, whose authenticity has recently been vindicated, could be read as showing that Edgar acknowledged that he held 'the land of Lothian and the kingdom of Scotland' not only by paternal inheritance but by the gift of his lord King William of England.[3] Alexander I, for his part, fought in Henry I's campaign in Wales in 1114, an enterprise in which he could have had no personal interest beyond his relationship with the king of England. In contrast, it will be recalled that David I's refusal of homage to King Stephen (1135–54) has been interpreted as an assertion of Scotland's independence.[4] The relationship thereafter between kings of Scots and kings of England has generally been presented as fluctuating from English feudal superiority to Scottish independence according to the relative strength and weakness of each king, with the added complication that, when David I and his successors held the earldom of Huntingdon of the king of England, it was possible to interpret homage as for lands in England alone, leaving Scotland out of the equation.

It is not necessary to enter the vigorous debate about the existence of 'feudalism' in order to appreciate that the relationship between kings of Scots and Norman kings of England cannot usefully be regarded from the outset as 'feudal'.[5] This has been shown by Rees Davies in his compelling re-assessment of submissions by 'Celtic' rulers to the king of England in this period.[6] He noted a qualitative change, when claims to jurisdictional superiority 'come to occupy centre stage in the definition of relationships between suzerain and client in the British Isles';[7] a process which began with the 'Treaty of Falaise' between William I, king of Scots, and Henry II in 1174 – the first occasion in which the independence of a subordinate kingdom was challenged directly and systematically. Before this point submissions had been political rather than legal affairs, and no-one had considered them as constituting a fixed agreement in which the client king and his heirs were deemed to 'hold' their kingdom as a grant from the king of England. In this chapter Professor Davies's insights will be extended into a more detailed discussion of how the Scottish kingdom was regarded by Scottish kings and churchmen in relation to the king of England. It will be possible to talk with some precision about the beginnings of Scottish independence: that is, when the status of the Scottish kingdom vis-à-vis England first became an issue with regard to the exercise of authority over Scottish society. The burden of the argument, however, is that this did not initially arise in the context of interaction between kings, but has its origins in the rebirth of the Church as a fully articulated unified institution whose authority embraced all of Latin Christendom. It was as part of this process that Scottish independence was first asserted in a text whose authenticity has only recently been established by the discovery of two manuscript witnesses.

Before this point is reached, we need to consider the nature of the relationship between kings of Scots and kings of England in the century after Mael Coluim's submission at Abernethy. Rees Davies has provided a compelling account of what he referred to as the 'patriarchal' or 'loose' overlordship that kings of England enjoyed in relation to their 'Celtic' neighbours before Falaise. Typically it involved not only a display of power by the king of England, such as his intervention in a disputed succession (as in William II's backing of Edgar against Domnall Bán), or, most brutally, a full-scale invasion (which is how William I forced Mael

Coluim to meet him at Abernethy in 1072), but also some face-to-face discussion between the principal parties leading to the establishment of friendship and peace. The process was completed by a public act of submission. Professor Davies emphasised that submission was 'essentially personal; it was not a treaty between states, nor was land mentioned'.[8] It would be misleading to refer to a 'Treaty of Abernethy' in 1072.[9] Meaning was conveyed by potent rituals and gestures. An important consequence of this was that, although the essential fact of the king of England's power had been unambiguously acknowledged, the detail of what might be involved could be open to more than one interpretation, and would not, in any case, be regarded explicitly as defining the relationship for ever and anon. In Rees Davies's words: 'these men were involved in defusing the crisis of the moment, not in composing footnotes in future textbooks of constitutional history'.[10] An essential feature of these submissions which Davies has identified is that, if they were to endure at all, 'the client must be made to feel that he was being treated as a friend not as a door mat'.[11] There would, usually, be demands made on the king who submitted, for example the surrender of hostages and payment of tribute. But there would also be important benefits for a king who enjoyed the friendship of a more powerful neighbour. He might expect that his own prestige 'at home' would be enhanced by such an association with a great ruler; indeed, he might need the support of the king of England in order to secure his own position as king against his rivals. It is this in particular which justifies the description of the king of England's overlordship as 'patriarchal'. It was also a 'loose' overlordship because there was no expectation that the king of England would cut across the client king's authority within his own kingdom. Far from being a threat to the client king's power over the people he ruled, the expectation was that the king of England would, if anything, help to make this more secure. In Rees Davies's words, submission 'inaugurated, formalised or continued what we may define as essentially a non-penetrative overlordship'.[12]

To what extent can these general observations be said to apply in the case of relations between kings of Scots and kings of England before the change to a more direct, interventionist overlordship? Older generations of historians might have objected, for instance, that in the twelfth century kings of Scots, unlike their Welsh and Irish counterparts, would have been familiar with feudal ideas, and that this would have influenced the nature of their dealings with their powerful southern neighbour. As backing for this, it might be protested, one could not deny the statement in Edgar's charter that the kingdom of Scotland had been given to him by his lord, King William II of England – a clear case, it would seem, of a link between subordination and tenure.

This is, indeed, a crucial document, and needs to be considered carefully. On closer inspection, it is far from clear in the charter's prose that William as Edgar's lord was deemed to have granted the kingdom of Scotland to his vassal.[13] The crucial passage reads:[14]

> *Edgarus filius Malcolmi regis Scottorum totam terram de Lodeneio et regnum Scotie dono domini mei Willelmi Anglorum regis et paterna hereditate possidens.*

> 'Edgar, son of Mael Coluim king of Scots, possessing the entire land of Lothian and the kingdom of Scotland by the gift of my lord William king of the English and by paternal heritage'.

Professor Duncan, in his defence of the charter against the charge that it is a later forgery, has pointed out that 'one could not possess something both by gift and by inheritance'.[15] He concluded, therefore, that this passage 'must mean that Edgar possessed all Lothian by Rufus's gift and *regnum Scotie* by inheritance'. He noted a similar contrast between land held as a grant and land possessed by paternal heritage in a charter of Duke Richard II of Normandy. The distinction between Lothian and Scotland in the charter therefore becomes crucial. Although it seems artificial today, it will be recalled from chapter 1 that the kingdom was identified specifically with Scotland north of the Forth, not with the whole realm ruled by the king.[16] In this light it is readily understandable that Lothian could be regarded as within the king of England's gift. The date of the charter, 1095, has nourished the greatest doubts about its authenticity, for there is no evidence that Edgar possessed the kingdom of Scotland at this stage: it was not until 1097 that Edgar drove his uncle from the kingship in an invasion supported by William Rufus. Professor Duncan has pointed out, however, that *regnum* in this period can readily be translated as 'kingship', referring to office or status, rather than 'kingdom', which implies territory. The statement that Edgar 'possesses the whole land of Lothian and the kingship of Scotland' can therefore be seen as saying merely that he had royal status as well as possessing Lothian.[17] Indeed, such an interpretation is invited by the contrast between *terra*, 'land', and *regnum*, 'kingship'.

It would not appear, therefore, that Edgar's dependence on William Rufus was regarded as establishing a formal tenurial relationship involving the Scottish kingship itself. There need be less doubt, moreover, that his successor Alexander I regarded his freedom to control his own kingdom as unaffected by his client relationship with Henry I. The reason for such confidence is that a contemporary writer has left a detailed account of his dealings with Alexander in which a key element was Alexander's view of his own kingship. The writer was Eadmer, who in his *Historia Novorum* reported and explained the events of his brief career in Scotland as bishop-elect of St Andrews from 1120 to 1121.[18] Eadmer had a wretched time. He was a monk of Canterbury, and a passionate advocate of Canterbury's claim to lead the Church throughout Britain. He was head-hunted by King Alexander, who arranged with the archbishop of Canterbury that Eadmer could be released to serve as *episcopus Scottorum*, 'bishop of the Scots' (which is how bishops of St Andrews were designated at that time). It was only after Eadmer had arrived that it became clear that Alexander and he had fundamentally different views about the status of the Scottish church. Eadmer held firm to his obedience to Canterbury, and asked that he might be consecrated there; Alexander, however, according to Eadmer, declared 'that he would never in his life consent that a Scottish bishop should be subject to the bishop of Canterbury', and insisted 'that the kingdom of Scotland owed no subjection to the church of Canterbury'.[19] Relations between the two men broke down completely. In desperation, Eadmer asked for advice from Bishop John of Glasgow and two monks of Canterbury who were with him. Eadmer's record of their assessment of the situation includes this graphic statement about King Alexander:[20] 'We know the man. He wishes in his kingdom to be all things alone, and will not endure that any authority have the least power in any matter, without his control.'

Eadmer was not an impartial observer in all this, of course. His portrayal of Alexander as both intransigent and exasperated could not be regarded as a complete picture of Alexander's character (and might equally be said of Eadmer himself). There is no need to doubt, however, that Eadmer has correctly reported the issues which lay at the heart of his dispute with the king: Alexander's insistence that he would not share authority over his kingdom with the archbishop of Canterbury or anyone else. In the light of this, it is inconceivable that Alexander would, for example, have led a contingent to fight in Henry I's invasion of Wales had this implied any diminution of his independence as ruler of his kingdom. At the same time there is no doubt that he was prepared to recognise the reality of Henry's power compared to his own. This not only took the form of military service, but also Alexander's marriage to Henry's illegitimate daughter, Sybil, which, it has been suggested, may have been arranged when the two kings were in Wales in 1114.[21] Such a match clearly indicated the inferior standing of the king of Scots. There is no reason to doubt that Alexander regarded his marriage in a positive light as marking friendly relations with Henry I.[22] Indeed, Alexander may have seen this as particularly welcome, given Henry I's close relationship with Alexander's brother David, who was not only a potential rival, but had won control of most of what is now southern Scotland despite Alexander's opposition.[23]

As far as this early period of submission of kings of Scots to kings of England is concerned, therefore, it is clearly misleading to view this as 'feudal'. Neither kings of England nor kings of Scots regarded Scotland as a feu granted by the king of England to the Scottish king and his heirs. There were, indeed, circumstances in which kings of Scots were not only clients of the king of England but owed their positions to him; but neither party would have thought of their relationship as defined in detail in a way that was necessarily meant to endure for ever. Certainly, in the normal run of events a king of England would be considerably more powerful than a king of Scots, and could quite naturally be regarded as the leading king in Britain. But the specifics of what a particular submission entailed would not have been imagined as constituting a permanent arrangement.

As long as subordination to kings of England was seen in 'feudal' terms it seemed natural to regard this as representing a loss of independence. A central point in Professor Davies's reassessment of the wider issue of Celtic rulers' submissions to kings of England, however, is that client kings retained their independence in relation to their kingdoms. Alexander I's insistence that he alone, and not some outside agency, should have authority in his kingdom would not have been unusual in this respect. The sense of being the ultimate source of authority for a named people or territory was what made a king. This was not compromised by submission to the king of England.

But this was to change. By 1216, as Rees Davies has made clear, the submission of Celtic rulers to the king of England was seen in a different light; it implied that a subservient king was little different in essentials from a major lord within England itself.[24] The first occasion in which the form and content of submission was radically reshaped was triggered by the capture of William I, king of Scots, at Alnwick on 13 July 1174 while invading northern England in support of a rebellion against Henry II.[25] The first departure from previous practice in the relationship between kings of Scots and kings of England was the sustained humiliation endured by William, who was taken, 'shackled under the belly of a horse', to meet Henry II at Northampton on 26 July.[26] William's discomfort continued when he was then taken in chains from Portsmouth to Normandy, arriving on 13 August.[27] He was held at Caen and Falaise, where he came to an agreement with his captor. The agreement was proclaimed publicly, and peace between the two kings formally restored, at Valognes on 8 December 1174.[28] The second departure from earlier practice was that this agreement was enshrined in a written document. The document may have been drawn up initially at Falaise; it was certainly issued when the agreement was formally proclaimed at Valognes.[29] It had an even more awesome public airing when, according to the terms of the agreement, King William, together with a full gathering of Scottish prelates and nobles, met Henry II at York on 10 August 1175. In full view of his leading subjects, the document was sealed by King William and David, his brother and heir, and then read out. This was immediately followed by the third departure from previous submissions. Not only was William himself obliged to perform homage to Henry II and his son and heir, but so too were the assembled Scottish prelates and nobles, who became vassals of the king of England and his son, and swore fealty and allegiance 'against all men'. This meant that, should King William 'draw back' from the terms of the agreement, they would remain loyal to the king of England against their own king. The same oath was to be extracted from those bishops and barons who were absent.[30] Such a direct intervention by an overlord in the relationship between a king and his people was unprecedented. So, too, was the stipulation that fugitives from justice in Scotland could be tried in England if they fled to England, while fugitives from justice in England must be handed over by the king of Scots and his vassals if they fled to Scotland. The final departure from previous submissions was that King William and his heirs were explicitly said to hold Scotland of the king of England and his heirs. This was announced in the document's first substantive statement:

> William, king of Scots, has become the liegeman of the lord king [of England] against all men, for Scotland and for all his other lands, and has sworn fealty to him as his liege lord in like manner as his [Henry's] other men are accustomed to do to him.[31]

It is true that Scotland was not referred to as a feu held of the English king, and that it was not symbolically surrendered and re-granted, but this did not alter the reality that (in Professor Barrow's words) the Scottish kingship itself 'was feudally subject to the king of England's lordship'.[32] From the moment of his capture William had been treated simply as a rebellious liegeman.[33]

Political reality, as before, continued to play its part in shaping the terms of a submission: the opportunity for such a comprehensive victory for the king of England did not arise again for over a hundred years. The implications of subordination, however, were changing fundamentally. Professor Davies has emphasised how the novel use of writing in this context was an essential element both in delimiting in painful detail the various and manifold consequences of William's submission, and also in offering the means to fulfill, potentially, the expectation that the agreement in all its clauses would define permanently the relationship between kings of Scots and kings of England. This could now only be redefined by another written agreement, which would explicitly supersede the earlier document. This is indeed what happened. After the coronation of Henry II's successor, Richard I, on 8 September 1189, William made arrangements to perform homage to the new king. When he met Richard at Canterbury on 2 December he succeeded in negotiating a new agreement which was intended to restore the relationship to its 'pre-Falaise' state: Richard conceded that William was released from all agreements and 'new charters' exacted by Henry II as a result of William's capture, and that the king of Scots 'shall do for us fully and completely whatever his brother Mael Coluim, king of Scotland, did of right, and ought to have done of right, for our predecessors . . .'[34] The original document of the Treaty of Falaise[35] was handed over to William, and presumably destroyed. This was all expressed in a new agreement, the 'Quitclaim of Canterbury', dated 5 December, which survives in the National Archives as a contemporary single sheet (although now, sadly, rather illegible).[36] A new pattern had been established, in which major issues between the kingdoms were settled by negotiations which, if successful, culminated in a treaty. Unfortunately the text of the next treaty in 1209 (the 'peace' of Norham), or of its renewal in 1212, does not survive: Professor Duncan has argued, however, that the lordship of English kings over Scotland was 'scarcely an issue'.[37] The experience of Welsh and Irish kings was not identical with William I's humiliation. The loose kind of overlordship was, however, eventually to become a thing of the past for them as much as for the king of Scots.[38] In time they, too, discovered that submission to the king of England on the king of England's terms now meant a surrender to intrusive overlordship defined in writing. Even if these documents were subsequently cancelled or were otherwise overtaken by political circumstances, they could still survive and inform future thinking or political posturing for generations to come. Although it had formally been rescinded, the Treaty of Falaise itself did not vanish into obscurity, but haunted Scottish claims to independence for centuries to come.

In reality King Henry did not exploit fully the opportunities for direct lordship over Scotland afforded him by the Treaty of Falaise; he did not even establish English garrisons in all the castles which William was required to surrender to him according to its terms.[39] Henry's jurisdiction was real enough, however: a writ of protection in Henry's name survives for Dunfermline, for example.[40] It was also clear, from the language of the Treaty of Falaise itself, that Scottish kingship was barely recognised: Professor Davies has pointed out that Scotland is referred to as a 'land' (*terra*), not a 'kingdom' (*regnum*), and that William's designation as 'king' contrasted with Henry's as 'lord king'.[41] The loss of independence was also keenly felt within King William's realm. A contemporary commented graphically on the recovery of independence in the 'Treaty' of Canterbury, declaring that 'by God's assistance, he [William] worthily and honourably removed his [Henry's] heavy yoke of domination and servitude from the kingdom of the Scots'.[42]

This was not, however, the first time in which the independence of the kingdom of the Scots had been called into question. The enforcement of a superior jurisdiction over Scotland had been attempted much earlier by archbishops of York and Canterbury. This was part of a wider process of consolidating the Church's authority which was initiated by Pope Leo IX (1049–54), and then galvanised by Pope Gregory VII (1073–85), who has aptly been described as 'the founding father of the high medieval papal monarchy'.[43] Before the mid-eleventh century the reality of episcopal jurisdiction and the operation of archi-episcopal authority had been variable, and sometimes negligible, with little or no intervention from the papacy. Gradually, in the period between Gregory and the next giant of the medieval papacy, Innocent III, this became firmed up into a clearly defined hierarchy of obedience embracing all the faithful. It was not always clear, however, what shape this structure should take. In some regions it needed to be established who should be archbishop, and/or what the limits of a diocese or province might be; another problem was the claims of primacy by one archbishop over others.[44] The outcome of these disputes was determined chiefly by two opposing factors: one was the power of the written word and other precedents in defining permanently enduring arrangements, and the other was the crucial part played by immediate circumstances.[45] As far as the former was concerned, the freedom of Scottish bishops from English archbishops seemed irredeemably compromised by the unambiguous testimony of so great an authority as Bede, who had clearly described Gregory the Great's intention that Britain should be divided between two archbishops, with northern bishops falling under the obedience of the archbishop of York.[46] This had surely been the basis for the earliest decision taken towards firming up a structure of ecclesiastical authority in Britain, which had been formulated initially when William I of England celebrated Easter at Winchester on 8 April 1072 with the archbishops of Canterbury and York and other leading English churchmen, and finally concluded at a council at Windsor on 27 May. A central figure in this process was the first papal legate to set foot in Britain, who had been sent by Pope Alexander II specifically for this purpose. In the document which was finally drawn up and copied to major churches across the country it was decided that the archbishop of York would have authority over all bishops north of the Humber 'as far as the outermost bounds of Scotland', and the archbishop of Canterbury would be acknowledged by York as primate of 'all Britain'.[47]

As the terms of this agreement made clear, the point at issue was the relationship between Canterbury and York, not the status of Scottish bishops. It is not surprising, therefore, that no Scottish bishops were present. The decision, nonetheless, had obvious implications for Scotland. Although the bishop of St Andrews had, probably since the beginning of the tenth century, been acknowledged as pre-eminent bishop of the kingdom (whatever this may have meant in practice), it was never going to be easy to obtain papal recognition of this as equivalent to metropolitan of a Scottish Church in the face of Bede's witness to Gregory the Great's intentions. The hopes of bishops of Glasgow, from Bishop John onwards, to escape York's jurisdiction must have seemed extremely remote, given that there were recent examples of bishops of Glasgow who had been within York's obedience.[48] It was hardly unexpected, therefore, that the papacy should have found York's claim to metropolitan authority over Scottish bishops to have been perfectly acceptable. The first extant letter from a pope to Scotland is that of Paschal II 'to the suffragans of York *per Scotiam*' written on the promotion of Gerard, bishop of Hereford, to the archbishopric of York in December 1100, in which the pope directed Scottish bishops to show obedience to their new archbishop.[49] This was ignored. The consecration of the formidable Archbishop Thurstan by Pope Calixtus II was the occasion of the start of a more vigorous papal letter-writing campaign insisting that York's authority be recognised in Scotland: a pair of letters was despatched on 19 November 1119, followed by two addressed to King Alexander, another pair of letters despatched on 15 January 1122, and a final missive to Bishop John of Glasgow. Successive popes wrote letters to the same effect, and with identical results: sustained prevarication or disobedience by the bishops of Glasgow and St Andrews, aided and abetted by their king. Only the bishop of Galloway yielded to York's authority, an indication of how Galloway in this period was not bound closely to the kingdom of the Scots.[50]

It is highly likely that, had the bishop of St Andrews or the bishop of Glasgow made a profession of obedience at this stage, then the game would have been 'up' for them.[51] The remaining Scottish bishops, whose sees and names were apparently unknown to the pope (and presumably York as well) until they were addressed personally by Pope Hadrian IV in 1155, would surely have fallen with St Andrews into York's obedience. What kept the cause of Glasgow and St Andrews and the others alive was a combination of politics and sheer good fortune. The most dangerous period was when a new bishop of St Andrews or bishop of Glasgow needed to be consecrated. Glasgow was particularly lucky that this coincided with vacancies in the archbishopric of York: both Bishop John and his successor Herbert were consecrated by the pope himself. This pattern was then continued even when there was no vacancy at York, when Herbert's successor, Ingram, was consecrated by Pope Alexander III and Ingram's successor, Jocelin, was consecrated at Clairvaux by the archbishop of Lund on the instructions of the pope sometime between 16 December 1174 and 15 March 1175.[52] The fate of St Andrews was decided more by politics. Its claim to archi-episcopal status meant that it could gain attention as part of the bigger picture of how the ecclesiastical structure of Britain and Ireland should be established. It has been pointed out, for example, that King David I in 1139–40 had contact with both Mael Maedoc Ua Morgair (St Malachy) and Bishop Bernard of St David's, who at that time were each seeking papal recognition for independent churches respectively in Ireland and Wales;[53] the success of one campaign against English metropolitan authority could have had positive implications for the chances of others.[54] The claim of St Andrews to archi-episcopal status, moreover, proved a crucial bargaining counter which could be used to persuade the archbishop of York to settle for a temporary compromise. Bishop Robert, for example, had been elected at the end of the reign of Alexander I, who died in April 1124. The new king, David, attempted to settle the matter by obtaining a pallium for St Andrews probably when he met the first papal legate to visit Scotland sometime in July or August 1125. Bishop John of Glasgow was later despatched to the Curia to press the case, arriving by Christmas 1125. In the end both sides agreed to shelve their claims temporarily when, at the behest of Henry I and David I, Archbishop Thurstan consecrated Robert early in 1127 without a profession of obedience. The role of the kings highlights another political dimension, for Henry I had been grateful for David I's support in securing the recognition of his daughter Matilda as his heir at Christmas in 1126.[55] After Bishop Robert's death in 1159, and the failure to persuade Waltheof, abbot of Melrose, to accept election to the see, the possibility of a pallium for St Andrews was raised again.[56] On this occasion, however, it has been suggested that papal politics played an important part in securing a further postponement of a final judgement on this and York's claims. Pope Alexander III, who succeeded Hadrian IV in September 1159 after a contested election (which has been described as a 'riotous and undignified spectacle'[57]), was challenged immediately by an imperially supported rival and had to withdraw from Rome. When the Scottish delegation reached the pope at Anagni before the end of November it is no surprise that Alexander may have been reluctant to make a decision which could have resulted in a loss of support.[58] He decided not to accede to King Mael Coluim's request with regard to St Andrews, but instead opted for a stop-gap solution by appointing one of the king's ambassadors, Bishop William of Moray, as papal legate for the whole kingdom of Scotland with a suggestion that William be made bishop of St Andrews.[59] In the end Arnold abbot of Kelso was appointed instead and consecrated bishop of St Andrews on 20 November 1160 by William as papal legate.[60] Before Alexander III was able to return to Rome in late 1165 the bishopric of St Andrews came to his attention again when Arnold's successor, Richard, needed to be consecrated: again, he avoided a direct confrontation by permitting the new bishop to be consecrated by other Scottish bishops at St Andrews on Palm Sunday, 28 March 1165.[61]

It was the accident of political events which eventually provoked Alexander III to adopt a distinctly anti-York, pro-Scottish position for the first time. The catalyst was the loss of Scottish independence following the Treaty of Falaise. The final stage in procuring full recognition of English jurisdiction over Scotland was at a council in Northampton, in January (or February) 1176, where Henry II attempted to force the subjection of Scottish bishops.[62] The bishops escaped from this awkward spot when the archbishops of York and Canterbury reopened the dispute about which of them should be their metropolitan. The Scots swiftly sent a delegation to Pope Alexander who came to their assistance with the bull *Super anxietatibus* on 30 July 1176. Alexander insisted that the 'bishops of Scotland' should regard the pope as their metropolitan until the issue was reopened by York, at which point a lasting resolution was anticipated.[63] The pontiff left no doubt what he thought of recent events, describing these as an affront to God and to Alexander himself: 'kings and princes', he declared, 'had no right to arrange ecclesiastical matters'.[64] York's defeat was not yet inevitable: independence was only finally guaranteed with the bull *Cum universi*, usually dated to 1192, although a strong case has been made for 1189.[65]

Although the struggle of Scottish bishops to escape the attentions of archbishops of York and Canterbury is clearly relevant to the general theme of the origins of Scottish independence, it might not seem immediately obvious that it was in this context that the independence of the *kingdom* was first conceived. It is generally recognised that, before the Gregorian Age, the Church was closely identified with secular power. That this was true in a Scottish context can readily be surmised by the fact that the title of the chief cleric paralleled that of the king: 'bishop of Scots' (*episcopus Scottorum*; *epscop Alban*) and 'king of Scots' (*rex Scottorum*; *rí Alban*). Nevertheless, the status of the Scottish kingdom has typically been regarded as essentially about the relationship between kings, rather than prelates. There is no shortage of accounts of how *ecclesia Scoticana* achieved its freedom; these, however, appear either in articles or books devoted specifically to Church History, or in designated sections on the Church in more general works.[66] It is hardly unexpected, therefore, that *Cum universi* does not appear in the indexes of two of the most important books on the history of the period 1100–1300 published in recent times, even though both have as their principal theme the English impact on Britain and Ireland and the response of societies at the receiving end of English domination.[67] Both books are avowedly secular in outlook; the claims of Canterbury and York over Scotland and elsewhere are not ignored, but they are not accorded any prominence.[68]

It has been remarked by Professor Geoffrey Barrow that Pope Alexander III was probably 'the first person to link the concept of liberty to the kingdom of Scotland'.[69] The occasion was a letter written in 1180 to King William in which Alexander warned the king to stop harassing the canonically elected bishop of St Andrews in favour of his own candidate.[70] The pope did not mince his words. In an obvious reference to his recent decision in *Super anxietatibus* to forbid the archbishop of York from exercising metropolitan authority in Scotland, Alexander declared that 'as we have laboured that your kingdom should have liberty, so we shall take care that it reverts to its original subjection'.[71] The idea that the kingdom's independence was at stake in the dispute with York and Canterbury, however, was not new. The York historian Hugh the Chanter, for example, described how Archbishop Thurstan in December 1125 thwarted the attempt to gain a pallium for St Andrews by persuading the pope that 'Scotland was part of the kingdom of England, and that the king of Scotland was the man of the king of England for Scotland'.[72] This is the earliest recorded instance in which the submission of kings of Scots was interpreted as subjecting Scotland itself to English lordship, clearly anticipating a central aspect of the Treaty of Falaise. It is also apparent that the independence of the Scottish kingdom was regarded as an issue in the disagreement between Alexander I and Eadmer, bishop-elect of St Andrews. In his last letter to Alexander, Eadmer, writing from Canterbury, insisted that it had not been his intention 'to detract in any way from the freedom and dignity of the kingdom of the Scots', and declared that he would no longer refuse Alexander's wishes.[73] This is almost certainly the earliest explicit reference to the kingdom's liberty.

All these references to Scottish independence are from non-Scottish sources. Nonetheless, there is no reason to doubt that Scottish kings and prelates would also have regarded York's and Canterbury's claims to metropolitan authority in a similar light. It will be recalled that Eadmer potentially affords us unparalleled access to Alexander I's thinking on this subject, and that, according to him, Alexander I saw the threat of Eadmer's consecration and obedience to the archbishop of Canterbury as not simply a matter of the status of the church of St Andrews, but in terms of his kingdom's subjection to Canterbury. When the first known request was made at the Curia for St Andrews to be recognised as an archbishopric, in Christmas 1125, we are told by Hugh the Chanter that it was argued 'by some people' (presumably the delegation from David I) that Scotland was not part of the kingdom of England.[74] It will be recalled that Archbishop Thurstan persuaded the pope otherwise. It was the Scottish delegation, however, who apparently raised this as the central issue.

It is now possible to gain a clearer impression of Scottish opinion from an early stage in this dispute thanks to the recent discovery of two manuscript witnesses of version 'A' of the St Andrews foundation legend.[75] This text, which was plainly written at St Andrews, had hitherto been known in full only in Archbishop James Ussher's *Britannicarum Ecclesiarum Antiquitates*, published in 1639.[76] Unfortunately the only previously known manuscript witnesses (one from the late twelfth century, the other from the mid-fourteenth century) were of a shorter version, minus the last fifth of the text printed by Ussher.[77] Ussher's text also showed a number of significant unique readings. It has not been surprising, then, that in the absence of any obvious way to verify the authenticity of Ussher's text as a twelfth-century recension of version 'A' of the foundation-legend, scholars have attached little or no significance to it. The two new manuscript witnesses have changed that. One is late-twelfth century in date, and the other might be either just before or after 1200.[78] Both contain the full extent of the text printed by Ussher, and share many of his variant readings. As a result, a strident statement of St Andrews' archi-episcopal status is rescued from scholarly limbo.

The first point to note in the restored text is that the significance of St Andrews in the kingdom is made plain. We are told that the Pictish king *Hungus* (almost certainly Unust son of Uurgust who died in 761) 'gave this place and this city to Almighty God and to St Andrew the apostle in freedom for ever, that it might be the head and mother of all churches which are in the kingdom of the Scots'. In the shortened version of the legend the contemporary force of this statement has been diluted by referring to the kingdom of the Picts rather than the kingdom of the Scots. The most striking part of the text, however, is at the end, where the main message is hammered home:

> And so the archiepiscopacy of all *Scotia* ought to be [exercised] from this city, where the apostolic seat is. No bishop ought to be ordained in *Scotia* without the approval of the elders of this place. Indeed, in relation to the first Rome this is the second; this is a preeminent city of refuge; this is the city of cities of *Scotia*, to which Our Lord gave these supports to help: that is, Archbishop Giric, Mac Bethad, and Gregoir, with other brothers of theirs.

St Andrews' archi-episcopal status is portrayed as a fact of life; moreover, it is not simply an archbishopric, but a 'second Rome', due to its special association with St Andrew. The text relates how his relics came to be housed at St Andrews, and how pilgrims from far and wide are drawn to them for a range of cures. The strident self-confidence of this statement, which has clearly been written in St Andrews itself, may arouse suspicion that it was produced when St Andrews' status was in question. These suspicions are strengthened considerably by the mention of Archbishop Giric, who appears (with some other names) between Fothad (d.1093) and Turgot (elected 1107) in the most accurate witness of the late-medieval list of early bishops of St Andrews.[79] His likely floruit of *ca* 1100 therefore coincides with the first extant papal communication with Scotland in which, it will be recalled, obedience to York was urged. It may be surmised that this was the occasion which provoked the writing of version 'A' of the St Andrews foundation-legend. If so, it can be read as a bold attempt to justify St Andrews' position as the premier see of the kingdom and to protect its freedom from any outside authority (except Rome itself). Seen in this light, it is also a statement of the kingdom's jurisdictional integrity: the first declaration of the kingdom's independent status in relation to another kingdom (specifically England).

It should not be forgotten, however, that already in the twelfth century someone had shorn the legend of its archi-episcopal pretensions by omitting the final section. The earliest manuscript of this truncated version may be dated on palaeographical grounds to the third quarter of the twelfth century.[80] It belonged to the Cistercian abbey of Newminster in Northumberland:[81] if this is an indication of the text's origins, then this might confirm a natural suspicion that the legend's sting had been pulled by someone sympathetic to the archbishop of York's claims. Our understanding of this version's genesis is complicated, though, by its appearance in the collection of Scottish historical items (including the longer Pictish king-list and the *Chronicle of the Kings of Alba*) in what Scottish scholars call the 'Poppleton manuscript'.[82] The collection was probably put together in more than one stage, beginning sometime between 1165 and 1184.[83] One of the pieces (a king-list including a eulogy of David I) betrays a particular affiliation with the Cistercian abbey of Melrose (just over sixty miles away from Newminster as the crow flies),[84] so it may be too hasty to assume that Newminster acquired its copy of the legend from an English church. The possibility cannot be ruled out that the idea of Scottish independence pursued by 'Archbishop' Giric and his successors at St Andrews may not have been shared by everyone in the Scottish realm. It will become apparent in the next chapter that such suspicions would not be unwarranted.

NOTES

1. A. D. M. Barrell, *Medieval Scotland* (Cambridge, 2000), 70; at 16 he explains what he understands by the term 'feudalism'.
2. For example, W. Croft Dickinson, rev. A. A. M. Duncan, *Scotland from Earliest Times to 1603* (Oxford, 1977), 60–1; A. O. Anderson, 'Anglo-Scottish relations from Constantine II to William', *SHR* 42 (1963) 1–20, at 11–13.
3. Duncan, *Scotland: the Making of the Kingdom*, 125. For the charter, see below, n. 14.
4. See above, 12.
5. The controversy was initiated by Susan Reynolds, *Fiefs and Vassals: the Medieval Evidence Reinterpreted* (Oxford, 1994): see 391–3 for Anglo-Scottish relations specifically, where she notes the special problems of fitting a kingdom into the model of fiefs and vassals. The debate in general about feudalism in Scotland has been joined by G. W. S. Barrow, 'Scotland's experience of feudalism in the twelfth century', *History Teaching Review Year Book* 14 (2000) 5–9, Susan Reynolds, 'Fiefs and vassals in Scotland: a view from outside', *SHR* 82 (2003) 176–93, and note especially Hector L. MacQueen, 'Tears of a legal historian: Scottish feudalism and the *ius commune*', *Juridical Review* (2003) 1–28.
6. R. R. Davies, *Domination and Conquest: the Experience of Ireland, Scotland and Wales 1100–1300* (Cambridge, 1990); and esp. Rees Davies,

' "Keeping the natives in order": the English king and the "Celtic" rulers 1066–1216', *Peritia* 10 (1996) 212–24.

7. Davies, *Domination and Conquest*, 103; in general, see 100–6.

8. Davies, ' "Keeping the natives in order" ', 215.

9. As, for example, in M. Brett, *The English Church under Henry I* (Oxford, 1975), 15; see also Oram, *David I*, 31.

10. Davies, ' "Keeping the natives in order" ', 215.

11. *Ibid.*, 216. This is not to say that some rulers did not suffer from harsh treatment: Dauvit Broun, 'The church and the origins of Scottish independence in the twelfth century', in *RSCHS* 31 (2002) 1–36, at 9 n. 24.

12. Davies, ' "Keeping the natives in order" ', 217.

13. The charter was almost certainly drafted and produced by the beneficiary, the monks of Durham.

14. The best edition is in A. A. M. Duncan, 'Yes, the earliest Scottish charters', *SHR* 78 (1999) 1–38.

15. *Ibid.*, 30. This is an important modification of his earlier interpretation in A. A. M. Duncan, 'The earliest Scottish charters', *SHR* 37 (1958) 103–35, at 129–31. The most coherent attack on the charter's authenticity is J. Donnelly, 'The earliest Scottish charters?', *SHR* 68 (1989) 1–22. See also Barrow, *Anglo-Norman Era*, 153 n. 42.

16. See above, 7–11.

17. Duncan, 'Yes, the earliest Scottish charters', 30–2. One might add that, from the point of view of the beneficiary of the charter (the cathedral priory of Durham, where the text was presumably drafted), they may have anticipated that Lothian would be ruled by the king of Scots (as had usually been the case for over a century); they may therefore have been keen that Edgar's kingship be specified in the hope that the terms of the charter would more readily be accepted by Edgar and his successors should he succeed in ousting his uncle, Domnall Bán, from the throne.

18. Martin Rule (ed.), *Eadmeri Historia Novorum in Anglia* (London, 1884). An important discussion of this work is Sally N. Vaughn, 'Eadmer's *Historia Novorum*: a reinterpretation', in R. Allen Brown (ed.), *Anglo-Norman Studies X: Proceedings of the Battle Conference, 1987* (Woodbridge, 1988), 259–89.

19. Rule (ed.), *Eadmeri Historia*, 284; *SAEC*, 143.

20. Rule (ed.), *Eadmeri Historia*, 285; *SAEC*, 144.

21. Judith A. Green, 'David I and Henry I', *SHR* 75 (1996) 1–19, at 9.

22. Alexander's marriage has often been viewed negatively by Scottish historians: it has even been claimed that Alexander was 'deliberately humiliated' (Gordon Donaldson, *Scotland: the Shaping of a Nation* (London, 1974), 28). This would only make sense, however, if it was assumed that Alexander regarded himself as Henry I's equal (which he obviously did not).

23. Green, 'David I and Henry I', 3. For a contemporary view of David as divisive, see Thomas Owen Clancy, 'A Gaelic polemic quatrain from the reign

of Alexander I, ca. 1113', *Scottish Gaelic Studies* 20 (2000) 88–96. It may be significant that, only months before Alexander's appearance in Henry's army, David's position had received a huge boost when Henry arranged his marriage to Matilda daughter of Earl Waltheof and bestowed on David the title of earl and possession of Northampton-Huntingdon: Green, 'David I and Henry I', 6.

24. Davies, ' "Keeping the natives in order" ', 220–1.

25. W. Stubbs (ed.), *Gesta Regis Henrici Secundis Benedicti Abbatis*, 2 vols (London, 1867), i. 72; *SAEC*, 254. For what follows, see Davies, ' "Keeping the natives in order" ', 220–1.

26. W. Stubbs (ed.), *Chronica Rogeri de Houedene*, 4 vols (London, 1868–71), ii. 64 (*sub ventre equi compeditus*). I am grateful to Matthew Strickland for suggesting to me that this may be interpreted to mean that William was placed on a mare (perhaps an old nag) with his feet tied together. Prof. Strickland has also pointed out to me that it may be inferred from Howden's account that William's humiliating presentation to Henry II was performed in front of a number of rebellious nobles who had recently submitted to Henry.

27. Henry G. Hewlett (ed.), *The Flowers of History by Roger de Wendover*, 3 vols (London, 1886–9), i. 101; *SAEC*, 255 n. 5.

28. W. Stubbs (ed.), *Radulfi de Diceto Opera Omnia*, 2 vols (London, 1876), i. 396; *SAEC*, 258.

29. It survives in two early-thirteenth-century transcripts (Stones (ed.), *Anglo-Scottish Relations*, 2–11). It was also copied by Roger of Howden (Stubbs (ed.), *Gesta*, i. 95–9; Stubbs (ed.), *Chronica*, ii. 80–2) with Falaise as the place-date; the other copies have Valognes. For a solution to this problem (and endorsement of Stones's suggestion that Howden was present) see John Gillingham, *The English in the Twelfth Century: Imperialism, National Identity and Political Values* (Woodbridge, 2000), 76 n. 54.

30. Stones (ed.), *Anglo-Scottish Relations*, 4–9; Stubbs (ed.), *Gesta*, i. 95–9; Stubbs (ed.), *Chronica*, ii. 80–2; *SAEC*, 260–2.

31. Stones (ed.), *Anglo-Scottish Relations*, 2–3.

32. Barrow, *Scotland and its Neighbours*, 28; see also Duncan, *Kingship of the Scots*, 101.

33. On the treatment of rebels see Matthew Strickland, *War and Chivalry. The Conduct and Perception of War in England and Normandy 1066–1217* (Cambridge, 1996), 240–57. Imprisonment was not uncommon; note also incidents in which the defeated party was humiliated in a way which involved horses or horsemanship (*ibid.*, 253).

34. Stones (ed.), *Anglo-Scottish Relations*, 13. Roger of Howden, a contemporary who was closely involved in Anglo-Scottish affairs, understood this to mean that William and his heirs were released from 'all allegiance and subjection concerning the kingdom of Scotland': (Stubbs (ed.), *Gesta*, ii. 98; Stubbs (ed.), *Chronica*, iii. 25). John Gillingam has argued persuasively that Howden's work may be regarded as essentially the journal of 'a clerk with

special expertise in Scottish and papal business, attached, as it were, to the Foreign Office, rather than to the Home Office or Treasury' (Gillingham, *The English in the Twelfth Century*, 90).

35. Its common designation as a 'treaty' (rather than an 'agreement') may be justified by the fact that it took the form of a written document concerning relations between kings (although, strictly speaking, it might therefore be more appropriate to call it the 'Treaty of Valognes': see n. 29, above).

36. Stones (ed.), *Anglo-Scottish Relations*, 12–17.

37. A. A. M. Duncan, 'John king of England and the kings of Scots', in S. D. Church (ed.), *King John: New Interpretations* (Woodbridge, 1999), 247–71, esp. 259–61, 263–4: quotation at 268. Duncan is not, however, suggesting that the possibility of English lordship over Scotland was never considered, commenting (at 268) that 'John's demands for [Scottish] castles in 1209 shows that he then considered re-establishing the 1174 vassalage ended in 1189, but was persuaded to settle for two lassies and 15,000 marks'.

38. Davies, ' "Keeping the natives in order" ', 220–1.

39. Duncan, *Scotland: the Making of the Kingdom*, 231.

40. *Ibid.*, 232; G. W. S. Barrow, 'A writ of Henry II for Dunfermline Abbey', *SHR* 36 (1957) 138–43.

41. Davies, *The First English Empire*, 14; Barrow, *Scotland and her Neighbours*, 28.

42. Joseph Stevenson (ed.), *Chronica de Mailros* (Edinburgh, 1835), 98; *ES*, ii. 322.

43. Robert Bartlett, *The Making of Europe. Conquest, Colonization and Cultural Change 950–1350* (London, 1993; repr. 1994), 244.

44. See, e.g., Barrow, *Kingship and Unity*, 68–9, for a valuable general account; Frank Barlow, *Durham Jurisdictional Peculiars* (London, 1950), ix–x, on diocesan authority in England; Lucien Musset, 'Les évêques normands envisagés dans le cadre Européen (Xe–XIIe siècles)', in Pierre Bouet and François Neveux (eds), *Les évêques normands du XIe siècle* (Caen, 1995), 53–65, at 53–6, for a brief survey of England, northern France and southern Italy; Gerd Tellenbach (trans. Timothy Reuter), *The Church in Western Europe from the Tenth to the Early Twelfth Century* (Cambridge, 1993), esp. 66, 72–3, on the pre-Gregorian papacy; Christopher Brooke, 'The archbishops of St David's, Llandaff and Caerleon-on-Usk', in [Nora K. Chadwick (ed.)], *Studies in the Early British Church* (Cambridge, 1958), 201–33, esp. 212–13, on claims of primacy.

45. The interplay of these factors can best be appreciated by examining case-studies. A particularly fine study of a famous case is Paula de Fougerolles, 'Pope Gregory VII, the archbishopric of Dol and the Normans', in Christopher Harper-Bill (ed.), *Anglo-Norman Studies XXI, Proceedings of the Battle Conference 1998* (Woodbridge, 1999), 47–66. See also the

discussion of Canterbury's claims to primacy over Britain in Michael Richter (ed.), *Canterbury Professions*, The Canterbury and York Society vol. 67 (1973), liv–lxxiv, lxxxvi–xcvi. Present needs could, of course, inspire the creation of written precedents from the past: an exemplary study is John Reuben Davies, *The Book of Llandaf and the Norman Church in Wales* (Woodbridge, 2003).

46. Bertram Colgrave and R. A. B. Mynors (eds), *Bede's Ecclesiastical History of the English People*, reprinted with corrections (Oxford, 1991), 104–7 (I.29). Another obstacle was the requirement in canon law that the seat of an archbishopric should equate with a Roman '*civitas*-capital': see de Fougerolles, 'Pope Gregory VII, the archbishopric of Dol', 52–3.

47. David Bates (ed.), *Regesta Regum Anglo-Normannorum. The Acta of William I (1066–1087)* (Oxford, 1998), no. 68 (surviving as a contemporary single sheet). A preparatory document (*ibid.*, no. 67) also survives as a contemporary single sheet.

48. John Durkan, 'Glasgow diocese and the claims of York', *IR* 50 (1999) 89–101. There is no evidence, however, to support the view that 'Scottish bishops were normally consecrated by the archbishop of York': R. W. Southern, *St Anselm and his Biographer. A Study of Monastic Life and Thought 1059–c.1130* (Cambridge, 1966), 135.

49. Robert Somerville, *Scotia Pontificia. Papal Letters to Scotland before the Pontificate of Innocent III* (Oxford, 1982), no. 1; James Raine (ed.), *The Historians of the Church of York and its Archbishops*, vol. iii (London, 1894), 22. For what follows, see Somerville, *Scotia Pontificia*, 3–10, 19–48 *passim*; A. D. M. Barrell, 'The background to *Cum universi*: Scoto-papal relations, 1159–1192', *IR* 46 (1995) 116–38; Watt, *Medieval Church Councils*, 13–30.

50. Richard D. Oram, 'In obedience and reverence: Whithorn and York *c*.1128–*c*.1250', *IR* 42 (1991) 83–100: at 95–6 there is a discussion of evidence of the involvement of kings of England in the appointment of bishops of Galloway in the twelfth and early thirteenth centuries.

51. Their most important weapon was the inability of the archbishop of York to make good his claims. Also, judging from the Irish and Welsh situations, occasional professions of obedience before independence became an issue were not fatal; it was rather different, however, if a profession of obedience was secured subsequently. The case of St David's is particularly instructive. The initial attempt by Bishop Bernard (1115–48) to gain papal recognition for St David's independence was effectively stymied by his profession to the archbishop of Canterbury and his behaviour as suffragan before his campaign for the pallium began sometime during the pontificate of Honorius II (1124–30): see Richter (ed.), *Canterbury Professions*, lxxxvii–xciii; M. Richter, 'Canterbury's primacy in Wales and the first stage of Bishop Bernard's opposition', *Journal of Ecclesiastical History* 22 (1971) 177–89.

52. See below, 137, 140.
53. It has been suggested that David I 'concerted the great attack on the Canterbury primacy from Scotland, Wales and Ireland in the 1140s': Denis Bethell, 'English monks and Irish reform in the eleventh and twelfth centuries', in T. D. Williams (ed.), *Historical Studies: papers read before the Irish Conference of Historians, VIII Dublin 27–30 May 1969* (Dublin, 1971), 111–35, at 132. I am grateful to Rees Davies for referring me to this paper. See also G. W. S. Barrow, 'King David I and the Honour of Lancaster', *EHR* 70 (1955) 85–9, esp. 89.
54. Marie-Thérèse Flanagan, *Irish Society, Anglo-Norman Settlers, and Angevin Kingship: Interactions in Ireland in the Late Twelfth Century* (Oxford, 1989), 32–8.
55. Green, 'David I and Henry I', 15–16.
56. Watt, *Medieval Church Councils*, 181–19. St Andrews' claim had also been raised in 1151/2.
57. Walter Ullmann, *A Short History of the Papacy in the Middle Ages* (London, 1972), 192.
58. Barrell, 'The background to *Cum universi*', 117; Stevenson (ed.), *Chronica de Mailros*, 76–7.
59. Somerville, *Scotia Pontificia*, no. 43.
60. Stevenson (ed.), *Chronica de Mailros*, 77. D. E. R. Watt and A. L. Murray, *Fasti Ecclesiae Scoticanae Medii Aevi Ad Annum 1638* (Edinburgh, 2003), 378.
61. Stevenson (ed.), *Chronica de Mailros*, 79; Watt and Murray, *Fasti*, 378.
62. D. Whitelock, M. Brett and C. N. L. Brooke (eds), *Councils and Synods, with other documents relating to the English Church, 1*: A.D. 871–1204 (Oxford, 1981), 997–8.
63. Somerville, *Scotia Pontificia*, no. 80.
64. *Ibid.*, at 79.
65. See below (next chapter, 143 and 157 n. 134).
66. An important contribution to the study of Church and kingship is Raymonde Foreville, *L'Eglise et la Royauté en Angleterre sous Henri II Plantagenet (1154–1189)* ([Paris], 1943): note especially her comment (at 504) concerning the Scottish struggle against the claims of Canterbury and York, that 'the opposition of the [Scottish] bishops already sometimes assumed the character of a genuine national resistance'.
67. Davies, *Domination and Conquest*, ix; Robin Frame, *The Political Development of the British Isles 1100–1400* (Oxford, 1990), 4.
68. Frame, *The Political Development of the British Isles*, 18, 52. The issue is given a more integrated treatment, however, in Flanagan, *Irish Society, Anglo-Norman Settlers, and Angevin Kingship*, ch. 1, and Davies, *The First English Empire*, ch. 2.
69. G. W. S. Barrow, 'The idea of freedom in late medieval Scotland', *IR* 30 (1979) 16–34, at 18.

70. On the dispute over the bishopric of St Andrews, see Duncan, *Scotland: the Making of the Kingdom*, 270–4.

71. *sicut laboravimus ut regnum tuum libertatem haberet, sic dabimus studium ut in pristinam subjectionem revertatur*: Stubbs (ed.), *Gesta*, i. 263; Stubbs (ed.), *Chronica*, ii. 212.

72. *Scociam de regno Anglie esse, et regem Scottorum de Scocia hominem esse regis Anglie*: Charles Johnson (ed.), revised M. Brett, C. N. L. Brooke and M. Winterbottom, *Hugh the Chanter, The History of the Church of York 1066–1127* (Oxford, 1990), 212; James Raine (ed.), 'History of Four Archbishops of York by Hugh the Chanter', in Raine (ed.), *The Historians of the Church of York and its Archbishops*, vol. ii (London, 1886), at 215; *SAEC*, 161.

73. *derogare libertati vel dignitati regni Scottorum*: Rule (ed.), *Eadmeri Historia*, 300; *SAEC*, 153.

74. Johnson and others (eds), *Hugh the Chanter, The History of the Church of York*, 212. For the three parties present at the Curia (those of David I, York and Canterbury) see Donald Nicholl, *Thurstan, Archbishop of York (1114–1140)* (York, 1964), 97–8.

75. For what follows, see Dauvit Broun, 'The church of St Andrew and its foundation legend in the early twelfth century: recovering the full text of Version A of the foundation legend', in Taylor (ed.), *Kings, Clerics and Chronicles*, 108–14.

76. James Ussher, *Britannicarum Ecclesiarum Antiquitates* (Dublin, 1639), 648–51.

77. M. O. Anderson, 'St Andrews before Alexander I', in G. W. S. Barrow (ed.), *The Scottish Tradition* (Edinburgh, 1974), 1–13: witnesses of the 'A' version of the legend are discussed at 9–10. The fourteenth-century manuscript of this shorter version, Paris, Bibliothèque nationale Latin 4126 (fos 31r–32r) has been the basis of all previous editions of this legend (most recently Anderson, *Kings and Kingship*, 258–60). No translation has yet been published.

78. London, BL Arundel 36 (fos 15vb–16va: pencil foliation) and London, BL Cotton Tiberius D iii (fos 93rb–94ra). The latter was badly damaged by fire on 23 October 1731.

79. Against normal expectations this is not Bower's *Scotichronicon* (where the list appears in book VI, ch. 24: John and Winifred MacQueen and D. E. R. Watt (eds), *Scotichronicon by Walter Bower in Latin and English*, vol. iii (Edinburgh, 1995), 342–5), but in Bower's own abbreviation of his great work, which is known to scholarship as the 'Book of Coupar Angus' (Edinburgh, NLS Adv. 35.1.7, p. 433). This has not been published before (although most of it was given in W. Goodall (ed.), *Joannis de Fordun Scotichronicon cum Supplementis et Continuatione Walteri Boweri*, 2 vols (Edinburgh, 1759), i. 339, n.*).

80. London, BL Additional 25014 (fos 118vb–119vb).

81. An erased *ex libris* is noted in Anderson, 'St Andrews before Alexander I', 9. Its provenance was also deduced as Newminster in N. R. Ker, *Medieval Libraries of Great Britain. A List of Surviving Books*, 2nd edn (London, 1964), 134, presumably on account of a note added on fo. 2v on how in 1333 a Scottish force sacked Newminster and destroyed 'our' dormitory and 'our whole abbey', but five days later was almost wiped out at the Battle of Halidon Hill ('Berwick').
82. See above, 66 n. 84, 77.
83. The evidence for this has not been published. It was presented in a paper on the *Chronicle of the Kings of Alba* I gave to the Celtic Department in the University of Aberdeen on 12 December 2005.
84. Anderson, *Kings and Kingship*, 69.

5

Whose Independence? Bishop Jocelin of Glasgow (1175–99) and the Achievement of Ecclesiastical Freedom

The ecclesiastical freedom of the Scottish kingdom had been secured for all time by *Cum universi* (usually dated to 1192, but 1189 should be seriously considered).[1] This did not, however, take the usual form of recognising the kingdom as a province of the Church under its own archbishop. Instead, each bishop was directly answerable to Rome. What had been established was not an independent entity corresponding (roughly) to the kingdom, but a group of independent dioceses. In this chapter the origins of this unique arrangement will be explored. It will be argued that the kingdom's ecclesiastical freedom was very far from being inevitable: *Cum universi* can be regarded as the brainchild of one man, Bishop Jocelin of Glasgow, who may personally be credited with changing the course of Scotland's history by this achievement. An examination of his motives, however, shows that the issue of independence, both in a Scottish and an ecclesiastical context, was much less straightforward than has previously been imagined.

The key to the background of *Cum universi* and an appreciation of Bishop Jocelin's achievement is an understanding of the aspirations of the bishops of Glasgow and their clergy during the second half of the twelfth century. The most obvious source for this is the *Life of Kentigern* by the expert hagiographer, Jocelin of Furness, at the behest of his namesake, Bishop Jocelin of Glasgow (1175–99).[2] There can be no doubt that Jocelin of Furness represented his patron's views, and presumably the views of the cathedral establishment, among whom he evidently spent some time while writing his work. There is also the account of St Kentigern's conception and birth written for Bishop Herbert (1147–64), often referred to as the 'Fragmentary Life'.[3] Another important source is the complete Office with Proper chants and readings for celebrating the feast of St Kentigern (13 January) preserved in a manuscript of the end of the thirteenth century known as the 'Sprouston Breviary'.[4] This allows us to hear, in both words and music, how the patronal saint was commemorated in a church within the diocese that had the resources for performing a full Office. The exact date of the Office is difficult to determine: it was presumably celebrated in the thirteenth century, but it may well draw on material that could be as much as a century older than the manuscript itself. Be this as it may, the Office at least shows how the cult of Kentigern in this period could be disseminated, reminding us that the view of the diocese promoted by the cathedral establishment was bound to be received by clergy in the parishes. Finally there are a few royal charters which were almost certainly drafted by episcopal clerks, and can offer some unexpected insights into the way these clerks thought about their bishopric. A striking feature of these texts is how, across a number of different genres, an attempt was made to present the diocese as different and distinct from Scotland or England. Let us examine each of these in turn.

In the *Life of Kentigern* by Jocelin of Furness, the diocese founded by Kentigern, with its cathedral at Glasgow, is described as extending 'according to the limits of the Cambrian kingdom', dividing Scotland from England.[5] A particularly vivid association of bishopric with kingdom is found in a remarkable passage in which the relationship between Kentigern and his patron, King Rhydderch, is defined:[6]

> [King Rhydderch], stripping away his royal robes, on bended knees and hands joined, with the consent and advice of his lords, gave his homage to St Kentigern, and handed over to him the dominion and rulership (*dominium et principatum*) over all his kingdom, and willed that he [Kentigern] be king, and himself [Rhydderch] the ruler of the country under him as his [Rhydderch's] father, as he knew that formerly the great emperor Constantine had done to St Silvester. Hence . . . so long as the Cambrian kingdom lasted . . . the ruler was always subject to the bishop.

This is as fictional as the legend of Pope Silvester and the emperor Constantine on which it was based.[7] It had an important outcome which was surely intended: the bishop, not the king, was presented as the true source of royal authority. Not only was the diocese portrayed as the kingdom, but the bishop was the real king: a much more immediate and compelling association with royalty than the claim in the earlier work commissioned by Bishop Herbert that Kentigern was from the stock of British kings.

This kingdom, moreover, was part of neither Scotland nor England. In the *Life of Kentigern* commissioned by Bishop Jocelin it is repeatedly called *Cambria*. This is consistent with the inquest conducted by David as *Cumbrensis regionis princeps*, 'ruler of the Cumbrian kingdom', re-establishing Glasgow's property-rights.[8] The inquest proper is preceded by a preamble which could have been written at any point between *ca* 1120 and Glasgow cathedral's old cartulary of the second quarter of the thirteenth century:[9] Professor Barrow has suggested sometime about the middle of the twelfth century.[10] Here *Cumbria* is defined as 'a certain kingdom (*regio*) situated between England and Scotland (*Scotia*)'.[11]

In the Office of St Kentigern in the 'Sprouston Breviary' a number of terms are used. Within the ninth responsory of Matins there is a *prosa* beginning *Gens Cambrina*;[12] but the opening of the responsory for First Vespers announces that Kentigern's holy church dwells in northern Wales (*in septemtrionali Wallia*), not far from Scotland (*Albania*).[13] Later, in one of the readings, it is described how Kentigern left his master (St Serf) and crossed a river (unnamed, but obviously the Forth) that divides Scotland (*Scocia*) from the kingdom of the Britons (*regnum Britannorum*).[14] In the account of Kentigern's conception and birth commissioned by Bishop Herbert, the last sentence to survive is a declaration that God should be thanked 'who has, among others, enriched our country Britain with such a patron' as Kentigern.[15] 'Our country Britain' (*patriam Britanniam*) probably means Strathclyde in a way comparable with the use of *Britannia* to refer to Wales.[16] Jocelin of Furness, by contrast, has none of this. For him, Kentigern's country is northern Britain or *Cambria*, and *Wallia* is distinguished from *Cambria* (for example, when Kentigern's journey from St Asaph's to Glasgow is described as going 'from Wales to Cambria; from exile to his own country', *de Wallia ad Cambriam; de exilio ad propriam patriam*).[17] There would seem in this respect to be a distinction between the precision of a professional writer like Jocelin of Furness, and more intensely local productions, like the surviving Office, or the account of Kentigern's conception and birth written for Bishop Herbert by a Glasgow cleric. If so, it would appear that Welsh and Brythonic identity was something that the cathedral establishment was happy to stress when left to its own devices.

Finally, it is striking that the very few royal charters which include a reference to Welsh in their address were all drafted by and for the bishopric of Glasgow. The significance of this only becomes clear if the charters are subjected to detailed examination. The 'racial address'[18] was a frequent, but never a regular, feature of royal charters; it is very rare in non-royal charters. It disappeared from English royal charters from the 1170s;[19] Scottish royal charters followed suit shortly afterwards.[20] It has been suggested that an effort was sometimes made to make the 'racial address' appropriate to the region concerned:[21] 'French and English' for Lothian, 'French, English and Scots' for Fife and 'French, English, Scots and Galwegians' for the South West. The only appearance of 'Cumbrians' in the address, for example, is in a charter of David I granting a mark of silver from his mill at Scotby to the monks of Wetheral in Cumberland; the charter also has Carlisle as its place-date.[22] There is no hard-and-fast pattern, however: Galwegians, for example, appear in the address of a charter relating to St Andrews.[23]

'Welsh' appear in the 'racial address' of four charters. One is quite incongruous: a charter of Mael Coluim IV confirming the grant of a chapel in Perthshire to St Andrews Cathedral Priory.[24] Why would Welsh be mentioned here? The answer is probably that this is a clerical error. The charter in question is one of a pair confirming gifts of churches to the priory by Richard, bishop-elect of St Andrews; Geoffrey Barrow in his edition of Mael Coluim's charters has suggested that they were 'probably of a date' with each other.[25] The other charter of this pair also has the 'racial address', except that *Gawelensibus* (Galwegians) appear instead of *Walensibus* (Welsh). Both charters survive only as cartulary copies. It is likely, therefore, that *Walensibus* is here a miscopying of *Gawelensibus*. If so, this leaves only three authentic appearances of 'Welsh' in the 'racial address'. These are all in charters for the bishop of Glasgow. They are:

1) a charter of Mael Coluim IV (1153–65) (without a place-date) (*RRS*, i. no. 258);
2) a charter of William I, datable to sometime between 1173 and *ca* 1191 (perhaps before *ca* 1180),[26] with Jedburgh as its place-date (*RRS*, ii. no. 179); and
3) another charter of William I, dated 6 July in the document, with Stirling as its place-date. It is datable to sometime between 1211 and 1214 (most likely 1212) (*RRS*, ii. no. 507).

All three are almost identical, except for the witness list and any dating clause they might have.[27] It is clear, then, that the second and third charters have been copied from the first, the charter of Mael Coluim IV. The racial address in the third charter (probably 1212) is an exact copy of the second (in or after 1173 and perhaps before *ca* 1180); while that in the second has evidently been modelled on the first (1153×65). This explains how the third charter came to sport a racial address even though this had been obsolete for more than thirty years. In effect, these three charters boil down to one charter-text in which 'Welsh' figured in the address.

It was clearly no ordinary text. In fact, it was the most important charter obtained by the bishop of Glasgow from Mael Coluim IV or his brother, William, and involves key aspects of the bishop's control over his diocese. In it the king ordered and urged all those within the diocese to obey and respect the bishop, archdeacon, and their officials, and render teinds and other ecclesiastical dues to their churches without opposition; also, that teinds were to be paid as fully as in any other diocese in the kingdom. Those who resisted would be fined by the king's sheriff; moreover, if the sheriff himself turned a blind eye, he would be fined and the teind paid in full.[28] There can be little doubt that the exemplar of this text was produced by the Glasgow cathedral establishment, not by royal clerks (although by 1212 the charter itself would have been produced by a royal scribe, presumably by copying the previous charter). The presence in the document of a rhetorical preamble is very rare in royal charters,[29] and almost certainly indicates that the text was written by the beneficiary. Also, the form of King Mael Coluim's name (*Malcolon'*) is paralleled only by *Malcolonus*, found uniquely in the great confirmation-charter of Kelso datable to 1159 (which survives as a magnificently impressive original single sheet).[30] The significance that was still attached to this text by the bishop and his associates by the time of its last extant copy in or about 1212 may be gauged from the fact that it was made on 6 July, the anniversary of the dedication of Bishop Jocelin's cathedral in 1197.

In the second half of the twelfth century, therefore, it appears that the cathedral establishment included explicit references to the bishopric's Welsh identity when a particularly important statement was made by them concerning the diocese and its cathedral, such as their patronal saint's *Life*, the liturgical celebration of his feast day, or a key royal document. They were also concerned to emphasise that the diocese was once a kingdom whose ultimate power continued to be represented by the bishop himself. How is this to be explained?

GLASGOW'S DISPUTED STATUS, 1100–75

First of all, it will be useful to take a wide focus encompassing the growth of the papacy from the mid-eleventh century as an effective source of authority flowing through a fully articulated hierarchy of obedience. It will be recalled that, by the late twelfth century, a coherent structure reaching from pope to parish was taking shape.[31] Glasgow's story can justifiably claim to be one of the most remarkable in this era of transformation and redefinition of roles and relationships within the Latin Church.

In the early twelfth century the bishop of Glasgow faced an almost unprecedented set of competing claims on his allegiance. Two arch-bishops, the archbishop of Canterbury and the archbishop of York, insisted that the bishop of Glasgow belonged to their province. This also involved the archbishop of Canterbury's attempts to consolidate his status as primate of Britain despite the recalcitrance of archbishops of York. We have met York's attempts to be recognised as Glasgow's (and Scotland's) metropolitan in the previous chapter, and also Canterbury's claim to jurisdiction over Scotland as argued by Eadmer in 1120 and by the archbishop of Canterbury at the council of Northampton in 1176. A specific claim to be Glasgow's metropolitan was also made by Ralph, archbishop of Canterbury (1114–22), in a letter to Pope Calixtus II in 1119 attacking the claim by Thurstan, the newly elected archbishop of York, that York did not owe obedience to Canterbury. Archbishop Ralph insisted that York was not a proper archbishopric because it lacked the number of suffragan bishops required to consecrate an archbishop. He backed this up by arguing that the bishop of Glasgow (whose predeces-sor, Michael, had acted as one of York's suffragans)[32] should by rights be subject to Canterbury according to Pope Gregory the Great's declaration that all the bishops of the British (*Brittaniarum*) should be under the authority of St Augustine, the first archbishop of Canterbury, as recorded in Bede's *Ecclesiastical History* (book I, chapter 27, section vii).[33] Finally, Glasgow was also involved with the concerted campaign by kings of Scots to gain papal recognition of his kingdom as a province in its own right with the bishop of St Andrews as its metropolitan: put simply, this would have meant (if the king had got his way) that all bishoprics in mainland Scotland would have been under the authority of an arch-bishop of St Andrews. It is not only these troubled waters that makes Glasgow's experience stand out, but also the final outcome. The bish-opric of Zamora in León, for example, was similarly caught between two established archbishoprics (Braga and Toledo, with the archbishop of Toledo also seeking to consolidate his position as primate of Spain); it was also coveted by the newly created archbishopric of Compostela, which was promoted to this rank in 1120 (and confirmed in 1124) at much the same time as the bishopric of Zamora itself was restored in 1121.[34] The ensuing dispute was played out at the Curia, with one side and then another gaining the upper hand, until 1199 when the music stopped and Compostela was left holding the prize.[35] Although Zamora enjoyed *de facto* independence at times during the conflict over its alle-giance, there was never any question that it would, in the end, become a bishopric within a province. What makes Glasgow exceptional is that, after seventy-five years of appearing to be destined to fall within the authority of an archbishop, the situation was suddenly transformed when Pope Alexander III, sometime early in 1175 (probably 30 April), made Glasgow an exempt diocese free of any archi-episcopal jurisdiction.[36] Despite some uncertainty at the outset,[37] this arrangement was to endure for nearly three hundred years.[38] In due course, as was noted at the outset, all Scottish dioceses were to achieve this status, enshrined in the famous bull *Cum universi*. It is important to emphasise that Glasgow was the first to gain formal recognition of its independence,[39] and for fourteen or seventeen years (depending on the dating of *Cum universi*) was the only Scottish diocese to enjoy this privilege.[40] Indeed, it will become apparent that *Cum universi* can be interpreted as essentially Bishop Jocelin of Glasgow's plan to secure the freedom of his diocese that he had so spectacularly gained at the beginning of his reign in 1175.

DIOCESES EXEMPT FROM ARCHI-EPISCOPAL JURISDICTION

Glasgow's achievement stands out not only in a Scottish context but more generally, too.[41] Exemption meant, in effect, that the pope acted as metropolitan: for example, the bishop-elect of an exempt diocese had to seek consecration directly from the pope, who might perform the ceremony himself or delegate it to someone else.[42] It is no surprise that the majority of exempt bishoprics were in Italy (or nearby), and that these were long established by the twelfth century.[43] Exempt dioceses were very unusual outside Italy (see the map on p. xiii). When Glasgow was made an exempt diocese, it became the most distant from Rome: in comparison to the next most distant (León), it was nearly 25 per cent further away as the crow flies. It was not only Glasgow's location that made it so remarkable. Even though papal recognition was extremely rare, and each case was the product of unusual circumstances, it is possible to identify some key contributory factors behind the creation or recognition of exempt dioceses in different periods. None of these characteristic features is present in the case of Glasgow, underlining the extraordinary nature of Jocelin's achievement in securing its independence. Let us explore this in more detail.

Outside Italy the greatest number of exempt dioceses on the Continent was in Spain. This was chiefly because, when Christian Spain was brought into the emerging structure of the Latin Church, the original Visigothic hierarchy was taken as its template. By 1100 archbishops were re-established at Toledo, Tarragona and Braga, and bishoprics assigned to them.[44] But this was not always a tidy process, not least because the old Visigothic hierarchy had collapsed many centuries earlier, and a number of new bishoprics had emerged in the interim, particularly at royal centres in what became the kingdom of León-Castile.[45] It was far from clear how these were to be accommodated in the new structure: in the end León, Oviedo and Burgos were confirmed as exempt dioceses, free of any archi-episcopal jurisdiction. The fate of the bishopric of Palencia in Castile offers an instructive contrast. It was founded in the 1030s, before an archi-episcopal structure was fully established, and was assigned to the province of Toledo by the pope in 1099. Its subordination to Toledo was resisted by a number of Palencia's bishops; but, because Palencia was a restored Visigothic see, there seems to have been no notion that it might become an exempt diocese. Instead its bishops claimed archi-episcopal rank on the basis that Toledo's metropolitan authority had been transferred to Palencia because Toledo was occupied by Saracens.[46] In the absence of royal support this strategy was doomed to failure. In Spain there was also the question of how to treat new or 'restored' dioceses in lands conquered from the Saracens. This could occasionally result in the creation of an exempt diocese. For example, the city of Mallorca (now called Palma) was recognised as an exempt see by Pope Gregory IX (1227–41) following its conquest in 1229 by King Jaime of Aragón.[47] In the south, the bishopric of Cartagena was restored after the city was reconquered in 1243;[48] in 1250 it was made exempt by Pope Innocent IV because (as he explained) a *contentio multiplex* had arisen between neighbouring metropolitans who each claimed Cartagena for their province.[49] The special problem here was that Cartagena had originally been metropolitan of the province which included Toledo, but had been conquered by Byzantium in the sixth century, allowing Toledo to emerge in its place.[50]

Outside Spain there were only three exempt dioceses on the Continent beyond Italy: Le Puy in the Upper Loire in Burgundy, Bamberg in Upper Franconia in Bavaria and Kammin (now Kamień Pomorski in Poland) on the east bank of the Oder (Odra) estuary in western Pomerania. Again, each escaped from archi-episcopal jurisdiction because of very unusual circumstances. Le Puy and Bamberg enjoyed a particularly close relationship with the papacy before the structure of archi-episcopal government had properly been consolidated, and this duly evolved into direct dependence on Rome. In the case of Le Puy, this appears to have originated in an instruction of Pope Sylvester II in 999 that the bishop should be consecrated by the pope.[51] The special relationship with the papacy became more explicit and enduring on Christmas Day 1051 when Pope Leo IX granted the bishop of Le Puy the 'right of the pallium, so that he be ordained by the Roman pontiff'.[52] It was explained in the bull that Pope Leo was moved to bestow this privilege out of reverence for the Virgin Mary, a reference to Le Puy's position as a centre of the cult of the Virgin.[53] Another indication of Le Puy's special relationship with the papacy is that it was the first port of call the next time a pope visited France, when Urban II came in 1095 to hold the Council of Clermont.[54]

Bamberg's bond with the papacy began when the diocese was created in 1007, when it was freed 'from all external power' by Pope John XVIII.[55] Bamberg owed its privileged position to the favour it was shown by King Henry II and his queen, Kunigunde, who established it as a royal residence and founded the church. In 1020 the church was offered to the papacy; the bishop thereafter owed the pope an annual tribute of a white horse with saddle.[56] This relationship with the papacy moved onto a new plane when a pallium was granted by Leo IX on 2 January 1053 at Henry III's behest, although with the caveat that the grant was made 'saving the metropolitan authority of the church of Mainz'.[57] It must be doubted whether Bamberg would have enjoyed so much papal favour if its patron had not been so powerful in relation to the papacy itself.

KAMMIN (KAMIEŃ POMORSKI)

The only diocese on the Continent north of the Alps to achieve exempt status after the eleventh century was the bishopric of Pomerania (whose see was established at Kammin by 1188). Again, a unique set of circumstances underlay this situation. This deserves some discussion not only because of its unusual complexity, but particularly because the definitive decision to recognise the bishop of Kammin's independence provides the closest parallel, chronologically and geographically, to the privileges of exemption gained first by Glasgow and then by the Scottish church.[58]

In 1109 the Polish Duke Bolesław Krzywousty conquered Pomerania, and reinforced this in 1120 after a rising against him. This reassertion of Bolesław's power was followed by Pomerania's conversion to Christianity in two missions led by Bishop Otto of Bamberg (1102–39).[59] On Otto's death a Pomeranian diocese was established whose see was initially at Wollin/Julin (now Wolin in Poland) and latterly at Kammin, and in 1140 a privilege of protection was obtained by its new bishop, Wojciech (Adalbert), from Pope Innocent II.[60] The kind of ecclesiastical or political ties that could have influenced the future allegiance of the Pomeranian church were, however, anything but straightforward. If the mother church of the Pomeranian mission had been the see of an archdiocese, or its bishop the suffragan of an archbishop, then there is a chance that the new diocese created on Otto's death might have been recognised as belonging to the same province. But, of course, Bamberg was the see of an exempt diocese. A more likely way that Pomerania's ecclesiastical identity could have been settled would have been according to the political allegiance of its rulers. It might therefore be expected, once the duke of western Pomerania (where Wollin and Kammin are situated) had recognised the overlordship of Duke Bolesław of Poland, that the new diocese would become part of the Polish church under the archbishopric of Gniezno.[61] As it happened, though, the nature of the relationship between Polish dukes and German emperors was contested in this period, and this inevitably spilled over into ecclesiastical politics, with the Polish church threatened by the archbishop of Magdeburg's claim to have authority over it.[62] When the new Pomeranian diocese was born, the ink was only a few years dry on Innocent II's bull of 1133 recognising the archbishop of Magdeburg as metropolitan of Poland and Pomerania, and his contrary bull of 1136 in favour of the archbishopric of Gniezno.[63] This confused situation in turn mirrored the competing ambitions in the region of Polish dukes and German emperors, which were eventually thwarted by the rise of Danish power in the Baltic. In 1181 the ruler of western Pomerania, Duke Bogusław of Szczecin, attempted to stave off Danish control by doing homage to Frederick Barbarossa, but three years later succumbed to Danish overlordship.[64]

It was in this new political landscape, which was to endure until the decline of Danish power after 1225, that the diocese of Kammin achieved recognition of its exempt status from Pope Clement III in a bull of 24 February 1188.[65] As far as Clement III was concerned the see's direct subjection to the Roman pontiff was a freedom which it had enjoyed from its inception, and he declared that this should continue inviolate for all time.[66] There is a strong suspicion that Bishop Zygfryd (Siegfried), who succeeded to Wojciech's episcopal throne in 1185, had lost no time in making the most of the opportunity afforded by Danish overlordship to escape from the clutches of both Gniezno and Magdeburg, and may have exaggerated the extent to which his see's freedom had been formally established at its foundation.[67] Certainly, the bull of protection obtained by Bishop Wojciech from Innocent II in 1140 makes no mention of any exemption from archi-episcopal authority.[68] On the other hand, Wojciech himself rather conspicuously drew attention to his consecration by Innocent II in the address of a charter in 1153.[69] It is possible, therefore, that there had been an aspiration to direct subjection to Rome from the outset, perhaps in imitation of the mother church of Bamberg.[70]

EXEMPT DIOCESES 1050–1250: A PATTERN OF DEVELOPMENT

Notwithstanding the rarity of exempt dioceses and the peculiar circumstances of how each came into being, it is possible to discern in outline a pattern of development, at least beyond Italy, in the key circumstances that could contribute to a bishopric's attainment of exemption from archi-episcopal authority. One obvious category is those, like Le Puy and Bamberg, whose enduring status as exempt dioceses was exemplified by their entitlement to receive the pallium from the pope. The pallium was the woollen shoulder band granted by the pope as a special symbol of his authority, and was by the eleventh century normally reserved for archbishops, for whom it was fast becoming the definitive marker of their metropolitan status. When the bishops of Le Puy and Bamberg were granted the pallium, its particular significance was not yet exclusively established: it was in essence the most distinguished item of papal attire which it was permitted for a prelate to imitate, and should be seen alongside concessions to wear, for example, the Roman mitre, gloves, sandals or slippers.[71] In this context Leo IX could regard Bamberg's pallium as not necessarily prejudicial to Mainz's metropolitan authority. Once the pallium had become the preserve of metropolitans, however, then it was no longer appropriate to grant them to bishops, even if they were exempt from archi-episcopal jurisdiction. For those who already received the pallium, it could now become a symbol of their independence: Mainz's claim on Bamberg was therefore effectively extinguished by Bamberg's continued entitlement to wear the pallium.[72]

The move away from the pallium as a privilege appropriate for a bishop can be gauged with reference to Spain. In 1095 Santiago de Compostela was the first Spanish diocese to have its exempt status recognised by the pope;[73] this was followed in 1104 by the grant of a pallium.[74] At this point León and Oviedo, in contrast, had only just reached the stage of having their independence recognised by the pope, in 1104 and 1105 respectively, having originally been assigned to the province of Toledo in 1099.[75] They did not go on to gain a pallium: in fact, no pallium was awarded to a bishopric that first achieved exemption in the twelfth century (or later). The status of León and Oviedo remained precarious for a generation or two: they both lost their independence in 1121 (a decision confirmed in 1125); León regained its exempt status within a decade, but Oviedo was only successful in 1157.[76]

Compostela, of course, went on to greater things, becoming an archbishopric provisionally in 1120, and then permanently in 1124.[77] This was not only due to the remarkable single-mindedness, political astuteness and good fortune of its bishop, Diego Gelmírez (1100–40). Like Le Puy, Compostela was favoured by the pope because of its particular importance as the centre of a major cult (in this case the cult of St James): this is made clear already in the bull establishing Compostela as an exempt diocese in 1095.[78]

Reverence for a cult was not a prominent factor in the creation of an exempt diocese in the twelfth century or later. Indeed, it is striking that, from the mid-twelfth century, the circumstances behind the recognition of a diocese's independence became, in one obvious sense, even more limited. The characteristic which all later examples (apart from Scotland) have in common is that they were newly established bishoprics in territory conquered from non-Christians. Although this was not the only factor which prompted each to become an exempt diocese – in the case of Kammin, for example, the complex experience of overlordship in western Pomerania appears to have been particularly significant – it remains true that the uncertainty about their place in the Church's hierarchy was due in the first instance to the fact that they were fresh creations (or re-creations) in newly Christian lands.[79] For the bishop of Kammin this at least enabled him to claim that the see had been directly subject to Rome from the time it was founded. Many new dioceses in lands conquered from non-Christians did not become exempt, of course.[80]

None of these cases provides a particularly close parallel to Glasgow's situation. As has been noted already, Glasgow was more similar to Zamora, a re-established diocese which was claimed by three provinces.[81] Disputed ecclesiastical allegiance, which was not a particularly rare experience in this period, had not hitherto been sufficient cause on its own for a diocese to gain exemption from archi-episcopal jurisdiction. It had, at best, been only a subsidiary factor in a few cases. When Glasgow's attainment of exempt status is seen in this light, it is hard not to regard it as a quite remarkable development.

GLASGOW AND ST ANDREWS

The most striking aspect of Glasgow's extraordinary achievement in becoming an exempt diocese is that this apparently only became an official episcopal objective a few weeks or months before it was granted in 1175. In what follows it will be argued that, although Glasgow had by that stage enjoyed a long period of *de facto* independence, it was very late in the day when it was decided by its bishop that this might be sought as a permanent arrangement. Before this point it would almost certainly have been unthinkable. In contrast, all exempt dioceses beyond Italy in the twelfth and thirteenth centuries, if they were not formally acknowledged as exempt soon after their foundation (with the exception of Kammin), had a history of seeking to retain their independence (if this was not already effectively established by the bishop's right to wear the pallium). Even in the case of Kammin there is some indication that direct dependence on Rome was an aspiration shared by its first bishop as well as its third bishop, Zygfryd (1185–1202).

Of all the bishoprics in the Scottish realm (not including Whithorn, re-established by December 1128),[82] Glasgow was in the weakest position for preserving its independence from York.[83] The strongest elements in York's favour, apart from consistent papal support until 1164 (at least),[84] was that two of the bishop of Glasgow's predecessors had been consecrated in the late 1050s by Archbishop Cynesige of York, and that the profession of obedience of another (Michael) was extant (and survives to this day in a copy):[85] Bishop Michael's known activity is, however, restricted to Cumbria in the north of England.[86] The only likely alternative to subjection to York was the creation of St Andrews as metropolitan of the kingdom. There can be little doubt that Glasgow was included in this plan. John, Bishop Michael's successor, was consecrated by Pope Paschal II on 21 January 1118 during a vacancy at York. He did not, therefore, make a profession of obedience as Michael had done. He did, however, play a key role in David I's effort to gain approval for an archbishopric of St Andrews, being dispatched to the Curia by the king in 1125 in pursuit of this goal.[87] Bishop John was unusually close to David I: he had been David's chaplain very early in David's career, and appears as a witness in so many of David's charters and brieves that he has justifiably been described as 'a court chaplain-bishop who also looked after his see'.[88] David would hardly have conceived the plan for an archbishopric of St Andrews without involving John, or asked John to promote this at the Curia if he did not have confidence in John's commitment to it. There is no indication that David I had a separate strategy for Glasgow, so it may be assumed that his intention was to include it as a suffragan of the hoped-for archbishop of St Andrews, and that Bishop John was a willing advocate of this arrangement. As we saw in the previous chapter, the status of the kingdom as a whole was at issue, not just Scotland in the restricted sense of the country north of the Forth.[89] It is also apparent that, even while David was 'ruler of the Cumbrians', Glasgow's status was regarded as a matter touching the Scottish realm: this would explain why Alexander I felt it behoved him to ask the pope that Bishop John be allowed to delay his return to the obedience of the archbishop of York.[90]

The final attempt to promote St Andrews as metropolitan was in 1159 following the death of the long-serving Bishop Robert. It will be recalled that the newly elected Pope Alexander III settled for a complex arrangement for a new bishop of St Andrews involving the appointment of a legate:[91] it is clear from the legate's designation that the whole kingdom was included.[92] Although Alexander III did not accede to the request that St Andrews become an archbishopric, he made it clear that the issue was open for further discussion. According to the terms of Alexander's bull, it might have been expected that the new bishop, Arnold, would have acted on the pope's suggestion that he should come to the Curia to have his status clarified. But nothing happened.[93] This may simply have been because Bishop Arnold died in 1162 less than two years after his election and consecration. His successor was the king's chaplain, Richard, elected in 1163 and consecrated with Alexander III's permission by Scottish bishops on 28 March 1165.[94] It seems, however, that the issue of St Andrews' claim to be archbishop of the realm was not pursued. This does not mean that St Andrews' aspirations had died down. They were potently expressed in the building of a new cathedral, begun in 1162 and continuing into the 1170s.[95] It has been argued compellingly that this deliberately rivalled the new choir at York Minster, 'and signalled that the Scottish Church was quite capable of administering its own affairs'.[96]

It is tempting to speculate whether the arrival of a new bishop of Glasgow at this time may have brought a change of attitude with regard to the plan for St Andrews. Bishop Herbert had died before mid-September 1164 when his successor, Ingram, was elected.[97] Ingram seems to have been more pro-active than Richard bishop-elect of St Andrews. With royal support he was received by Alexander III at Sens and consecrated by the pope by 1 November that year.[98] Unfortunately we can only guess Ingram's attitude to the future of his diocese. It is tempting to associate him with the archetypal royal charter for Glasgow which included Welsh in the racial address. Ingram combined the offices of king's chancellor and archdeacon of Glasgow for nearly three years before he was elected bishop in September 1164,[99] so it would have been particularly easy for him to obtain this document in an attempt to facilitate his job as archdeacon.[100] Be this as it may, there is no doubt whatever about his successor's determination to promote Glasgow's independence. The most straightforward interpretation of the evidence is that this specific goal became episcopal policy more or less as soon as Bishop Jocelin was consecrated, and that it should therefore be seen as his initiative.

SPECIAL DAUGHTER OF ROME

The final unusual aspect of Glasgow's achievement in becoming an exempt diocese was the way this was expressed: a few key words in an otherwise regular document. The crucial papal bull obtained by Bishop Jocelin early in 1175 was otherwise identical in nature to the privilege of protection procured from the same pope, Alexander III, by his predecessor Ingram, dated 5 April 1170.[101] This earlier text took the standard form of receiving the church into the pope's protection and confirming its properties and other rights. Ingram was not the first Scottish bishop to obtain a bull of this kind: the earliest extant example is in favour of Bishop Edward of Aberdeen in 1157,[102] followed by another in favour of Dunkeld in 1163 (the original of which survives).[103] What made the privilege procured by Bishop Jocelin so important was the addition of five words in the clause granting the pope's protection: the church of Glasgow was described as *specialem filiam nostram nullo mediante*, 'our special daughter with no-one coming in between'.[104] When Bishop Jocelin obtained a renewal of this privilege in 1179 the phrase was altered to read *specialem nullo mediante Romane Ecclesie filiam*, 'special daughter of the Roman church with no-one coming in between':[105] the possible significance of this new formula will be discussed in due course. Repetitions of the bull of 1179 were procured from different popes in 1182 and 1186.[106]

It has been suggested that 'the phrase "special daughter" is one used by Alexander to demonstrate papal protection for a particular purpose, and has no significance beyond that'.[107] By way of an example of this, it has been pointed out that the abbot of Kelso was also described by Pope Alexander III as a special daughter in a letter of 1165.[108] Drawing attention to the numerous privileges of protection granted by popes to monastic houses is very helpful for clarifying the significance of the key words in the bulls procured by Bishop Jocelin in 1175 and 1179. This only serves, however, to confirm their crucial importance. Many monasteries obtained privileges of protection; only a few of these privileges went as far as granting exemption from episcopal authority. Initially this distinction was not always made clear in the terminology used in papal bulls. During the pontificate of Innocent II (1130–43) the phrase 'special daughter with no-one coming in between' or versions of it began to be used; and in due course this came to be applied consistently for exempt houses during the pontificate of Alexander III (1159–81).[109] This can be seen in the case of the bull of 1165 for Kelso. Earlier Kelso, in its privilege of protection by Hadrian IV dated 1155, had been confirmed as 'free and immune from all subjection except to the Roman pontiff'.[110] Now it was referred to by Alexander III as 'a special daughter of the Roman church'. In the same bull it was also granted by Alexander III that the abbot could wear a mitre, a symbol of the house's independence from episcopal authority.

There can be little doubt, therefore, that when Alexander III countenanced the use of the phrase 'our special daughter with no-one coming in between' to describe Glasgow in 1175 he understood this to mean that Glasgow was exempt from all other ecclesiastical authority except his own as pope. The only unusual aspect is that it was applied to a bishopric rather than a monastery. The same formula was not used to describe other exempt dioceses. Another form of words had been fashioned for this purpose by the Curia in the bull in favour of Compostela in 1095: here the bishop and his successors were told that 'they were to be subject to no-one except the Roman metropolitan; and all who will succeed you in that see will be consecrated by the hand of the Roman pontiff as special suffragans of the Roman see'.[111] Although this was deployed in other grants and confirmations of exemption, it is not found in Clement III's bull for Kammin, or later in the cases of Mallorca and Cartagena, so the failure to use it in the bull for Glasgow in 1175 is not necessarily significant. The key words in the bull for Glasgow, moreover, are not wholly unprecedented in relation to exempt dioceses. 'Special suffragan' in the bull for Compostela and its derivatives is clearly reminiscent of 'special daughter' in the bull for Glasgow. Apart from this, the closest parallel to the Glasgow formula in a grant of exemption to a bishop is Gregory IX's pronouncement that 'the church of Mallorca pertains to the apostolic see with no intermediary'.[112] Nowhere else apart from the bull for Glasgow (and later *Cum universi*), however, as far as I am aware, are the ideas of 'special suffragan' and 'no intermediary' put together; and nowhere else is the phrase 'special daughter' deployed, even though this had become a standard formula in relation to exempt monasteries.

Did these particular words originate in the mind of the papal clerk who drafted the bull for Bishop Jocelin in 1175? The alternative is that the phrase 'special daughter with no-one coming in between' was coined by Jocelin or his agents, and that the papal clerk has simply reproduced what he found in Jocelin's petition. This seems particularly likely if it is recalled that the bull is otherwise in essence a repeat of an earlier privilege of protection (except for changes in the list of possessions and rights). Glasgow's exemption is so anomalous, even when compared with other instances of this rare phenomenon, that it has to be regarded as

Jocelin's initiative, not the pope's.[113] In general terms, too, it is easy to see Jocelin as masterminding the whole project, bearing in mind that it seems to have originated with him, rather than with previous bishops.

JOCELIN'S COUP

How did Jocelin pull off this astonishing coup? He was elected bishop on 23 May 1174, and was consecrated on the instructions of the pope by the archbishop of Lund at Clairvaux sometime between 16 December 1174 and 15 March 1175.[114] Before he obtained the famous privilege that Glasgow was Rome's special daughter (taking 30 April to be the correct date of that bull), he had already succeeded (on 15 March) in gaining from the pope 'a special privilege of liberty' for as long as Jocelin lived, namely that no-one but the pope or his special representative could promulgate the ecclesiastical censures of interdict, suspension or excommunication against him or the church of Glasgow.[115] In this earlier bull we can see some of the strings that Jocelin was able to pull in the cause of his diocese. Pope Alexander III explained that he was moved to honour Jocelin because of the support Jocelin and the Cistercian order had given him;[116] Jocelin, before becoming bishop of Glasgow, had been abbot of Melrose, the premier Cistercian house in Scotland. Alexander III was certainly very well disposed towards Cistercians at this time: the previous year he had authorised the canonisation of Bernard of Clairvaux, the most prominent Cistercian of the age.[117]

The most important factor in Jocelin's favour, however, was that any surviving plan for an archbishopric of St Andrews must by then have been shelved. Any potential thought of Glasgow's independence would have been stifled as long as there was royal support for the bishop of St Andrews as the kingdom's hoped-for metropolitan. But such aspirations for St Andrews were now no longer sustainable in the aftermath of King William's capture at Alnwick in July 1174. According to the terms agreed at Falaise in December for William's release, which centred on the fact that William now recognised Henry II as his liege lord 'for Scotland and all his other lands', it was stated that Bishop Richard of St Andrews and other leading churchmen 'have granted that the church of England shall also have the right in the church of Scotland which it lawfully should, and that they will not oppose the right of the church of England . . .'[118] The studied ambiguity of this prose has often been commented upon. It is not difficult, however, to see in these words Henry II's determination to settle once and for all that Scottish bishops would be subject to an English archbishop. It would have been fruitless in these circumstances for William to have maintained any designs for an archbishopric of St Andrews against his liege lord's wishes. If he was no longer able to support St Andrews' cause, he would have had no reason to block Jocelin's ambition to secure Glasgow's independence. The threat of Henry II's taking control of the Scottish church, in turn, would also have strengthened Jocelin's hand with Pope Alexander, who would have had no desire to allow ecclesiastical organisation to be dictated by the king held responsible for the murder a few years earlier of Thomas Becket, archbishop of Canterbury.

Did Jocelin get all he wanted? As is so often the case in this period, it is only possible to guess the nature of a petition from its outcome. It cannot always be assumed, of course, that a papal bull is an exact mirror of what was sought. Frequently a petitioner might end up with less than he hoped. It is unlikely, though, that Jocelin attempted to gain more than recognition of Glasgow as an exempt diocese. There were no grounds for Glasgow to mount a credible claim to become an archbishopric (although the play made by Jocelin of Furness of Kentigern's founding of St Asaph's and his brief mention of Kentigern's see having once been at Hoddom could be read as a piece of later kite-flying). A shortage of suffragans may not have been a critical issue earlier in the century, but it would have been fatal in 1175.[119] Jocelin would need to have pitched his request for the privilege of exemption in a way that would have been regarded as worthy of serious consideration. He was, after all, asking for something unprecedented: the granting of independence to a diocese that had hitherto shown no aspirations to this status in the previous seventy-five years of contact with the Curia.[120] It is perhaps not too fanciful, therefore, to see the neat phrase 'special daughter with no-one coming in between' added to an otherwise unremarkable privilege of protection as Jocelin's masterly presentation of something new in terms with which the Curia of the day would have been very familiar.[121]

JOCELIN AND *CUM UNIVERSI*

We need not doubt that Jocelin was acutely aware that something so novel and so recently bestowed was vulnerable. Privileges could be withdrawn,[122] and the political situation might be transformed so that a future pope might deem it necessary either to placate a king of England bent on securing suffragans for York, or please a king of Scots committed anew to the creation of an archbishopric of St Andrews. Exempt bishoprics were, in any event, frequently threatened by neighbouring archbishops.[123] What made Glasgow's position especially vulnerable was that the status of almost all the other bishops in the Scottish realm had yet to be determined once and for all. Apart from Glasgow (and Galloway which had been recognised as a suffragan of York), this involved eight bishops (with a ninth, Argyll, created before the end of the century): more than enough to constitute a province, or make up for York's lack of suffragans.

The first inkling that all these Scottish bishops might become directly subject to Rome arose the year after Jocelin gained the privilege of exemption; in his bull of 30 July 1176, *Super anxietatibus*, Alexander III dramatically reversed earlier papal support for York's claim to Scotland by instructing Scottish bishops to obey no-one by metropolitan right except the pope himself until such time as the archbishop of York wished to pursue his claim at the Curia.[124] This was only intended as a temporary arrangement: it is tempting with hindsight to regard it almost as a rough draft of *Cum universi*, but it should probably be seen as the best way Alexander could have stayed York's authority without making a commitment to an archbishopric of St Andrews. *Super anxietatibus* was a very welcome development from a Scottish point of view, but it must have been problematic for Glasgow. How could Glasgow retain its freedom if the question to be determined was the status of the Scottish church as a whole? Glasgow's fate would run a serious risk of becoming entangled with that of the other Scottish bishops, so that the issue would again centre on the question of whether there should be a Scottish province (and all provinces up to this time had a metropolitan, who in this case would have been the bishop of St Andrews), or not (in which case Glasgow could have ended up with the other bishoprics as suffragan sees of York).

The best that Jocelin might realistically have hoped for was that the 'Scottish question' would not come to a head after *Super anxietatibus*, and that all Scottish bishops (except, of course, Galloway) would *de facto* remain directly subordinate to Rome. But this was hardly a secure position. It would be understandable, therefore, if Jocelin feared that an attempt to resolve Scotland's status once and for all might be made, and that this prompted him to take the unusual step, in the weeks following the Third Lateran Council of 1179, of seeking another bull of exemption from Alexander III.[125] The 'Scottish question' may, indeed, have been raised at the council. There is a notice in a York inventory of an instruction to Scottish bishops to obey the archbishop of York 'until they come to a council to receive justice in this matter'; if this is not simply a distorted summary of a known document, then it may (as Robert Somerville has suggested) refer to a lost bull sent in the lead up to the Third Lateran

Council of March 1179.[126] Be this as it may, Scotland's status had almost certainly been on the agenda of Alexander III's legate, Cardinal Vivian, who visited Scotland in 1176 and 1177.[127] Jocelin may have scored a spectacular success in 1175; but by 1179 he may well have felt that this needed to be bolstered.

This could account for the difference in wording between the bulls of 1175 and 1179. It will be recalled that in 1175 Glasgow was described by Alexander as 'our special daughter'. Unfortunately this could be read as applying to Alexander III only, not to popes in the future. Whether or not this was what was actually intended,[128] Jocelin may have been aware of this weakness, and sought to have the phrase redrafted. This, certainly, is what was achieved by the only change to the text of the bull of 1175 (apart from updating and redrafting the list of Glasgow's rights and possessions): in the bull of 1179 the key phrase now read 'special daughter of the Roman church'. There could now be no doubt that the relationship was meant to apply to all popes. Such a clarification may have been very helpful for Jocelin; but he must still have realised that by far the best way to guarantee this for the future would be to have Glasgow's independence embedded within the framework of a definitive settlement for the Scottish Church as a whole.

This, as is well known, was secured in the bull *Cum universi*.[129] It will be recalled that according to its terms the issue of the position of Scottish bishops in the Church's hierarchy was resolved by determining that the Scottish Church was subject to no archbishop or any foreign interference and was answerable directly to the pope. There is a strong suspicion that this was Bishop Jocelin's fully worked-out plan, based on his initial breakthrough in 1175, as well as on the interim measure of the pope as the Scots' metropolitan articulated in *Super anxietatibus*.[130] There is no indication that any other Scottish bishop included in the provisions of *Cum universi* sought such independence; they were probably accustomed to regard St Andrews as their chief bishop, or at least regarded a province of St Andrews as their best bet.[131] Certainly *Cum universi* was a blow to St Andrews. Not only had its archi-episcopal claims been denied, but it was now placed on an equal footing with bishops who it had regarded as traditionally under its authority.[132]

The most poignant indication that *Cum universi* was a descendant of the bull of exemption obtained by Jocelin in 1175 is that its central idea was expressed in the phrase 'special daughter with no-one coming in between'. It will be recalled that this formula was peculiar to the bulls of 1175 and 1179 that made Glasgow an exempt diocese: if it was not in fact a feat of Jocelin's own draftsmanship, it would certainly have been cherished by him. On one level such a textual link is unremarkable: it was natural for documents to be modelled on others relating to the same subject (as was seen in the case of bulls of exemption to Spanish bishops in the twelfth century).[133] But *Cum universi* was not simply about the exemption of a diocese. What makes the link between *Cum universi* and the bulls of exemption for Glasgow noteworthy is that it shows an ability to take a key phrase from one context and apply it to a novel (if related) situation. This ability is seen equally in Jocelin's unparalleled use of the language of monastic exemption in Glasgow's bull of 1175 as in the use of the same key phrase in articulating the extraordinary notion of an exempt province in *Cum universi*. Once it is appreciated that *Cum universi* represented Glasgow's aspirations much more than anyone else's, it seems likely that we have here another example of Jocelin's carefully judged pitch for acceptance of an unprecedented idea: that the church in a kingdom should be deemed to consist only of exempt dioceses.[134]

CONCLUSION: BISHOP JOCELIN AND GLASGOW'S WELSH IDENTITY

Looking back at the texts produced by or for the cathedral establishment at Glasgow in the second half of the twelfth century, the need to sustain the diocese's independence after 1175 can readily be recognised in the *Life of Kentigern* commissioned by Bishop Jocelin from Jocelin of Furness.[135] It was not enough simply to be 'between Scotland and England': for example, in the case of St Andrews a key question was whether Scotland was part of the English realm or was an independent kingdom.[136] In Glasgow's case there was by this time no king of Strathclyde and, in that sense, no kingdom. This problem was met head-on by representing the diocese as the kingdom and the bishop as the source of royal power. It is surely no coincidence, moreover, that after the account of King Rhydderch's transfer of rulership to St Kentigern, Glasgow's status as an exempt diocese is immediately called to mind by claiming that Kentigern sought and received from the pope a privilege that 'he should be subject to no bishop, but rather should be styled and actually be the vicar and chaplain of the pope'.[137]

The promotion of a specifically Welsh identity in this period cannot, however, be attributed solely to the reign of Bishop Jocelin. It is true that the idea in the Office of Kentigern that Glasgow was in 'northern Wales' could belong to material that might be as old as the last quarter of the twelfth century, and that this could represent a conscious attempt by Bishop Jocelin to conjure up images of a language and a culture different from those of the Scots and the English. An instructive parallel would be the campaign by Bishop Bernard of St David's in the 1130s and 1140s to become archbishop of Wales; he could not refer to a kingdom corresponding to the bounds of his proposed province, but emphasised instead how the Welsh were different in language and culture from the English.[138] The only definite evidence that a Welsh identity for the diocese was articulated during Jocelin's episcopate (and afterwards) is the racial address of William I's charter for Glasgow, datable to sometime between 1173 and perhaps *ca* 1180.[139] The fact that this was copied from a charter of Mael Coluim IV shows that this aspect of the portrayal of Glasgow as different from Scotland and England must predate 1175: the production of this charter may, indeed, be associated with Jocelin's predecessor, Ingram, who could have initiated it as archdeacon of Glasgow, and approved it as the king's chancellor (remembering that Ingram held both offices simultaneously before he became bishop of Glasgow).[140]

It is clear, therefore, that the Welsh identity of the diocese of Glasgow was the result of more than just a 'propaganda campaign' by Bishop Jocelin. Although Bishop Jocelin may be recognised as the genius behind the idea that Glasgow should be an exempt diocese, the articulation of a Welsh identity (on the back of an earlier British or Cumbrian identity), at least since the 1160s, points to something more than simply personal advancement as the motive for Jocelin's ambitions for his diocese. It suggests, rather, that Jocelin was able to tap into a sentiment that he shared with the cathedral establishment: a feeling that Glasgow was not 'like' other dioceses in the kingdom, and should be regarded as a cut or two above the average.[141] This would not have been unjustified. Glasgow's cathedral at this time may have been 'meagre and narrow'[142] (especially if compared to the splendid structure being built at St Andrews from 1162),[143] but at least it was staffed by a chapter, which no other potential suffragan see of St Andrews could boast in the twelfth century.[144]

It was common for major churches to be acutely conscious of their own dignity. This did not, of course, normally lead to expressions of ethnic distinctiveness, because this could only have been made by a few (for example, by claiming to be the chief church of a people defined in the present by language and custom or by texts and 'traditions' from the past). Even among the small number of major churches that had this option, ethnicity was not always used in contexts where it might have been appropriate. There is no indication, for example, that the ecclesiastical powers at St Andrews drew attention to the predominantly Gaelic character of their putative province as a way of countering the metropolitan authority of the archbishop of York. After the failure to gain recognition in 1159, the principal expression of their aspirations was evidently architectural.[145] In Glasgow's case, the appeal to a distinct British or 'Cambrian' past through the hagiography of its patron was coupled with a contemporary invocation of Welshness. The re-imagining of the past was achieved in some style and conjured up some striking precedents, but of itself is not particularly remarkable. What stands out especially are the self-conscious (if fleeting) references to a Welsh identity in the present, as when it is declared in First Vespers that the cathedral 'dwells in northern Wales', and a deliberate decision has been taken to include 'Welsh' among the diocese's inhabitants in the address of a key royal charter. It is this, above all else, which suggests that the sense of being 'different' was important to Glasgow's cathedral establishment at least in the 1160s and later, and was not simply a fading remnant of an earlier era when Glasgow was the see of the 'bishop of the Cumbrians': the fact that neither they, nor probably any of their flock, could speak Welsh by this time was neither here nor there. This sense of Welshness also offers a perspective on how the cathedral establishment of Glasgow may have grown unhappy (after 1159, at least) with the prospect of the bishop of St Andrews as their metropolitan. At the very least it suggests that they were ambiguous about being Scottish in this context.[146] The continued failure to resolve the issue of independence in favour of St Andrews had, it seems, provided the opportunity for alternative sentiments and aspirations to take root and flourish. Meanwhile, as the legal framework of ecclesiastical relationships became tighter, there may have been a sharpening awareness of particular patterns of jurisdiction (such as the increasingly standardised exemption of some monasteries from episcopal authority) that made it possible for Jocelin to conceive of his diocese's independence and articulate this in a way that could receive papal approval. Glasgow cathedral's Welsh identity can be recognised as an expression of a keener sense of its own importance and distinctiveness, which was eventually given substance within the emerging structure of the Church as a whole by the ingenuity, opportunism and tenacity of Bishop Jocelin.

NOTES

1. See A. D. M. Barrell, 'The background to *Cum universi*: Scoto-papal relations, 1159–1192', *IR* 46 (1995) 116–38, at 128–37; Karen Miller, 'Ecclesiastical Structural Reform in Ireland and Scotland in the Eleventh and Twelfth Centuries', unpublished Ph.D. dissertation (University of Aberdeen, 2004), 192–4.

2. Alexander Penrose Forbes (ed.), *Lives of S. Ninian and S. Kentigern compiled in the Twelfth Century* (Edinburgh, 1874), 27–119, 159–242.

3. *Ibid.*, 121–33, 243–52.

4. Greta-Mary Hair and Betty I. Knott (eds), *Vespers, Matins and Lauds for St Kentigern, Patron Saint of Glasgow* (Glasgow, forthcoming). The manuscript is National Library of Scotland Adv.18.2.13b. I am extremely grateful to Greta-Mary Hair and Betty Knott for allowing me access to their edition prior to publication, and I am especially grateful to Greta-Mary Hair for her patience and generosity in explaining the technical aspects of the text to me.

5. Forbes (ed.), *Lives of S. Ninian and S. Kentigern*, 55, 182–3.

6. *Ibid.*, 94, 218.

7. For further discussion, see A. A. M. Duncan, 'St Kentigern at Glasgow Cathedral in the twelfth century', in Richard Fawcett (ed.), *Medieval Art and Architecture in the Diocese of Glasgow* (Leeds 1998), 9–24, at 18–19.

8. Barrow (ed.), *Charters of David I*, no. 15.

9. *Glas. Reg.* i. 3–4; Edinburgh, National Library of Scotland, MS Acc. 10301/1.

10. Barrow, *The Kingdom of the Scots*, 2nd edn, 203.

11. *Glas. Reg.*, i. 3. For *regio* as 'kingdom', see Barrow, *The Kingdom of the Scots*, 2nd edn, 205.

12. Hair and Knott (eds), *Vespers, Matins and Lauds for St Kentigern*; Forbes (ed.), *Lives of S. Ninian and S. Kentigern*, c.

13. Hair and Knott (eds), *Vespers, Matins and Lauds for St Kentigern*; Forbes (ed.), *Lives of S. Ninian and S. Kentigern*, xciv.

14. Hair and Knott (eds), *Vespers, Matins and Lauds for St Kentigern*; Forbes (ed.), *Lives of S. Ninian and S. Kentigern*, xcix.

15. Forbes (ed.), *Lives of S. Ninian and S. Kentigern*, 133, 252.

16. For Wales as *Britannia*, see above, 80.

17. Forbes (ed.), *Lives of S. Ninian and S. Kentigern*, 91, 216.

18. For example, 'Mael Coluim, king of Scots, to bishops, abbots, earls, and nobles, and all his worthy men, French, English, and Scots of his whole realm, greeting': *RRS*, i. no. 235.

19. Leopold Delisle (ed.), *Recueil des Actes de Henri II, Roi d'Angleterre et Duc de Normandie*, vol. i (Paris, 1909), 208.

20. *RRS*, ii. 77.

21. *RRS*, i. 74; *RRS*, ii. 77.

22. Barrow (ed.), *The Charters of King David I*, no. 76.

23. *RRS*, i. no. 239.

24. *Ibid.*, no. 240.

25. *Ibid.*, 260 n. 1.

26. Note that the issue dealt with in the charter was also the subject of two papal letters both issued on the same day in 1178/9: Somerville, *Scotia Pontificia*, nos 88 and 89 (the discussion of no. 89 points clearly to 1178/9).

27. Also, the racial address in the William I charters lists 'French and English, Scots and Galwegians and Welsh'; in the charter of Mael Coluim IV the same peoples are named, but Welsh come before Galwegians.

28. For a specific problem of payments see *RRS*, ii. no. 374 (*ca* 1193x5).

29. *RRS*, i. 76–7; *RRS*, ii. 79.

30. *RRS*, i. 69–70, 72; no. 131.

31. The Fourth Lateran Council held in 1215 is typically regarded as marking a major step in achieving this objective. A crisp account is given in D. E. R. Watt, 'The provincial council of the Scottish church, 1225–1472', in Alexander Grant and Keith J. Stringer (eds), *Medieval Scotland: Crown, Lordship and Community. Essays presented to G. W. S. Barrow* (Edinburgh, 1993), 140–55, at 141.

32. N. F. Shead, 'The origins of the medieval diocese of Glasgow', *SHR* 48 (1969) 220–5, at 223–4.

33. Colgrave and Mynors (eds), *Bede's Ecclesiastical History of the English People*, 88–9 (bk. I, ch. 27, section vii).

34. R. A. Fletcher, *The Episcopate in the Kingdom of León in the Twelfth Century* (Oxford, 1978), 38, 43.

35. *Ibid.*, 195–203, esp. 186–7.

36. Somerville, *Scotia Pontificia*, no. 76; *Glas. Reg.*, no. 32. The dating clause is faulty: see discussion in Somerville, *Scotia Pontificia*, no. 76, and A. W. Haddan and W. Stubbs (eds), *Councils and Ecclesiastical Documents Relating to Great Britian and Ireland*, vol. ii, part i (Oxford, 1873), 41–3 and n. *b*.

37. See below, 141–4.

38. Until St Andrews finally became the archi-episcopal see of the Scottish kingdom on 17 August 1472, although Glasgow's independence was restored when it, too, became an archi-episcopal see on 9 January 1492: Watt and Murray, *Fasti*, 187, 376.

39. It has been suggested that when Gregory, bishop of Dunkeld, attended the Council of Tours in May 1163 (he was the only Scottish bishop to do so, and the first known to have attended such a council), 'he won the right to sit among a group of other exempt bishops': Watt, *Medieval Church Councils*, 20; see also R. Somerville, *Pope Alexander III and the Council of Tours 1163* (Berkeley, California, 1977), 135 (where Gregory is described as sitting 'with or beside the exempt churches'), and G. W. S. Barrow, review of Somerville, *Pope Alexander III*, *SHR* 58 (1979) 196, where Gregory is described as attending 'as or in a "contingent" distinct from York'. The evidence for this is a near contemporary manuscript from Chichester in which a sederunt of a church council (shown by its editor, Timothy Reuter, to have been Tours) follows a chronicle. Bishop Gregory is found at the end of the list in a category of his own, entitled *De Scotia*, which follows the list of exempt bishops (misleadingly entitled *De Hispania*, which Reuter suggests should have read *De provincia Romana*): Timothy Reuter, 'A list of bishops attending the

Council of Tours (1163)', *Annuarium Historiae Conciliorum* 8 (1976) 116–25, at 125 and n. 65. Had Gregory been regarded as exempt, then he would presumably have been listed along with the bishops of León, Burgos and Le Puy (see discussion of exempt dioceses, below 131, 134), who appear misleadingly as *De Hispania* in the text. Gregory's isolation in the sederunt was no doubt because his status was recognised as disputed, which would explain how he succeeded in sitting apart from the archbishop of York.

40. In 1176 Alexander III instructed Scottish bishops to treat him as their metropolitan, but this was only an interim measure pending a final resolution of their status vis-à-vis York: see below, 142.

41. Previous comment on this in a Scottish context has been based on L. Duchesne and P. Fabre (eds), *Le Liber Censuum de l'Église Romaine*, 3 vols in 2 (Paris 1889–1952): e.g., Watt, 'The provincial council of the Scottish church', at 140 n. 2, citing Duchesne and Fabre (eds), *Le Liber Censuum*, i. 243, 249, and ii. 105–6; but this provides only a snapshot, and is in general not wholly reliable (see comments in Barrell, 'The background to *Cum universi*', 117 n. 5).

42. A wider remit is taken in Anzelm Weiss, *Biskupstwa bezpośrednio zależne od Stolicy Apostolskiej w średniowiecznej Europie* [The Exempted Bishoprics Subject to the Papacy in Medieval Europe] (Lublin, 1992), who includes those whose status is uncertain (e.g., before the hierarchy was consolidated in the eleventh century), or whose exemption was only conceived as a temporary measure (e.g., 'missionary bishoprics'). My attention is confined to bishoprics before the fourteenth century whose exempt status was recognised by the pope in a way that was intended to endure (and was effective as such): i.e., those which it would be relevant to compare with Scotland. I am extremely grateful to Dr Emilia Jamroziak for bringing this book to my notice, and for going through it with me and translating the title. Weiss gives only a brief discussion of Scotland: *ibid.*, 211–14.

43. Josef Engel (ed.), *Grosser Historischer Weltatlas*, vol. ii, Mittelalter (München, 1970), 72; see also Angus Mackay and David Ditchburn (eds), *Atlas of Medieval Europe* (London, 1997), 48–9, 112–13. In the list of archbishoprics and bishoprics drawn up by Cardinal Albinus towards the end of the twelfth century, seventy-three in Italy are listed as directly subordinate to Rome; near Italy there was one in Dalmatia, and three in Corsica and Sardinia: Duchesne and Fabre (eds), *Le Liber Censuum*, ii. 105–6.

44. Fletcher, *The Episcopate in the Kingdom of León*, 24, 135–8.

45. León was the main royal centre of the kingdom of León until the expansion of the kingdom in the reign of Alfonso VI; Burgos was the main royal centre of the kingdom of Castile. Oviedo had declined in significance since the early tenth century: see Fletcher, *The Episcopate in the Kingdom of León*, 68–9, 72–5. This may account for why the bishop of Oviedo had to work harder to maintain his exempt status: see Barton and Fletcher, *The World of El Cid*, 68–71, and below, 134.

46. The bishop of Palencia may, indeed, have functioned briefly as metropolitan of the kingdom of León-Castile early in the reign of Alfonso VI (1065/72–1109), but Alfonso's plan for a metropolitan for his kingdom focused on Toledo after its conquest in 1085. For all this, see A. D. Deyermond, *Epic Poetry and the Clergy: Studies on the 'Mocedades de Rodrigo'* (London, 1968), 101–5, 117–22. A claim to metropolitan status based on transfer from Toledo was also attempted at one stage by the bishop of Oviedo, but this was set in the ninth century: see Simon Barton and Richard Fletcher, *The World of El Cid: Chronicles of the Spanish Reconquest* (Manchester, 2000), 70.

47. For details and references see Broun, 'Welsh identity', 147 n. 154, and also below, 139.

48. Derek W. Lomax, *The Reconquest of Spain* (London, 1978), 149.

49. Potthast no. 14032; Elie Berger (ed.), *Registres d'Innocent IV*, 4 vols (Paris, 1884–1921), ii. no. 4783.

50. Rachel L. Stocking, *Bishops, Councils and Consensus in the Visigothic Kingdom, 589–633* (Ann Arbor, Michigan, 2000), 16 n. 105, 121 n. 13; E. A. Thompson, *The Goths in Spain* (Oxford, 1969), 159–60, 320–1.

51. JL no. 3906; *PL*, cxxxix. col. 274.

52. JL no. 4265; *PL*, cxliii. col. 681.

53. On the shrine of Notre Dame du Puy, see for example William D. Paden, jr., Tilde Sankovitch and Patricia H. Stäblein (eds), *The Poems of the Troubadour Bertran de Born* (Berkeley/Los Angeles, 1986), 24, and n. 48 where reference is made to Francisque Mandet, *Histoire du Velay*, vol. ii, *Notre-Dame du Puy: Légende, archéologie, histoire* (Le Puy, 1860).

54. Note R. Somerville, 'The Council of Clermont (1095) and Latin Christian society', *Archivum Historiae Pontificae* 12 (1974) 55–90, at 57–8.

55. JL no. 3954.

56. JL no. 4030. In due course this could be commuted to a payment of twelve marks: see Duchesne and Fabre (eds), *Le Liber Censuum*, i. 162.

57. JL no. 4287. Leo had two months earlier also given permission for the bishop of Bamberg to wear the Roman mitre, a concession which was linked to the translation to Bamberg of the body of Pope Clement II (1046–7) who had been the second bishop of Bamberg: JL no. 4283.

58. For what follows, see Pierre David, *La Pologne et l'Évangélisation de la Poméranie aux XIᵉ et XIIᵉ siècle*, Etudes Historiques et Littéraires sur la Pologne Médiévale (Paris, 1928), esp. 44–65. I have not been able to access Gerard Labuda (ed.), *Historia Pomorza*, vol. i in two parts [volume on Pomeranian history to 1466], (Poznań, 1969). A more popular account is provided in Gerard Labuda, *Wielkie Pomorze w Dziejach Polski* [Greater Pomerania in Polish History] (Poznań, 1947), esp. 18–21 for western Pomerania in the twelfth century. A useful outline of the history of the Church there may be accessed at http://www.diecezja.szczecin.opoka.org.pl/dzieje.htm#_ftn15 (Grzegorz Wejman, *Wybrane zagadnienia z*

dziejów Kościoła katolickiego na Pomorzu Zachodnim do 1945 roku).

59. David, *La Pologne*, 44–55; see also Weiss, *Biskupstwa*, 260–74 (I am very grateful to Dr Emilia Jamroziak for this reference).

60. Carl Friedrich Wilhelm Hasselbach, Johann Gottfried Ludwig Kosegarten and Baron Friedrich Ludwig Carl von Medem (eds.), *Codex Pomeraniae diplomaticus oder Sammlung der die Geschichte Pommerus und Rugens* (Greifswald 1843/1862), no. 14; JL no. 8102; *PL*, clxxix. cols 518–19. Duke Bolesław (probably in coordination with the Pomeranian Duke Warcisław) seems to have originally intended founding two sees – one at Wollin, the other at Stettin: Józef Dobosz, *Monarchia i Możni wobec Kościoła w Polsce do początku XIII wieku* (Poznań, 2002), 209. I am very grateful to Dr Emilia Jamroziak for supplying me with this reference, and for discussing with me the bibliographical peculiarities of *Codex Pomeraniae*, ed. Hasselbach and others.

61. David, *La Pologne*, 59, argued that it was the intention of Bishop Otto of Bamberg and Duke Bolesław of Poland that a diocese of Pomerania should be bound to the Polish metropolitan.

62. See Dobosz, *Monarchia i Możni wobec Kościoła*, 202–9, for how this affected Pomerania. I am very grateful to Dr Emilia Jamroziak for supplying me with this reference and for guidance on this point.

63. Hasselbach and others (eds), *Codex Pomeraniae*, nos 12 and 13; JL nos 7629 and 7785; *PL*, clxxix. cols 183–6. Innocent's initial decision in favour of Magdeburg was born of his dependence on Lothar III and Poland's support of Innocent's rival, Anacletus II; by 1136 Poland had abandoned Anacletus for Innocent. See Dobosz, *Monarchia i Możni wobec Kościoła*, 222–5. I am very grateful to Emilia Jamroziak for supplying me with this reference. See also David, *La Pologne*, 61–2.

64. A. Gieysztor, 'Medieval Poland', trans. K. Cękalska, in Stefan Kieniewicz, *History of Poland* (Warsaw, 1968), 29–165, at 108.

65. JL no. 16154; *PL*, cciv. cols 1301–3; Hasselbach and others (eds), *Codex Pomeraniae*, no. 63; David, *La Pologne*, 64–5.

66. . . . *libertatem quoque qua sedes ipsa* [Wollin] *soli fuit Romano pontifici a prima sui institutione subjecta, sicut est hactenus observata, ratam habemus et perpetuis temporibus inviolabilem permanere sancimus . . .* : *PL*, cciv. col. 1302. Gniezno's claims were, nonetheless, still a source of contention much later: see I. Sułkowska-Kuraś and S. Kuraś (eds), *Bullarium Poloniae* (Rzym, 1982), no. 29 (letter of Urban VI, 1380).

67. A different view is taken in Weiss, *Biskupstwa*, 270–1, but this is appropriate for his looser definition of exemption (see above, n. 42). I am grateful to Dr Emilia Jamroziak for translating this section of Weiss's book for me.

68. As noticed by David, *La Pologne*, 63. Weiss, *Biskupstwa*, 270, however, emphasises the failure in the bull to mention a metropolitan.

69. Hasselbach and others (eds), *Codex Pomeraniae*, no. 21: . . . *communis eorundem principum* [Bolesław of Poland and Wartisław of Pomerania]

electio et domini pape Innocentii consecratio me, quamvis indignum, primum Pomeranie prefecit episcopum. . .

70. There is an account of how Otto of Bamberg sent a ring to Pope Honorius II (1124–30) that it might be consecrated and returned, but it is difficult to know what significance should be given this: David, *La Pologne*, 55–6 (and 56 n. 3 for the text). Weiss, *Biskupstwa*, 270 refers to Wojciech's receipt in 1140 of a ring from Otto of Bamberg.

71. See, for example, JL nos 4281 (1052) and 4300 (1053); and Carl Sachsse, 'Tiara und Mitra der Päpste', *Zeitschrift für Kirchengeschichte* 35 (1914) 481–501.

72. In 1139 Pope Innocent II, when he sent a pallium to the new bishop of Bamberg, confirmed Bamberg's privileges, and granted additionally that the bishop could process with a cross carried before his face, 'saving, of course, the *reverentia* of the metropolitan of Mainz': JL no. 8048; *PL*, clxxix. cols 483–4. This is not the same as reserving Mainz's metropolitan authority: neither was the same caveat attached by Innocent to the wearing of the pallium. In the list of bishoprics and archbishoprics by Albinus, the diocese of Bamberg appears in the province of Mainz; in the more accurate list by Censius, however, it is given as directly subject to Rome (still owing a white horse with saddle every year, or twelve marks): Duchesne and Fabre (eds), *Le Liber Censuum*, i. 161–2; ii. 98. The bishop of Bamberg's continued entitlement to wear the pallium was confirmed by Pope Gregory IX in 1235: Potthast no. 9955.

73. JL no. 5601; R. A. Fletcher, *St James's Catapult. The Life and Times of Diego Gelmírez of Santiago de Compostela* (Oxford, 1984), 195–6.

74. JL no. 5986; Fletcher, *St James's Catapult*, 196–7.

75. Fletcher, *The Episcopate in the Kingdom of León*, 68–9, 72–3.

76. Ibid., 69, 73–5. The bull restoring León's freedom is lost, but its exempt status was recognised by 27 December 1135 when it was upheld by Innocent II in a letter rebuking the archbishop of Compostelo and referring to Toledo's presumption: JL no. 7735; *PL*, clxxix. cols 249–50. Oviedo may have had to work harder to preserve its independence because it had ceased since the early tenth century to be a royal centre and had become 'something of a backwater' (Barton and Fletcher, *The World of El Cid*, 69).

77. JL no. 7160; Fletcher, *St James's Catapult*, 196–212.

78. JL no. 5601; *PL*, cli. cols 440–1.

79. This is true also of Cartagena, which shares with Glasgow the fact that its provincial identity was disputed (see above, 131).

80. For a quick appreciation of how many new bishoprics were created in Spain and eastern Europe in this period, and of the pace of expansion, see Bartlett, *The Making of Europe*, maps 2 and 3.

81. Although the bishopric of Zamora was not part of the Visigothic hierarchy, it was not a new creation in 1121. It originated in the ninth century, but

ceased to have a bishop in the eleventh: Fletcher, *The Episcopate in the Kingdom of León*, 42–3.

82. Professor Watt argued cogently that the context for the creation of a diocese of Galloway obedient to York is David I's agreement with Henry I and Archbishop Thurstan in 1126–7 in which David secured the consecration of Robert, bishop of St Andrews, without professing obedience to Thurstan: Watt, *Medieval Church Councils*, 14. A case for Fergus, lord of Galloway, as prime mover has recently been made (Oram, *The Lordship of Galloway*, 171–3), although the weight placed by Oram on the bishop of Galloway's obedience to York fails to persuade in the light of Watt's discussion.

83. Although the case for regarding Glasgow as a suffragan of Canterbury was articulated vigorously by Archbishop Ralph to Pope Calixtus II in 1119 (James Raine (ed.), *The Historians of the Church of York and its Archbishops*, 3 vols, ii (London, 1886), 241), and was reactivated in 1176 (see above, 112), this never received papal backing.

84. 1164 is the earliest possible date of Somerville, *Scotia Pontificia*, no. 68.

85. Durkan, 'Glasgow diocese and the claims of York', 89–90.

86. N. F. Shead, 'The origins of the medieval diocese of Glasgow', *SHR* 48 (1969) 220–5, at 221.

87. Charles Johnson and others (eds), *Hugh the Chanter*, 212–13.

88. Duncan, *The Kingship of the Scots*, 89.

89. See above, 113–14.

90. Somerville, *Scotia Pontificia*, no. 10.

91. See above, 112.

92. Somerville, *Scotia Pontificia*, no. 43; Duncan, *The Kingship of the Scots*, 95–7.

93. *Ibid.*, 97.

94. Somerville, *Scotia Pontificia*, no. 57 and comment.

95. E. Cambridge, 'The early building-history of St Andrews Cathedral, Fife, and its context in northern transitional architecture', *Antiquaries Journal* 57 (1977) 277–88.

96. Malcolm Thurlby, 'St Andrews Cathedral-Priory and the beginnings of Gothic architecture in northern Britain', in John Higgitt (ed.), *Medieval Art and Architecture in the Diocese of St Andrews* (Leeds, 1994), 47–60, at 56. See also C. Wilson, 'The Cistercians as "missionaries of Gothic" in northern England', in C. Norton and D. Park (eds), *Cistercian Art and Architecture in the British Isles* (Cambridge, 1986), 86–116, at 97.

97. Watt and Murray, *Fasti*, 188.

98. Somerville, *Scotia Pontificia*, no. 54.

99. *RRS*, i. 29.

100. Presumably he could have performed both offices with the help of clerks and officers, and need not be regarded too literally as an absentee archdeacon, *pace* Watt and Murray, *Fasti*, 196.

101. Somerville, *Scotia Pontificia*, no. 62; *Glas. Reg.*, no. 26.
102. Somerville, *Scotia Pontificia*, no. 39.
103. *Ibid.*, no. 48 and frontispiece. Bishop Gregory of Dunkeld attended the Council of Tours which met on 19 May, and took this opportunity to obtain the privilege of protection (dated 7 June). There is no indication that he sought exempt status for himself (see n. 39 above): the most notable feature of the privilege he obtained was a concern to limit the election of his successors to the 'canons of Dunkeld' (a problematic phrase: see Watt and Murray, *Fasti*, 132).
104. As noted in Haddan and Stubbs (eds), *Councils and Ecclesiastical Documents*, ii (i). 43 n. *b*.
105. Somerville, *Scotia Pontificia*, no. 86; *Glas. Reg.*, no. 51 (as noted in Haddan and Stubbs (eds), *Councils and Ecclesiastical Documents*, ii (i). 45).
106. Somerville, *Scotia Pontificia*, nos 111 and 135; *Glas. Reg.*, nos 54 and 62.
107. Durkan, 'Glasgow diocese and the claims of York', 98.
108. Somerville, *Scotia Pontificia*, no. 59; *Glas. Reg.*, no. 467.
109. I. S. Robinson, *The Papacy 1073–1198: Continuity and Innovation* (Cambridge, 1990), 234–5; Kenneth Pennington, *Pope and Bishops: the Papal Monarchy in the Twelfth and Thirteenth Centuries* (Philadelphia, 1984), 155–6.
110. Somerville, *Scotia Pontificia*, no. 35, evidently following earlier privileges (*ibid.*, nos 24 and 32), which are lost but implied in no. 35.
111. *nulli præter Romano metropolitano subjecti sint; et omnes qui tibi in eadem sede successerint, per manum Romani pontificis tanquam speciales Romanæ sedis suffraganei consecrentur*: JL no. 5601; *PL*, cli. cols 440–1. The bull for Oviedo in 1105 has almost identical wording: *nulli unquam præter Romanum metropolitano subjecti sint, et omnes qui tibi in eadem sede successuri sunt per manum Romani pontificis tanquam specialis* [sic] *Romanæ sedis suffraganei consecrentur*: JL no. 6039; *PL*, clxiii. cols 168–9. Note also the bull of 1105 confirming the bishop of Le Puy's right to the pallium: *nulli præter Romanum metropolitano subjecti sint, et omnes qui tibi in eamdem* [sic] *sede successuri sunt per manum Romani pontificis tanquam speciales Romanæ sedis suffraganei consecrentur*: *ibid.*, cols 155–6. Another example is Alexander III's confirmation of the bishop of León's privileges in 1163: *nulli unquam metropolitano debeatis, nisi tantum Romano pontifici subjacere, et omnes qui tibi in eadem sede successerint per manus* [pl.] *Romani pontificis tanquam speciales Romanæ sedis suffraganei consecrentur*: JL no.10859; *PL*, cc. cols 219–22.
112. In Mallorca's case the textual situation is complicated. (The documents discussed below are published in Ferrer Flórez, 'Mallorca y la teocracia pontificia', *Analecta Sacra Tarraconensia. Revista de Ciencias Histórico-Eclasiásticas* 23 (1950) 15–30.) The earliest extant papal definition of Mallorca's status is in letters of Innocent IV, one to the bishop of Mallorca

and another to the archbishops and bishops of Spain, both dated 1 April 1248. The latter document provides the closest parallel to the phrase 'special daughter of the Roman church with no-one coming in between' used of Glasgow in the bull of 1179. In his letter to Spanish bishops and archbishops, Innocent IV reported that Gregory IX declared it 'to pertain to the apostolic see with no intermediary', *ad Sedem Apostolicam . . . nullo medio pertinere*. Gregory IX was pope when Mallorca was conquered from the Moors and a new diocese created. That it was Gregory IX himself who first used these words is confirmed by notarial instruments of May 1267 recording Mallorca's defence of its independence from the archbishop of Tarragona. Here a very similar phrase is used repeatedly: *Maioricensis Ecclesia ad Romam Ecclesiam nullo medio pertinet*, 'the church of Mallorca pertains to the apostolic see with no intermediary'. In one place this phrase is attributed directly to Gregory IX.

113. It is probably fruitless to guess how Jocelin came to know of the existence of exempt bishops and of the phrase 'special daughter' applied to monasteries: the former must have been known of in Scotland at least since Bishop Gregory met the bishops of León, Burgos and Le Puy at the Council of Tours in 1163 (see above, n. 39); and Jocelin could have picked up the latter from the abbot of Kelso (who he must have known, especially when Jocelin was abbot of Melrose a dozen miles from Kelso).

114. N. F. Shead, 'Jocelin, abbot of Melrose (1170–1174) and bishop of Glasgow (1175–1199)', *IR* 54 (2003) 1–22, at 3, 6.

115. Somerville, *Scotia Pontificia*, no. 74; *Glas. Reg.*, no. 37.

116. Alexander was referring to the difficult beginning of his pontificate, when he was threatened by a rival pope supported by the emperor (the second antipope to be known as Victor IV), and had to wait for nearly a year before being recognised by England and France: Scotland was among the first to support Alexander.

117. Stevenson (ed.), *Chronica de Mailros*, 87.

118. Stones (ed.), *Anglo-Scottish Relations*, 4–5.

119. Michael Richter, 'Canterbury's primacy in Wales and the first stage of Bishop Bernard's opposition', *Journal of Ecclesiastical History* 22 (1971) 177–89, at 179–81; Michael Richter, *Giraldus Cambrensis: the Growth of the Welsh Nation*, rev. edn (Aberystwyth, 1976), 39.

120. Beginning with Pascal II's injunction to Scottish bishops in 1100/1 to obey the archbishop of York as their metropolitan: Somerville, *Scotia Pontificia*, no. 1.

121. It is a moot point, however, whether the formula 'our special daughter' represented Jocelin's 'pitch', or a rewording of 'special daughter of the Roman church', which Jocelin may have asked for, and which he finally achieved in the bull of 1179. For the difference between these formulae, see below, 143.

122. Robinson, *The Papacy 1073–1198*, 237–9.

123. This continued to be a problem after the twelfth century: see Broun, 'Welsh identity', 163 n. 225.
124. Somerville, *Scotia Pontificia*, no. 80.
125. By this stage Jocelin's chief opponent would have been Roger, archbishop of York; the death of Richard, bishop of St Andrews, in 1178 initiated a decade of disputed succession during which time an archbishopric of St Andrews would have been off the immediate agenda. An important discussion of the bull of 1179 is Barrell, 'The background to *Cum universi*', 119–22, although his suggested redating of the outbreak of the disputed succession at St Andrews to 1177 rather than 1178 is unconvincing: see Paul C. Ferguson, *Medieval Papal Representatives in Scotland: Legates, Nuncios, and Judges-Delegate*, Stair Society (Edinburgh, 1997), 56, n. 153.
126. Somerville, *Scotia Pontificia*, no. 80, commentary. Barrell, 'The background to *Cum universi*', 121, has argued that Alexander III may have resumed a pro-York stance in April 1178, although the evidence is a bull that is not dated to a pontifical year: this document must be regarded as different from the item noted in a York inventory, which does not fit readily with any known text.
127. Barrell, 'The background to *Cum universi*', 120; Stubbs (ed.), *Gesta*, i. 117. For Vivian as legate in Scotland, see Ferguson, *Medieval Papal Representatives*, 53–5.
128. It may also be recalled (see 140 above) that Alexander III, at about the same time, gave Jocelin a 'special privilege of liberty' for the duration of Jocelin's episcopate. Was the 1175 bull of exemption also intended by Alexander to be a personal measure, limited to his own pontificate? If so, this was not spelt out in the same way as it was made clear in the special privilege for Jocelin. In Howden's account of the council of Northampton in 1176 in his *Chronicle* (Stubbs (ed.), *Chronica*, ii. 92) Jocelin is reported as referring to Glasgow as *specialis filia . . . Romanae ecclesie*; but this is not included in the account of the council given in Howden's earlier work (Stubbs (ed.), *Gesta*, i. 111–12).
129. Somerville, *Scotia Pontificia*, no. 156, datable to either 1189 or 1192: see n. 1, above.
130. It has been suggested that *Super anxietatibus* may have been Jocelin's initiative; note the comment in Ferguson, *Medieval Papal Representatives*, 52, that 'it is perhaps indicative of the premier role which the see of Glasgow under bishop Jocelin appears to have played in obtaining papal support against York that the text of the bull is preserved only in the *Registrum Vetus* of Glasgow'.
131. On Bishop Gregory of Dunkeld at the Council of Tours in 1163, see above, n. 39.
132. Broun, 'The church of St Andrews and its foundation-legend'.
133. See above, 139 and 154 n. 111.

134. The moving chairs of royal politics and ecclesiastical vacancies would have been decidedly more favourable for Jocelin if 1189 were accepted as the date of *Cum universi*: see Broun, 'Welsh identity', 167 n. 236.

135. Unfortunately this cannot be dated with any precision within Jocelin's episcopate. It has been suggested that it may be the earliest of Jocelin of Furness's four extant hagiographical works: George McFadden, 'The *Life of Waldef* and its author, Jocelin of Furness', *IR* 6 (1955) 5–13, at, 9–10.

136. See above, 113–14.

137. Forbes (ed.), *Lives of S. Ninian and S. Kentigern*, 95, 219; see also Duncan, 'St Kentigern at Glasgow Cathedral', 18. For speculation about this as possible kite-flying for a pallium, see Broun, 'Welsh identity', 168 n. 239.

138. W. S. Davies (ed.), *Giraldus Cambrensis: De Invectionibus*, in *Y Cymmrodor: the Magazine of the Honourable Society of Cymmrodorion* 30 (1920), at 142. There is, by the way, no suggestion that Bernard included Glasgow in his plans!

139. *RRS*, ii. no. 179; see n. 26 for the possibility of dating this to 1178/9.

140. See above, 137.

141. Jocelin was no stranger to his diocese, of course. Not only had he been a monk of the Cistercian abbey of Melrose all his adult life, becoming abbot in 1170, but his family can be linked to Clydesdale: Shead, 'Jocelin', 2.

142. These words (*exilis . . . et angusta*) were probably used of Bishop John's cathedral (dedicated in 1136) in a charter of William I (datable to 1189×95, and probably drafted by a Glasgow clerk) supporting Jocelin's fund-raising effort for a new cathedral after the old one had been destroyed by fire: *RRS*, ii. no. 316; see also Barrow, *The Kingdom of the Scots*, 2nd edn, 213. Jocelin is reported to have 'gloriously magnified' the cathedral in 1181 (Stevenson (ed.), *Chronica de Mailros*, 91). For the archaeological evidence for Bishop John's and Bishop Jocelin's cathedrals, see now S. T. Driscoll, with contributions by Susan Bain and others, *Excavations at Glasgow Cathedral 1988–1997* (London, 2002).

143. See n. 96, above.

144. The first reference to a dean and chapter of Glasgow is in a papal letter of 7 March 1161 (Somerville, *Scotia Pontificia*, no. 73): see Barrow, *The Kingdom of the Scots*, 2nd edn, 212, and n. 48, plus N. F. Shead, review of Barrow, *David I and the Church of Glasgow*, in *SHR* 76 (1997) 264–5, at 265, for 1161 in preference to Somerville's 1175. There were six prebends by the time of Bishop John's death in 1147, and another was created by Bishop Herbert: Barrow, *The Kingdom of the Scots*, 2nd edn, 211. It may be recalled (see n. 39 above) that canons were referred to in Dunkeld in Alexander III's bull of protection in 1163; however, a collegiate chapter (as opposed to a synodal one) was only established under Bishop Gilbert (1229/30–6): Watt and Murray, *Fasti*, 132.

145. See above, 137.

146. Their Scottish identity is discussed below, 163–4.

PART III

Sovereign Kingship

6

The Inauguration of Alexander III (1249) and the Portrayal of Scotland as a Sovereign Kingdom

On the face of it, Scottish independence had finally been secured by the end of the twelfth century. In the Quitclaim of Canterbury, Richard I had agreed that the objectionable Treaty of Falaise be cancelled, while in *Cum universi* the papacy had recognised that the kingdom was not part of England. This is all very well as far as it goes. On closer examination, though, it is not at all clear that anyone in 1200 thought of Scottish independence in a straightforward sense that we might recognise today; Scotland was not yet seen by its leading figures as a single jurisdiction under a sovereign ruler. *Cum universi* may have rescued the kingdom from the authority of foreign archbishops, but it did not give *Ecclesia Scoticana*, the Scottish Church, an institutional identity of its own as a province with its own metropolitan. It is true that, at least in the ecclesiastical sphere, there had been those who had pressed for the kingdom to be recognised as an independent entity in the normal way with an archbishop of St Andrews; but, as we have seen, this was not universally welcomed, and in the end a rather different notion of ecclesiastical independence had won the day. The Quitclaim of Canterbury, for its part, signified the restoration of the previous relationship between the kings, not a recognition that the king of Scots stood on an equal footing with his neighbour. There is nothing to suggest that William saw himself as anything other than a client of Richard I. When it came to performing homage to Richard's successor, John, in November 1200, there is no reason to suppose that William was uncomfortable with the special arrangements John made for the event: an impressive gathering of the great and good of the Angevin realm were invited to Lincoln to witness William's act of subordination on a conspicuous mound outside the city walls.[1] What William had foremost on his mind was that he should regain the northern counties of England which his brother, Mael Coluim IV, had agreed to hand over to Henry II in 1157. He may, indeed, have hoped that, now that John had made such a conspicuous display of becoming his superior, John might be ready to offer 'good lordship' and acknowledge William's claims – a hope that was frustrated in the 'long discussion' which immediately followed. There is no evidence that William felt that any special arrangements were needed to safeguard his royal dignity, or that he felt demeaned by the way the ceremony of homage itself had been staged.

There are clear indications of a fundamental change by the reign of William's grandson, Alexander III (1249–86). When Alexander finally did homage to Edward I on 28 October 1278, the setting and choreography were markedly different from the events at Lincoln in 1200. This time the status of Scottish kingship was indeed the paramount cause of concern. In the protracted diplomacy leading up to the homage which Alexander could not avoid rendering to Edward for his English possessions, extreme care was taken by Alexander to avoid the formal subordination of his kingship.[2] Although the ceremony took place during parliament at Westminster, it was performed in the king's chamber rather than in a more public space (albeit in front of at least thirty-four witnesses). After Edward had received Alexander's homage, it was conceded, in deference to his royal status, that Alexander would not swear fealty in person, but that Robert Bruce, earl of Carrick, would take the oath on Alexander's soul. This much presumably had been planned, and is as far as the official English record of the event goes.[3] It may also have been agreed that, in future, kings of Scots would not be summoned to perform homage at a particular time and place, but that the king of England would receive it at a place and time of the king of Scots' choosing.[4] In a Scottish account (which there is no good reason to doubt), however, the issue of the king of England's claim to homage for the kingdom of Scotland was raised in an unscripted intervention by the bishop of Norwich. Alexander's reply was an unambiguous denial of English lordship: 'nobody but God alone has the right to the homage for my realm of Scotland, and I hold it of nobody but God alone'.[5] Professor Duncan has argued that this formula had been agreed and rehearsed when the king and a sizeable gathering of Scottish leaders met at Roxburgh earlier in October prior to Alexander's departure for Westminster. The idea that Scotland was held by the king of God alone may not have been brand new, of course. It is also found in the account of a healing miracle at St Margaret's shrine in Dunfermline abbey at the time of the Battle of Largs (1263), and in the reported response of Bishop Robert Wishart of Glasgow to Edward I's claim to suzerainty over Scotland at Norham on 10 May 1291.[6] Be this as it may, if it is put together with the Treaty of Perth (1266) and its statement about how 'the laws and customs of the kingdom of Scotland' were to be applied to all,[7] it is clear that Scottish independence had come to be understood by Alexander and his leading men in terms of a sovereign king ruling a unified territory.

When did this idea first take root among those close to the kingship? In this chapter it is argued that the inauguration of Alexander III on 13 July 1249 can be regarded as the earliest extended expression of the claim that Scotland was a sovereign realm. It was much more than a few carefully chosen words. Indeed, this particular occasion can be recognised as an ingenious piece of theatre designed to proclaim the kingship as on a par with any other despite the handicap of being denied the most obvious props of coronation and anointment. A similar resourcefulness and creativity in articulating an enhanced image of Scottish kingship has been noticed in the remarkable small seal of Alexander III's minority, whose matrix was struck within a year of the inauguration.[8] The seal and the inauguration were both exceptionally potent opportunities for expressing the nature of a kingship's authority. But the inauguration was particularly significant, not only because it was a bigger and more flexible medium for making symbolic statements, but also because it was presented to a gathering of those near the kingship – both in relation to their social and political standing and their location – who could potentially, as a body, share its message. It can also be regarded as a more coherent single statement of sovereign kingship than the seal of minority, which, at some stage not long after it was first struck, appears not to have been deemed to present an entirely satisfactory or full statement of Alexander III's royal authority: it has been shown that it was not until sometime between June 1250 and June 1252 (probably after the destruction of the Great Seal in January 1252) that the legend *Rex Scottorum Dei Gratia* was added in the field which bore the king's image,[9] presumably as an explicit claim to the status normally conferred by anointment.[10]

Before Alexander's inauguration is examined further, we will return to the bishopric of Glasgow, where it is possible to trace this changing perspective on the Scottish kingdom, albeit in a more learned and less certain context. It can be argued that the see which had been so keen to preserve its freedom came, by the 1260s, to base its aspirations on a new conception of Scotland's ancient territorial integrity which embraced the diocese of Glasgow, rather than on an idea that Glasgow was not part of 'Scotland'.

GLASGOW'S SCOTTISH IDENTITY

Even when Glasgow's cathedral establishment was projecting an image of the diocese as somewhere distinct from Scotland, this had not precluded it from also seeing itself as 'Scottish'. This may seem paradoxical. It foreshadowed the fact, though, that in the end it was as part of *Ecclesia Scoticana* that Glasgow's independence had finally been secured by the provisions of *Cum universi*. The articulation of its Scottishness can, moreover, be found side by side with expressions of Welsh identity. In the same responsory for First Vespers in which Glasgow was located 'in northern Wales not far from *Albania*', Kentigern's breath is likened to a torch burning in *Scocia*. This recalls Jocelin's *Life*, in which Kentigern is portrayed as an evangelist in *Albania* (i.e., Scotland north of the Forth) as well as in Galloway after he had become bishop of Glasgow.[11] This Scottish profile for Kentigern and his see is also found in the remarkable poem composed by a clerk of Glasgow, William, celebrating the killing of Somairle (Somerled) in battle at Renfrew in 1164.[12] The poem must have been written very soon afterwards, for it has been interpolated into Cambridge, Corpus Christi College MS 139 in a hand of this period (probably soon after the manuscript was produced in 1164 × 6).[13] In it Kentigern is repeatedly referred to as a 'Scottish saint' (*sanctus Scotticanus*). There is an important distinction drawn in the poem, however, between two Latin words meaning 'Scottish': *Scotticanus* and *Albanicus*. Kentigern is *Scotticanus*; but it was 'a Scottish force' (*uis Albanica*), along with the men of Argyll and the Isles, who constituted a 'barbarous host threatening the gentle' (*minatur mites manus barbara*) in the years of oppression leading up to the battle. Glasgow was quite distinct from *Albania*, the historic core of the kingdom north of the Forth; but it could still be Scottish. This appears to be a precocious attempt to articulate a Scottish identity for the kingdom as a whole at a time when 'Scotland' (i.e., the region between the Forth and the Spey) was routinely regarded as simply one of a number of 'countries' in the realm of the king of Scots.[14] A similar distinction between *Scocia* (the kingdom as a whole) and *Albania* ('Scotland' north of the Forth) may also be detected in the responsories (but not the readings) in the Office of St Kentigern in the Sprouston Breviary. The fact that this apparent distinction between 'Scotland' and 'Scottish' in an inclusive sense (*Scocia, Scotticanus*), meaning '(of) the realm of the king of Scots', and 'Scotland' and 'Scottish' in a restricted sense (*Albania, Albanicus*), as pertaining to the region north of the Forth, only works in Latin suggests that this was not a widely held view. Presumably it was important to the cathedral establishment at the time. It could have made it easier for them to reconcile their allegiance to the king of Scots with their desire to distance themselves from the putative Scottish province with St Andrews as its metropolitan.

Succeeding generations of the cathedral establishment inhabited a very different ecclesiastical landscape in which being Scottish would, for them, lose its earlier ambiguity. A crucial development was the setting up in 1225 of a Scottish provincial council as the organ of government for the Scottish Church.[15] This meant that the diocesan independence enshrined in *Cum universi* was finally placed on an enduring practical footing. The diocese of Glasgow, like any other in the kingdom at that time (except Galloway, which was excluded from the provisions of *Cum universi*), functioned from then on within a specifically Scottish structure. This allowed it, without compromising its freedom from archi-episcopal authority, to operate effectively as part of the wider Church by responding to the decrees of legatine or general councils, to requests for financial contributions or demands for taxation, as well as to the ever-present need to maintain discipline and settle disputes. The Scottish provincial council also changed the nature of the relationship between king and bishops, permitting the king to exercise influence over them all at once, making it much easier for him to maintain and implement policies relating to the Church (for example, on papal taxation).[16] Since the time of Bishop John there had been a close link between bishops of Glasgow and kings of Scots. The Scottish provincial council created a new framework for that relationship, a framework which would presumably have reinforced the fact that Glasgow was now part of the Scottish Church. At the same time there would, in this pattern of relationships, have been little need to emphasise Glasgow's distinctiveness.

It is difficult to pinpoint when the Welsh element in Glasgow's identity lost its vitality. At a more general level, it can be shown in the Chronicle of Melrose that, around 1220, monks at Melrose, on the fringe of the diocese, began to regard the south-east of the kingdom, where they were situated, as part of 'Scotland'.[17] Before this point it is likely that they would have regarded themselves as living in part of 'England' in the kingdom of the Scots.[18] Finally, at some stage between the late 1260s and late 1280s, they began to identify themselves as 'Scots' (rather than as 'English').[19] This probably reflected the point when a kingdom-based Scottish identity became widespread in the diocese as a whole. From then on 'Scotland' and 'Scottish' would, in the various vernaculars spoken by the king's subjects, have meant the territory of the kingdom and that which pertains to it – meanings which we can recognise today.

JOHN OF CHEAM'S CLAIM TO CARLISLE AND THE SIGNIFICANCE OF STAINMORE

There is one tantalising indication that, by the second half of the thirteenth century, what had been Welsh may have been replaced by this growing kingdom-centred Scottish identity. Bishop John of Cheam, a remarkable Englishman who had probably never set foot in Scotland before becoming bishop of Glasgow in 1259, decided at some point towards the end of his reign, around 1265, to insist that his diocese should extend south to the Rere Cross at Stainmore, thereby incorporating the diocese of Carlisle in its entirety. Professor Barrow has observed that Cheam was 'effectively claiming that the Glasgow bishopric was coterminous with the kingdom of Strathclyde'.[20] Is this what John of Cheam had in mind? Or was his scheme fuelled by some other kind of historical precedent?

There is, unfortunately, no extant statement from Cheam justifying this bold move: it is said in the Lanercost Chronicle merely that it was based on 'ancient right' (*ius antiquum*).[21] The bishopric of Carlisle had been founded by Henry I of England in 1133: there is some evidence that Bishop John of Glasgow and his predecessor, Michael, performed episcopal functions in Cumberland and Westmorland before this date.[22] This may have been what Cheam had in mind. The specific mention of Stainmore, however, could suggest another inspiration for Cheam's claim to Carlisle, one that would not have been available much earlier than the mid-thirteenth century. In order to reveal what this was, we need to embark on a brief sojourn into the text-history of king-lists and chronicles.

The key here is the unexpected appearance of Stainmore deep in Scotland's imagined past. In book III chapter 2 of Fordun's chronicle contradictory accounts are given of the bounds of the kingdom ruled by Fergus (son of Erc), who was regarded as the first Scottish king according to king-lists current in Scotland during the thirteenth century. It is the first of these accounts that concerns us. Here it is claimed that Fergus held sway from Stainmore in the south as far as Orkney in the north. A similar statement is found in the oldest extant manuscript of Wyntoun's *Original Chronicle*, except that Drumalban (i.e., the mountain range on the eastern bounds of Argyll) is mentioned rather than Orkney.[23] These accounts of the limits of Fergus's realm have been derived ultimately from a version of the Scottish king-list which can be dated to the reign of Alexander II (1214–49).

If these statements in Fordun and Wyntoun are set alongside the copy of the king-list that is most closely related to them (which is known to scholarship as king-list 'D'),[24] a clear progression can be discerned: first, the realm is limited to Argyll in the king-list ('beyond Drumalban' is viewed from the east); then Stainmore is introduced (as in Wyntoun); and finally Drumalban is replaced by Orkney (as in Fordun).

KING-LIST D:[25]

Fergus son of Erc reigned first in Scotland for three years beyond 'Druchin' [an inherited garbling of Drumalban], and from 'Druchin Albane' as far as 'Scuagh muner' and up to 'Inchgal' [i.e., the Hebrides].

WYNTOUN'S *ORIGINAL CHRONICLE*, BOOK IV, CHAPTER 8:[26]

. . . Fergus Erthswne, that thre yhere
Made hym beyhond the Drwm to stere
Oure all the hychtis evyrilkane,
As thai ly fra Drwmalbane
Tyll Stanmore and Inchegall,
Kyng he mad hym oure thaim all.

FORDUN'S *CHRONICLE OF THE SCOTTISH PEOPLE*, BOOK III, CHAPTER 2:[27]

In the space of less than three years after this [the expulsion of Romans and Britons] Fergus held under his sway all regions of the kingdom north and south of the Scottish Water [i.e., the Firth of Forth] that had been in the possession of his ancestors from ancient times, that is the lands from the Stony Moor [Stainmore] to 'Inchegal' [i.e., the Hebrides] and the Orkney islands.

This is *not* to say that Fordun was here copying Wyntoun, or that Wyntoun copied king-list D: Fordun completed his work sometime between 1384 and 1387, Wyntoun sometime between 1408 and 1424, and king-list D is in the hand of James Gray, secretary to William Shevez and James Stewart, archbishops of St Andrews respectively in 1476–97 and 1497–1504.[28] The progression is between their (lost) sources. The

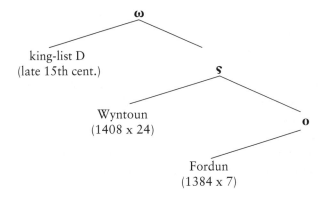

best way to appreciate these interrelationships is in a diagram, using Greek letters to indicate texts that do not survive, and are therefore hypothetical.[29] The latest date for ω is probably 1306 or not long thereafter.[30]

It may be noted in passing that o can be identified as one of three versions of the Scottish king-list used in the construction of Fordun's chronicle. It is potentially of great significance, and will be discussed in more detail in chapter 9.

The decision to make Stainmore one of the kingdom's limits occurred in the middle of this progression, in the text dubbed ς in the diagram. In order to attempt to understand why this happened it is necessary to examine the difficult passage in Wyntoun more closely. We are told here that Fergus ruled beyond Drumalban, and from Drumalban to Stainmore and the Hebrides. This only makes sense if we are to suppose that Drumalban was conceived as a mid-point, with the realm stretching in one direction as far as the Outer Isles, and in the other direction down to Cumberland. Perhaps this is what Wyntoun intended, hence his remark that Fergus 'ruled all the heights', as if Drumalban was mentioned because it was a central or notable range of mountains. Wyntoun's source (ς), however, was almost certainly a more prosaic text, like king-list D, in which the bounds of Fergus's realm were given without comment. Is it possible that Stainmore was introduced in ς without realising that it made nonsense of Drumalban as one of the kingdom's limits?

The answer is probably yes. It is more than likely that the statement of the bounds of Fergus's kingdom as found in king-list D was, at best, incompletely understood. The problem was the name rendered in king-list D as 'Scuagh muner'. A comparison with other witnesses of the king-list suggests that this was earlier rendered as 'Stuaghmuner'; if the sequence of minims in '-mun-' is reanalysed, then this can be read as 'Stuaginnuer', a possible spelling of *Stúag* (or *Túag*) *in (n)ber*, the mouth of the River Bann (remembering that *b* in *in(n)ber* would be pronounced like 'v' and written as 'u' in medieval Latin).[31] The Bann was a notable early medieval boundary; it denoted the western limit of the reduced province of Ulaid (including Dál Riata, whose western limit was nearby at the River Bush).[32] 'Stuaginnuer' may have been comprehensible to the scholar responsible for the earliest Latin Scottish king-list to include kings of Dál Riata (datable to the reign of William I: 1165–1214); he (or a source) certainly seems to have known what they were doing in describing Dál Riata's eastern and northern limits as Drumalban and the Hebrides. The various ways in which 'Stuaginnuer' was treated in subsequent king-list texts, however, suggests that it soon become meaningless to scribes in eastern Scotland. In some it was simply omitted;[33] in king-list E it was amended to the 'Irish Sea';[34] in others it became even more unintelligible, such as 'Sluagh muner' and 'Sluaghmaner'.[35] In this context the interpretation of something like 'Stuaghmuner' as Stainmore in ѕ can readily be appreciated as an attempt to find a meaningful form for what had become an incomprehensible name. The resulting sentence may not have made immediate sense; it could, nonetheless, be seen as an improvement on what would have been found in its exemplar, which no-one could have understood, given how 'Stuaginnuer' had degenerated into gibberish.

With Stainmore adopted instead of 'Stuaginnuer', the awkwardness of the bounds of Fergus's kingdom reported in ѕ would have represented a stark challenge for anyone who used it as a source. The problem was how to make sense of Drumalban. A tidy solution was adopted by the source of the passage quoted from Fordun's chronicle (dubbed **o** in the diagram above); Drumalban was jettisoned and the sentence recast so that it was made explicit that Fergus's realm encompassed all Scotland. This image of the kingdom's ancient territorial integrity was a bold development: in Fordun's chronicle itself the preferred option (even though contradictory accounts are given in the text) was to regard the Scottish kingdom as confined at this stage to Argyll and the Isles.[36] The ambitiousness of the claim made for the extent of Fergus's kingdom should not, however, obscure the likelihood that this was inspired by the appearance of Stainmore in its exemplar, and by a desire to make the exemplar's statement about Fergus's realm less awkward. The only necessary impulse for these changes, therefore, was a desire to make an important historical text make sense. True, one ingredient was probably an assumption that Scotland in its primeval past must have been much the same as Scotland in the present – a different manifestation of the same Scottish identity based on the kingdom as a whole that is visible in the Chronicle of Melrose. There is no need, certainly, for the appearance of Stainmore here to have been made with any knowledge of John of Cheam's claim to extend his diocese.

Could John of Cheam have been moved to action as a result of reading something like ѕ or **o**? An important point in favour of this possibility is that, although the Rere Cross at Stainmore is repeatedly referred to by scholars as the south-eastern boundary of the kingdom of Strathclyde, the references given in support of this lead to no convincing evidence.[37] It is perfectly possible, in fact, that the text dubbed as ѕ was the earliest statement that Stainmore was the long-established southern boundary of a kingdom. If this possibility is to be pushed further, it is necessary to argue that ѕ predated John of Cheam's attempted annexation of Carlisle. There is nothing in the diagram of textual relationships (given above) that offers much hope that the latest lost text (**o**) need be any older than the four-teenth century. As will become apparent in chapter 8, this part of Fordun's chronicle was probably in existence by 1285.[38] Although 1285 is about a generation later than John of Cheam's reign, it would certainly make it easier to envisage that ѕ or **o** could be as old as the 1260s if the account of Fergus's kingdom stretching from Stainmore to Orkney could be shown to have been part of the proto-chronicle on which Fordun based his work. It would also make it much easier to propose that ѕ was the ultimate source of all statements that the Rere Cross of Stainmore was a long-established boundary of the kingdom of Strathclyde.

The tantalising possibility remains, therefore, that John of Cheam may have been inspired by a statement about the primeval bounds of the Scottish kingdom stretching south to Stainmore – a notion which prob-ably originated as a textual amendment by a redactor of a Scottish king-list. If this is indeed how Cheam's claim to Carlisle arose, then it must have grown into something more than just the personal hobby-horse of a foreign bishop who (let us imagine) stumbled on this supposed 'ancient right' when he was reading up on the history of his adopted country. The insistence elsewhere in Fordun's chronicle that the diocese of Glasgow ought 'now' to extend to Stainmore suggests that this was a cause that was espoused by others who presumably identified themselves with Glasgow.[39] If all this is accepted, then it would be a striking illustration of how Glasgow's clerical establishment at this time could identify itself with the kingdom of Scotland. It would mean that its claim to the diocese of Carlisle was based not on any memory that the kingdom of Strathclyde (or the diocese of Glasgow prior to the creation of the bishopric of Carlisle in 1133) once stretched to the Rere Cross of Stainmore;[40] the claim would instead have been grounded on the establishment's assump-tion that, if Fergus first king of Scots ruled as far south as Stainmore, then its diocese should likewise extend to the kingdom's ancient southern limit. If this was indeed the basis of John of Cheam's campaign, then it makes a vivid contrast with the attempts by Bishop Jocelin to advance the cause of his diocese by emphasising its association with a kingdom and people that were distinct from Scotland and the Scots.

THE INAUGURATION OF ALEXANDER III: THE SOURCES

The currency of a clear-cut idea of Scottish sovereignty by the mid-thirteenth century could by no means be said to be demonstrated compellingly if, as evidence, there was only the suggestion that John of Cheam may have been infected by assumptions about Scotland's territorial integrity transmitted through a lost king-list of uncertain date. Also, even if this explanation of Cheam's claim to Carlisle could be substantiated conclusively, it hardly amounts to an extended statement of how Scotland was perceived. Its interest lies chiefly in what it may suggest about how a straightforward notion of Scotland's jurisdictional integrity could have taken root even in a context where there had once been profound ambiguity about promoting the kingdom's unity.

For much more substantial evidence of a clear-cut expression of Scottish sovereignty in this period, we should turn to the inauguration of the seven-year-old Alexander III on 13 July 1249. There are no fewer than three surviving descriptions which can (with varying degrees of conviction) claim to preserve contemporary information about what took place.[41] There is more than enough material here for modern scholars to get their teeth into; and many have, from W. F. Skene onwards.[42] The fullest and most impressive study is that by Archie Duncan as recently as 2002, who has succeeded more than anyone else in extrapolating a detailed account of what occurred, and what might have occurred, and placed this in the wider context of royal inaugurations elsewhere. If it is not too simplistic to characterise Archie Duncan's achievement as a maximalist interpretation of the evidence, then it would not be unfair to describe the approach I will adopt on this occasion as minimalist. A reader might be forgiven for forgetting how problematic and uncertain much of this evidence is, given how rare it is to have three Scottish accounts of such an important event in this period. One way to deal with this is to face the difficulties of the evidence head on and grapple with the most important textual challenges. The objective is a reconstruction of the earliest account of the inauguration ritual (which is indebted to Professor Duncan's work); the result is that important innovations in the ceremony can be identified which can be recognised as part of a concerted attempt by Scottish leaders to project a new image of their kingdom. There is also an important by-product. The process of stripping away textual accretions in order to reveal the earliest account enables a commentary on the ritual to be identified which was likely to have been in writing by 1285, a year before the end of Alexander III's reign. This will bring us back to the question of Scotland's imagined ancient past in a much more compelling way than can be suggested for the putative source of John of Cheam's claim that the diocese of Carlisle should be incorporated into Glasgow.

It will be useful to begin with a brief account of the three Scottish descriptions of Alexander III's inauguration, and of their limitations as sources. One has the merit of originating from Scone itself: it is a depiction of what must be this event on the large seal of Scone Abbey.[43] The king wears a crown and is seated out of doors, holding a sceptre in his right hand and pulling the fastening of his mantle with the index finger of his left hand. At his side two churchmen hold his mantle: one is certainly a bishop. Behind them stand two knights, while above the clerics are two figures, one holding out a box and the other grasping something long and thin. Behind the latter figure lurks another who has been squeezed into the remaining space. He is almost too small and uncertain to be recognised as a person, but may represent someone sitting; whatever he may be, he was evidently too important to be omitted, despite the lack of room. Below the king's feet there are three shields: the middle one bears the royal arms of the lion rampant, the one on the left has three vertical lines, while the one on the right has two chevrons. This enables the two knights to be identified as the earls of Fife and Strathearn. If there were no written accounts of Alexander III's inauguration it would be difficult to identify the other figures with certainty, and even more of a challenge to reconstruct the ritual. It might very reasonably be guessed that the clerics are the bishop of St Andrews and the abbot of Scone, and that the box held out by the figure above the bishop is a *scrinium* or relic-case for the swearing of oaths. Another problem is that it is difficult to determine when the seal was made. It is found on a document of 1296, and may well by that time have been in use for decades. Could it be contemporary with the inauguration of Alexander III? It has been noticed that the image of the king holding a sceptre in his right hand and the fastening of his mantle with his left is similar to Alexander III's second great seal of about 1260, suggesting that this may have been a model for the Scone seal.[44] It is likely, then, that the Scone seal was created at least ten years later than the event depicted on it. Was it simply based on the memory of eye-witnesses? Or was a written source used?

The independent value of the Scone seal is boosted by the fact that there is no extant written account which could readily have furnished all its details. The oldest written source is the extensive material (known to modern scholarship as *Gesta Annalia*, 'Yearly Deeds') appended to John of Fordun's *Chronica Gentis Scottorum* ('Chronicle of the Scottish People') in some manuscripts.[45] The layers of textual activity that can be detected will be discussed in due course. Suffice to say at this stage that, in general terms, *Gesta Annalia* here cannot readily be traced back earlier than 1285. In it we are told that, after the whole clergy and people had 'with one voice' assented to making Alexander king, he was led by the earls of Fife and Strathearn and others to a cross in the abbey's cemetery where he was placed on the royal throne and consecrated as king by the bishop of St Andrews. The earls and other nobles, on bended knee, then strewed their garments at the feet of the king sitting on his throne, 'that is, the stone . . . kept for the consecration of kings of Alba'. This was followed by the arrival of a 'certain highland Scot' who greeted Alexander in Gaelic and read out his pedigree 'from man to man . . . until he came to the first Scot, namely Éber Scot'. Much of this can be recognised in the scene depicted on the large seal of Scone abbey: the out-of-doors setting, the key roles of the earls of Fife and Strathearn, and of the bishop of St Andrews; it has very plausibly been suggested that the figure grasping something long and thin is the 'highland Scot' reading the genealogy (who can be recognised as the king's poet, *ollam ríg*).[46] This level of corroboration makes it easier to have confidence in those features which are unique to either source. Confidence in *Gesta Annalia*'s account is also increased by its mention of Bishop Geoffrey of Dunkeld who died on 22 November 1249. He is one of three clerics named in *Gesta Annalia* as present at the inauguration of Alexander III.[47] What is particularly striking is that Bishop Geoffrey is not only named, but is given a eulogy: 'a man beloved in many ways as much by clergy as people, keenly engaged in temporal and spiritual affairs, who showed the friendly side of himself to all, the great as much as the poor, but a terrifying side to evil-doers'. A possible explanation of this very unusual feature would be that the original account was written shortly after his death, and that the author had a close association with him.[48]

Finally, there is the longer account in Bower's *Scotichronicon*, composed in the 1440s. It is known in general terms that Bower used *Gesta Annalia* as a source, and that he did not simply copy it, but adapted its prose and added other material to it. This is certainly true here. Before Alexander is led to the cross in the cemetery we are told that he was girded with the belt of knighthood by the bishop of St Andrews, who then 'set out the rights and promises that pertain to a king, first in Latin, then in French', before proceeding to the king's 'blessing and ordination'. It has been pointed out that administering the oath in French as well as Latin is unlikely to have been a feature of Scottish inaugurations and coronations later than the thirteenth century, and is therefore an important indicator that here, at least, Bower was using an earlier source.[49] After this point *Gesta Annalia*'s account can readily be recognised, but it has been changed. For example, instead of the earls and nobles casting garments at the feet of the enthroned king, they start settling down on stools at the king's feet in readiness to listen to a sermon before being interrupted by the arrival of the 'highland Scot'. Also, Bower adds that Alexander at this point had a crown and sceptre, and that the king's poet was 'a venerable, grey-haired figure' who, 'though a wild highlander, was honourably attired after his own fashion'. It has been suggested that Bower had a different account which he regarded as 'superior' to that in *Gesta Annalia*.[50] As far as this section is concerned, however, it is much more likely that Bower has simply 'improved' on *Gesta Annalia* by heightening its rather bare prose. It is also apparent that he has joined an account which featured the bishop of St Andrews administering the oath in Latin and French to *Gesta Annalia* by making out that it was the custom, 'after the solemn ceremony of the king's coronation', to bring the king to the cross in the cemetery. In *Gesta Annalia*'s account, however, the enthronement at the cross is presented as the constitutive act: Alexander is 'a king soon to be' (*rex mox futurus*) as he is led there. In sum, it appears that Bower has put together two independent accounts of the inauguration, and probably rewritten parts of both of them (certainly *Gesta Annalia*) according to what he thought made sense – even though the point of enthroning Alexander at the cross in the cemetery is thereby lost (which may be why he repackaged it as a change of scene for the purpose of hearing a sermon and the old Highlander). Neither *Gesta Annalia* nor the other account were evidently written as full descriptions of what happened (as can be verified by referring to information unique to the Scone seal), and they were not necessarily mutually exclusive; each simply concentrated on different aspects of the ceremony.

The account in *Gesta Annalia* can therefore be recognised as the most authoritative written source for Alexander III's inauguration. It also has the potential to be more contemporary than the depiction of the ritual on Scone abbey's seal. It is with this prospect in mind that we can now examine it in more detail.

RECONSTRUCTING THE ORIGINAL ACCOUNT OF ALEXANDER III'S INAUGURATION

In the light of recent work, a plausible reconstruction of the original text used as the source for Alexander III's inauguration by *Gesta Annalia*'s author can be attempted, making it possible to be appreciably more certain about some key aspects of what occurred when Alexander III was installed as king at Scone on 13 July 1249.[51] The process of reconstruction will chiefly involve the identification and removal of later interpolations. The discarded material will not be forgotten, however. It offers vital clues to the identification of the earliest sustained narrative of the

Scottish kingship's ancient past, and is examined in detail in chapter 8. It is also appropriate to delay until chapter 8 a discussion of *Gesta Annalia*'s complex development, where more of the text than simply its account of Alexander III's inauguration will be under review. Suffice to say at this stage that, although *Gesta Annalia*, as published by Skene in his edition, runs up to 1363 (with a patchy continuation of events between 1371 and 1385 in some manuscripts), this conceals the fact that it was originally divided in two by a dossier of documents relating to Scottish independence, headed by the Declaration of Arbroath (1320), and some other items, placed after the notice of the embassy sent by Alexander III to France in February 1285 to seek a new wife. This and other considerations point firmly to the conclusion that *Gesta Annalia* from Alexander III's second marriage in October 1285 to 1363 was added at a later stage. To make this clear, *Gesta Annalia* up to February 1285 will be referred to as '*Gesta Annalia* I' (or '*GAI*' for short), and the material from October 1285 to 1363 as '*Gesta Annalia* II' (or '*GAII*'). The author of *GAI* therefore ceased to write sometime after the embassy was despatched on 2 February 1285. There is also an indication that his work can be dated to sometime during the following two months.[52] At the end of the chapter describing how a dispute over the earldom of Menteith arose in 1260, it is commented that the case was 'still under discussion';[53] it was not finally resolved until a 'great assembly' at Scone on 9 April 1285.[54]

The identification of *GAI* as a work from towards the end of Alexander III's reign clearly adds value to its account of the beginning of the reign. As long as Fordun himself was regarded as author of *Gesta Annalia*, all that could be said was that (as it stood) the description of Alexander III's inauguration could not with confidence be dated earlier than Fordun's career (and all that is known with any certainty about Fordun is that he was working sometime between 1384 and 1387), but that it is apparent that Fordun based his account on a very well-informed source. It is now possible to suggest that the description of Alexander III's inauguration is likely to have been in writing by April 1285, and to have been based on an even earlier account.

Why suppose that there was necessarily an earlier account at all? The text of Alexander III's inauguration does not read as a homogenous piece of prose, but has evidently been added to and adapted.[55] In *Gesta Annalia* the events at Scone on that day are given as two chapters (which in Skene's edition appear as nos 47 and 48): one (Skene's 48) for the inauguration itself, and the other (Skene's 47) in which we are told of a dispute between Walter Comyn, earl of Menteith, and the justiciar, Alan

Durward, which broke out after everyone had assembled for the inauguration (the point at issue being whether Alexander should be knighted by Durward beforehand). Professor Duncan has argued compellingly that this material has been separated into two chapters, resulting in some awkward phraseology; it is possible to rectify these clumsy features, thereby restoring something much closer to the original text. He also argues cogently that the author of the account as it survives evidently sought to make clear the Stone of Scone's significance, and in the process he 'ties his prose in knots' in 'passages which conspicuously interrupt the flow of his description'.[56] The identification of Alexander's throne (*cathedra*) with the Stone is repeatedly made in what looks like glosses to the original, and a key passage explaining the significance of the Stone of Scone has been intruded.

There can be little doubt that whoever added this material was writing before the Stone's removal to Westminster in 1296, because the present tense is used when referring to how the Stone is reverently kept at Scone.[57] There is also a less obvious clue which points to the author of GAI as the interpolator. Scone is not named at the outset: it is merely referred to as 'the same monastery'. On investigation this suggests that whoever interpolated the passage on the Stone's significance also divided the narrative of what happened that day into two chapters. Because Scone is not actually named, the reader would have to recall from the beginning of the previous chapter that Scone was intended – which is awkward, to say the least. The use of *idem*, 'the same', however, implies that what was being referred to was reasonably close to hand in the text. As it happens, the nearest appearance of Scone is not in the text itself, but in the rubric of this chapter (Skene's 48), which reads: *De Coronatio Regis Alexandri apud Sconam*, 'Concerning the Coronation of King Alexander III at Scone'. The same person who added the passage explaining the Stone's significance is likely, therefore, also to have been responsible for that chapter's rubric, in which case it follows that they were also responsible for separating the narrative of Alexander's inauguration into two chapters. It may be noted that chapters are only very occasionally given headings in GAI. Only eleven out of one hundred and seven are so adorned (according to Skene's edition): four of these are in the first six chapters, and, of the remaining seven, four highlight 'coronations' (Mael Coluim IV, William, Alexander II and Alexander III). Chapter-headings are much more common in GAII.

The organisation of this material into two chapters can surely therefore be attributed to the author of GAI. This is not the only indication that he was responsible for interpolating the passage explaining the significance of the Stone of Scone. This will become clear in chapter 8. Suffice to say at this stage that this passage betrays the same concern to draw attention to Scone as the 'seat of the kingdom of Alba' established by ancient kings as is found elsewhere in *GAI*. Of course, the idea that Scone was founded of old as a centre of kingship was doubtless well known. What is significant here is the shared emphasis, and the use of similar terms of reference (particularly the use of *Albania* rather than *Scotia* at this point). This reinforces the suspicion that this passage, and therefore all the awkward asides about the Stone, were written by the author of *GAI*, and were not originally part of the account of Alexander III's inauguration.

Thankfully, the interpolations and adaptations which the author of *GAI* made to the account of Alexander's inauguration seem sufficiently obvious to allow a meaningful attempt to be made at reconstructing the original description of the ceremony itself by excluding the interpolated material. Following on from Professor Duncan's reconstruction of the original text before its division into separate chapters, the result would read as follows. (Round brackets indicate probable interpolations, which are also underlined, and have been omitted from the translation; angled brackets indicate alterations I have made to the text for the sake of grammatical sense; and square brackets indicate words added in the translation to improve comprehension. Spelling has been standardised.)[58]

Comites, scilicet dominu<s> Malcolmu<s> com<es> de Fyff et dominu<s> Malisiu<s> com<es> de Stratherne, et ceter<i> plures nobiles Alexandrum regem mox futurum ad crucem in cimiterio ex parte orientali ecclesie stantem adduxerunt, quem ibidem in regali cathedra positum, pannis sericis auro textis ornata, episcopus Sancti Andree et ceteri coadiuuantes in regem ut decuit consecrarunt. Ipso quoque rege super cathedram regalem (scilicet lapidem) sedente, sub cuius pedibus comites ceterique nobiles sua uestimenta (coram lapide) curuatis genibus sternebant. (Qui lapis in eodem monasterio reverenter ob regum Albanie consecrationem servatur. Nec uspiam aliquis regum in Scocia regnare solebat, nisi super eundem lapidem regium in accipiendum nomen prius sederet in Scona, sede vere superiori, videlicet, Albanie constituta regibus ab antiquis.) Et ecce, peractis singulis, quidam Scotus montanus ante thronum subito genuflectens materna lingua regem inclinato capite salutauit (hiis Scoticis uerbis) dicens: 'Benach de Re Albanne Alexander mac Alexander mac Uleyham mac Henri mac Dauid, et sic pronunciando regum Scottorum genealogiam usque in finem legebat. (Quod ita Latine . . .)

The earls, namely lord Mael Coluim, earl of Fife, and lord Mael Ísu, earl of Strathearn, and many other nobles, led Alexander, soon to be king, to a cross standing in the cemetery at the east part of the church, whom they placed in the royal seat adorned with silk cloths woven in gold; the bishop of St Andrews and other assistants with him consecrated [Alexander] as king, as was proper. Also, while the king was sitting upon the royal seat ( ), earls and other nobles on bended knee ( ) spread their garments under his feet. ([Passage on the significance of the Stone of Scone attributable to the author of *GAI*.]) And behold, after they one by one were finished,[59] a certain highland Scot, kneeling suddenly before the throne, greeted the king in the mother tongue,[60] bowing his head, saying ( ): *Bennachd Dé, rí Albana<ch>, Alexanndar mac Alexannda<i>r m<ei>c Uilleim m<ei>c Énri m<ei>c Dauid*,[61] and by proclaiming in this way read the genealogy of the kings of Scots to the end.

The remaining part of the chapter is taken up with a Latin translation of the passage in Gaelic, which is continued with a Latinate rendering of the royal genealogy step by step back to 'Fergus son of Feredach or Ferchar' (with some discussion of the variable patronymic), followed by a statement that the genealogy was read out back to the 'first Scot' (identified as Éber 'Scot' son of Gaedel Glas son of Nél, and of Scota daughter of Pharaoh). This was obviously not the text read out as part of the inauguration (which we are told was Gaelic); it has been copied from an earlier Latinate version of the genealogy closely related to the text which is found in *Imagines Historiarum* by Ralph of Diss.[62] It is clearly dangerous to regard any of this (from *Quod Latine sonat . . .*) as part of the original account of Alexander's inauguration. Indeed, the statement that the highland Scot 'read the genealogy of the kings of Scots to the end' seems to overlap unnecessarily with what then follows. It seems more natural to regard this as the end of the original account which has then had a Latinate version of the genealogy tacked on together with a little commentary, rather than to regard the whole as part of the original record of Alexander III's inauguration. In the light of this, *hiis Scoticis uerbis* may be regarded as an interpolation; it certainly adds nothing to what we have just been told (namely that the king was addressed in the mother tongue), but could have been added to balance the statement introducing the version in Latin (*hiis Scoticis uerbis dicens . . . Quod ita Latine sonat*, 'saying these words in Gaelic . . . Which sounds thus in Latin . . .').

It will be useful at this point to summarise these suggestions about the composition of the description of Alexander III's inauguration in *Gesta Annalia*. Only a small amount of the text as we have it relating to the ceremony may be accepted as a contemporary account (it has been tentatively reconstructed above). This has been considerably enlarged and to some extent rewritten, most probably by the author of *GAI* no later than April 1285. It was he, evidently, who reorganised the original account to form the basis of two chapters of his work, and who included the material in which the Stone's significance and its identification with Alexander's throne was emphasised. Presumably it was he also who added the Latinate version of the royal genealogy.[63] It may be observed that, according to this analysis, the account of Alexander III's inauguration in *Gesta Annalia*, which was once regarded as manifestly superior as a source to that in Bower's *Scotichronicon*, seems now to share with Bower's account the character of a small core of contemporary information which has been embellished and enlarged at a later stage. The source behind Bower's account, however, does not lend itself so readily to the kind of reconstruction attempted here and by Professor Duncan.

It is apparent from Professor Duncan's work on the other sources for the inauguration ritual performed in 1249 that the contemporary core in the *Gesta Annalia* account is probably a selective record of what occurred. Even if its author was a witness to the ceremony, he has not attempted to give a complete description of what he saw, but has, in his abbreviated and beguilingly matter-of-fact version of events, quietly betrayed what he deemed to be significant. For a more explicit statement about the significance of elements of the inauguration ritual, however, we must turn to the material which may be attributed to the author of *GAI*, namely the commentary on the Stone and the extended treatment of the royal genealogy. It is this which affords a unique opportunity not only to appreciate in more detail how the kingship's past was portrayed by a contemporary writer before the end of Alexander III's reign, but also to show that *GAI* is but a fragment of a more extensive work on the kingship's history.

INNOVATIONS IN ALEXANDER III'S INAUGURATION

The author of the original account of Alexander's inauguration evidently regarded the Stone of Scone as playing a central role (as, indeed, did the author of *GAI*). The vision of the Stone as the core element of an age-old ritual would be broadly accepted by many scholars today. The ceremony at Scone, moreover, was strikingly different compared with what was increasingly the norm in Latin Christendom in the thirteenth century. There was no crown, and no anointment as such by the kingdom's leading bishop, symbolising the king's transformation into his new status by the infusion of divine grace. The ritual at Scone (at least in the original account used by the author of *GAI*) was more secular in tone, with the bishop of St Andrews moving centre-stage only after the earls of Fife and Strathearn had enthroned the king on the Stone. It is easy to see the

Scottish ceremony as belonging to an earlier age, an example of a more primitive, even pagan, form of inauguration. One scholar, for instance, has described the Stone as 'by far the most ancient seat of royalty still in use in Britain' in this period.[64] Another has commented that 'the enthronement [on the Stone] links this ceremony with one of the most archaic in Ireland, a survival of the primitive Indo-European idea of kingship into historical times . . . Lacking the equivalent of Middle Irish literature,' he continues, 'we have in this ceremony at Scone an invaluable anthropological glimpse of the pagan sacral kingship which lingered on . . . [in some form] until the 1290s'.[65] The archaic idea behind this and similar inauguration rituals in Ireland was, in Katharine Simms's words, 'a "kingship-marriage" (*banais ríghe*) whereby the new king was wedded to the *tuath*, that is, to the territory itself and the people who occupied it'.[66]

It is readily acknowledged by these scholars that it is difficult to gauge how far such ancient notions of kingship may have still been understood in the thirteenth century.[67] Those governing in the young Alexander III's name, for their part, were clearly dissatisfied with the inauguration ritual, and wished to replace or adapt the existing ceremony with a papally sanctioned coronation and anointment. A failed attempt to procure this was made before early 1251, probably within the first year of the new king's reign.[68] The issue was raised again unsuccessfully in 1259 when Alexander III began his personal reign,[69] but then lay dormant until Pope John XXII acceded to Robert I's petition in 1329.[70] The chief attraction of coronation and anointment for Scottish leaders was that it would have represented unambiguous recognition within Latin Christendom that Scotland was jurisdictionally on a par with any other realm: in short, that it was a sovereign kingdom. Kings of England were equally keen to prevent this, however, and made representations to the pope that the king of Scots was subject to the king of England.[71] The fact that the papacy refused Scottish requests does not, however, necessarily mean that they always accepted the English view of the status of the kingship of the Scots; it did not make sense politically for the pope to antagonise the king of England needlessly by striking what would have been a mortal blow to English pretensions to superiority over Scotland. In particular, after the death of the emperor Frederick II in December 1250, leaving an illegitimate youth to succeed him as king of Sicily, the papacy was keen to reassert its claim that the Sicilian kingdom was a papal fief: a project in which Henry III of England would in due course become embroiled, with disastrous consequences.[72]

Presumably, had the much desired papally sanctioned coronation and anointment been achieved, the Stone of Scone would have remained (in some form) the inaugural throne, as it was to become in England and has remained up to the present day. The ceremony of inauguration itself, however, would undoubtedly have changed fundamentally. We must conclude that, as far as contemporaries were concerned, the ritual was not something fixed and ancient, but could be adapted to reflect current concerns. It was too important an opportunity to miss for making a dramatic statement about the kingship. This was particularly true for Alexander III's inauguration, where it is possible to detect some features which can claim to have been devised specifically for that occasion. It is striking, for instance, that Alexander III was enthroned not on the Moot Hill, as might naturally be expected, but at a cross in the graveyard.[73] This innovation was almost certainly never repeated, and may therefore have been a 'one off'.[74] The next royal inauguration, that of John Balliol in 1292, was celebrated in the abbey church itself, which was doubtless another innovation.[75] There is an implicit contrast between the inauguration under a cross (in which the association with God is focused on the king and his enthronement) and inauguration in a church (in which the religious association relates more generally to the whole ceremony and all its participants). Be this as it may, it must be suspected that the purpose of inaugurating Alexander under a cross was to demonstrate the king's sovereignty by expressing symbolically what Alexander himself is said to have declared in Edward I's presence in 1278: that he held the kingdom of Scotland of God alone.[76] Such an attempt to remould the ceremony to present Alexander III as a sovereign king despite the lack of coronation and anointment would also explain another unusual feature: the nobles' strewing of their garments at the feet of the newly enthroned king. The most pertinent parallel with this otherwise unprecedented piece of theatre is to be found in the Book of Kings.[77] At the inauguration of King Jehu we are told that, after Jehu was announced as anointed by God as king over Israel, 'they hastened and, each taking off their cloak, placed [it] under his [Jehu's] feet in the likeness of a raised platform, and they sounded the trumpet and said "Jehu reigned" '.[78] The nobles were enacting a recognition of Alexander as 'anointed by God', an anointing which, of course, had not taken place, but whose essence would have been conveyed metaphorically by Alexander's enthronement under the cross in the cemetery. Instead of the final declaration that 'Jehu reigned', it was wholly appropriate that, as soon as the last noble had cast his cloak at the king's feet, the king's poet arrived to perform the time-honoured announcement that Alexander was now king by proclaiming his pedigree.

The established elements of enthronement and a reading of the genealogy had been skilfully blended with new features so that, together, participants and onlookers might understand that the king of Scots was as much a king as any other monarch in Latin Christendom. These innovations were almost certainly a foretaste of the requests for coronation and anointment made on Alexander's behalf to Pope Innocent IV (1243–54), and then (when Alexander's minority was coming to an end) to Pope Alexander IV (1254–61). They were, as has already been noted, unsuccessful; but were they a complete failure? It is unlikely to be a coincidence that Alexander III received bulls from Innocent IV and Alexander IV affirming the 'rights and liberties of the king and kingdom'. If these bulls amounted to *de facto* recognition of Scottish sovereignty, then it may no longer have seemed necessary for Alexander to pursue the matter further. In 1259 he may, as an adult king, have got the substance of what he required, but without the trappings, and decided that this was as much as could be hoped for in the teeth of English opposition. A note of caution must be sounded, however. Unfortunately Innocent IV's and Alexander IV's bulls do not survive; all that exists is a brief mention of them in the inventory of the muniments in the royal treasury in Edinburgh made in 1282,[79] so there cannot be certainty about their content.[80] There can be no doubt, however, about Innocent IV's view that the kingdom of Scotland was as much a kingdom as any other. He made this clear in a letter of 6 April 1251 to Henry III in which he explained that he could not accede to Henry's request to be granted a tenth of ecclesiastical revenues from Scotland 'because it is altogether unheard of that this [privilege] should be granted to anyone within the kingdom of another'.[81]

The kingdom's independence had initially become an issue with regard to the Church. It was eventually recognised in *Cum universi*, if not by Clement III (1187–91), then certainly by Celestine III (1191–8), and in re-issues of the bull by Innocent III (1198–1216) and Honorius III (1216–27).[82] Scottish independence had only been brought directly into question in the context of relations between the Scottish and English kings with the Treaty of Falaise (1174); but then the previous pattern of the king of Scots' subordination while exercising control of his own realm had been formally re-established by the Quitclaim of Canterbury (1189). The papacy was occasionally involved in relations between the two kings, most notably during the minority of Henry III: a papal legate played a pivotal role in arranging the settlement between Alexander II and Henry III at York in 1220.[83] As far as the issue of their relative status was concerned, the pope's view at that time was that the king of Scots was subject to the king of England, although this was not the subject of a formal pronouncement addressed to either Alexander or Henry.[84] This changed with the accession of Gregory IX (1227–41), who in 1235, at the instigation of Henry III of England, wrote to Alexander II specifically in support of the provisions of the Treaty of Falaise.[85] When, therefore, Innocent IV explained to Henry III that it was unthinkable for him to be permitted to collect ecclesiastical taxation in another kingdom, Scotland, it was the first time (beyond the issue of the status of the Scottish church itself) that the pope had recognised Scottish independence directly in the arena of the relationship between the kings themselves. The Scottish embassy, which not long before had failed to persuade Innocent to grant coronation and anointment, had not been entirely unsuccessful, if it had at least convinced the pope that the king of Scots should be regarded in this context as *de facto* on a par with any other sovereign.

NOTES

1. Stubbs (ed.), *Chronica*, iv. 141; *SAEC*, 324–5; Davies, *The First English Empire*, 16.
2. Duncan, *Scotland: the Making of the Kingdom*, 589–90.
3. Stones (ed.), *Anglo-Scottish Relations*, 76–81.
4. H. R. Luard (ed.), *Annales Monastici*, 4 vols (1864–9), iv. 277–8; *SAEC*, 383–4.
5. Stones (ed.), *Anglo-Scottish Relations*, 80–3; see esp. Barrow, *Scotland and its Neighbours*, 5–6; Duncan, *Kingship of the Scots*, 161–3.
6. Robert Bartlett (ed.), *The Miracles of St Æbbe of Coldingham and Saint Margaret of Scotland* (Oxford, 2003), 86–9; Shead, Stevenson and Watt (eds), *Scotichronicon*, vi. 28–9, and F. J. Amours (ed.), *The Original Chronicle of Andrew of Wyntoun*, 6 vols (Scottish Text Society, 1903–14), v. 212–13. Both Wishart and the abbot of Dunfermline were probably present at Roxburgh in October 1278 (Duncan, *Kingship of the Scots*, 160–1), so it is possible (but hardly necessary) to imagine that the formula originated there and was recalled at Dunfermline and Norham.
7. See above, 2.
8. Grant G. Simpson, 'Kingship in minature: a seal of minority of Alexander III, 1249–1257', in A. Grant and K. J. Stringer (eds), *Medieval Scotland: Crown, Lordship and Community* (Edinburgh, 1993), 131–9; see also A. A. M. Duncan, 'Before coronation: making a king at Scone in the thirteenth century', in R. Welander, D. Breeze and T. O. Clancy (eds), *The Stone of Destiny. Artefact and Icon* (Edinburgh, 2003), 139–67, at 149–50.
9. *Ibid.*, 150 and Duncan, *Kingship of the Scots*, 133 n. 28 and plate IV, show that *Rex Scottorum Dei Gratia* was a later addition. For the destruction of the Great Seal, see Duncan, *Scotland: the Making of the Kingdom*, 561–2. The Great Seal had been used instead of the seal of minority by Durward's

government in 1251: see Duncan, *Kingship of the Scots*, 154.

10. The claim may have been too obscurely stated in the seal's legend as originally struck: ESTO PRVDENS VT SERPENS ET SIMPLEX SICVT COLVMBA, 'Be prudent as a serpent and innocent like a dove': see Duncan, *Kingship of the Scots*, 152–3.

11. Forbes (ed.), *Lives of S. Ninian and S. Kentigern*, 96, 220.

12. Skene (ed.), *Johannis de Fordun Chronica*, 449–51; Clancy (ed.), *Triumph Tree*, 212–15.

13. The poem is on an inserted folio, fo.135: see D. N. Dumville, 'The Corpus Christi "Nennius", *BBCS* 25 (1974) 369–80, at 371.

14. See above, 7–11.

15. Watt, 'The provincial council of the Scottish church', 141–2.

16. Watt, *Medieval Church Councils*, 99–101.

17. See above, 7.

18. Dryburgh was described by its prior as *in terra Anglorum, et in regno Scotorum*: Adam of Dryburgh, *De tripartito tabernaculo*, in *PL* cxcviii. cols 609–792, at col. 723.

19. Broun, 'The Declaration of Arbroath', 8; for the dating, see Broun and Harrison (eds), *The Chronicle of Melrose*, vol. i (forthcoming).

20. Barrow, *The Kingdom of the Scots*, 2nd edn, 299.

21. Stevenson (ed.), *Chronicon de Lanercost*, 65.

22. Nicholl, *Thurstan*, 17, 140–2; Shead, 'The origins of the medieval diocese of Glasgow', 224.

23. David Laing (ed.), *The Orygynale Cronykil of Scotland by Androw of Wyntoun*, 3 vols (Edinburgh, 1872–9), ii. 214. The manuscript represents the second edition of Wyntoun's work, according to the scheme proposed in Amours (ed.), *Original Chronicle*, i. section 8. In the oldest manuscript of the first edition Stainmore has been garbled as 'Cammore', while in the third edition this section has been extensively rewritten and the kingdom's bounds jettisoned: Amours (ed.), *Original Chronicle*, iii. 86–7.

24. Anderson, *Kings and Kingship*, 264–8.

25. Translated from *ibid.*, 264.

26. Laing (ed.), *Orygynale Cronykil*, ii. 214: '. . . Fergus son of Erc, who made himself ruler beyond the Drum for three years. Over all the heights, each and every one, as they lie from Drumalban to Stainmore and Inchgall: he made himself king over them all.'

27. Skene (ed.), *Johannis de Fordun Chronica*, 88; Skene (trans.), *John of Fordun's Chronicle*, 79; MacQueen and MacQueen (eds), *Scotichronicon*, ii. 4–5, 7.

28. Anderson, *Kings and Kingship*, 64.

29. The letters are compatible with Broun, *Irish Identity*, 63–174. Presumably **o** represents the king-list related to Wyntoun and king-list D from which the idea that Scottish kings preceded the Picts was cited (as an alternative to his preferred option) in Fordun's chronicle: see *ibid.*, 107–8.

30. *Ibid.*, 126–7; Anderson, *Kings and Kingship*, 67.
31. Dauvit Broun, 'The Picts' place in the kingship's past before John of Fordun', in Edward J. Cowan and Richard J. Finlay (eds), *Scottish History: the Power of the Past* (Edinburgh, 2002), 11–28, at 22 n. 38.
32. Thomas Charles-Edwards, *Early Christian Ireland* (Cambridge, 2000), 54; Francis John Byrne, *Irish Kings and High-kings* (London, 1973), 109, 120–1.
33. For example, king-lists K and N: Anderson, *Kings and Kingship*, 286, 290.
34. *Ibid.*, 253.
35. In lists 'F1' and 'F2' respectively: *ibid.*, 270.
36. Broun, 'The Picts' place in the kingship's past', 17–18.
37. For example, Charles Phythian-Adams, *Land of Cumbrians. A Study in British Provincial Origins*, AD *400–1200* (Aldershot, 1996), 194 n. 56, referring to Alfred P. Smyth, *Warlords and Holy Men: Scotland* AD *80–1000* (London 1984; repr. Edinburgh, 1992), referring to Kirby, who discusses the point in D. P. Kirby, 'Strathclyde and Cumbria: a survey of historical development to 1092', *TCWAAS* 62 (1962) 71–94, at 90–1, referring to Skene (ed.), *Chronicles*, 204. This is king-list K: its lack of credibility as a source in this context is discussed in Broun, 'Welsh identity', 178–9.
38. See below, 216–17.
39. Skene (ed.), *Johannis de Fordun Chronica*, 115; Skene (trans.), *John of Fordun's Chronicle*, 107.
40. Although this is not to deny that bishops Michael and John once operated in the area: Shead, 'The origins', 221.
41. Duncan, 'Before coronation', 144–7, 150–66; Duncan, *Kingship of the Scots*, 131–50.
42. See W. F. Skene, 'The coronation stone', *PSAS* 8 (1869) 68–99, at 73 n. 1; M. D. Legge, 'The inauguration of Alexander III', *PSAS* 80 (1948) 73–82, at 78–81.
43. Duncan, 'Before coronation', 158, who shows that there is no need to doubt that one of the shields of arms is the earl of Fife's (and suppose, therefore, that the inauguration depicted on the seal was John's in 1292: G. W. S. Barrow, 'Observations on the Coronation stone of Scotland', *SHR* 76 (1997) 115–21, at 115–17).
44. Duncan, *Scotland: the Making of the Kingdom*, 556–7. He points out that the stool throne and beardless king could have been modelled on the seal of minority.
45. Skene (ed.), *Johannis de Fordun Chronica*, 293–5.
46. Duncan, *Kingship of the Scots*, 147; John Bannerman, 'The king's poet and the inauguration of Alexander III', *SHR* 68 (1989) 120–49.
47. Simon Taylor and D. E. R. Watt, with Brian Scott (eds), *Scotichronicon by Walter Bower in Latin and English*, vol. v (Aberdeen, 1990), 192–3.
48. This does not necessarily mean that the author belonged to Dunkeld itself; he could (for instance) have been at Inchcolm (in the diocese of Dunkeld,

where some bishops of Dunkeld were buried, although not Bishop Geoffrey). But Geoffrey had been a member of the royal household, holding the office of clerk of the liverance, before he became bishop in 1236, and would presumably have remained well connected in royal circles. A less personal notice of his achievements, and the epitaph on his tomb, is recorded in Taylor and Watt (eds), *Scotichronicon*, v. 192–3.

49. Taylor and Watt (eds), *Scotichronicon*, v. 438; Duncan, *Kingship of the Scots*, 134.

50. Taylor and Watt (eds), *Scotichronicon*, v. 435, and followed in Duncan, *Kingship of the Scots*, 146–8. See Donald Watt's discussion in Taylor and Watt (eds), *Scotichronicon*, v. 435–41, esp. 435 and 438 (at lines 56–7).

51. See in particular Duncan, 'Before coronation', 144–5, and Dauvit Broun, 'A new look at *Gesta Annalia* attributed to John of Fordun', in B. E. Crawford (ed.), *Church, Chronicle and Learning in Medieval and Early Renaissance Scotland* (Edinburgh, 1999), 9–30.

52. There is at least a formal possibility that the person writing between early February and mid-April 1285 was simply a continuator, and that *GAI* was largely written earlier. In the absence of a thoroughgoing investigation of *Gesta Annalia* and its sources this cannot be ruled out. As far as this discussion is concerned, however, this would simply mean that the rewriting of Alexander III's inauguration may have occurred earlier, whenever it may be supposed that *GAI* first took shape.

53. *sub discussione lis adhuc pendet*: Taylor and Watt (eds), *Scotichronicon*, v. 334, and see suggestion at 459 (for lines 10–19).

54. Amours (ed.), *Original Chronicle*, v. 138–9; Duncan, *Scotland: the Making of the Kingdom*, 609.

55. What follows could not have been written without Duncan, 'Before coronation', 144–5.

56. Duncan, 'Before coronation', 146.

57. Also, it may be noted that references to the Stone of Scone written by Scots after 1296 regularly refer to its removal by Edward I.

58. The angled brackets indicate changes to nominative (as subject of *adduxerunt*) from accusative (as object of *adiungentes* in the passage immediately preceding that 'has a clumsiness which is striking', and serves to link this chapter to the previous one: Duncan, 'Before coronation', 144).

59. Duncan, 'Before coronation', 146, has commented how *Et ecce . . .* follows naturally once the passage *Qui lapis . . . ab antiquis* is recognised as an interpolation. This also allows *peractis singulis* to refer to the spreading of their clothes by each of the nobles in turn. Previously it has been interpreted as referring to the ceremony of inauguration as a whole (Felix Skene translated it 'when all was over'), despite the fact that the ceremony was palpably not over.

60. This is usually translated 'his mother tongue', although there is no possessive pronoun. Given that Gaelic in this period was regularly referred to as *Scotica*, it would not be odd for Gaelic to be described as 'the mother

tongue'.

61. It appears that nominative forms have been used indiscriminately, including *Albanne* which I take to represent *Albanaig* (nom. pl. of *Albanach*, 'Scot') rather than *Alban* (gen. of *Alba*, 'Scotland'): the translation into Latin which follows immediately renders *re Albanne* as *rex Albanorum*, 'king of Scots'. *Dauid* is found in medieval Gaelic texts. See Dauvit Broun, 'Gaelic literacy in eastern Scotland, 1124–1249', in Huw Pryce (ed.), *Literacy in Medieval Celtic Societies* (Cambridge, 1998), 183–201, at 199 nn. 10, 22. (Note that my transcription of this passage is slightly different from that at 184.)

62. See Broun, *The Irish Identity*, 180–3. Diss's own manuscript, begun in 1188, still survives (London, Lambeth Palace MS 8: the genealogy is at fo. 107va32–b28).

63. This is especially likely if (as suggested below, 218–19) the only other person who wrote parts of the extant *GAI* made only a few additions which related specifically to the wars of independence. Without the genealogy the chapter would have been unusually short in relation to others in *GAI*.

64. G. W. S. Barrow, *Robert Bruce and the Community of the Realm of Scotland*, 3rd edn (Edinburgh, 1988), 151 (in his account of Robert I's inauguration in 1306).

65. Duncan, *Scotland: the Making of the Kingdom*, 115–16.

66. Katharine Simms, *From Kings to Warlords* (Woodbridge, 1987), 39.

67. Best on this is *ibid.*, 27–34 (esp. 32). Note A. A. M. Duncan, *The Nation of the Scots and the Declaration of Arbroath (1320)*, Historical Association Pamphlet (London, 1970), 8: 'The king . . . so modified the more ancient inauguration ritual that its ritual significance was forgotten and a new legend concocted to explain the ritual objects still in use.'

68. See Duncan, *Kingship of the Scots*, 151–2.

69. Duncan, *Scotland: the Making of the Kingdom*, 576.

70. Pope John XXII's bull is published in facsimile, transcribed and translated in Cosmo Innes (ed.), *Facsimiles of the National Manuscripts of Scotland*, 3 parts (Southampton 1867–71), ii. no. xxx. See also James Cooper, *Four Scottish Coronations*, special issue of the Aberdeen Ecclesiological Society and the Glasgow Ecclesiological Society (Aberdeen, 1902), 47–9.

71. Stones (ed.), *Anglo-Scottish Relations*, 34–7, 58–9 (bull of Gregory IX, in which Henry III's claim was endorsed, and bull of Innocent IV, in which Henry III's attempt to have a veto on any decision to award coronation and anointment to the king of Scots was rejected).

72. Summarised in Carpenter, *The Struggle for Mastery*, 345–7.

73. The illustration accompanying Bower's account in his working copy (Cambridge, Corpus Christi College MS 171), drawn in the 1440s, has erroneously situated the cross on the mound, presumably because the Moothill was such an obvious site; perhaps James I had been inaugurated on the Moothill in 1424. For a discussion of the illustration, see John Higgitt,

'Bower's working text: Corpus MS. Decoration and illustration', in Watt (ed.), *Scotichronicon*, ix. 157–85, at 172–4. The whole picture thus represents a curious mix of incompatible elements.

74. Duncan, 'Before coronation', 145–6, notes that no medieval written source says that the inauguration took place on the Moot Hill, and suggests that this absence reflects a real state of affairs. He prefers to see the cross as marking the original site; in Duncan, *Kingship of the Scots*, 144, he speculates that it might have replaced a sacred tree. Although there is evidence in Ireland for sacred inaugural trees, there is abundant evidence for the use of mounds (like the Moot Hill), and for stones on mounds. See Dauvit Broun, 'The origin of the Stone of Scone as a national icon', in R. Welander, D. Breeze and T. O. Clancy (eds), *The Stone of Destiny: Artefact and Icon* (Edinburgh, 2003), 183–97, at 191, citing Elizabeth FitzPatrick, 'The Practice and Siting of Royal Inauguration in Medieval Ireland', 2 vols, unpublished Ph.D. dissertation (Trinity College, Dublin, 1997). See also Elizabeth FitzPatrick, *Royal Inauguration in Gaelic Ireland c.1100–1600: a Cultural Landscape Study* (Woodbridge, 2004), esp. table 2 (at 228–9), where mounds are the principal feature in fourteen of twenty-five attested sites whose locations are known.

75. Duncan, 'Before coronation', 147.

76. See above, 162.

77. I am grateful to Walter Ullmann for pointing this out to me. It was first mentioned in print in Cooper, *Four Scottish Coronations*, 9; he also suggested a parallel with the reception the disciples gave Christ described in Matthew 21:8.

78. 2 Kings 9:12–13; translation of Vulgate adapted from Duncan, *Kingship of the Scots*, 146.

79. *APS*, i. 107.

80. Alexander IV's might perhaps relate to the provision of John of Cheam as bishop of Glasgow in 1259 against the king's will. It is noteworthy that no such bull is noted from Urban IV (1261–4), whose representative came to York in 1263 in an attempt to settle the disputed succession to the earldom of Menteith, something which Alexander III objected to strongly because the case was to be heard in a foreign kingdom and he, in any event, regarded succession to an earldom as falling within his jurisdiction: Shead, Stevenson and Watt (eds), *Scotichronicon*, v. 332–5.

81. Stones (ed.), *Anglo-Scottish Relations*, 58–9.

82. Text and translation of Honorius's bull (1218) in Stones (ed.), *Anglo-Scottish Relations*, 28–33; see 29 n. 2 for Innocent III's bull (1200).

83. A. D. M. Barrell, 'Scotland and the papacy in the reign of Alexander II', in Richard D. Oram (ed.), *The Reign of Alexander II, 1214–49* (Leiden, 2005), 157–77, at 158–60.

84. See below, 203.

85. Stones (ed.), *Anglo-Scottish Relations*, 34–7.

7

From Client King to Sovereign

Royal Charters and the Status of Scottish Kingship in the Reigns of William I (1165–1214) and Alexander II (1214–49)

The inauguration of Alexander III was the first occasion when Scottish leaders as a group would, by their participation in the ritual, have identified themselves explicitly with the idea of sovereign kingship. It was also, presumably, the first opportunity for this to have been communicated to a large audience. The symbolism of enthronement at the cross and the casting of garments at the new king's feet would doubtless have been explained to all and sundry, perhaps in a homily during a post-inaugural mass,[1] and those who performed these acts would presumably have been briefed about their significance. The ability of those at the heart of the kingship to respond so quickly and imaginatively to the sudden and unexpected opportunity of a royal inauguration in 1249 is impressive: Alexander II died on 8 July on the island of Kerrera, just under a hundred miles from Scone, and the inauguration of his seven-year-old son and heir took place on 13 July. We may guess that Scottish sovereignty was already well established in their minds for them to have agreed so swiftly on the innovative features in the inauguration.

Is it possible to say when this idea began to take root among those closest to the king, and to see whether it grew gradually, or if it was first espoused in response to a particular event? A contrast has been drawn between the Quitclaim of Canterbury (1189), in which King William's position as a client king in unfettered control of his own realm was restored, and the idea enacted at Alexander III's inauguration of Scotland as a realm of equal status with any other kingdom. How had Scottish thinking about their kingship changed so fundamentally in sixty years? The Quitclaim and the inauguration were each provoked by the accident of events, and offer only a rough guide to when and how the attitudes and aspirations they articulated had evolved. If the question is to be answered, then some other kind of source-material will have to be used which goes beyond the carefully chosen words of formal documents or the theatre of ritual. A clear answer would also hold out the promise of securing some vulnerable parts of the argument so far. It has been assumed that no attempts were made at Alexander II's inauguration in 1214 to portray him as a sovereign king, but this cannot be demonstrated conclusively for lack of sufficient detail about the ritual on that occasion.[2] The assumption is based largely on the idea that William I was happy to regard himself as a client king, but there is no direct evidence that this was so, or that he maintained this view until his dying day. It has simply been inferred, chiefly from events such as his homage to John at Lincoln in 1200. This is not a sound basis for discussing deep-seated aspirations, not least because events are dictated as much by circumstances as by intentions. Also, it must be recognised that the Quitclaim of Canterbury is not a simple expression of William's view on his relationship with the king of England: it is formally a statement of what both he and Richard were able to agree on this issue.

In studying the development of ideas of independence in relation to the Church, it was possible to recover the broader picture by looking beyond formal statements which were made on a particular occasion. There were texts produced at a little more leisure as part of a campaign on behalf of a church (like Jocelin's *Life of Kentigern* or the St Andrews foundation-legend), which offered a vivid insight into the aspirations of those for whom they were written; and also a work like the Office of Kentigern, composed in response to a more regular need, which revealed almost in passing a concern about Glasgow's place in relation to Scotland. Of particular value, however, was an incidental detail in a relatively mundane context, such as the inclusion of 'Welsh' in the racial address in a few significant royal charters in favour of Glasgow drafted by its clerks. We need not doubt that this was a carefully calculated act; but it was so simple to put into effect that it had the potential to reflect even the most general attitudes and assumptions in a direct and meaningful way. Something similar is required if we are to trace with greater clarity the change in thinking of kings of Scots, and those closest to them, about their kingship in the context of relations with the king of England. There is one type of evidence from the heart of the royal household which has the potential to meet this need: the evidence of the diplomatic of royal charters. This can seem a rather technical subject. It will inevitably involve some discussion of apparently trifling details about formulaic elements in charters, and also some consideration of aspects of the seemingly dry topic of royal administration. It is argued in this chapter, however, that changes in the way charters of kings of Scots were dated and in the use of the 'royal we' repay close scrutiny. What is revealed is the gradual dawning of the novel idea that the king of Scots was no longer subordinate to the king of England, but was of equal status. It is also apparent that such an idea was unthinkable to William I and his entourage, who continued to hanker after the old pattern of independent kingship under the British overkingship of the king of England.

A CHANGE IN THE DATING CLAUSE OF ROYAL CHARTERS IN 1195

At the centre of this discussion of Scottish royal diplomatic is an attempt to solve a puzzle. Shortly after Easter in 1195, probably by 17 April, while William I was residing at Clackmannan, a standard form of dating royal charters was determined which, with some very rare exceptions, was adhered to until it began to be modified in 1221.[3] The immediate inspiration was a change a few years earlier in English practice. This was not replicated precisely by Scottish royal scribes, however. Instead, a curious variation was adopted which has defied a satisfactory explanation.

From the outset of Richard I's reign (even before his coronation on 3 September 1189),[4] English royal charters conferring or confirming perpetuities concluded with a dating clause giving the place, the day of the month, and the regnal year; this was preceded by a statement, beginning with the words *per manum* ('by the hand'), identifying the chancery official who produced the charter. It has long been recognised that this was, in effect, a less elaborate version of the dating clause in papal solemn privileges and that something very similar was found in French royal diplomas.[5] Before Richard I's reign it had been customary for royal charters to finish with a place-date only; a time-date was a rare luxury, appearing only sporadically, and in various forms. There are also a few charters with a *per manum* clause towards the end of Henry II's reign.[6]

The practice adopted by Scottish royal clerks was a much less elaborate version of Richard I's dating clause. From April 1195, with only one or two exceptions before the end of William's reign, royal charters were given a time-date as well as the usual place-date.[7] The time-date, however, consisted of only the day of the month (e.g., 17 April): there are no examples where the day of month is followed by the regnal year or the year of the Incarnation. Professor Barrow has shown that for the remainder of William's reign the day of the month time-date almost always took the same form in those charters which survive as contemporary single sheets (for example, *xvij. die Aprilis*).[8] There is only one example of a *per manum* clause, which, instead of preceding the dating clause (as in English royal charters), follows it; indeed, it has been placed at the foot of the document and appears detached from the rest of the text.[9] (Another highly unusual feature in this particular charter is that the *per manum* clause is followed by the year of the Incarnation, which is thus quite separate from the day of month.)

Before the simple time-date was adopted in 1195, William's charters had only ever sported a place-date: earlier sporadic and varied attempts to supply a time-date were abandoned in William's reign.[10] It is likely that the last extant charter before the adoption of a time-date is the one with a Clackmannan place-date which Professor Barrow suggests, in his edition of William's *acta*, was produced in '1195?', publishing it immediately before the first charter with a time-date.[11] This can be affirmed not only by the Clackmannan place-date (previous charters with a Clackmannan place-date are no later than about 1170),[12] but by the fact that the witness list includes two individuals who otherwise appear frequently in royal charters with the new time-date formula: this charter is the only occasion in which William de Valognes, who succeeded his father, Philip, as king's chamberlain in 1215, and Alexander son of Thor, sheriff of Clackmannan, are found in a royal charter without a time-date.[13] Before we get too attached to Clackmannan's special place in the history of Scottish diplomatic, however, it should be stressed that the nature of the dating clause makes it possible that the charter dated 'at Clackmannan, on 17 April', regarded as the first extant example of this time-date, was not from 1195: it could conceivably be as late as 1199.[14] It is necessary to note, therefore, that the earliest certain example of a charter with the new time-date is one produced at Jedburgh on 4 July 1195.[15]

There can be little doubt that the new standard dating clause in Scottish royal charters was adopted in the light of recent practice in Richard I's chancery. It may be guessed that William's entourage in his two visits to Richard's court would have had the opportunity to become aware of English chancery practice; certainly William, on each occasion, departed with a document from Richard I in his hands (the Quitclaim of Canterbury, 5 December 1189, and a letter patent of 17 April 1194 establishing arrangements for future visits of a king of Scots to the English royal court).[16] Both documents, of course, sported the new English dating clause complete with regnal year as well as the day of the month. Now, it might not seem too odd that, when this dating clause was adopted and adapted by the Scottish royal chapel, the *per manum* clause was deemed to be dispensable. It appears very strange, however, that it was decided to eschew the regnal year completely, even in the most formal charters. The possibility cannot be denied absolutely that an occasional example might once have existed, like the lone surviving instance of the *per manum* clause. Nonetheless, in the face of the unanimous evidence of all 145 extant charter-texts for the remainder of William's reign (fifty of which are contemporary single sheets), and more than fifty extant charter-texts of Alexander II before the dating clause began to be modified in 1221, it would not be unduly rash to assume that it was consciously determined that the regnal year should be avoided, and that this was adhered to scrupulously until the time-date came under review in 1221.

EXPLAINING THE NEW DATING CLAUSE OF ROYAL CHARTERS: AN AID TO RETRIEVING COPIES KEPT BY ROYAL CLERKS?

The only serious attempt hitherto to account for the adoption of a time-date in Scottish royal charters serves, if anything, to heighten the sense that the failure to use regnal years was a curiously perverse decision. Geoffrey Barrow has commented that 'it seems impossible to explain this practice [of using a time-date] save on the assumption that from this point in the reign onwards the clerks of the chapel began to copy acts on rolls which were made up, or freshly headed, for each regnal year'.[17] Professor Barrow goes on, however, to note that 'the form in which it was added . . . must have been slightly inadequate even for contemporary clerks'.[18] If part of the intention was to provide a way of authenticating charters by enabling any single sheet to be matched with an enrolled copy, then this would, indeed, have been made unnecessarily difficult by omitting the regnal year from the single sheet itself. It would be a mistake, though, to put too much weight on this. It should be noted, for example, that safeguarding against forgery cannot have been the chief purpose of the patent rolls and close rolls maintained by the English chancery in the early thirteenth century; the close rolls were filled with copies of documents which typically included only the day of the month, and not the regnal year. The regnal year was also frequently omitted from the documents enrolled in the patent rolls. It was only in the third (and earliest) of the rolls maintained by the English chancery, the charter rolls, that each item was consistently adorned with the regnal year.[19]

The existence of some Scottish administrative records by 1195 is not in question. Unfortunately, this is impossible to quantify, given that all such records were lost when Edward I attempted to ship them down to England; but an inventory of the holdings in Edinburgh Castle was made in 1296 under the direction of Hugh Cressingham, Edward I's treasurer in Scotland.[20] One item can certainly be identified as earlier than 1200, and it can be inferred from another that records may have been kept as early as 1182 (if not earlier).[21] Not surprisingly Treasurer Cressingham's inventory is concerned principally with records of royal revenue. If we want to find any detail about rolls of other types of document, it is necessary to turn to an even more jejune inventory of the documents in Edinburgh Castle, compiled in 1292.[22] Here mention is made of a large roll containing sixty-two 'pieces' which included, *inter alia*, copies of charters and confirmations by 'various kings'; and another roll, consisting of twelve membranes, concerning 'ancient charters' and other documents from the reigns of William I and Alexander II.[23] This is all frustratingly elusive. It might be added, though, that where there is reference to the date of any rolls (and this is confined to those concerning royal revenue), there is no indication that regnal years were used. AD dates are the order of the day, except for one roll (at least) in which dates were also given according to a nineteen-year cycle.[24]

Even if it was agreed that some charters, at least, were enrolled from some point in King William's reign onwards, it is questionable whether this can bear the burden of explaining the adoption of a time-date in Scottish royal charters. The adoption of time-dates by the English chancery has no obvious relationship with the practice of keeping copies. The first of the charter rolls belongs to the first year of John's reign (1199–1200); a separate roll for letters patent was not begun until John's third year; and the earliest extant roll for letters close, which is incomplete, is for John's second year.[25] The rolls of ancient charters are another kettle of fish: whatever their purpose was, it cannot be said to represent a systematic attempt at enrolment.[26] The practice of giving each document issued by the chancery a time-date, initiated by Richard I, does not, therefore, have any apparent relationship with record keeping. There can, in any event, be no explanation within the practical concerns of day-to-day administration for the conscientious omission of regnal years by Scottish royal scribes. This, and indeed the whole issue of the adoption of a time-date as a regular feature of royal charters, naturally inhabits the world of charter diplomatic rather than record-keeping. Thankfully, this means that the problem can be investigated by examining a considerable body of texts, and a critical mass of contemporary single sheets plus some well-preserved seals, rather than by groping in the inadequate traces of a lost archive.

THE ADOPTION OF ENGLISH FEATURES IN SCOTTISH ROYAL CHARTERS

The most relevant background here is the development of Scottish royal charters in relation to their model, the charters of English kings. From the earliest charter of a Scottish king which may be discerned as the work of a royal scribe, it is clear that English royal charters provided ready-made exemplars of what a document in a king's name might contain and what it might look like.[27] A notable example of this in William's reign is the adoption of *Dei gratia* ('by the grace of God') in the royal style some-time between August 1173 and December 1174 soon after it had been adopted in English royal charters sometime between May 1172 and February 1173.[28] Professor Barrow has regarded this change as 'prompted by the king of Scots' desire to demonstrate that he was as much a true king as Henry fitzEmpress'.[29] Certainly, it is particularly poignant that the earliest use of the new royal style in an extant single sheet by one of King William's scribes has Northampton as its place-date, which suggests, as Professor Barrow has pointed out, that the charter was produced sometime in December 1174 when William was on his way back from his humiliation at Falaise.[30] As is well known, William had there agreed to become Henry II's vassal for Scotland in a treaty in which a careful contrast was made throughout its prose between Henry as 'lord king' (*dominus rex*) and William as simply 'king' (*rex*).[31]

There are, however, dangers in interpreting any change in charter practice in isolation. For example, later in the same decade Scottish royal clerks were not slow to follow their English counterparts in abandoning the 'racial address', which is last found in current use in a charter which may probably be dated to 1179.[32] Professor Donaldson took this to mean that the 'various races' had now become 'simply subjects of the king of Scots, and therefore themselves Scots'.[33] This would anticipate a development which, in the English south-east of Scotland, is attested in the Chronicle of Melrose a century later.[34] A less dramatic, but surely more plausible interpretation would be that here, as in other instances where the more intimate twists and turns of English chancery practice have been followed, the main concern was that a Scottish royal charter should maximise its credibility by conforming with the readily apparent exemplar of royal authority provided by documents of the English Crown. A similar motivation could also account for the adoption of *Dei gratia* so soon after it became a regular feature of English chancery practice.

Given the importance of English royal charters as a model, it is especially noteworthy when Scottish practice appears deliberately to have chosen a different course. A particularly striking example, as far as the charter text is concerned, is the increasing preference in the reigns of David I and Mael Coluim IV for *probis hominibus* ('to men of standing') in the address as the catch-all term for the king's subjects, rather than *fidelibus suis* ('to his faithful') favoured by English chancery scribes.[35] It is difficult to determine the significance of this. It is much easier, however, to appreciate differences in the visual representation of kingship on the seal. Professor Duncan has pointed out that, although the design of the portrayal of the king was modelled on the English royal seal, William I and his son Alexander II (1214–49) were represented without a crown:[36] indeed, it is likely that neither Alexander I (1107–24), David I (1124–53) nor Mael Coluim IV (1153–65) sported a crown on their seals either.[37] It is also striking that the legend advertised them as *Deo rectore rex Scottorum*, 'by God the ruler, king of Scots', rather than *Dei gratia*, 'by the grace of God', as in the English royal seal, and, as we have seen, despite the fact that *Dei gratia* had become part of the standard royal style in the charter text itself from no later than December 1174 onwards.[38] Professor Duncan makes the convincing suggestion that the avoidance of *Dei gratia* on the seal in conjunction with the lack of a crown on the depiction of the king in majesty 'indicates that the designer of the seal had in mind the absence of anointing and coronation from the ceremony of royal inauguration'.[39] It might be objected that the lack of coronation and anointment did not prevent Alexander III (1249–86) from sporting a crown on his seals, or from *Dei gratia* replacing *Deo rectore* in the recast small seal which was used during his minority (probably after the destruction of the great seal in January 1252).[40] By this stage, however, there was evidently a conviction among those closest to the kingship that the king of Scots should be portrayed as a king in the fullest sense, enjoying all the established symbols of royal dignity insofar as this could be engineered in the face of the papacy's failure to cooperate.[41]

As far as the absence of coronation and anointment is concerned, it might be objected that this was beyond the control of the Scots; it might therefore be dangerous to see the lack of a crowned king and avoidance of *Dei gratia* in the seal's legend before 1249 as indicative of limited aspirations, rather than simply a willingness to accept reality. A charter-text, however, offered a variety of opportunities to indicate kingship in the fullest sense in ways which need not have been limited by the lack of coronation and anointment; moreover, it seems that there was greater freedom of expression, insofar as it was obviously deemed appropriate to adopt *Dei gratia* as a regular feature in the charter-text but not on the seal. If there was a consistent desire to present King William as the equal of the king of England, then there was certainly scope to do so.

The overall impression, however, is that King William and his chapel of scribes did not see themselves as in the same league as the English king.

For example, the adoption of *Dei gratia* in the royal style must be balanced against a failure to employ the first person plural, the 'royal we', which was a routine feature of the charters of Richard I and his successors, lending greater dignity to the written utterances of the monarch.[42] Again, Scottish royal scribes cannot have been ignorant of this development, and would surely have appreciated its significance. The fact, then, that King William persisted until the end of his reign in speaking in the first person singular in his charters, with only very few exceptions, suggests that the Scottish royal chapel had consciously decided not to recalibrate the prose of royal charters in this way, and were ready to accept that, in this respect at least, the king of Scots would appear a notch lower than the king of England.

CHARTERS OF WILLIAM I WITH THE PLURAL OF MAJESTY

Unfortunately matters cannot be allowed to rest there. There are some exceptions to the use of the singular 'I' and 'my' which it would be indecent to ignore, and which demand some explanation. This is particularly pressing in the case of one charter where the 'royal we' is pervasive. This charter (which I will refer to as no. 493, its number in Barrow's edition of William's *acta*) has led to the suggestion that there was a time when 'the royal chapel had made a firm decision to change from the older singular usage to the newer plural usage'.[43] The charter is dated at Stirling on 22 June, probably 1210, and confirms agreements between Melrose and Kelso abbeys. What makes no. 493 particularly significant is that it survives as a contemporary single sheet by a royal scribe. If this does show a change of policy, however, Professor Barrow acknowledges that it must have been brief. If we follow Barrow's chronological arrangement of the charters, then there are no further examples of the plural of majesty in the nine charters after no. 493 surviving as contemporary single sheets produced by royal scribes: moreover, all nine are in the hand of Gilbert of Stirling, the same scribe as no. 493 itself.[44]

An examination of the very few other charters of King William which use the first person plural suggests another explanation for its appearance in no. 493; namely that a draft text, including the plural of majesty, was produced elsewhere and was taken to the royal chapel for copying and sealing. (By this stage all charters appear to have been produced physically by the royal chapel: see below.) This would imply that some of the king's subjects were prepared to go further than the royal chapel itself in the dignity accorded to their king in the prose of these charters. Leaving no. 493 aside, there are four other charters with the plural of majesty (not including one which is suspect and another which has the plural form inconsistently in the first dispositive clause, and the singular in the second).[45] Three of the four are for the bishop of Glasgow and his cathedral establishment, and were evidently drafted by Glasgow clerks. This is obvious in one case, dated at Roxburgh and datable to sometime between 1189 and 1195,[46] because the text is so untypical: it is, in Geoffrey Barrow's words, 'couched in an altogether unusually rhetorical style and could almost be said to constitute one long harangue'.[47] We have met the two other Glasgow examples in a previous chapter:[48] they are the almost verbatim copies of a charter of Mael Coluim IV which sported the Welsh in its unique version of the racial address. It will be recalled that these, too, had a Glasgow origin, and that the text had apparently been presented on each occasion by the bishop and copied by a royal scribe (if it was not simply recopied by one of the bishop's clerks and presented for sealing), with only the witness list and dating clause being cast afresh. The fourth and final example is a charter which poses some problems which have recently come under Professor Duncan's scrutiny.[49] This is a confirmation of Bishop Jocelin of Glasgow's grant of a church to Melrose on the king's advice following a dispute between the king and the bishop over patronage. Its place-date is Melrose. Professor Barrow gives it a date-range of 1193×1195, with a tentative preference for 1193, while Professor Duncan has argued for late 1195, after 10 September, despite the lack of a time-date and other hidden difficulties.[50] The dating is important because the scribe has been identified as Gervase, who began his career as a clerk of Bishop Jocelin before transferring to the royal chapel 'c.1194–5'.[51] Is this, then, an example of Gervase's work as an episcopal clerk or as a royal scribe? The simplest answer may lie in the clear attempt to give the script the appearance of a papal document, something which would be more in character for an episcopal clerk than a royal scribe.[52] Certainly the influence of a papal model would be sufficient to explain the unusual use of the plural of majesty. According to this line of argument this would be another example of a royal charter drafted by a Glasgow clerk.

Returning again to no. 493, there is one internal feature which could lend weight to the suggestion that the text was drafted by someone outside the royal chapel. This is found in the witness list, where King William's sons, Alexander and Robert of London, are each referred to as *filius domini regis*, 'son of the lord king'. The usual formula is *filius meus*, 'my son' (which would have become *filius noster*, 'our son', in this case). The choice of words would at least be consistent with a document drafted by someone who was unaccustomed to speaking for the king, as it were, and who naturally referred to him in an objective way, rather than in the first person as royal clerks had learnt to do. It would be difficult to insist on this feature as certain evidence that a text was drafted outside the royal chapel.[53] It is instructive, however, in the case of King William's brother David and his son Alexander, at least, that out of the seventy royal charters in which they appear as a witness, they are described as 'the king's brother' or 'the king's son' (rather than 'my brother' or 'my son') in only five. Four of these five charters were almost certainly drafted by the beneficiary. Two are even in the hand of a beneficiary's scribe (the same Melrose scribe in both cases);[54] the other two (which survive only as cartulary copies) are general confirmations for religious houses (Dunfermline and Arbroath) which are each modelled very closely on previous general confirmations.[55] This points to a scenario similar to that suggested above for the Glasgow charters repeating an earlier text; moreover, the general confirmation for Dunfermline is, uniquely for William I, in the form of a diploma, a type favoured by Dunfermline for this kind of document.[56] The only example that cannot be accounted for so confidently as a text drafted outside the royal chapel is a confirmation of a grant to Huntingdon priory in the first years of William's reign; this also survives only as a cartulary copy.[57]

The lack of the regnal year in Scottish royal charters, after a time-date was adopted as a standard feature, can therefore be explained as a carefully calibrated statement of the kingship's status. It was not simply that English chancery practice was followed only minimally. The key here is an important variation in the dating clause of papal documents (which was imitated by Richard I's chancery), whereby the pontifical year was used consistently only for solemn privileges and grants of perpetuities. Ephemeral letters and instructions, in contrast, were typically endowed with a shorter dating clause in which the time-date was reduced to the day of the month. By the end of the twelfth century, therefore, the royal household would have been accustomed to associating a time-date restricted to the day of month with documents of lesser significance emanating from the ultimate authority in Christendom. This, then, indicates where the Scottish kingship placed itself in the spectrum of prestige and authority: it did not claim to be a supreme power, but regarded itself as a kingship nonetheless, exhibiting a lesser kind of dignity in the diplomatic of its charters.

CHANGES IN THE DIPLOMATIC OF ROYAL CHARTERS IN THE REIGN OF ALEXANDER II

This has obvious implications for what the adoption of the regnal year in Alexander II's charters signified. It is noteworthy, moreover, that this occurred at about the same time as the plural of majesty became a regular feature: indeed, *anno regni nostri* ('in the year of our reign') was the formula used in the earliest charters which featured the regnal year in the time-date. Before examining this in a little more detail I should warn that there is no published collection of Alexander II's charters, so any comments about them should, strictly speaking, be regarded as provisional. The task of producing the *Regesta Regum Scottorum* volume for Alexander II is in the masterly hands of Keith Stringer, however, and I am very grateful to him for notifying me of charters which have a bearing on the discussion that follows. It should also be said at the outset that the first extant document in Alexander II's name to bear a regnal year cannot be regarded as representing a change of practice by the king's chapel. This was a written undertaking Alexander gave to Henry III of England, at York on 15 June 1220, which was paired with a written undertaking by Henry to Alexander.[58] Both documents are identical in terms of their diplomatic, which conforms with English practice, and were presumably drafted at the same time by an English chancery clerk.

A year later Alexander was back in York, marrying Joanna, Henry III's sister, on Saturday 19 June, 1221. It is in connection with this occasion that we see the first clear sign of dissatisfaction with the dating-clause used by the royal chapel since 1195. On 18 June the tocher assigned by Alexander to Joanna was recorded in a charter which, as well having the day of the month, had the novelty of an *Anno Domini* date in its time-date.[59] This was not a flash in the pan. The same combination of AD date and day of the month was used in the next three charters in Scoular's hand-list, each for a different beneficiary: the last was on 22 February 1222.[60] By 20 April 1222 a new practice had been established: the regnal year displaced the AD date, and thereafter (at long last) it became a standard feature of the dating-clause of royal charters.[61] A few months later the transition to a fuller expression of royalty was achieved when the plural of majesty was adopted as a standard feature after 10 July and in or before 21 July 1222.[62] Finally, it is noteworthy that the regnal year appears regularly on brieves from at least 10 April 1224.[63] There is, unfortunately, no way of telling whether there are any extant brieves from between April 1222 and April 1224 which lacked the regnal year: very few brieves survive, and among those that do survive from the first decade of Alexander's reign, there are two which have been assigned date-limits of 1215×1225 by Scoular.[64]

At the end of this period of transition, from no later than mid-June 1221 to mid-July 1222, Alexander II's charters had not become a carbon copy of current English chancery practice: for example, no attempt was made to introduce a *per manum* clause into the dating clause. Nonetheless, his written utterances had become that of a king in the fullest sense, at least insofar as the charter-text was concerned: on his seal, of course, Alexander remained uncrowned. The fact that the regnal year was adopted only after nearly a year's experimentation with the AD date might, however, suggest that there was some hesitation. Once the ball was set rolling, though, it did not stop where it had arrived in mid-July 1222. The dating clause itself was altered so that the regnal year was no longer *anno regni nostri* ('in the year of our reign') but became *anno regni domini regis* ('in the year of the reign of the lord king'): at first this formula was deployed intermittently, but by 24 April 1229 it had become a consistent feature.[65] This was an indigenous development, without an English parallel, and remained a consistent feature for the remainder of Alexander II's reign (although it did not long outlast it).[66]

COMPARISONS AND CONTRASTS: THE CHARTERS OF LLYWELYN AP IORWERTH

An important perspective on these changes is offered by a brief consideration of the charters of the rulers of Gwynedd. They also attempted to improve the dignity of their charters, but did not go as far as Alexander II. What they did, and what they did not do, reinforces the impression that the consistent use of a time-date, and particularly the regnal year, was regarded as particularly significant in the period under review. It must be admitted, however, that the documents of the rulers of Gwynedd cannot be discussed with the same ease as those of their Scottish counterparts. There are much fewer charter-texts, let alone contemporary single sheets, to work with.[67] Also, the most unusual (and interesting) documents diplomatically are often the most problematic. Nevertheless, two significant developments are discernible in charters relating to perpetuities. The first is the regular use of the plural of majesty from 1223, with some examples in the previous two decades.[68] The second is the use from the 1240s (with very few exceptions) of a time-date consisting of the day of the month (according to either ecclesiastical or Roman calendar) and AD date.[69] There are earlier examples in 1221, 1229, 1230, 1237 and 1238,[70] but four of these are all for the same beneficiary, the priory of Ynys Lannog (Priestholm), and may only be taken to reflect what Ynys Lannog thought was appropriate for documents of the ruler of Gwynedd and his heir.[71] (It will be recalled that some Scottish church establishments may have endowed the king of Scots with more dignified prose than did the king's scribes.) Two charters must, however, be mentioned, because they give the year of Llywelyn ap Iorwerth's principate as well as day of the month and AD date.[72] Both are for the abbey of Aberconwy, and were purportedly produced on the same occasion. Charles Insley has shown that neither is likely to be authentic as they stand, a view endorsed by Huw Pryce.[73] The dignity of a year of principate, moreover, is balanced by another charter in Llywelyn's name with a remarkable dating-clause: 'at Rhuthin in the octave of St Martin in the tenth year of the reign of Henry the younger, king of England', i.e., 18 November 1225.[74] The dating by the king of England's regnal year is a striking statement of subordination, comparable with the occasional use of the king of Scots' regnal year in private charters in Scotland during William's reign.[75] Again, however, there are doubts about authenticity. The most recent assessment is that 'the probable incompatibility of the prince's style with the dating clause renders the document's authenticity suspect', particularly with regard to the protocol or the dating clause.[76]

Although the use of the plural of majesty was found much more frequently in Llywelyn ap Iorwerth's charters in the first decades of the thirteenth century than it was in the charters of Scottish kings, it is striking that anything like a policy towards including a time-date only became established very much later.[77] The time-date that was eventually adopted, moreover, was of a kind (with some variation in how the day was identified) that was beginning, by the 1240s, to catch on in private charters in Scotland: for example, in a charter of Richard of Leicester, burgess of Perth, in 1240,[78] a charter of Mael Domnaich, earl of Lennox, in 1238[79] and another charter by Affrica, lady of Strathnith, in 1227.[80] Some, if not all, of these are likely to have been drafted by the beneficiary. By the time Llywelyn ap Gruffudd was at the zenith of his power in 1267 it was becoming common for private documents in Scotland to be adorned with dating-clauses which were as dignified as those in the charters of the 'Prince of Wales and Lord of Snowdon'.

It might be objected that the absence of the year of his principate from the standard dating clause of the ruler of Gwynedd's charters may be linked in some way to the fact that king-lists were not maintained in Wales in this period or earlier.[81] In a culture where reign-lengths were not calculated, the regnal year might not have come to consciousness in the dating of a charter as readily as in Scotland, where not only was the king-list an established genre, but the current king's regnal year might be known in as 'remote' a place as Deer.[82] The existence of the year of principate in two Aberconwy charters, regardless of their status, may go some way towards allaying such doubts (for they were almost certainly produced at Aberconwy itself, albeit probably *ca* 1283 and 1284×1332 respectively). As far as the special importance of the regnal year for Alexander II is concerned, however, there is, fortunately, a clear indication that he at that time wished to advance his status far higher than any ruler of Gwynedd is known to have dreamt of attempting.

ALEXANDER'S REQUESTS TO THE PAPACY FOR CORONATION, AND THE DAWNING OF SCOTTISH SOVEREIGNTY

Sometime early in 1221 James of St Victor, the pope's legate *de latere* for Scotland and Ireland, arrived in Scotland, holding a council at Perth on 9–12 February, and leaving sometime after 21 April 1221.[83] At some point (it is not clear when) Alexander diverted the legate's gaze from ecclesiastical concerns with a bold request: that he should crown him king. The legate contacted Pope Honorius for instructions. Honorius's response survives, and was a bitter blow to Alexander. Not only was coronation refused, but the legate was told that this was none of his business because the king of Scotland was said to be subject to the king of England; the matter was up to the king of England and his councillors to decide.[84] Paul Ferguson has pointed out that Honorius's reply is one of four undated letters recorded among those of June 1221 in the register for Honorius's fifth year.[85] It is not certainly known, therefore, when Alexander would have become aware of the pope's answer. It may safely be assumed, however, that the adoption of the regnal year and plural of majesty in 1222 was effected after the pope's blunt affirmation of Alexander's inferior status had been thoroughly digested.

This incident might also offer a more precise understanding of Alexander's conception of his kingship at this time. It will be recalled that some hesitation was discerned in the assumption of the trappings of full kingship in the text of Alexander's charters. Perhaps this could be explained as a reaction to the rebuff from the pope. A strict reading of Pope Honorius's reference to Alexander's request would suggest that Alexander did not seek coronation and anointment, but coronation alone. This may be to read too much into silence, but it contrasts with Innocent IV's reference to a Scottish request thirty years later, in which both coronation *and* anointment are specified.[86] It appears, then, that in early 1221 Alexander may not have been aiming for exactly the same degree of dignity as that enjoyed by the king of England.[87] Again, the significance of this can be debated: he must have known that politically he had no chance of persuading the pope to grant him coronation *and* anointment. Nonetheless, it is possible overall to view Alexander in 1221–2 as feeling his way towards an outcome that was initially uncertain, and to contrast this with the confident assertiveness of those in charge of government at the beginning of Alexander III's reign, who clearly had no doubts that their monarch was as much a king as any other in Christendom.

To conclude: the addition of a time-date in 1195, which seems superficially to be so odd when taken on its own, can most readily be understood by being considered alongside the changes to the time-date in 1221–2 rather than by being examined in the light of the fragmentary evidence for enrolments by the Scottish chapel in the late twelfth century. The case for seeing the evolution of the dating clause as first and foremost a matter of diplomatic can also be justified by the close association between the introduction of the plural of majesty and the adoption of the regnal year as standard features of Scottish royal charters. To say this is not, however, to say that these are simply disinterested changes in clerical fashion whose greatest virtue for historians is that they supply a mechanism for testing the 'authenticity' of charters. I would argue, rather, that they give us unprecedented access to how the king and his household regarded their own kingship. Although the process of producing a charter can, as we have seen, be far from straightforward, there can be no doubt that a new standard feature would only have been initiated on the chancellor's authority.

Our understanding of the significance of these changing perceptions of kingship would be enhanced if a convincing political context could be found for them. This is difficult to achieve. It might be argued that the kingship's status was most likely to be reappraised when relations with England were particularly topical, as they were to some extent in 1195, and certainly were at the time of Alexander's marriage to Henry III's sister. In any case, a redefinition of the status of the Scottish kingship must inherently involve its relationship with kings of England, not least because they consistently sought to limit Scottish aspirations. Nevertheless, these changes cannot be represented in a two-dimensional way as simply a Scottish response to English dominance, culminating in defiant declarations of sovereignty at the outset of Alexander III's reign. Alexander II, in fact, had been treated as Henry III's equal throughout the protracted negotiations leading to his marriage to Joanna. The inauguration of a boy king nearly thirty years later would have been an anxious time for those in government, but their fears are likely to have been fuelled by domestic considerations as much as by any imagined threat from the English king. There is, moreover, no apparent connection between relations with England and the change from *anno regni nostri* ('the year of our reign') to *anno regni domini regis* ('the year of the reign of the lord king') in April 1229.

It should not be forgotten, of course, that the main audience for charters was domestic. It may be significant, therefore, that the new time-date in 1195 could be seen as part of a review of clerical practice in the chapel which was responsible for another important innovation at about this time. Professor Barrow has shown that all William's charters in the final decades of his reign which survive as contemporary single sheets were scribed by royal clerks. From April 1195 (including the charter immediately prior to the adoption of the time-date) up to William's death in December 1214 there are fifty-one 'originals', representing a third of all known charters from this period: all of them are by six royal scribes.[88] It appears that, at some point, it was insisted that all royal charters should be scribed (at least) in the royal chapel. Any hope of dating this decision with any precision is unfortunately bedevilled not only by the issue of the uneven survival of originals but also by the lack of the time-date before April 1195. There is some indication, however, that it had occurred sometime between 1193 and April 1196.[89]

Although a specific context for each and every change seems allusive, it may still be valid to sketch a broad brush-stroke background. In the light of what Rees Davies has recently taught us about the dominant role within Britain and Ireland exercised by Henry II and subsequent kings of England it should come as no surprise that William I was viewed by his household, and presumably saw himself, as in a lower league of kingship. It will be recalled, however, that the nature of this dominance had begun to change fundamentally when William's submission in December 1174 was recorded in writing.[90] What was spelt out for everyone to read was how, for the first time, the independence of a subordinate kingdom had been systematically subverted. No longer was the king of Scots deemed 'in his kingdom to be all things alone, . . . [unwilling to] endure that any authority have the least power in any matter, without his control' (to quote a contemporary's assessment of Alexander I's view of what it meant to be king of Scots).[91] The king of England now sought to bind not just William to him, but also William's subjects, and to insist that no-one could escape his justice by fleeing to Scotland. The distinction between overkingship and kingship was fading rapidly: a new pattern had emerged whereby a ruler who submitted to the king of England would have to make some formal recognition of superior jurisdiction.

It might, perhaps, be thought that the tendency to view overkingship as having a jurisdictional element would have provoked a reaction in the way subordinate kingships presented themselves. There can be no doubt that Alexander I's dictum that the king in his kingdom should be all things alone was shared by William and Alexander II, as seen, for example, in their dealings with the Church.[92] It was not until the reign of Alexander III, however, that this was articulated as a full and clear statement of Scottish sovereignty, when an attempt to achieve coronation and anointment was made, the image of the king was remodelled on his seal, and the royal inauguration was adapted to portray the new king as divinely ordained. This, however, seems to have been inconceivable for King William and his household. They seem, rather, to have hankered after the old pattern of subordinate kingship and overkingship, as if the clock had been turned back once the objectionable Treaty of Falaise had been rescinded. Even when the kingship's status was reappraised in 1221–2, it may not be too fanciful to see in the step-by-step enhancement of royal diplomatic the uncertain dawning of a new idea: that Scotland was a sovereign kingdom.

NOTES

1. The earliest reference to a post-inaugural mass is in 1292, but it can be inferred on earlier occasions (especially given that Scone Abbey was 'on site'): Duncan, 'Before coronation', 165.

2. W. W. Scott, 'Fordun's description of the inauguration of Alexander II', *SHR* 50 (1971) 198–200.

3. Easter Day was 2 April. King William would presumably have celebrated this in a major church. The evidence for Clackmannan as the place where this decision was made is discussed below.

4. Pierre Chaplais, *English Royal Documents King John–King Henry VI, 1199–1461* (Oxford, 1971), 14.

5. C. R. Cheney, *English Bishops' Chanceries 1100–1250* (Manchester, 1950), 86–7.

6. Chaplais, *English Royal Documents*, 14; V. H. Galbraith, 'Seven charters of Henry II at Lincoln Cathedral', *Antiquaries Journal* 12 (1932) 269–78.

7. *RRS*, ii. 82. The only certain exception is no. 405, datable to 1198×1200, a re-grant of lands to William son of Philip de Valognes (who had been William's chamberlain). It survives as a contemporary single sheet by a royal scribe identified by Geoffrey Barrow as Hugh de Sigillo (*ibid.*, 89). The omission appears to have been a simple oversight. Professor Duncan's redating of no. 365 to late 1195 (A. A. M. Duncan, 'Roger of Howden and Scotland, 1187–1201', in B. E. Crawford (ed.), *Church, Chronicle and Learning* (Edinburgh, 1999), 135–59, at 135–9) would make this another exception. See below, 198, for further discussion of this pivotal charter.

8. *RRS*, ii. 82.

9. *Ibid.*, no. 434. This bears comparison with contemporary French royal diplomas: see A. Giry, *Manuel de Diplomatique* (Paris, 1894), 755. I am grateful to Huw Pryce for this suggestion. There is one episcopal charter (of

Bishop Roger of St Andrews, 17 June 1200) which has the complete set of *per manum* clause, date of month and pontifical year: Thomas Thomson (ed.), *Liber Cartarum Prioratus Sancti Andree in Scotia* (Edinburgh, 1841), 153–4.

10. Barrow, *Scotland and its Neighbours*, 100.
11. *RRS*, ii. no. 375: it survives as a contemporary single sheet, and is the earliest attributed by Barrow to the royal scribe, Hugh de Sigillo (*ibid.*, 89). Unfortunately this is the same scribe who accidentally omitted the time-date on one occasion: see n. 7, above.
12. *Ibid.*, nos 102 (1165×72) and 103 (1165×70).
13. *Ibid.*, *ad indicem*. For Alexander as sheriff of Clackmannan, see *ibid.*, 64, n. 90.
14. *Ibid.*, no. 376. It is witnessed by Hugh, the chancellor, who died on 10 July 1199.
15. *Ibid.*, no. 379.
16. Published in Stones (ed.), *Anglo-Scottish Relations*, 12–23.
17. *RRS*, ii. 58.
18. *Ibid.*, 82.
19. Nonetheless, Henry III in 1272 felt able to pronounce that if the dating clause of a certain letter patent did not agree with his itinerary, then the document must be false: Chaplais, *English Royal Documents*, 18.
20. *APS*, i. 117–18.
21. The 'roll of Abbot Archibald' (concerned with 'ancient renders in money and ancient waitings') must refer to Archibald, abbot of Dunfermline from probably 1178 until his death in 1198, who appears in a number of charters as someone active on the king's business: *RRS*, ii. 58–9. The other item is seven pieces containing accounts from 1202 to 1215, beginning with what is described as the 'twentieth account of Philip' (at which point some text has been lost): see *ibid.*, 58, and esp. Duncan, *Scotland. The Making of the Kingdom*, 214.
22. *APS*, i. 113–17 (with facsimile between 112 and 113).
23. *Ibid.*, 114.
24. The earliest extant administrative records are some accounts for 1262–6: John Stuart with George Burnett (eds), *The Exchequer Rolls of Scotland*, vol. i, AD *1264–1359* (Edinburgh, 1878).
25. Chaplais, *English Royal Documents*, 4 n. 1, where it is suggested that the series of close rolls may have begun in John's first year.
26. Lionel Landon (ed.), *The Cartæ Antiquæ, Rolls 1–10, Printed from the Original MSS*, Publications of the Pipe Roll Society vol. lv (new series, vol. xvii) (London, 1939), xiii–xvii.
27. Barrow, *Scotland and its Neighbours*, 102.
28. *RRS*, ii. 75–6 (where the earlier sporadic appearance of *Dei gratia* is also noted); L. Delisle (ed.), *Recueil des Actes de Henri II, Roi d'Angleterre et Duc de Normandie*, vol. i (Paris, 1909), 12–38.

29. *RRS*, ii. 76.

30. *Ibid.*, no. 146 (comment).

31. Barrow, *Scotland and its Neighbours*, 28.

32. *RRS*, ii. 77; for England see Delisle (ed.), *Recueil des Actes de Henri II*, i. 208. The charter of probably 1179 is *RRS*, ii. no. 218, which must date from sometime after Arnold was blessed as abbot of Melrose on 6 January 1179: D. E. R. Watt and N. F. Shead, *The Heads of Religious Houses in Scotland from the Twelfth to Sixteenth Centuries* (Edinburgh, 2001), 149. The charter confirms Walter the Steward's grants to Paisley, and is unlikely therefore to be much later than Walter's death in 1177. An isolated late example of the racial address is no. 507 (*ca* 1212) where it has been inherited from its model: see 127, above.

33. Gordon Donaldson, *Scotland: the Shaping of a Nation*, 3rd edn (Nairn, 1993), 23. Note also Alexander Grant, 'Aspects of National Consciousness in Medieval Scotland', in Claus Bjørn, Alexander Grant and Keith J. Stringer (eds), *Nations, Nationalism and Patriotism in the European Past* (Copenhagen, 1994), 68–95, who comments (at 79) that this change 'reflects the development of Scottishness and, south of the Border, Englishness which transcended ethnic and linguistic origins'.

34. See below, 275.

35. *RRS*, i. 73. It remained a standard phrase through to the reigns of William II and Anne: Barrow, *Scotland and its Neighbours*, 104. Another important difference is that, although *rex Anglie* replaced *rex Anglorum* as the English royal style from 1199, *rex Scottorum* was retained by Scottish kings (with the exception of John, 1292–1304). For discussion, see *ibid.*, 35–6.

36. See Duncan, *Kingship of the Scots*, plate 2B, and Duncan, 'Before coronation', 161, for excellent reproductions of Alexander II on his seal.

37. There is some controversy about whether there is a crown depicted on the matrix of the seal used by Alexander I, reused for David I, and copied for Mael Coluim IV. The best extant example is of Alexander I. According to W. de Gray Birch, *History of Scottish Seals*, vol. i (Stirling and London, 1905), 19, Alexander I wears a 'close-fitting, cap-shaped crown', adding that 'the details of the crown are very indistinct'. J. H. Stevenson and M. Wood, *Scottish Heraldic Seals* (Glasgow, 1940), i. 3, refer simply to a 'small crown'. More recently, Barrow (ed.), *Charters of King David I*, 30, refers to David I as depicted crowned on his seal, and this has been followed in Oram, *David I*, 205. Professor Duncan, however, has stated that Alexander I on his seal 'wears a simple hair-band with meaningless pendants' (Duncan, *Scotland. The Making of the Kingdom*, 553), and more recently has commented that the seal was based on that of William Rufus, but without a crown (Duncan, *Kingship of Scots*, 146). I have examined Professor Duncan's slide of Alexander I's seal, and am inclined to agree with him that there is no crown. I am grateful to John Hudson for bringing this problem to my attention.

38. Duncan, *Scotland. The Making of the Kingdom*, 553.
39. *Ibid.*
40. *Ibid.*, 556; Simpson, 'Kingship in miniature'. See above, 163.
41. It has been pointed out that this includes the depiction of Alexander III holding a sceptre on his 'seal of minority', a feature absent from Scottish royal seals since 1107: Simpson, 'Kingship in miniature', 138.
42. *RRS*, ii. 82–3; Chaplais, *English Royal Documents*, 13 and n. 6.
43. *RRS*, ii. 83.
44. *Ibid.*, 90. Gilbert of Stirling's career in the royal chapel spanned more than twenty-five years, beginning in the late 1190s.
45. *Ibid.*, 83. The suspect charter is no. 505 (a letter to King John of England in an English chancery hand of the mid-thirteenth century); the charter with both plural and singular usage is no. 388, and survives only in *APS*, i. 89. Barrow notes (in his comment on no. 388) that the substance of the charter, addressed to Geoffrey *Blundus* and the burgesses of Inverness, resembles a Flemish liberty more than an English one; this observation relates to its first dispositive sentence in particular. He also notes that a Geoffrey *Blundus* was a citizen of London in the household of Richard I's chancellor. Could a draft of the first dispositive sentence have been produced on behalf of Geoffrey and his Flemish colleagues, which reflected their expectations of royal prose?
46. *RRS*, ii. no. 316.
47. *Ibid.*, 79.
48. *Ibid.*, nos 179 and 507.
49. *Ibid.*, no. 365, where it is noted (in the comment) that this seems to confirm a transaction noted in the Chronicle of Melrose *s.a.* 1193, although the confirmation by the Glasgow cathedral chapter cannot be earlier than 10 September 1195. Duncan, 'Roger of Howden and Scotland', 138–9 (see next note for discussion).
50. One difficulty hinges on the scribe, and is discussed two notes below. The other is the appearance of Walter de Berkeley, rather than Philip de Valonges, as royal chamberlain in the witness list. Philip de Valonges (who is also a witness) evidently replaced Berkeley before 1195, hence his appearance as chamberlain in five charters without time-dates (none can be earlier than 1189), and in four (possibly five) charters which were probably produced in and between 17 April and 17 September 1195. (In fact, he is chamberlain in what is likely to be the last extant charter before the time-date was introduced, as well as the probable first with a time-date: *RRS*, ii. nos 375 and 376.)
51. *Ibid.*, 88–9.
52. This is not broached directly in Duncan, 'Roger of Howden and Scotland', 138–9; however, he asks 'Is there defiance or mockery in the way the king's charter . . . apes the pope's bull?', which must mean that he regards Gervase as still an episcopal, not a royal, clerk. But this creates a problem for

Duncan's dating of this charter. If Gervase only became a royal clerk some-time in (or after) late 1195, then it would need to be explained why eight of the eleven single sheets in his hand, which he could only have produced as a royal scribe, have no time-date.

53. Note *RRS*, ii. no. 209, a charter of 1178×95 confirming land held of Arbroath abbey by the king's brewer, in which Robert of London appears in the witness list as *filius regis*. It survives only as a copy in an Arbroath cartulary. It is not inconceivable that this was produced by an Arbroath scribe, but there is no particular reason, beyond the use of *filius regis*, for suggesting that it was.

54. *Ibid.*, nos 264 and 265. Barrow (at 88) comments that the scribe has affin-ities to other Melrose hands. No other royal charters are attributed to him.

55. *Ibid.*, no. 513 (based on no. 197), and no. 30 (compare with *RRS*, i. no. 118).

56. See comment in *ibid.*, 59–60; also *RRS*, ii. 69.

57. *Ibid.*, no. 51 (1165×71).

58. Thomas Rymer (ed.), *Foedera, Conventiones, Literæ et cujuscunque generis Acta Publica inter Reges Anglie et Alios . . .* vol. i (London, 1704), 240–1.

59. James Scoular, *Handlist of the Acts of Alexander II, 1214–1249* (Edinburgh, 1959), 16; Rymer (ed.), *Foedera*, i. 252.

60. Scoular, *Handlist*, 16–17; Cosmo Innes (ed.), *Registrum Episcopatus Moraviensis* (Edinburgh, 1837), no. 52 and Cartae Originales no. 4; Cosmo Innes (ed.), *Liber S. Thome de Aberbrothoc*, 2 vols (Edinburgh, 1848–56), i. no. 131.

61. Cosmo Innes (ed.), *Liber S. Marie de Calchou* (Edinburgh, 1846), no. 7; Scoular, *Handlist*, 17–49 (note that the undated acts, *ibid.*, 50–4, are undated because the text is defective, most commonly because the witness list is lost and, along with it, the dating clause: see *ibid.*, 1).

62. The earliest extant charter in which this had become a standard feature was produced on 21 July 1222, at Kinross (J. Raine (ed.), *The History and Antiquities of North Durham* (London, 1852), appendix, no. 63, where the date is mistakenly given as 26 July: I am very grateful to Keith Stringer for the correct date). The previous charter was produced on 10 July 1222 at Roxburgh (Innes (ed.), *Liber S. Marie de Calchou*, no. 183). A rare return to the first person singular is found in an unpublished charter dated 5 April 1223 (Scoular, *Handlist*, no. 69): I am very grateful to Keith Stringer for pointing this out to me.

63. Scoular, *Handlist*, 20; Innes (ed.), *Liber S. Marie de Calchou*, nos 6, 16, 393, a brieve against poinding goods of Kelso abbey.

64. Scoular, *Handlist*, 11; Innes (ed.), *Liber S. Thome de Aberbrothoc*, i. nos 105 and 106. They have the same place- and time-date, and were presum-ably issued on the same occasion.

65. Innes (ed.), *Liber S. Thome de Aberbrothoc*, i. no. 110. I am very grateful to Keith Stringer for informing me in detail about the 'stop go' deployment

of *anno regni domini regis* from its first extant appearance in a pair of unpublished charters of 5 November 1223 (Scoular, *Handlist*, nos 75 and 76).

66. The last example, as far as I am aware, is a charter of 23 April 1252: Joseph Robertson (ed.), *Liber Collegii Nostre Domini . . . Accedunt Munimenta Fratrum Predicatorum de Glasgu* (Edinburgh, 1846), 149.

67. Huw Pryce (ed.), with the assistance of Charles Insley, *The Acts of Welsh Rulers 1120–1283* (Cardiff, 2005), table 9 (at 53). Only forty-six charters (of which a mere five are originals) survive before 1283 (see *ibid.*, 79), although this does not include letters patent (which are in many key respects similar: see *ibid.*, 59).

68. *Ibid.*, 63. Note also (at 67) the use of the first person during the early 1240s, coinciding with a period of weakness in relation to the king of England.

69. *Ibid.*, 67, 69.

70. *Ibid.*, nos 250, 260, 272, 286 and 288.

71. See *ibid.*, 139, for a discussion of the possibility of beneficiary production in these cases, where it is pointed out that there is significant variety in other aspects. The two in the name of Llywelyn ap Iorwerth (nos 250 and 272) use the royal 'we'; the two in the name of Llywelyn's heir, Dafydd (nos 286 and 288), do not.

72. *Ibid.*, nos 218 and 219.

73. Charles Insley, 'Fact and fiction in thirteenth-century Gwynedd: the Aberconwy charters', *Studia Celtica* 33 (1999) 235–50; Pryce (ed.), *Acts of Welsh Rulers*, 248–71.

74. Pryce (ed.), *Acts of Welsh Rulers*, no. 256.

75. For example, Earl Gille Brigte of Strathearn's foundation charter for Inchaffray, which has an elaborate dating-clause: William A. Lindsay, John Dowden and J. Maitland Thomson (eds), *Charters, Bulls and Other Documents relating to the Abbey of Inchaffray* (Edinburgh, 1908), no. 9. An exotic example is a charter of Richard, abbot of Kelso, and the convent of Kelso, for Melrose, which is dated 'at Kelso, in the year of the Lord's incarnation 1208, in the forty-third year of the reign of our lord, William, king of Scots, and the tenth year from the birth of Alexander, son of King William': Innes (ed.), *Liber Sancte Marie de Melros*, i. no. 146.

76. Pryce (ed.), *Acts of Welsh Rulers*, 242.

77. There is only one document in Llywelyn ap Iorwerth's name (*ibid.*, no. 231) which gives the day of the month without the year, but this is paired with the age of the moon on that day, and is clearly not comparable with the dating clause of Scottish charters.

78. Lindsay, Dowden and Thomson (eds), *Charters, Bulls and Other Documents relating to the Abbey of Inchaffray*, no. 69.

79. Cosmo Innes (ed.), *Registrum Monasterii de Passelet* (Edinburgh, 1832), 160–1. Note the use of the plural of majesty here and in a later document of Earl Maol Domhnaich (*ibid.*, 171–2, dated 1250).

80. Cosmo Innes (ed.), *Registrum Episcopatus Glasguensis*, 2 vols (Edinburgh, 1843) i. no. 142.

81. Dumville, 'Kingship, genealogies and regnal lists', 96–7.

82. Kenneth H. Jackson, *The Gaelic Notes in the Book of Deer* (Cambridge, 1982), 31 (trans. at 34).

83. Ferguson, *Medieval Papal Representatives*, 86.

84. *Ibid.*, 87–8; Joseph Robertson (ed.), *Concilia Scoticana*, 2 vols (Edinburgh, 1866), i. xlv n. 2; W. H. Bliss (ed.), *Calendar of Entries in the Papal Registers relating to Great Britain and Ireland: Papal Letters*, vol. i, *1198–1304* (London, 1893), 83; A. D. M. Barrell, 'Scotland and the papacy in the reign of Alexander II', in Richard D. Oram (ed.), *The Reign of Alexander II, 1214–49* (Leiden, 2005), 157–77, at 162.

85. Ferguson, *Medieval Papal Representatives*, 87 n. 145.

86. Stones (ed.), *Anglo-Scottish Relations*, 58–9 (which shows that the request was made not long before April 1251). Note also M. Bloch, 'An unknown testimony on the history of coronation in Scotland', *SHR* 23 (1925–6) 105–6. Coronation alone is mentioned in the notification by Henry III in 1233 of an appeal by the archbishop of York against what must have been another request to the papacy: *ES*, ii. 491 n. 2.

87. Note Bloch's comment that 'the unction, and the unction only, was thought to be able to confer on kings a truly sacred character': Bloch, 'An unknown testimony', 105.

88. *RRS*, ii. 88–90. Hand Dc is identified in three charters (not four, as *ibid.*, 89; no. 295 is a later cartulary copy). The other five scribes are Da (thirteen examples), Db (eight examples; Barrow suggests that Db may be the same hand as Da), Dd (eleven examples), De (five examples), Df (twenty-eight examples, not including no. 495 which is not an original).

89. See Dauvit Broun, 'The absence of regnal years from the dating clause of charters of kings of Scots', in John Gillingham (ed.), *Anglo-Norman Studies XXV: Proceedings of the Battle Conference 2002* (Woodbridge, 2003), 47–63, at 62 n. 98.

90. See above, 106–8.

91. Rule (ed.), *Eadmeri Historia Novorum*, 285; *SAEC*, 144. See above, 105.

92. William I had a protracted struggle over the appointment of a bishop of St Andrews (see, e.g., Duncan, *Scotland. The Making of the Kingdom*, 270–4), while Alexander II introduced a procedure whereby a case in an ecclesiastical court could be stopped by a claim that the matter in dispute was secular (see Hector L. MacQueen, 'Canon law, custom and legislation: law in the reign of Alexander II', in Richard D. Oram (ed.), *The Reign of Alexander II, 1214–49* (Leiden, 2005), 221–51, at 236–7, although it is stressed that 'the picture of conflict between church and state should not be over-dramatised'.

PART IV

National History

8

The Principal Source used by John of Fordun for his Chronicle of the Scottish People

What impact did this new sense of Scotland as a sovereign kingdom have on how the kingship's early history was imagined? It was argued in chapter 2 that an important way in which the highest secular authority was given substance in the minds of the learned and their audiences was by the articulation of a sustained narrative of a kingship, rooting it in the deep past, and creating the expectation that it would exist in the future. As long as this was written in a way which was memorable or enjoyable it had the potential to become a key part of the infrastructure of a society's shared imagination. It was argued that Scotland was remarkable in that it lacked a narrative of this kind focused on Scotland, long after this had been provided for the English, Irish and Welsh by their historians in the period between the mid-eleventh and mid-twelfth centuries. When did Scotland finally gain a sustained account of its kingship from ancient times? And what is revealed in it about the way the kingdom was perceived?

Until recently it has seemed natural and wholly unexceptionable to follow W. F. Skene, the only person to attempt an edition of Fordun's *Chronicle of the Scottish People*, in regarding Fordun's work as 'the first detailed and systematic history of Scotland'.[1] It can be dated to sometime between early 1384 and late August 1387,[2] and was certainly very influential. Before the histories of John Mair (1521) and Hector Boece (1527), Fordun's chronicle was the bedrock of all attempts to write a history of Scotland in Latin. But some doubts have recently been aired about Fordun's standing as the 'father of Scottish history'.[3] It has been noted, for example, that Scottish procurators at the papal curia in 1301 appear to have been familiar with a particularly distinctive part of his narrative relating to the beginning of the Scottish kingdom.[4] This, at the very least, suggests that an account of the kingship's ancient past (which was more than a mere king-list) already existed before Fordun was born. In the following chapter we will return to discuss what the procurators' source may have been.

The main evidence for the existence of a pre-Fordunian extended narrative of the kingdom's history, however, lies in Fordun's own text, and in *Gesta Annalia* which only survives in some manuscripts of Fordun's chronicle. This inescapably requires us to embark on an ever deeper exploration into the darker recesses of textual archaeology as layer on layer of writing and rewriting is identified, sifted and extracted. One key prize of all this endeavour is that the structure of Fordun's narrative is revealed as belonging to the same work as '*Gesta Annalia* I' ('GAI'), which (it will be recalled) was probably in writing sometime between 2 February and 9 April 1285. Not only does this enable at least one potentially important stage in the consolidation of a vision of Scotland as a sovereign kingdom to be identified, but it also sheds light on small-scale efforts to articulate an image of the kingship's significance through the construction of its ancient past. The most striking of these is the king-list discussed in chapter 6 in which it was claimed that the realm of the first king of Scots stretched from Orkney in the north to Stainmore in the south. A much more substantial enhancement of the kingdom's past which emerges a little more clearly from the shadows is a pro-Scottish recasting of material from Geoffrey of Monmouth's *History of the Kings of Britain* that has been identified in Fordun's chronicle by John and Winifred MacQueen.[5] In many cases the existence of these works, or of texts like them, is already known. Their contents cannot be completely recovered, although some progress is possible. If it could be shown that they were used as sources by the author of *GAI*, however, then this would at least enable them to be dated to probably no later than 1285.

GESTA ANNALIA

All this depends critically on how and when *Gesta Annalia* is thought to have taken shape.[6] This was mentioned briefly in chapter 6; it is now necessary to tackle the issue head-on. As noted already, Fordun's chronicle proceeds chronologically no further than the death of David I, son of St Margaret and Mael Coluim III, in 1153; *Gesta Annalia* consists of an account of St Margaret's ancestors and descendants which continues (in its earliest recoverable form) up to 1363. It was Skene's opinion that *Gesta Annalia* represents Fordun's first draft.[7] There is no good reason, however, for regarding it as Fordun's work. It has been shown – on the basis of the text's distribution within manuscripts and a comparison with similar material used by Wyntoun in his *Original Chronicle* (written 1408×24) and in a brief chronicle found in Edinburgh University Library MS 27 – that *Gesta Annalia* is directly derived from two separate chronicles: one supplied a record of events from October 1285 to 1363, while the other began with St Margaret's English royal ancestors, and gave an account of her Scottish royal descendants up to Alexander III's embassy to France on 2 February 1285. These represent two stages in the development of *Gesta Annalia*. The first stage (up to 1285), *GA*I, we have met already; the second stage, which may be dubbed '*Gesta Annalia* II' (or *GA*II), was added later as a continuation up to 1363.

But this is not the whole story. There was evidently a further stage when some material referring to events between 1290 and Robert I's liberation of Scotland was added to *GA*I. This may also have included the pieces of Bruce propaganda in *GA*II, which sit uneasily alongside the more non-committal posture found elsewhere in *GA*II.[8] Certainly, one of these additional items in *GA*I refers to the death of Margaret 'the Maid' in *GA*II, so this material would seem to represent a final significant stage in the text's development after *GA*I had been added to *GA*II. Another stage which can readily be detected is the addition of a dossier of documents relating to Scottish independence beginning with the Declaration of Arbroath (1320). This was presumably before *GA*II had been tacked on at the end, because the dossier is followed not by *GA*II but by a haphazard assemblage of texts which are likely to represent a period of piecemeal accretion. (A particular piece of evidence for this is discussed below.) *Gesta Annalia* as a whole, therefore, should properly be regarded as a text which has grown in at least four stages. It will be useful to take one step back and two steps forward in the argument by summarising each stage and supplying some additional information.

1) *GA*I represents a history of St Margaret's ancestors and descendants up to 2 February 1285, and probably completed within the following two months. An important source was an earlier history of St Margaret's ancestors and descendants which is chiefly known in a text written in Dunfermline shortly after Alexander II's death in 1249.[9] A close relationship with a lost chronicle, which was in turn related to the Chronicle of Melrose, is also apparent.[10]

2) A dossier of documents on Scottish independence, with the Declaration of Arbroath as its first item, was added to *GA*I.

3) Other documents and texts were also added, but probably later and in piecemeal fashion.[11]

4) *GA*II was tacked on at the end. It was derived from a putative St Andrews source which ceased at 1363.[12]

At some point the text of *GAI* has been 'enhanced' by someone with a particular interest in Scottish independence. This has the potential to disturb our confidence in identifying material from the earlier '1285' layer of the text, so it will be useful to consider this in more detail before returning to the account of Alexander III's inauguration.

Four items fall readily into this category:

(i) A passage on Robert I's birth added to the account of the irregular circumstances of his parents' courtship and marriage at the end of chapter 60 in Skene's edition of *Gesta Annalia*.[13] It concludes with a stanza of hexameters marking the year of Robert's birth.[14] It is possible that the story of Robert's parents could also have been added at this stage: it is told in a way which seeks to exonerate Robert I's father, and may represent a Bruce family legend.

(ii) Following the account of the death of Prince Alexander (28 January 1284) in chapter 63 in Skene's edition there is a retrospective mention of the death of his younger brother, David, in 1281, and how both deaths were 'the beginning of Scotland's future woes'; this is immediately followed by an outburst of lamentation which concludes with a pithy saying in a hexameter.[15] (The narrative then resumes with the arrival of Flemish knights seeking the return of Prince Alexander's widow, Marguerite of Flanders.)

(iii) In chapter 64 in Skene's edition – which relates the marriage of Alexander III's daughter Margaret to the king of Norway (misnamed as 'Hangow'), her death leaving a daughter Margaret ('the Maid') and her husband's request for his daughter Margaret to be supported by lands in Scotland – the first mention of Margaret 'the Maid' is followed by a comment that 'when she had arrived at years of maturity'[16] she also died 'as is said below' (a reference to chapter 69 in Skene's edition, which is part of *GAII*).

(iv) Skene's chapter 65 describes Edward I's conquest of Wales.[17] At the end it is said that 'this chapter has briefly been inserted there in case any neighbouring people, reading this said account, unchastened by the example of the Welsh, should fall unwarily into a most wretched servitude under the lordship of the English'.[18]

All these appear to be interpolations; indeed, we are more or less told as much in the case of the last item. Are there other parts of *GAI* which can be identified as similar attempts to enhance the text? One obvious candidate is chapter 15 in Skene's edition: this is a dramatic (and unhistoric) account of a speech by a certain Gilbert, a Scottish cleric, at the Council of Northampton (in January 1176), protesting at the subjugation of the Scottish Church. It has been pointed out by Donald Watt that it is out of place chronologically and is not attached to the notice of the Council of Northampton given earlier (in the correct chronological context) in *Gesta Annalia*. He concluded that it seems to have been intruded.[19] It certainly shares a couple of features with the other interpolated items noted above: it is directly concerned with the issue of independence, as in items (i) and (iv); and it concludes with a pithy hexameter, as in item (ii).[20] It may also be noteworthy that it uses the phrase 'wretched servitude', *misera seruitudo*, which is also found in item (iv).[21]

Although these items are fairly obvious interpolations, it is impossible to be sure that the same person who made them did not also seek to enhance *GAI* (and *GAII*) with less conspicuous changes. As things stand, though, this remains no more than a formal possibility. As far as the dating of *GAI* is concerned, it might be inferred from the failure in the pre-interpolated version of Skene's chapter 64 to allude to the death of Margaret 'the Maid' that it was written before late 1290. It has earlier been noted that, in one of the passages attributable to the author of *GAI* in the account of Alexander III's inauguration (see further below), the Stone of Scone is referred to in the present tense as in Scone, pointing to a date before its removal in 1296. Therefore, although the dating of *GAI* to before 9 April 1285 depends on a single moment in the text, these other indications of date increase our confidence in it, even if they do not provide direct corroboration.

THE ACCOUNT OF ALEXANDER III'S INAUGURATION AND THE AUTHOR OF *GESTA ANNALIA* I

In chapter 6 it was argued that a near-contemporary record of Alexander III's inauguration had been enlarged and repackaged by the author of *GAI*, and that, in order to reconstruct the original account of Alexander III's inauguration, it was necessary to strip out those elements which had been added by him. It is to these additional elements that we will now turn. They consist chiefly of two passages. The first is an explanation of the Stone of Scone's significance: I will refer to it as interpolation A.

> *Qui lapis in eodem monasterio reuerenter ob regum Albanie consecrationem seruatur. Nec uspiam aliquis regum in Scocia regnare solebat, nisi super eundem lapidem regium in accipiendum nomen prius sederet in Scona, sede uere superiori, videlicet, Albanie constituta regibus ab antiquis.*

This stone is reverently kept in the same monastery for the consecration of kings of Alba. And none of the kings were accustomed to reign anywhere in

Scotland if he had not first, on receiving the title of king, sat upon that same royal stone at Scone, which had, indeed, been established by ancient kings as the sovereign seat, namely of Alba.

The second is a Latin rendering of the royal genealogy for nearly sixty generations. I will refer to this in its entirety as interpolation B. Its concluding passage is particularly notable:[22]

> *. . . filii Fergusii primi Scotorum regis in Albania. Qui quoque Fergusius fuit filius Feredach, quamuis a quibusdam dicitur filius Ferechar, parum tamen discrepant in sono. Hec discrepantia forte scriptoris constat uicio propter difficultatem loquele. Deinde dictam genealogiam idem Scotus ab homine in hominem continuando perlegit donec ad primum Scotum uidelicet Iber Scot peruenit. Qui quidem Iber fuit filius Gaithel Glas filii Neoili regis quondam Athene genitus ex Scota filia regis Egipci Centhres Pharaonis.*

> *. . .* son of Fergus, first king of Scots in Alba. This Fergus, moreover, was son of Feredach, although 'son of Ferchar' is stated by some – but there is little difference in sound. Perhaps this discrepancy consists of a scribal error due to language difficulty. Then the same Scot read the said genealogy to the end, continuing from man to man, until he reached the first Scot, namely Éber Scot. This Éber was son of Gaedel Glas son of Nél (at one time king of Athens), begotten of Scota, daughter of Pharaoh Centhres, king of Egypt.

The identity of the kings in interpolation A who originally made Scone the time-honoured centre of Scottish kingship is revealed earlier in *GAI*, in an account of the foundation of Scone as an Augustinian priory. There it is said that Scone was 'where ancient kings, from Cruithne first king of Picts, established the seat of the kingdom of Alba'.[23] It has been noted earlier (in chapter 6) that the same concern for Scone's primeval significance is apparent in interpolation A. It was also remarked upon that a similar choice of words is found in both statements. The comment on Scone in the account of the founding of the abbey reads in Latin: *ubi antiqui reges, Cruthne primo Pictorum rege, sedem regni Albanie constituerant. Albania* is simply Alba in Latin clothes: it is very unusual to find it in the thirteenth century or later (except, eventually, with reference to the 'duke of Albany', a title created in 1398). It also appears in the material following the Latin version of the royal genealogy, given above: *filii Fergusii primi Scotorum regis in Albania.* Finally, looking again at interpolation A and the comment made on Scone in the section on the abbey's foundation, the use of the same verb *constituere* – although it may not be so striking as sharing *Albania* – is still worth noting. All this serves to strengthen the identification of these passages in the account of Alexander's inauguration as the work of the author of *GAI*.

These are not the only links between interpolations A and B and other parts of *GAI*. In the account of the acquisition of the Hebrides by Magnus Barelegs in 1098, we are told that Fergus son of Feredach was a Scottish king who first reached 'Albion' about 1,500 years earlier:

> from the time of Simón Brecc's great-grandson, King 'Ethdaci Rothai' [genitive], who was the first of the Scots to settle the islands, the Scots have continually held these same islands [the Hebrides], without any break, up to this point for a space of two thousand years or more, and nearly five hundred years before the king of Scots, Fergus son of Feredach, reached the soil (*solum*) of Albion (*Albionis*).[24]

The most striking feature is 'Ethdaci Rothai' (genitive). This is a strangely inaccurate rendering of Gaelic *Echdach Buadaig* (nominative: *Eochaid Buadach*) originating in a Latinate recension of the royal genealogy that only survives in full in Ralph of Diss's *Imagines Historiarum* (written towards the end of the twelfth century).[25] This version of the genealogy was the one given in interpolation B (although not as far as 'Ethdaci Rothai');[26] another copy was added by Fordun to the end of book V of his chronicle (but omitting the section with 'Ethdaci Rothai').[27] Again, the simplest explanation for this connection between one part of *GAI* and an addition to the account of Alexander III's inauguration is that they were both written by the same person: the author of *GAI* himself. The idea of naming Fergus's father as Feredach rather than Ferchar could also have come from this text of the genealogy used by the author of *GAI*:[28] in Diss we find 'filii Forgso filii Feredach', in which 'Feredach' represents a nominative where genitive *Feredaig* would be expected.[29] In Gaelic this would have been *meic Forgo meic Feredaig*.[30] It is no surprise, if 'Forgso' was taken as Fergus, that Feredach is mentioned as a possible version of the name of Fergus's father at the end of the extensive extract of the royal genealogy given in interpolation B: 'filii Forgso filii Feredach' is presumably what the author of *GAI* found in his exemplar.

THE KINGSHIP'S PAST IN THE ACCOUNT OF ALEXANDER III'S INAUGURATION

It will be recalled that *GAI* is an account of St Margaret's royal ancestors and descendants. Ostensibly it lacks much chronological depth, and what there is is concerned with English kings. It is apparent, however, that its author also had a keen interest in Scotland's ancient history. What emerges from an examination of his references to figures from the deep past is that he saw both Scots and Picts as part of that history: Cruithne first king of Picts established Scone as the kingship's seat, while the Scots had had kings in Scotland for around a millennium and a half. It may be surmised that the author of GAI envisaged a primordial territory which, before the Scots conquered the Picts, comprised two ancient kingdoms: one in the east founded by Cruithne, and another in the west founded by Fergus son of Feredach. Fergus son of Feredach was not only an ancient king, however, but was identified with Fergus son of Ferchar, who is otherwise unknown except in a legend of how the Stone of Scone was taken by him from Tara (in Ireland) to Scotland. The earliest extant form of this legend is in passages embedded in Fordun's chronicle attributed to a *historia* or *legenda* of St 'Congal'.[31] Putting all this together, it seems that the author of GAI had developed an impressively neat view of the ceremony of inauguration as a synthesis of the two most enduring elements of the kingship's heritage: Cruithne's Pictish kingdom lived on in Scone's status as the royal centre of Alba, while the kingship of *Scoti* established by Fergus was represented by the Stone itself. He could not have made it clearer that both aspects were essential when he insisted in interpolation A that any would-be king, as soon as he had accepted the title, had to go to Scone to be seated on the Stone. It must also be suspected that he took equal care in his choice of *Albania* as the Latin word for the kingdom's territory. He evidently did not regard this as originally either Pictish or 'Scottish', and may have wished to avoid *Scotia* for that reason alone; but, equally, he may have wished to bring to mind the image of the mainland north of the Forth. It will also be recalled that, in the late twelfth century (and from a Glaswegian point of view, at least), *Albania* could be used in Latin to distinguish 'Scotland' north of the Forth from *Scotia*, 'Scotland', the realm ruled by present-day kings of Scots.

When adding material to the account of Alexander's inauguration, the author of GAI also reveals an interest in Scottish origins prior to the Scots' arrival in Scotland. He states in interpolation B that Éber Scot was the 'first Scot', and claims that he was the final person named in the reading out of the king's pedigree. There is nothing to suggest that this was taken from his source. Indeed, it is inherently unlikely that the pedigree would have stopped at this point without going on to Éber's father, Gaedel Glas (or on to Noah, as in Diss, or even to Adam 'son of the living God', as in the genealogy of William I in the 'Poppleton manuscript').[32] Éber Scot appears in the Latinate version of the royal pedigree found in Diss, so it might be wondered whether the author of GAI was moved to describe him as the first Scot simply because of his eponym. But Éber was not the earliest figure to be called 'Scot'. If the text of the royal genealogy used by the author of *GAI* was essentially the same as Diss's, he would presumably have noticed 'Richaith Scot', great-grandson of Noah.[33] There must be some other reason, apart from his eponym, why he was so keen to emphasise Éber Scot as the first Scot and the ultimate royal ancestor proclaimed at Alexander's inauguration. The only context in which this would readily make sense is as a reference to the account of Scottish origins in which Ireland was portrayed as virgin territory divinely ordained for the *Scoti* which Éber was the first to settle.[34] This is a potent representation of Ireland, not Scotland, as the Scottish 'homeland' which will be considered in due course. Again, it may be suspected that the author of *GAI* has deftly accommodated two different ideas of Scottish territory: one focused on the kingdom in which he presented Alba in terms of the kingdom's origins; the other focused on the people and in which Ireland was where the Scots first became Scots. This latter point is heightened by the mention of Éber's parents, Gaedel Glas and Scota, and grandfathers Nél and Pharaoh 'Centhres'; it was the association with Ireland, not their ancestry from Scota, which made the Scots Scots.[35]

FORDUN'S CHRONICLE AND THE AUTHOR OF *GESTA ANNALIA* I

When all the material on Scottish origins in *GAI* is put together, it emerges that its author must have known something very like Fordun's chronicle. If *GAI* should be dated to 1285, however, then its author cannot have seen Fordun's chronicle itself, which must date from sometime between 1384 and 1387. How is this conundrum to be explained? The answer becomes starkly apparent if the scraps showing what the author of *GAI* knew and understood are compared with those small parts of the chronicle which are indubitably Fordun's own work.

To begin with, let us recap on the Fordunian *dramatis personae* of Scottish origins that demonstrably were known to the author of *GAI*. First there is Gaedel Glas, son of Nél, and his wife Scota, daughter of Pharaoh 'Centhres', and Éber Scot. Then there is Simón Brecc (mentioned in the passage on the annexation of the Hebrides by Magnus Barelegs). Simón Brecc is only found as a person of any significance in the first 'half' of the legend of the Stone of Scone (referred to earlier in connection with Fergus son of Ferchar), where he features as a son of a king of Spain who brought the Stone to Ireland and established it at Tara. Next there is Eochaid 'Rothai', who we are told was Simón Brecc's great-grandson, and who is presented as the first Scot to settle the Hebrides. He is followed by Fergus 'son of Feredach or Ferchar', the first Scottish king on mainland Scotland. It will be recalled that this reference to Fergus as son of Ferchar shows knowledge of the second 'half' of the legend of the Stone of Scone, in which the Stone is brought from Ireland to Scotland. This is almost a full list of leading characters from Fordun's chronicle as far as the arrival of the Stone of Scone in Scotland. The only absentees are the sons of Míl (who lead another early invasion of Ireland from Spain); but there was little opportunity, in the very brief allusions to Scottish origins in GAI, for them to be mentioned, so this omission is hardly significant.

It is also striking how the author of GAI shows a secure understanding of the carefully contrived structure of Scottish history expounded in Fordun's chronicle. On the one hand, there is the staged arrival of the Scots, who first settled the islands (led by Eochaid 'Rothai', who we are told is the eponym of Rothesay), and then established a kingdom on the mainland west of Drumalban, with Fergus son of Ferchar as the first king in 330 BC (book I, chapters 28 and 34, and book II, chapter 12). On the other hand, there is the concern to portray Picts and Scots as originally two separate kingdoms within the same country, *Albania*. Furthermore, the interest in dividing Scottish history into 500-year chunks seen in the passage in GAI referring to Eochaid 'Rothai' and Fergus (in connection with the loss of the Hebrides to Norway in 1098) is also apparent in Fordun's chronicle (although 500 years is stated explicitly only for the initial period of 'joint kingdoms', while a thousand years is stated in book I chapter 31 as the period between the Pict's expulsion of their Scottish in-laws shortly after arriving in Scotland and the destruction of the Picts by the Scots).

If we wish to examine Fordun's own understanding of these matters, and so gauge whether he could have been responsible himself for constructing the narrative of Scottish history in his chronicle, or whether he is more likely to have based it on an existing work, it is necessary to isolate sections that can demonstrably be regarded as his own prose. This may seem a rather tall order, but there are two parts of his chronicle where Fordun's handling of early Scottish history is exposed. Both are in book V.

The most obvious place to find Fordun at work is where GAI was his principal source, from chapter 9 (the accession of Mael Coluim III) until chapter 35 (when Aelred's account of David I's death takes over). Now, it might be thought that there is not much scope here for Fordun to reveal anything about his understanding of the early Scottish past. All he needed to do was copy what he found in GAI, which is essentially what he did with the passage on the Norwegian takeover of the Hebrides in

1098 in which mention is made of Eochaid 'Rothai' and Fergus 'son of Feredach'.[36] Much worse, however, is Fordun's treatment of *GAI*'s statement on Scone's origins in the account of the foundation of the priory there by Alexander I. It will be recalled that, in *GAI*, we are told that Scone was 'where ancient kings, from Cruithne first king of Picts, established the seat of the kingdom of *Albania*'.[37] Fordun rephrased this passage so that Scone became the place 'where kings from ancient times, both Picts and Scots, established the chief seat of the kingdom'.[38] The intrusion of Scots here cuts across the idea that Scotland was anciently divided between distinct Pictish and Scottish kingdoms, and thereby undermines a fundamental feature of the chronicle's structure.

The worst example of Fordun's failure to deal competently with Scotland's early history as this was presented in his chronicle is in the second instance where there can be no doubt that Fordun's voice can be heard. This is in the copy of David I's genealogy in book V chapter 50 which Fordun says he obtained 'a little while ago' (*dudum*) from Walter Wardlaw, 'cardinal of Scotland' and bishop of Glasgow (who became cardinal on 23 December 1383 and died probably on 21 or 23 August 1387).[39] What Wardlaw possessed was evidently a copy of the same Latinate text found in Diss's *Imagines Historiarum* and used by the author of *GAI* in interpolation B in the account of Alexander III's inauguration.[40] Fordun himself must therefore have been responsible for the pieces of commentary in the genealogy referring to material earlier in the chronicle. These amount to three brief explanations of a particular figure in the genealogy (two of which are unexceptionable),[41] and two longer passages. The two longer passages coincide with points where Fordun has skipped parts of the genealogy, directing the reader instead to chapters where equivalent sections can be found: Cinaed mac Ailpín's descent from Fergus son of Erc (book IV chapter 8) and the descent of Fergus son of Ferchar from Simón Brecc (book I chapter 26). It might be imagined that these cross-references would be straightforward affairs. As it happens, this is true of neither of them.

Cinaed's lineage in book IV chapter 8 has, in point of fact, been derived from a king-list, and would have differed from Wardlaw's text in having a block of three extra generations (as well as different name-forms).[42] The two would not have been incompatible, though, so this hardly matters too much. It is more disconcerting that the section of pedigree in book I chapter 26 (which is a genuine section of the same Latinate recension of the royal genealogy) is not what Fordun says it is: instead of a section from Fergus (son of Feredach/Ferchar) back to Simón Brecc, what is actually to be found is the pedigree of Simón Brecc back to the sons of Míl of Spain. Fordun is also not particularly accurate when he refers to Fergus as 'leading the Scots out of Ireland'. Although it is reported in book I chapter 34 that Fergus brought youths with him, he is clearly represented as coming to Scotland to rule over the Scots who were already there, expelled by the Picts from their midst.

These are minor aberrations, and suggest carelessness more than ignorance of the chronicle's contents. The same cannot be said, however, for Fordun's identification of 'Rothacha' as 'the first to inhabit the islands of *Scotia*'. It will be recalled that in the chronicle, and also in *GAI*, this role is attributed to Eochaid 'Rothai' (inspired, no doubt, by the epithet, which made it possible to regard him as eponym of Rothesay).[43] In both, Eochaid is described as the great-grandson (*pronepos*) of Simón Brecc, which agrees with the Latinate version of the royal genealogy from which Eochaid 'Rothai' originated (as a mistake for Eochaid Buadach). In the genealogy, however, 'Rothacha' is much more venerable, appearing nine generations *before* Simón Brecc. Although Eochaid 'Rothai' belonged to one of the two omitted sections of Wardlaw's text (which means that the exact reading is lost), Fordun would (at the very least) have known of Eochaid as the first to settle the Hebrides and as great-grandson of Simón from the passage in *GAI* which he copied in book V chapter 24. It may be suspected, therefore, that he spotted 'Rothacha' as a potential eponym for Rothesay in Wardlaw's text of the genealogy, and could not resist the temptation of giving the Scots an even longer history in Scottish territory, and perhaps (in particular) of furnishing an astonishing claim to antiquity for one of the ancestral seats of the reigning king, Robert II. Be this as it may, it made a nonsense of the chronicle's chronology. It was perfectly plain in book I that Simón Brecc's ancestors were meant to be in Spain in anticipation of Simón's taking the Stone of Scone to Ireland and establishing it at Tara.[44] The proposition that one of his ancestors superseded Eochaid 'Rothai' as the first Scot to reach the islands off Scotland was therefore an ignorant subversion of the chronicle's structured account of Scottish origins.

In the light of all that can be discovered about Fordun's own treatment of the ancient Scottish past, it is impossible to accept that he could have created the skilfully crafted chronology found in the chronicle that bears his name. Fordun is exposed as simply too crude and careless to be capable of such an achievement. Worse still, he seems not to have been familiar with the key elements of the chronicle's narrative. In contrast, everything that can be gleaned about the author of *GAI*'s knowledge of this material shows that he understood it well and was sensitive to its finely tuned framework. Fordun's blunt insistence that Scone was established by Scots as well as Picts, and his heedless back-projection of the Scottish settlement of the Hebrides, seem cack-handed by comparison.

GESTA ANNALIA I AS A FRAGMENT OF FORDUN'S PRINCIPAL SOURCE

This is not to deny that significant parts of the work known to scholarship as Fordun's chronicle could not have been Fordun's own contribution. It has also been noted, with regard to his treatment of material in *GA*I, that some of the prose in the chronicle is Fordun's choice of words, even when he was largely reproducing material from his source. Fordun's chronicle cannot simply be regarded as a carbon copy of an earlier work. There can be no doubt, however, that this earlier work existed, and that Fordun depended on it heavily, not least for the structure of his narrative. It would also appear that this earlier work (which may be referred to for convenience as 'proto-Fordun') was the creation of the author of *GA*I. This is suggested not only by the treatment of early Scottish history in *GA*I, but also by a small but powerful indication that *GA*I itself is a final fragment of 'proto-Fordun'.

The evidence that *GA*I was once part of a lost larger work has been known since Skene's edition, but its importance has not been appreciated, perhaps because, in the absence of any context which could support an explanation, there has been little apparent alternative to regarding it as simply a quirk. Once the existence of 'proto-Fordun' is taken on board, however, then this curious feature becomes readily intelligible and highly significant. The strange item is this: after the death of Mael Coluim IV in 1165, all manuscripts of *Gesta Annalia* (except one highly abbreviated version) read that 'book V ends; book VI begins'. This cannot be book V of Fordun's chronicle, which in all the manuscripts is advertised, in a listing of chapters at the beginning of the book, as ceasing at David I's death in 1153 with an account of his ancestry. Unfortunately, the manuscript which preserves the original distribution of material after Fordun's chronicle (known to scholarship as 'C' or 'FC') has evidently lost a book division, while the other principal manuscript has evidently had book divisions altered in line with the removal of *GA*I to precede *GA*II. In MS C only one further book division appears after the death of Mael Coluim IV: at the end of the dossier of documents we are told, 'the pleading ends which is called Baldred's: book VII finishes here'.[45] A book division is also found here in the other principal manuscript, so it must be an original feature. In both manuscripts, moreover, no *incipit* appears here for a following book, which would suggest that the overall work at that point went no further. It is clear, then, that the book divisions would have existed at least by 'stage 2' out of the four outlined initially in this chapter. There is nothing to say if they existed at an earlier stage, or whether the dossier was, in effect, added as an additional book. Unless the addition of the dossier was only a small part of a much more complex process of compilation and composition than has been guessed hitherto, the most natural conclusion is that it was added to a work which was approximately two-thirds bigger than *GAI*, and that *GAI* is all that survives of it.

A number of points can now be brought together. Fordun must have used an earlier recension of his chronicle ('proto-Fordun') as his principal source, and is known to have used *GAI* as his chief source in book V. *GAI* appears to be only the final part of a much larger work, and the author of *GAI* shows knowledge and understanding of the content and structure of the narrative of Scottish origins preserved in Fordun's chronicle (in contrast to Fordun himself, who could display astonishing ignorance of this). All this leads to the same conclusion: that 'proto-Fordun' was written by the author of *GAI* (presumably completing the task sometime between 2 February and 9 April 1285), and that all that remains of this independently of Fordun is its final part (referred to for convenience as *GAI*), from its account of St Margaret's English ancestors and Scottish descendants up to Alexander III's embassy on 2 February 1285. There is only one serious objection to this. As it stands *GAI* does not read like it begins at the mid-point of a longer narrative. It will be recalled that *GAI* is chiefly an account of St Margaret's ancestors and successors. It is wholly appropriate, therefore, that it should open with the very beginning of Margaret's genealogy, starting at Adam. The work, in short, gives every impression that it was originally conceived as beginning where it does. How can this be explained in the light of all the evidence that it is, in fact, the surviving final portion of something akin to John of Fordun's chronicle? A dramatic solution to this conundrum will emerge at the end of chapter 9. This will also help to explain why only this part of proto-Fordun has survived.

One piece in the jigsaw remains which reinforces this connection between *GAI* and 'proto-Fordun'. It has been noted elsewhere that Fordun's chronicle includes a number of different and often contradictory accounts of Scottish origins which have been skilfully synthesised into a coherent narrative by adopting a copy of the Latinate version of the royal genealogy as its chronological backbone.[46] This particular version of the pedigree was quarried for names that could be matched with key figures in the various accounts: some names were genuinely identical, if spelt slightly differently (such as Gaedel Glas), while others were wholly contrived (such as the identification of 'Rether' in the genealogy with Bede's 'Reuda'). As we have seen, Fordun's poor grasp of his chronicle's chronological structure means that he himself cannot be credited with this achievement. It will be recalled that the author of *GAI* had a copy of this Latinate version of the genealogy, which he quoted at length in interpolation B in the account of Alexander III's inauguration. This, plus his own sensitivity to the chronicle's structure, would suggest that he was the synthesist. But this is not all. At one point he betrays a particular concern to match a figure from the origin-legend material with someone in his text of the genealogy. In interpolation B, at the end of his quotation of the royal genealogy, he explained that 'Fergus, moreover, was son of Feredach, although "son of Ferchar" is stated by some – but there is little difference in sound. Perhaps this discrepancy consists of a scribal error due to language difficulty'.

The possibility that Fergus's father might be Feredach rather than Ferchar only appears in *GAI*, so this was not an attempt to resolve an important variant detail in different accounts of Fergus as first king of Scots. Neither was it an idle piece of scholarly obfuscation as far as the author of *GAI* was concerned: in the passage on the acquisition of the Hebrides by Magnus Barelegs Fergus's father is given simply as Feredach, so this must have been his preferred option. The answer to why he should have been so keen to identify Fergus's father as Feredach is because the source for Feredach was his copy of the Latinate version of the royal genealogy. Only someone striving to connect the origin-legend material with this version of the genealogy would have insisted that this Fergus's father was Feredach rather than Ferchar. In the passage from the account of Alexander's inauguration we can see the author of *GAI* struggling to achieve this; and in this struggle he reveals himself as the synthesist.

TAILPIECE: FORDUN AND THE TREATMENT OF THE NAMES *FEREDACH* AND *EOCHAID*

Sadly, it is not possible to say whether the author of *GAI* also explained his struggle to identify Ferchar with Feredach when Fergus son of Ferchar first appeared in proto-Fordun (in the equivalent of book I chapter 34 and book II chapter 12 of Fordun's chronicle). In Fordun's text, as it stands, Fergus is named on his first appearance as *filius Ferechad siue Ferchardi*, 'son of "Ferechad" or "Ferchard" ', and is thereafter only Fergus son of 'Ferchard'.[47] 'Ferechad' is simply 'Feredach' with the 'ch' and 'd' swapped round. This could happen accidentally (either in speech or in writing). It may be suspected, though, that it was a later attempt to tidy up this problem, perhaps suggested by a claim (similar to that given in *GAI*) that the two names did not differ much. If so, it was not realised, presumably, that making Feredach into 'Ferechad' meant that the name no longer had a match in the royal genealogy.[48]

It is not possible to say, of course, that Fordun himself was necessarily responsible for this. What indications there are tend to suggest, in fact, that he was not. It is noteworthy, for instance, that he was prepared to copy out *GAI*'s 'Feredach' without alteration in the passage on the annexation of the Hebrides just mentioned. This on its own might not count for much, but there is other evidence that someone prior to Fordun took an interest in at least one other aspect of proto-Fordun's name-forms. It has been shown elsewhere that, although in Fordun's chronicle as it stands *Eugenius* is used as the Latin equivalent of both Gaelic *Eógan* and *Eochaid*, in proto-Fordun *Eugenius* was used only for *Eógan*, and that the few instances where *Eochaid* (genitive *Echdach*) survives, it has either been left without an attempt at a Latin case-ending (for example, 'Echach'),[49] or has been rendered as 'Echadius', 'Eochodius' or 'Ethdacus'.[50] That the two names were originally distinguished is made clear by the fact that, in the account of the expulsion of the Scots in 360 (included as part of the synthesis),[51] a brother of 'Echadius' (i.e., *Eochaid*), Fergus's grandfather, was concocted for the sake of the narrative, and was named 'Eugenius'. It has been assumed hitherto that Fordun himself failed to realise that 'Eugenius' in his source stood for *Eógan*, not *Eochaid*, and caused confusion by changing most instances of *Eochaid* to *Eugenius*. But this does not take account of the appearance of Eochaid 'Rothai' as 'Eugenius Rothay' in the account of the Treaty of Perth (1266) in *GAI* (remembering that *GAI* represents a stage in the text's development prior to Fordun's chronicle). It would be inaccurate, therefore, to imagine that the adoption of *Eugenius* for *Eochaid* was done by Fordun as he was writing. It must belong to an earlier stage.

As for Fordun himself, it cannot be demonstrated that, before embarking on work on his chronicle, he had no involvement with proto-Fordun (including *GAI*) – say, as a glossator or corrector. There is no necessity at all to think that he did, however. As far as the change of *Eochaid* to *Eugenius* is concerned, all that is required is that, in Fordun's exemplar (or at an earlier stage, of course), someone had crossed out forms of *Eochaid* and replaced them with *Eugenius*, but failed to do this systematically.[52] The same could have occurred in the case of the putative change of 'Feredach' to 'Ferechad' (also with a couple of instances overlooked). But this is obviously only a speculative suggestion.

NOTES

1. *Chron. Fordun*, i. lxxviii; and e.g., Bruce Webster, 'John of Fordun and the independent identity of the Scots', in Alfred P. Smyth (ed.), *Medieval Europeans: Studies in Ethnic Identity and National Perspectives in Medieval Europe* (Basingstoke, 1998), 85–102, at 85.
2. See below, 262.
3. For example, Nicola Royan, 'Hector Boece and the question of Veremund', *IR* 52 (2001) 42–62, at 61–2.
4. Broun, 'Birth of Scottish History', 15–20: see below, 253–4.
5. MacQueen and MacQueen (eds), *Scotichronicon*, i. xxviii–xxix.
6. For what follows, see Dauvit Broun, 'A new look at *Gesta Annalia* attributed to John of Fordun', in B. E. Crawford (ed.), *Church, Chronicle and Learning in Medieval and Early Renaissance Scotland* (Edinburgh, 1999), 9–30. The title *Gesta Annalia*, 'Yearly Deeds', is no more than a convenience: it was adopted by W. F. Skene, the only modern editor of Fordun's chronicle. I will use it to refer to all the chronicle-material which follows Fordun's chronicle: strictly speaking Skene used *Gesta Annalia* only for part of this material, beginning with the accession of Mael Coluim IV in 1153.
7. *Chron. Fordun*, i. xxxiii.
8. For example, the wholly fictitious account of how Robert Bruce (grandfather of the future king) had the stronger claim, but refused the award of the throne if it meant doing homage for it to Edward, unlike John Balliol, who agreed to Edward's terms (*Chron. Fordun*, i. 313–14, ii. 308–9), contrasts with the studiously neutral statement, following a detailed and unadorned account of the descent of the royal family, that 'having seen these things, let learned men seek and investigate which of the suitors had the stronger right' (*Chron. Fordun*, i. 315–18, ii. 309–12). I am grateful to Dr Alexander Grant for originally pointing this out to me.
9. See Donald Watt's discussion in MacQueen, MacQueen and Watt (eds), *Scotichronicon*, iii. xvii–xviii; for the dating of the text see Broun, *Irish Identity*, 196. It may also have been a source of interpolations into king-list E on Matilda, Christina and Edmund, children of Margaret and Mael Coluim (Anderson, *Kings and Kingship*, 255), which would suggest that the extant Dunfermline text is only an abbreviated form of the original, extended *ca* 1250.
10. See esp. A. A. M. Duncan, 'Sources and uses of the Chronicle of Melrose', in Simon Taylor (ed.), *Kings, Clerics and Chronicles in Scotland, 500–1297* (Dublin, 2000), 146–85.
11. Broun, 'A new look at *Gesta Annalia*', 16.
12. *Ibid.*, 14, 18, 19.
13. *Chron. Fordun*, i. 304–5, ii. 300.
14. The first line (which gives the year 1274) can work as a hexameter if its first words, *Anno Domini*, are excluded.

15. *Chron. Fordun*, i. 307, ii. 302.
16. *cum ad annos maturitatis peruenerat*; this may seem inappropriate, given that Margaret died aged seven, but *maturitas* here is presumably in relation to infancy.
17. *Chron. Fordun*, i. 308–9, ii. 303–4.
18. *Hoc igitur insertum est breuiter ubi capitulum, ne qua gens comprouincialis* (as in MSS B and C; other MSS read *prouincialis*), *dictam perlegens historiam, exemplo Gualencium incastigata decidat sub Anglorum incaute dominio misserime seruitutis.*
19. D. J. Corner, A. B. Scott, W. W. Scott and D. E. R. Watt (eds), *Scotichronicon by Walter Bower in Latin and English*, gen. ed. D. E. R. Watt, vol. iv (Edinburgh, 1994), 527.
20. Verse is in general a rare feature in *GAI*: there is a verse on comets, couplets on Alexander II's death, some more on the death of King Hákon in Orkney and his successor, Magnús, and a full poem on the death of Mael Coluim IV.
21. Gilbert talks of the English bringing down the Scottish church, its mother, 'into extreme and wretched servitude', *in ultimam deduceres miseram seruitudinem*. The phrase 'wretched servitude' is not found in set-piece declarations of freedom in contrast to slavery in Fordun's chronicle (such as Gaedel Glas's speech to his sons, I.16, and the reply of the kings of Picts and Scots to Julius Caesar, II.15, discussed below, 248–51). For example, compare *sub execrabilis onere subieccionis* (in Fordun's chronicle, I.16: Broun, *Irish Identity*, 45, at XVI.i).
22. *Ibid.*, 183–7 (at 187 for edition of the passage).
23. *ubi antiqui reges, Cruthne primo Pictorum rege, sedem regni Albanie constituerant*; *Chron. Fordun*, i. 430 ('Early Gesta' chapter 31). In Fordun's chronicle (book V, chapter 28; *Chron. Fordun*, i. 227; see also MacQueen, MacQueen, and Watt (eds), *Scotichronicon*, iii. 106–7) this was significantly rephrased: Scone was the place 'where kings from ancient times, both Picts and Scots, established the chief seat of the kingdom' (*quo reges antiquitus tam Scoti quam Picti sedem regni primam constituerunt*).
24. *Chron. Fordun*, i. 427–8. It was repeated almost verbatim in Fordun's chronicle (V.24): *ibid.*, i. 223–4, ii. 213–14.
25. Broun, *Irish Identity*, 71, 180–2.
26. *Ibid.*, 183–7 for edition.
27. *Chron. Fordun*, i. 251–2, ii. 244–6.
28. See further, below 229, where it is pointed out that Fergus 'son of Feredach' is not found anywhere else.
29. Broun, *Irish Identity*, 186 n. 197; see also 70.
30. As can be deduced, for instance, from the genealogy of William I in the 'Poppleton manuscript', where Gaelic name-forms have been retained: see Broun, *Irish Identity*, 178 lines 56–7.
31. *Ibid.*, ch.5.

32. *Ibid.*, 176–80.
33. *Ibid.*, 186 n. 197.
34. *Ibid.*, 117–18.
35. For the application of a similar principle, but to Scotland (so that Scots are simply said to be called from *Scotia*), see Broun, 'Birth of Scottish History', 115.
36. Fordun made some minor alterations, recasting *GAI*'s statement that Eochaid 'Rothai' settled the islands 2,000 years ago 'or more' to read 'almost' 2,000 years ago, and making Fergus's arrival 'about' 500 years rather than 'nearly' 500 years later.
37. *ubi antiqui reges, Cruthne primo Pictorum rege, sedem regni Albanie constituerant*; *Chron. Fordun*, i. 430.
38. *quo reges antiquitus tam Scoti quam Picti sedem regni primam constituerunt*; *Chron. Fordun*, i. 227, ii. 208; MacQueen, MacQueen and Watt (eds), *Scotichronicon*, iii. 106–7.
39. Watt and Murray (eds), *Fasti*, 191. There is no reason to suppose (*pace* Skene) that this chapter was added later by Fordun, in which case the terminal dates for his work would be sometime between early 1384 (when the news of Wardlaw's elevation would have reached Scotland) and late August 1387 (given that it might be expected in a passage like this, which advertises some kind of a personal connection between Fordun and Wardlaw, that some reference to Wardlaw's death would have been made had it occurred).
40. Broun, *Irish Identity*, 180–2.
41. They concern Erc father of Fergus, and Gaedel Glas.
42. Both Diss and *GAI* make Eochaid (father of Aed Find) a son of Domnall Brecc, whereas in book IV chapter 8 Domnall Brecc is father of Domangart ('Dongard'), father of Eochaid ('Eugenius'), and father of 'Findan' (known only to a recension of the king-lists), who is father of Eochaid (called 'Eugenius') father of Aed Find. See Broun, *Irish Identity*, 180 n. 117.
43. It will be recalled (above, 221) that 'Rothai' is a misrendering of *Buadaig* in the archetype of the Latinate recension shared by Diss as well as the author of *GAI* and Wardlaw. The idea that the eponym of Rothesay played such a significant role in Scotland's imagined past need only have had a textual origin, although an interest in Bute's name could suggest more interest: see below, 260.
44. Broun, *Irish Identity*, 65–8, 73.
45. There is a lacuna (noted in *Chron. Fordun*, i. 283 n. 1) from before the end of Skene's chapter 32 to midway in chapter 36 which might account for this, although a book-division here would not be entirely natural and might seem premature. At the end of *GAI*, a note has been added in a hand contemporary with the text hand to say that 'book VII' is finished later on, resuming where *GAII* begins. This is a natural response to the interruption caused by *GAI*'s ending with messengers sent to find Alexander III a new bride, and *GAII*'s beginning with the wedding. Where, though, did he think that book

VII began? Not being in the text hand, the status of this addition is uncertain.

46. Broun, *Irish Identity*, 63–72.
47. Broun, *Irish Identity*, 59 (XXXIV. c); 60–1.
48. There can be no doubt that 'Feredach' was the original form, not only because that is what is found in the Latinate version of the genealogy, but also because it is the form given in the passage in *GAI* on the annexation of the Hebrides by Magnus Barelegs in 1098 which Fordun repeated without comment.
49. *Chron. Fordun*, i. 74.
50. *Chron. Fordun*, i. 87, 112, 427. Broun, 'Birth of Scottish History', 18–20.
51. See below, 254.
52. A parallel could be drawn with the incomplete replacing of *Picti* with *Scoti* in a manuscript of the St Andrews foundation-legend version B: see Broun, 'Picts' place in the kingship's past', 15 and n. 14.

9

The Scots as Ancient and Free: 'Proto-Fordun', 'Veremundus' and the Creation of Scottish History

Before proceeding further, it will be useful to take stock briefly and retool so that we have the terminology that will equip us best for a trek into the increasingly shadowy world of lost texts. The intention is to keep the necessity of groping about in the gloom of uncertainty to a minimum by concentrating on those areas which offer the clearest visibility as belonging to the synthesis identified as proto-Fordun. This will include those parts of Fordun's chronicle relating to the chronological structure of early Scottish history, as well as those sections of the narrative of Scottish origins where two or more contradictory passages have been juxtaposed (especially where the passages have been advertised as coming from different sources). Also, it is possible to reconstruct the narrative outline (but not necessarily the very words, of course) of some of the lost sources that have been used by the synthesist. This is relatively straightforward where passages have been attributed to the same text (such as the *legenda* or *historia* of St Congal which is the earliest detectable statement of the legend of the Stone of Scone featuring Simón Brecc and Fergus son of Ferchar). It is also possible, in the case of material attributed simply to 'a chronicle' or 'another chronicle', to use contradictions between passages as a way of distinguishing one source from another, and to reconstruct at least the narrative outline of a few of them by matching together passages that share specific details. Fortunately this task of recovering the narrative shape of some of the lost texts used by the synthesist has already been accomplished in an earlier study, so that it will be necessary on this occasion simply to draw on its conclusions.[1] The tools we have can only take us so far, however. Even so, when our way becomes impassable, there will still be an opportunity to shoot an occasional glance towards what is barely discernible in the distance. In particular, it would be unforgivable, after trekking so far into the unknown, not to scan the horizon for at least a glimpse of that most elusive and controversial of early historical texts: the narrative from Scottish origins to Mael Coluim III attributed to 'Veremundus'. If this could be sighted, it may be feasible to find a way to get much closer to it than has hitherto been thought possible. As things stand it lies on the outermost limits of our scholarly field of vision. Both Hector Boece and David Chalmers claimed to have used it in the sixteenth century,[2] but its existence has until recently been either dismissed or regarded as lacking any evidence with which to decide the matter.[3] Nicola Royan, however, has rescued it from scholarly oblivion by making a compelling case, based on a detailed consideration of Boece's sources, that it is easier to regard 'Veremundus' and his history as real rather than fabricated.[4] It was pointed out by Skene that Veremundus could be identified with Richard Vairement, a *céle Dé* of St Andrews Professor Barrow has shown to have been active between 1239 and 1267.[5] If Vairement was the author of this work, and if it existed at all, then it would clearly have a claim to be regarded as the earliest sustained narrative of a distinct Scottish past.

We can begin, then, with a summary of the discussion so far, fleshing this out with a resumé of lost texts. Fordun's chronicle has been recognised as an impressive synthesis of diverse sources into a chronologically coherent account of Scottish history from its ancient origins. But it has been shown that Fordun cannot have created this himself. Instead, he has (to some unknown extent) rewritten and expanded an earlier work, which I have dubbed 'proto-Fordun'. The only part of this that survives is the text I have dubbed '*Gesta Annalia* I' (or *GA*I for short). The author of *GA*I was therefore the author of 'proto-Fordun', and the internal evidence for dating *GA*I to sometime between 2 February and 9 April 1285 is therefore also evidence for the date of 'proto-Fordun'. The identity of *GA*I as a fragment of proto-Fordun can usefully be consolidated in our minds by referring to its author as the 'synthesist', which also serves to highlight the text's chief identifiable characteristic.

Before proceeding further, some explanation of terms of reference may be helpful. In particular, a Greek letter denotes a lost archetype (meaning in this case a copy of a text of the king-list or origin-legend which has undergone some detectable modification, either deliberately or by accident: this is a broader definition of archetype than usual). The Greek letter serves to alert the reader that the existence and contents of these archetypes are ultimately hypothetical. A Roman capital, in contrast, denotes an extant manuscript-witness of one of these texts. Altogether there are four texts to bear in mind:

α

An assemblage of two accounts of Scottish origins (one is the legend of the Stone of Scone attributed to a *historia* or *legenda* of St Congal), followed by a king-list in which it was made clear that the early Scottish kings were parallel with Pictish kings. No attempt appears to have been made to iron out differences or confront contradictions between the various texts. The king-list in the assemblage must have reached at least as far as Alexander II, so that the whole work can be dated to sometime after 1214.[6]

The 'Éber account'

This is a rewriting of the origin-legend material in **α** into a coherent narrative.[7] It would have told how the Scots, a combination of Greek and Egyptian nobles expelled from Egypt led by Gaedel Glas, swore to seek uninhabited land as their new home; but they first attempted to settle in Spain, despite the fact it was already inhabited, and were threatened with extinction or servitude due to the relentless pressure of the Spaniards. Gaedel Glas therefore resolved to renew the quest for uninhabited territory, and dispatched sailors to explore the seas. The sailors returned with reports of a most beautiful land (Ireland), and Gaedel, now at the point of death, exhorted his sons not to miss such a glorious opportunity. Éber responded, and colonised Ireland. It is likely that this account also told how, later, the Stone of Scone was brought up from the sea bed by Simón Brecc, and was subsequently taken to Scotland by Fergus son of Ferchar when he became king of the Scots who had been expelled from their midst by the Picts. The Picts had taken Scottish wives from Ireland, and these Scotswomen had brought their relatives who the Picts in due course drove out. The author of the Éber account would also have had to confront the problem (left unresolved in **α**) of having two Ferguses as first king of Scots: Fergus son of Ferchar in the origin-legend material, and Fergus son of Erc in the king-list. At this stage it is difficult to discern how he dealt with this.

o

This is the text discussed in chapter 6 in which the realm of Fergus son of Erc was portrayed as stretching from the Orkneys in the north to Stainmore in the south and the Hebrides in the west.[8] It can be identified as a king-list descended ultimately from **α**, but with some fundamental modifications. The synthesist was aware of an astonishing claim that the succession of Scottish kings from Fergus son of Erc to Ailpín (father of Cinaed mac Ailpín) preceded, *en bloc*, the succession of Pictish kings. This was presumably derived from a king-list in which the early kings of Scots and Pictish kings were misconstrued as a single succession (leading ultimately to the reigning monarch), with Scots preceding Picts, and finishing with Cinaed mac Ailpín and his successors after the destruction of the Picts.[9] (The first text of this kind is denoted as β in the stemma below.) This would naturally have encouraged the view that the bounds of Fergus's kingdom should be reinterpreted as corresponding to the thirteenth-century kingdom (as in **o**), rather than to historic Dál Riata (chiefly Argyll), as delineated in **α**. But, as we saw when discussing the basis of Glasgow's claim in the 1260s to the diocese of Carlisle, it took a number of stages in the text's development before this point was reached. The identification of **o** as the king-list which was the source of these ideas in proto-Fordun is wholly consistent with its relationship to Wyntoun and king-list D as discussed in chapter 6. It may, however, have contained only the king-list from the archetype it shared with Wyntoun.[10]

The 'Partholón account'

Partholón was taken from Geoffrey of Monmouth's *History of the Kings of Britain*, where he appears as leader of a band of wanderers who submit to a king of Britain and are granted Ireland. In this account Partholón became, instead, the leader of a desperate people who settled Ireland as their perpetual possession, in freedom, after having endured severe hardship in Spain under their king rather than submit to their enemies.[11]

The 'Scottish Monmouth'

This source has been identified by John and Winifred MacQueen as a history based loosely on Geoffrey of Monmouth written from a decidedly Scottish point of view.[12] It will be referred to for convenience as the 'Scottish Monmouth'. It shows all the signs of having been a full-bodied narrative extending from the first settlement of Scots in Ireland to at least the early centuries AD. Its treatment of the earliest stages of Scottish origins would seem naturally to be represented by the Partholón account, which can readily be identified as a reworking of Geoffrey's text from a Scottish point of view.[13] A more likely alternative will be suggested in due course.

The relationship between the texts derived from **α** can be represented diagrammatically, showing also their relationship with Wyntoun and king-list D, as well as with other texts which have not been discussed: king-list K (in Grey's *Scalacronica*)[14] and the first poem in *Liber Extravagans* (attached to Bower's *Scotichronicon*).[15] (It should be noted, to avoid any confusion, that lines do not necessarily mean direct connections without intermediary copies or recensions, and that it is in any case perfectly feasible for items high up the stemma to be used in texts much later than items lower down the stemma: a stemma does not have the chronological parameters of the generations in a family tree.[16]) For the sake of clarity, I have boxed those datable specifically to the reign of Alexander III (1249–86).

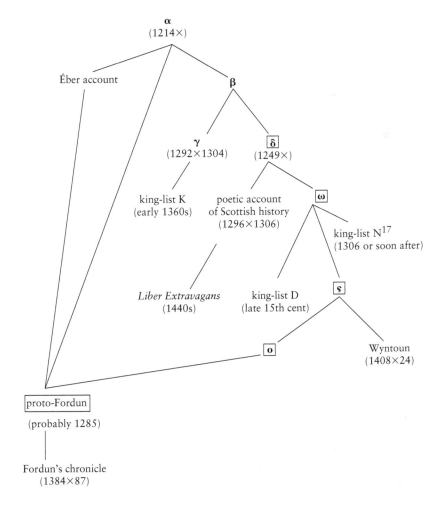

Other chronological markers that may be noted are John of Cheam's (probable) awareness, around 1265, of either ʂ or o,[18] and a likely reference by the Scottish procurators at the curia in 1301 to material in Fordun's chronicle, suggesting that they had access either to proto-Fordun or one of its sources. (This will be investigated towards the end of this chapter.[19])

'PROTO-FORDUN' AND THE VISION OF AN ANCIENT SCOTTISH KINGDOM

Although proto-Fordun was hugely significant as providing the structure of the sustained narrative of the kingship's past adopted in Fordun's chronicle and its derivatives, there are obvious difficulties in trying to detect its author's view of the nature of Scottish kingship. Only certain features of Fordun's text can with confidence be regarded as derived from proto-Fordun. Unfortunately these are chiefly in areas where the choices made by the synthesist are likely to have been driven by his desire to create a chronologically coherent and all-embracing narrative, rather than because he wished to promote a particular vision of the kingship's past. It will be recalled, however, that there were specific elements to which he drew attention in *GAI*, such as the establishing of Scone as the kingdom's seat by the first king of the Picts. Even if he cannot be shown to have created all these elements, he must at least have felt sufficiently strongly to want to make a point of referring to them. Where these elements also involved the harmonisation of radically different views, it may be assumed that the synthesist at least contributed to the text as we have it. The example that will be discussed is the question of who settled in Scotland first: the Scots or the Picts. He appears to have pushed his material as far as he dared to in order to sustain the view that they arrived more or less simultaneously. This chimes directly with his careful portrayal in *GAI* of the kingship as derived from both Pictish and Scottish roots. It is important to bear in mind, though, that a similar attitude to the claims of Picts and Scots to primacy may be detected in one of his sources, the Éber account.[20] This was not, therefore, in origin necessarily the synthesist's idea, although he seems to have been keen to promote it.

A different benefit of the synthesist's work, however, is what it can tell us about other views apart from his own, and it is to this that we will turn first. His overriding desire to bring together disparate accounts allows us to see two or more perspectives on some highly charged moments in the kingship's imagined past. A particularly significant example is the treatment of Fergus son of Erc, who was universally regarded as 'first king of Scots', either in his capacity as the first in the current succession of kings (as in proto-Fordun), or (more straightforwardly in the king-lists) as the first king of Scots in Scotland. Here the synthesist seems to have had special difficulty in embracing contradictory accounts, each with its own special emphasis on the kingdom's territorial identity.[21] It helps, in navigating our way through this, to bear in mind that Fergus was accorded a reign of three years in all king-lists, but sixteen in Fordun's chronicle. The reasons for this difference will become apparent towards the end of this chapter.

In book III chapter 2 the reader of Fordun's chronicle is confronted by a range of contradictory accounts of Fergus's kingdom. We are told that

(i) within three years after his arrival Fergus son of Erc had extended his realm to embrace the kingdom of his fathers on both sides of the Firth of Forth, namely from Stainmore to the Hebrides and to Orkney. We are then told that

(ii) forty-five kings (possibly forty was the original reading)[22] reigned from Fergus son of Ferchar to Fergus son of Erc; but these (it is explained) are not going to be given individually.

(iii) Fergus son of Erc reigned for sixteen years; in the last three years he was the first king of Scottish descent to reign in the land of the Picts beyond Drumalban, that is, from the mountains to the 'Scottish sea' (Firth of Forth).

The chapter finishes by noting raids made jointly by Scots and Picts on the Britons' kingdom of *Britannia*.

The statements in (i) and (iii) are incompatible on two counts. One says that Fergus ruled in the east as his fathers had done; the other maintains that his dominion in the east was unprecedented for a Scottish king. The second is that Fergus either conquered the east within three years of 403 (as in (i)), or in the last three years of his reign (413–16) (as in (iii)). This is evidently a strained attempt to integrate statements about Fergus from different versions of the king-list (where he would have been accorded, as usual, a three-year-reign) with the sixteen-year reign given to Fergus as part of the process of dating his advent to 403. We have already met the king-list source of (i), namely **o**. The source of (iii), for its part, has been identified elsewhere as the Éber account,[23] although it could just as well be the synthesist's interpretation of the standard statement in king-lists that Fergus ruled 'beyond Drumalban' (so it could, in fact, have been derived from **α**). What is immediately noteworthy in (iii) is that, although the bounds of Fergus's kingdom have been interpreted as including the east, the Firth of Forth remains the southern limit. The image of an ancient territory is confined to the idea of combining the original Scottish and Pictish kingdoms. The statement in (i) derived from **o**, therefore, stands out as the only attempt to delineate the original kingdom of the Scots as essentially the same as the territory of the Scottish kingdom at the time these texts were written around the middle of the thirteenth century.

Although it may not be possible to detect where the synthesist's sympathies lay between the two narratives of defining Fergus's realm, he was evidently keen to stress that the Picts and Scots arrived in Scotland at much the same time. This parity gave legitimacy to both, and therefore allowed the reigning king of the moment to be portrayed as ruling a realm which, by projecting back from the present, could be regarded as having existed from the beginning, not only since the conquest of the Picts by Cinaed mac Ailpín. It is particularly striking that the synthesist rejected the idea that the Scots could have settled in Scotland a couple of centuries (at least) before the Picts (which was the clear inference from the king-list in β and its derivatives, including **o**). The emphasis was on Scotland the territory (and specifically the landmass north of the Forth), not on the Scots. Characteristically, he still found an ingenious way of accommodating the portrayal of a pre-Pictish Scottish kingdom that he would have found in **o** with the idea that Scots and Picts had arrived in Scotland more or less simultaneously. The way this was achieved was by picking up on a statement in the king-lists that the first Pictish king, Cruithne, was a judge.[24] On the basis of this it was proposed that the Picts initially did not have kings but judges, so that Scottish kings may have predated Pictish *kings* but the Scots did not necessarily predate the arrival of the Pictish *people*.

The same concern to promote the parity of Scots and Picts as Scotland's original inhabitants can also be traced in the stress on an ancient unity and amity between these peoples as the chronicle's narrative unfolds. To begin with they are mixed together, because the Picts bring Scottish wives from Ireland with them when they first settle in Scotland (and with the wives came the in-laws and other kinsfolk); but the Picts find so many in-laws intolerable and eject the Scots, who roam unoccupied tracts of the country until Fergus son of Ferchar hears of their plight and becomes their king (book I chapters 29–31 and 34).[25] The two kingdoms become close allies. In book II, chapter 37, however, we are told that, not long before the accession of the emperor Diocletian in 287, a period of 500 years in which Scots and Picts had 'reigned together in peace, everywhere protecting their kingdoms with combined strength', came to an end.[26] Unity is restored on the accession of Fergus son of Erc as king of Scots in AD 403, but in due course this gives way to intermittent warfare until, in 839, the Picts are finally conquered by Cinaed mac Ailpín (book IV, chapters 3, 4 and 8).[27] In the end, the breakdown of the peaceful concord between Scots and Picts leads to the forcible unification of the two kingdoms when the Scots destroy the Picts. Although none of this was necessarily written by the synthesist himself, it would all have been consistent with his concern to promote a sense of Scotland north of the Forth as a single entity from the beginning. His particular interest in this narrative thread, however, can be seen in *GAI*. The mention of an initial 500 years of peace between Picts and Scots calls to mind the passage in *GAI* on the annexation of the Hebrides by Magnus Barelegs in 1098, in which a figure of 'nearly 500 years' was given between the arrival of Eochaid 'Rothai' and Fergus son of Ferchar, and '2,000 years or more' between Eochaid and 1098.[28] This not only suggests a predilection for 500-year periods, but also a particular concern for the chronicle's chronological structure, with each approximate 500-year period representing a new stage in the narrative.

A determination to present this image of the kingdom's ancient territorial integrity was only part of the picture, however. The other side of the coin was the king as ruler of a people: the Scots. Here Ireland, rather than Scotland, was highlighted. In both the 'Éber' and 'Partholón' accounts of Scottish origins, for example, Ireland was portrayed as the God-given and perpetual home of the Scots under rulers of their own people.[29] It has been argued that the key here was the royal pedigree which traced the king's ancestry back to a series of prehistoric figures who were understood to have been kings of Ireland.[30] This identification with Ireland as a way of authenticating the kingship was well established by the time of Alexander III's inauguration. As far as proto-Fordun is concerned, the dual emphasis on Ireland as homeland of the Scots and on Scotland north of the Forth as the kingdom's primordial territory is consistent with what has been gleaned from the account of Alexander III's inauguration about the synthesist's vision of an ancient Scottish past. The inauguration on the Stone at Scone seemed to promote a view of the present-day kingdom (before the Stone's removal in 1296) as the heir of parallel realms of Picts and Scots in the remote past; while, at the same time, the attention drawn to Éber as the 'first Scot' suggested knowledge and approval of the representation of Ireland in the Éber account as the divinely ordained homeland of the Scots.[31]

It has been noted that the synthesist did not betray a clear preference for one or other definition of the bounds of Fergus son of Erc's kingdom. There is equal difficulty in pinning him down about the original Scottish and Pictish realms, particularly when it comes to their southern limit. Unfortunately the key section in Fordun's chronicle was not evidently composed of extracts from different sources, and is therefore much less certainly drawn from proto-Fordun. Book II chapter 7 is an account of the extent and nature of *Scotia*, and is (as far as any hope of identifying it with proto-Fordun is concerned) a frustratingly homogenous piece of prose.[32] It begins with an explanation of how Scotland was initially bounded by the Firth of Forth, but later reached as far south as the Humber, 'where *Albania* also began'.[33] We are then told that the southern limit was later defined by the wall built as far as the River Tyne by Severus (i.e., Hadrian's Wall), but that it is now the River Tweed. On the face of it there is no way of telling whether this is the work of Fordun or the synthesist. It does, however, seem to be of a piece with the next two chapters, on the topography and economy of the Lowlands and Highlands (chapter 8), and on the cultural and social differences between the peoples of these zones (chapter 9).[34] The last includes the oft-quoted description of the Gaelic-speaking inhabitants of the Highlands and Islands as 'a wild and untamed race, primitive and proud, given to plunder and the easy life', contrasting this with the 'home-loving, civilised, trustworthy, tolerant and polite' 'Teutonic' speakers who lived beside the sea and on the low-lying lands. This, as the earliest extended statement of the 'Highland/Lowland' divide, is commonly regarded as inconceivable before the 1360s (on the grounds that it was based on a real linguistic and social divide for which there is no evidence until Fordun's day).[35] This would seem to put beyond doubt that book II chapter 9, and the related chapters which precede it, are also Fordun's own work. But there are possible objections. In general terms it is debatable (to say the least) that it would have been impossible for someone to think along these lines in Scotland in the thirteenth century.[36] More specifically, there are signs of a similar attitude to Gaelic-speakers in *GAI*. The most telling point here is not that Gaelic-speakers are labelled as 'brutes' and 'beasts' when ravaging Northumberland with Galwegians in 1173; it is not even that the term *Scotus montanus*, 'highland Scot', is used twice (in the same passage as 'brutes' and 'beasts', and in the account of Alexander III's inauguration):[37] it is that Gaelic-speakers are *not* regarded as inveterate savages. In a celebrated passage in book II chapter 9 it is observed that they are 'loyal and obedient to king and kingdom, if ruled, and also readily subject to laws'. This qualification of the stereotype of Gaelic (or Celtic) barbarity is unusual. It is noteworthy, therefore, that an example of such a loyal and obedient Gael is found in *GAI* in its account of the killing of Uhtred of

Galloway by his brother: we are told that this was 'because he had shown himself a true Scot and could not be deflected from this stance' by his brother and his supporters who had 'made a conspiracy, dividing themselves from the kingdom of Scotland in the same year' that William had been imprisoned at Falaise (1174).[38] This suggests that the same person who interpreted Uhtred's fate in this way could also have penned the depiction of Gaelic-speakers in book II chapter 9. The knock-on effect of this is that it would at least become conceivable that the earlier chapters in this section of Fordun's chronicle, including the account of Scotland's borders in book II chapter 7, were present in proto-Fordun. Although it is stated there that the Firth of Forth was the southern frontier in the beginning, what is emphasised is how it had fluctuated over time: a practical and realistic response to this vexed issue which was not typical of other attempts to describe the kingdom's limits in the deep past.

Overall, the vision of the kingship's primordial past in proto-Fordun (insofar as this can be identified with reasonable certainty), not only as portrayed by the synthesist himself, but also in his sources, suggests that only a very limited attempt was made in the thirteenth century to relate an image of the kingdom's original territory to its current bounds. The only unambiguous statement would have been the portrayal of Fergus son of Erc's kingdom in o (remembering that in this text Fergus son of Erc would have been the first in a single succession of more than 110 kings, including Picts, before reaching Alexander III). This would also have been the only deliberate expression of this idea if all known texts before 1290 are taken into account.[39] Instead, it was more common to project back an image of a single territory bounded by the Firth of Forth in the south by presenting the current kingdom as originating in parallel Scottish and Pictish realms. The first indication of this idea is during the reign of Alexander II (1214–49), when a Pictish king-list was added to the Scottish king-list (which had itself only been extended back to Fergus son of Erc during the reign of William; this was in due course incorporated into α).[40] This king-list (given the siglum ξ in the overall scheme) was the first occasion in which the reigning king was presented explicitly as simultaneously successor to both Pictish and Scottish kingdoms.[41] This failure to embrace current political reality more conclusively, and the decision to concentrate instead on the essential unity of the territory north of the Forth, can most readily be explained as illustrating the continuing hold on the historical imagination of the image of the Forth as a geographical divide. This was not the only respect in which little had changed. The legitimacy of a long succession ruling a territory defined by the Forth was complemented by a sense of being the kingship of a people with an Irish pedigree, and Ireland as its home. The genealogical link with kings of England through St Margaret was also actively maintained: it is the dominant feature of the first part of *GAI*, and is also witnessed at the beginning of Alexander III's reign by a dynastic history written at Dunfermline as a continuation of an earlier text on Margaret's English ancestors and her children.

On the face of it, proto-Fordun represents an important development in the infrastructure of how the Scottish kingdom was conceived by those closely associated with it: a continuous account of the kingship's past had been constructed which, in its chronological scale and substance, could stand alongside the extended narratives which the English, Irish and Welsh had boasted for over a century. Instead, however, of completely refashioning the kingship's history into a pure statement of Scottish sovereignty, it also served to perpetuate the significance of the image of an ancient realm originally confined to Scotland north of the Forth, the umbilical tie with Ireland, and the dynastic link with English kingship and the idea of Britain. It is little wonder that, when Scottish lawyers and politicians during the first war of independence sought to justify Scotland's claim to be an independent, sovereign kingdom, they abandoned the synthesist's meticulously crafted structure and created their own chronologically cruder statements of Scottish origins, banishing the Picts from the scene as soon as the Scots arrived in Scotland, and either omitting Ireland altogether from the Scots' primeval journey to their homeland, or imagining that Scota herself brought the Stone of Scone directly to Scotland.[42] The perpetuation of the older framework of the kingship's legitimacy in proto-Fordun was partly a consequence of its design as a synthesis of different accounts, of course; but it is also apparent that much of this appealed to the synthesist himself, both from his insistence on the essential territorial integrity of Scotland north of the Forth, and from his claim that Alexander III's pedigree was read back to Éber the 'first Scot'. The only one of his sources identified so far that presented the current kingdom in a blatant way as having a distinct and ancient history on a par with the English, Irish and Welsh was king-list o; but the synthesist went to some trouble to diminish its claim for the precedence of the Scots in relation to the Picts. In contrast, the author(s) of the Declaration of Arbroath regarded this differently, and embraced the central idea of king-list o (which was shared with other texts derived from β) that the current king was the latest in a single succession of more than 110 kings.

PROTO-FORDUN, THE SCOTTISH MONMOUTH AND SCOTTISH FREEDOM

It would be a mistake, though, to regard king-list o as the only one of the synthesist's sources to project a forceful image of Scottish sovereignty. It has been pointed out, for example, that the key themes in the Partholón account were the hardship endured by the Scots in their quest for 'perpetual settlements in freedom' (which they found in Ireland), and the independence they enjoyed from the beginning: these are so deeply embedded in the narrative that they cannot plausibly be regarded as later additions or embellishments (by Fordun or anyone else).[43] For this reason, it was argued that a particularly significant statement about freedom found at the end of a section drawn from the Partholón account could be regarded as originally part of this source rather than necessarily an embellishment by Fordun. After the Scots are described as eking out a wretched existence in the desert places and forests given to them by the Spaniards, it is declared that, 'in all these ills and difficulties [the people] could never be bowed into submitting or answering to a foreign king, but chose rather to lead this bestial life, with freedom alone, always humble and loyal under their own king'.[44] An even more clear-cut expression of sovereignty lies at the heart of the Éber account, however. The narrative hinges on the vow taken by Gaedel and his followers on leaving Egypt that they will seek out uninhabited lands to settle: their lingering in Spain, fighting against the Spaniards who had settled there already, leads to divine disapproval and the threat of servitude or extinction which is only relieved by their discovery and settlement of an uninhabited island (Ireland) as their divinely ordained possession.[45] The governing idea here is that every people has its own God-given country which they were the first to settle. According to this general principle, the Scots could not be regarded as in any way subject to the king of England. We can also go further, and see in this an assumption that all kingdoms are of equal status.

But how was Scotland made to fit into this paradigm, given that Ireland was presented as homeland of the Scots? It has been argued that the Éber account continued with the arrival of the Picts in Ireland, who were persuaded by the Scots to settle the previously uninhabited northern part of Britain, taking Scots as their brides.[46] As a result, Scotland became the primordial home of Picts and Scots in combination: not exactly a new people, but distinctive enough to mean that Scotland's first inhabitants were endowed with a unique character. This depended crucially on the notion that the Scots and Picts arrived simultaneously –

an idea which (it will be recalled) the synthesist himself was keen to promote. Perhaps he gained the idea from the Éber account, where the Scots and Picts as joint settlers would have been crucial in creating an appropriate profile for Scotland within its narrative scheme.[47]

The ancient and enduring freedom of the Scottish kingdom was also proclaimed in what I have called the 'Scottish Monmouth'. John and Winifred MacQueen have argued compellingly that most of the narrative of book II of Fordun's chronicle came from this work.[48] It is difficult to conceive how this could have been created by Fordun himself, given that he includes quotations directly from Geoffrey of Monmouth which sometimes relate to the same episodes drawn from the 'Scottish Monmouth': why write a Scotticised version of Geoffrey's *History of the Kings of Britain* if it was also Fordun's intention to quote from the original for the same material? The most sustained exposition of the idea of freedom attributable to this source is in book II chapters 14–16 during an episode which has clearly been modelled on Geoffrey of Monmouth's work.[49] It is described how Julius Caesar, on reaching the southern bank of the Firth of Forth, sent letters demanding the submission of the Picts and Scots, but was compelled to leave Britain before he could take further action. The centrepiece is a defiant letter to Caesar sent jointly by the king of the Picts and the king of the Scots (chapter 15) which (as the MacQueens have observed)[50] takes its inspiration from book IV chapter 2 of Geoffrey's *History of the Kings of Britain*, which is a letter in similar vein sent by Cassivelaunus, king of the Britons, to Julius Caesar in response to his demand that the Britons should pay tribute and owe obedience to Rome.[51] The letter of the Pictish and Scottish kings is written to match the vivid style of Geoffrey of Monmouth's prose in the letter of Cassivelaunus, and finishes with a resounding declaration of Scotland's everlasting freedom:

> For after our death we will hand over to our sons the freedom handed down by our ancestors, which we must value above gold and topaz: in our judgment it transcends by far all worldly things, both necessities and pleasures, incomparably and infinitely; the freedom which our big-hearted fathers preserved from the beginning unsullied for us, their sons, right up to death, and which we similarly and exceedingly . . . will preserve inviolate for our sons, and without the least taint of servility. Farewell.

> *Nam auie tradicionis libertatem, que diligenda nobis super aurum est et topazion queque nostro iudicio cunctas longe mundanas et incomparabiliter opes transcendit et infinite iocalia, quam ab inicio magnanimes patres incontaminatam nobis filiis et usque ad mortem servabant, egregie similiter et*

nos . . . nostris post obitum filiis inuiolatam seruabimus, et absque seruili quoquam scrupulo transferemus. Ualeas.

Can it be shown that the Scottish Monmouth was used not by Fordun, but by the synthesist? The best place to look for an answer is in book I of Fordun's chronicle, which exhibits the most tell-tale features of the synthesist's work: it consists chiefly of passages juxtaposed from different (and often contradictory) sources held together by skilful use of the royal genealogy to create a coherent chronological framework. There are, in fact, not one but two origin-legend sources used by the synthesist which have taken their inspiration from Geoffrey of Monmouth (which is not altogether surprising, given how popular Geoffrey's work was among readers of Latin in the middle ages). Is there one which is clearly more likely to be part of the Scottish Monmouth than the other?

We have briefly met the two origin-legend sources already: they are the 'Éber' and 'Partholón' accounts. Let us look at them now in more detail. The Partholón account, as it stands, is a recasting of Geoffrey's tale of how a group of Basques, expelled from Spain, were wandering the oceans with their leader, Partholón, looking for somewhere to settle: Gargunt Babtruc came upon them, and Partholón did homage to him, and was granted Ireland, which (we are told) was uninhabited at that time.[52] The Partholón account (insofar as this can be reconstructed) was an attempt to retell this episode without any reference to Gargunt or to homage. Instead, freedom was emphasised, not only in its version of how Ireland became their perpetual possession, but also in its account of the Scots' commitment to maintaining their independence despite having to live like beasts in the wilderness and forests of the Pyrenees. This episode was evidently modelled on the section in book I chapter 4 of Geoffrey's history in which Brutus takes the Trojans out of servitude among the Greeks and leads them deep into the forests where they prefer to live as though they were wild beasts, in freedom, rather than remain under the Greeks' yoke of slavery.[53] The Éber account, in contrast, is not so obviously based on Geoffrey of Monmouth as to have taken its leading figure from the cast of Geoffrey's history. Éber and his parents, Gaedel and Scota, originate (ultimately) from Gaelic sources, as do other details in its narrative.[54] Its chief connection with Geoffrey of Monmouth is that its central idea – that the Scots set off from Egypt seeking uninhabited land which had been assigned to them by the gods – finds a particularly close parallel in Geoffrey's account of Brutus's quest for Britain. In book I chapter 11 of Geoffrey's history it is told how Brutus, on leaving Greece, sought the help of the goddess Diana, who foretold that he would find an uninhabited island waiting for him and his people.[55] In book I chapter 15 the Britons' destiny as settlers of Britain is reinforced in a way that is very similar to the account of Gaedel's troubles in Spain and decision to revert to the mission to settle in divinely approved land.[56] Geoffrey tells how Brutus lingered in Gaul, but found that his people were outnumbered and threatened with extinction; anxious about this worsening situation, Brutus resolved to return to the quest for the empty island that the gods had prophesied would be his. The *dramatis personae* may be different between the two, but the plot of the Éber account has evidently been drawn from Geoffrey's history.

There are three further considerations which point to the Éber account as part of the Scottish Monmouth. The first is that, when the sources behind the account of Scottish origins in Fordun's chronicle were analysed on a previous occasion, the Éber account was reconstructed as extending as far as the arrival of Fergus son of Ferchar to rule the Scots who had been expelled by the Picts from their midst.[57] This leads without a break into the remainder of the narrative in book II (and beyond) which, it will be recalled, was drawn chiefly from the Scottish Monmouth. The second consideration is that the detail between the end of the Éber account of Scottish origins and the beginning of material attributed to the Scottish Monmouth in book II dovetails comfortably together: both imagine Scotland as anciently inhabited by Picts and Scots together, and regard it as initially confined to the mainland north of the Forth. Finally, it is notable that, in book I of Fordun's chronicle, the material chosen as the first version of each episode is drawn from the Éber account, and that, towards the end of book I, it is even more obviously the source of the chronicle's narrative thread. This is a trend which continues in book II with material drawn from the Scottish Monmouth. Putting all this together, it appears that the Éber account and then the Scottish Monmouth was used by the synthesist as his chief narrative source into which everything else was integrated thanks to his deft use of the royal genealogy. There is no reason whatever to think that the Éber account and the Scottish Monmouth were ever separate from each other: they are simply different sections of the same work.

Bearing all this in mind, we can now turn to a key passage which has been attributed on firm grounds to the Éber account/the Scottish Monmouth. It gives the clearest indication that the most colourful expressions of the idea of freedom in the early parts of Fordun's chronicle should not be assumed to be embellishments by Fordun himself.[58] The passage occurs in book I, chapter 16, and begins with Gaedel Glas on his deathbed addressing his sons, recounting how they had suffered in Spain because they had not heeded the just wishes of the gods that they should settle an uninhabited land. He urges them to accept the gift of an empty land offered by the gods, and to go and settle Ireland where they would be able[59]

> to live noble and free, since it is the highest nobility of men, and of each honourable heart the joy most desired of all things, or rather it is the most precious gem rightly to be preferred to all the pleasures in the world, to suffer the authority of no foreign rule, but to enjoy of one's own accord only the power of one's own nation in due succession.

This deathbed speech has clearly been tacked onto an extract attributed to a *legenda* of St Brendan. In the passage from the *legenda* it is stated that Ireland was already inhabited before the Scots arrived – which is, of course, incompatible with a central tenet of Gaedel's speech that Ireland was the uninhabited land assigned to the Scots by the gods. This tolerance of juxtaposed inconsistencies is a characteristic of the synthesist's work. If Fordun had added Gaedel's speech, it is very difficult to see why he would have placed it here rather than at the end of chapter XV, where it would have followed the section from the Éber account/the Scottish Monmouth on the discovery of uninhabited Ireland. There is also at least a suspicion of significant similarity in expression between Gaedel's speech and the letter of kings of Picts and Scots to Julius Caesar. It will be recalled that, in the latter, it was announced that freedom 'transcends by far all worldly things, both necessities and pleasures, incomparably and infinitely' (*cunctas longe mundanas et incomparabiliter opes transcendit et infinite iocalia*), which compares closely with Gaedel's deathbed declaration that freedom 'is the most precious gem rightly to be preferred to all the pleasures in the world' (*gemma cunctis mundi merito preferenda iocalibus*). It has been assumed that celebrations of freedom such as these should be understood as particularly appropriate for Scots following their experience of English conquest and occupation during the wars of independence.[60] It should not be forgotten, however, that the kingdom's liberty was expressly what was at stake in the twelfth century when most of Scotland was threatened with falling under the control of an English archbishop, and that it would have remained a living issue when efforts to gain formal recognition of the kingship's sovereign status from the papacy were repeatedly thwarted by the king of England's insistence that the king of Scots was his man for Scotland. Freedom was also celebrated (if not quite so vividly) in Geoffrey's history. Although it cannot be said, of course, that Fordun simply reproduced all the words of his sources exactly as he found them, there is no reason to suppose that the sentiments (at least) in these passages, if not some of the prose itself, did not originate in the Scottish Monmouth via proto-Fordun.

THE 'SCOTTISH MONMOUTH' AND VEREMUNDUS

A close examination of Fordun's chronicle, and an intimate appreciation of the work of synthesis that lies just below its surface, has allowed a rewriting of material from Geoffrey of Monmouth's *Historia Regum Britannie* from a Scottish perspective (dubbed the 'Scottish Monmouth' for convenience) to emerge from the shadows as the earliest sustained narrative of the earliest Scottish past. Fortunately it is possible to say more about this pioneering work, and gain a clearer impression of the extent of the synthesist's indebtedness to it. It is also possible to identify who probably wrote it. The key here is a couple of significant clues in the work of Baldred Bisset and his fellow procurators who defended Scottish independence at the curia in 1301.

It has already been suggested that the Scottish Monmouth was apparently more than just a retelling of substantial sections of Geoffrey's history of British kings, and probably also consisted of the Éber account (consisting of the story of Gaedel, Scota and the settlement of uninhabited Ireland by their son, Éber, the discovery of the Stone of Scone by Simón, the settlement of the previously uninhabited northern part of Britain by Pictish men and their Scottish brides, and the Stone of Scone's arrival with Fergus son of Ferchar in Scotland). The Éber account is a rewriting of the origin-legend material in the small collection of items which have been referred to as α. This would mean that the author of the Scottish Monmouth had access to its king-list material, too. The synthesist must also have used it for some of the origin-legend material which he added to what we can now recognise as the account of Scottish origins given by the Scottish Monmouth. As long as the Scottish Monmouth was seen as only one element among others in the synthesis behind Fordun's chronicle, it would have been natural to see the main narrative of Scottish kings that has been constructed from the king-list in α as the synthesist's work, rather than originating in the Scottish Monmouth. Now, however, that the Éber account – the main strand in the synthesist's compendium of origin-legend material – can be recognised as part of the Scottish Monmouth, the question naturally arises about how much more of the synthesist's narrative is also from the Scottish Monmouth, thinking especially of the account of Scottish kings from the advent of Fergus son of Erc in 403. Is it possible to resolve this?

The answer leads us straight to Veremundus. There is at least a fingerprint's worth of evidence in Baldred Bisset's pleading that has been identified as indicating that the forty kings between Fergus son of Ferchar and Fergus son of Erc, described graphically by Boece but passed over by Fordun, were known in outline at least to the Scottish procurators at the curia in 1301.[61] The crux is Bisset's claim that there were thirty-six Christian kings in Scotland before the conversion of the English.[62] This can be explained, with uncanny precision, partly by assuming that Boece's Donald I king of Scots was intended, who reigned when Pope Victor was reputed to have sent a mission to convert the Scots.[63] But how could Bisset in 1301 have known of Boece's *History of the Scots* (1527)? The answer must be that they shared a source; and the source cited by Boece for Donald and the other forty kings between Fergus son of Ferchar and Fergus son of Erc is Veremundus.[64] Bisset would need also to have known of Pope Victor's equally legendary mission. The earliest mention of this is in Fordun's chronicle, where it has been identified by the MacQueens as another example of Geoffrey of Monmouth's history being adapted to Scottish taste: the mission in 203 has plainly been inspired by the mission to the Britons attributed by Geoffrey to Pope Victor's predecessor, Pope Eleutherius.[65] This would suggest that the Scottish Monmouth and Veremundus are one and the same.

Bisset could only have found twenty-three of his thirty-six Christian kings this way before the conversion of the English, however: the other thirteen would have been Pictish kings.[66] The uncanny explanation of Bisset's figure involves not only knowledge of Pope Victor and King Donald, but of a suitable account of the conversion of the Picts. This, it has been pointed out, takes us again into legend, this time the foundation-legend of St Andrews, where Regulus is said to have brought the apostle's relics in the mid-fourth century.[67] Here the Pictish king was identified as King 'Hungus', but no king with this name appears in the appropriate place in the Pictish king-list. Instead there is the remarkable Drest who reigned (according to the king-lists) for a hundred years. It has been pointed out that in a draft document (known misleadingly as the 'Instructions'), written by the Scottish procurators as preparation for Bisset's pleading,[68] mention is made at one point of 'Durst or Hurgust' as king of the Picts when St Andrew's relics arrived in Scotland.[69] Bisset and his team therefore had a source to hand in which a crude attempt had been made to match the legend of Regulus and the Pictish king-list by giving both kings together. The foundation-legend of St Andrews features prominently in Fordun's chronicle in its account of the fourth century, and one detail in particular immediately catches the eye: the legend's Pictish king 'Hungus' has become 'Hurgust', exactly as in the draft document of Bisset and his team.[70] It may be concluded, then, that they were looking at a source shared by Fordun's chronicle.[71] In Fordun's chronicle itself, though, the alternative 'Durst' is not mentioned here, presumably because a solution to the chronological conundrum has been found so that the awkwardness of saying it was either Hurgust or Durst could be avoided. Given Fordun's track record on such matters, it is more likely that this was achieved by the synthesist rather than by Fordun himself. It would follow from this that Bisset and his team had to hand a source used by the synthesist.

If it is accepted that Bisset used the Scottish Monmouth in calculating his figure of thirty-six Christian kings before the conversion of the English, then the Scottish Monmouth would be the obvious choice for his knowledge of 'Hurgust or Durst', too. If a circular argument is to be avoided, however, then everything would rest on the coincidence of 'Hurgust' as the spelling of 'Hungus' found in Fordun's chronicle and in the material prepared by Bisset's team. Help is at hand if we return to the passage where 'Durst or Hurgust' is mentioned by the procurators led by Bisset. As well as saying that one of these reigned over the Picts when St Andrew's relics arrived, we are also told that the king of Scots at this time was 'Erth' son of 'Echadius brother of Eugenius'.[72] It has been pointed out elsewhere that this shows knowledge of a key episode in Fordun's chronicle which has been created as a solution to a problem: how to present Fergus son of Erc as 'first king of Scots' (because of his pole position in king-lists) despite his being a distant successor of Fergus son of Ferchar, first king of Scots in the origin-legend? This was achieved by making out that the Scots were expelled from Scotland for a while before Fergus son of Erc led them back and became the first in the current succession of kings. The telling detail here is that the exile coincided with the arrival of St Andrew's relics. This means that all the Scottish royalty named by Bisset's team at this juncture – 'Erth' (i.e., Erc), his father 'Echadius' and King Eugenius his fictional uncle – could only have come from a prior version of Fordun's chronicle (where they all duly appear in this position).

Can we be more specific about this prior version of Fordun's chronicle? A couple more steps in the argument take us to the Scottish Monmouth. The crucial first step is Steve Boardman's observation that Sulgentius in Geoffrey's history, a British leader who opposed the Roman emperor Severus, has been developed in the Scottish Monmouth into a more significant figure called Fulgentius who allies with the Scots and Picts, and who is endowed with descendants who appear later in the narrative as asserting their right to England north of the Humber, which is described as Fulgentius's patrimony.[73] The most significant of these is Grim, whose daughter marries Fergus son of Erc. As Steve Boardman points out, this has the effect of making kings of Scots the heirs of Fulgentius. Grim's significance for Scottish history is underscored by the author of the Scottish Monmouth by placing him at the centre of the action in book III, chapters 4 and 5, where he appears as regent for his grandson Eugenius (who succeeds Fergus in 419 while still a minor) and as guardian of the kingdom.[74] In this capacity he leads an invasion in pursuit of his heritage north of the Humber, breaking down Antonine's Wall in the process.[75] It is explained that the wall is known to this day as 'Grimisdik' (i.e., Grim's wall). In reality the opposite is true, of course: the author of the Scottish Monmouth has created Grim's name from 'Grimisdik', which shows that his existence as a fictional character is inseparable from the account of his destruction of Antonine's Wall, which in turn is dependent on his role as governor of the kingdom.

The fact that the author of the Scottish Monmouth, as Grim's creator, based this section of his narrative on Grim's role as Eugenius's regent is crucial for what follows. There is no Eugenius (in any guise) in this part of any king-list. He is one of three additional kings in Fordun's narrative who have been created to solve a chronological problem. The date of 403 for Fergus's return had been arrived at from a king-list by taking the stated year-totals of Fergus to Alpin (father of Cinaed), and of Cinaed to the accession of Alexander II in 1214, and subtracting them from 1214. In the case of the king-list in α it is likely that this would have yielded the calculation $1214 - 811 = 403$.[76] But the actual reigns in the king-list could not fill this space. In order to maintain a narrative line, therefore, it was necessary to make some serious adjustments. This was achieved with some flair by creating three kings, one of whom was Grim's young charge. There can be little doubt, then, that not only Grim, but Eugenius too, was created by the author of the Scottish Monmouth.

Once this is all put together, a strong case emerges for identifying the Scottish Monmouth with Veremundus. Grim is an integral part of the narrative in book III of Fordun's chronicle which was created to bridge the gap caused by placing Fergus as early as 403. This treatment of Fergus should therefore be regarded as an innovation of the Scottish Monmouth, not the synthesis. It follows that the entire story of Fergus's return after the exile of his father and grandfather and the killing of his granduncle, another King Eugenius, by Picts and Britons, was also created by the author of the Scottish Monmouth. Turning now to Bisset and his team, the reference made by them to Fergus's father, 'Erth', and his grandfather and granduncle, is further evidence that they had access to the Scottish Monmouth. This makes it more straightforward to accept that the Scottish Monmouth was also their source for the Pictish kings, 'Durst or Hurgust' (remembering that this cannot plausibly have come from the synthesis lying behind Fordun's chronicle, and so must have featured in a source used by the synthesist). It will be recalled that 'Durst or Hurgust' coincided with the conversion to Christianity attributed by Bisset's team to the arrival of St Andrew's relics, and that this was one of the two vital ingredients which can provide a strikingly precise explanation of Bisset's figure of thirty-six Christian kings before the conversion of the English. The other ingredient was the mission of Pope Victor to the Scots in the reign of King Donald, which requires that Bisset saw Donald in the series of forty kings whose names today are known only from Boece. The Scottish Monmouth can therefore be identified as the source of both ingredients; and, if that is so, it follows that it contained (in some form) the forty legendary kings attributed by Boece to Veremundus. In the light of Nicola Royan's work on this aspect of Boece, it is now easier to accept that there was such a thing as the history of the Scots from their origins whose author was known as Veremundus. That being so, the identification of this work by Veremundus with the Scottish Monmouth becomes practically irresistible.

This has a dramatic effect on our understanding of the relationship between the Scottish Monmouth and the synthesist. If the author of the Scottish Monmouth wrote the account of the expulsion of the Scots and their return led by Fergus son of Erc, and fleshed out the chronological gaps this created by inventing kings and providing colourful episodes, then he is very likely to have been ultimately responsible for the rest of the narrative of Scottish kings in Fordun's chronicle. The same capacity for creating kings to sustain the overall story-line is also in evidence, for example, in the treatment of 'Cumbria' as the possession of each king's designated successor in the tenth century, a device which not only serves to explain how the Scottish realm came to include the kingdom of Strathclyde, but also provides momentum for the royal narrative.[77] The identification of the Éber account as part of the Scottish Monmouth would mean that this significant element in Fordun's chronicle can also be regarded as an example of his ability to produce something coherent and vivid from contradictory and meagre resources. All in all, a skilful weaver of narrative emerges who, as well as displaying some flair for the dramatic and rhetorical, also shows sensitivity in his handling of his sources, using them as a springboard for his fiction rather than ignoring or subverting them. It is hard to resist forming the impression, therefore, that Fordun's chronicle is not only substantially a reiteration of the synthesis datable to 1285, but that the synthesist, in turn, did little more than repeat this earlier work stretching from Scottish origins to kings of Scots in the tenth century and beyond, carefully integrating it with other material by creating a more secure chronological framework based on the Latinate version of the royal genealogy.

Before finally taking the plunge and suggesting that we should refer for evermore to this earliest continuous narrative of Scottish history as the work of Veremundus/Vairement, it is important to check it against Boece's description of it. Boece refers to it twice. On one occasion he talks of 'an ancient history of our past, written by Veremundus, formerly archdeacon of St Andrews, from the origin of the Scottish people to King Mael Coluim "Canmor", embracing everything abundantly, although from a rather unpolished age'.[78] Mael Coluim 'Canmor' was, of course, Mael Coluim III (1058–93).[79] On another occasion he adds that Veremundus was Spanish, and that he had dedicated his work to Mael Coluim III.[80] On the face of it there seems no good reason to question the identification of Veremundus with Richard Vairement, *céle Dé* of St Andrews and chancellor of Queen Marie de Couci, who is visible in Scottish sources from 1239 to 1267, and who almost certainly arrived in Scotland in her household.[81] This would mean that Boece's description of Vairement is roughly on target, but certainly not on the bull's eye: a member of the ecclesiastical establishment at St Andrews, yes, but not the archdeacon; a native of the Continent, yes, but not a Spaniard. It would also follow, of course, that Vairement could not have dedicated his history to a King Mael Coluim: this much would have to be pure fiction. Nicola Royan did not, however, dismiss it altogether. In order to tidy this up conclusively, some explanation is required of the statement that the work finished with Mael Coluim III.

Help is at hand if we return to *GAI*. It will be recalled that this was identified as the only extant part of 'proto-Fordun' (i.e., the synthesist's work).[82] There was a serious objection, however: *GAI* as it stands does not appear to begin in mid-flow. It is chiefly an account of St Margaret's ancestors and successors, and gives every impression that it was originally conceived as beginning where it does. This could readily be explained, however, if the synthesist's role was chiefly confined to adding chunks of material to Veremundus. Most of *GAI* could, then, have originated as a discrete work on St Margaret's ancestors and successors which was simply tacked on by the synthesist to his principal source. What makes this scenario particularly attractive, then, is that all the pieces of the jigsaw fit together: the statement that Veremundus finished with Mael Coluim III, the impression that most of *GAI* once had a separate existence and the indications that *GAI* is, nonetheless, the remains of proto-Fordun. This would suggest that Veremundus may have ceased at the point where Fordun's chronicle becomes a rewriting of *GAI*: that is, with the accession of Mael Coluim III. If it was still obvious in proto-Fordun that the main text ended there and that a new text (now *GAI*) began, then this would help to explain why the material in *GAI* relating to the period between Margaret and David I was originally copied alongside Fordun's chronicle, despite so much overlap: it was copied because it was recognised as an integral part of a work beginning where it does today with the first chapter of *GAI*.

SCOTTISH HISTORY FROM VAIREMENT TO FORDUN

It will be useful to consolidate what has emerged about the development of a continuous regnal history prior to Fordun's chronicle by summarising each stage from Vairement to Fordun. This will also be a good opportunity to tie up a few loose ends.

(i) Richard Vairement's history of the Scots from their origins to Mael Coluim III

This can now be recognised as Scotland's first continuous narrative. The hypothetical texts which have previously been identified as the Éber account and the Scottish Monmouth were simply parts of this work, and had no separate existence. Vairement's history ran from Scottish origins to the accession of Mael Coluim III, and was based chiefly on Geoffrey of Monmouth and α (a small collection of three texts: an account of the travels of Gaedel, Scota and Éber from Greece and Egypt to Ireland; the legend of the Stone of Scone featuring Simón Brecc and Fergus son of Ferchar; and a bare king-list, save for details of each king's death and burial from Cinaed mac Ailpín, in which it was made clear that the early Scottish kings were parallel with Pictish kings). Presumably he would have been aware of something like the Dunfermline dynastic history of Margaret's ancestors (from Æthelred) and successors, which would have included treatments of the reigns of Scottish kings from Mael Coluim III. His intention, then, may have been to create a full account of Scottish history that could be read alongside the dynastic history of Margaret and Mael Coluim's descendants (which was probably the only narrative of Scottish kings in existence that was more than a king-list with death-details). If so, this would reinforce the significance of his work as supplying an alternative focus for the kingship's past from Margaret's English royal ancestors by creating an exclusive history of the Scots and their kings from ancient times. The descent of recent kings of Scots from English forbears was not negated or downplayed, of course. The significance of a continuous narrative of a distinct Scottish past, however, was that in Vairement's hands it provided a way of articulating the idea of Scottish freedom in terms of a sovereign people and kingdom.

Vairement produced his narrative by repackaging material from Geoffrey of Monmouth to create a vision of immemorial Scottish freedom, a theme he extended into his retelling of Scottish origins. He appears to have promoted the idea that the Scots and Picts were allies from the beginning, seeing the ancient realm in terms of the landmass north of the Forth which was, at first, shared between them, followed by a period of separation and hostility before, finally, Cinaed mac Ailpín destroyed the Picts. For Scottish kings between Fergus son of Ferchar and Fergus son of Erc he seems (if Boece's names are accepted) to have drawn on the royal genealogy.[83] There is room to doubt, though, whether Vairement did anything more than create a list: certainly the negative portrayal of kings which is such a prominent feature of Boece's narrative runs counter to the generally positive image of kingship in everything else in Fordun's chronicle which may be attributed to Vairement.[84] From Fergus son of Erc his narrative is largely fictional, spun from the meagre resources of the king-lists in α. It is very likely that he was responsible for the idea that 'Cumbria' was held by the designated successor to the throne in the tenth century, and so came to be incorporated into the realm. He seems also to have incorporated a version of the longer St Andrews foundation-legend in his account of the conversion of the Picts to Christianity; he had already described the conversion of the Scots by a mission sent by Pope Victor in 203.

As far as the dating of Vairement's work is concerned, a number of pieces of internal evidence have been commented on in Fordun's chronicle as suggesting a context a century or more before Fordun himself. Steve Boardman has pointed out that the material on Fulgentius and Grim has evidently been told with claims of the king of Scots to northern England in mind.[85] Alasdair Ross has argued that Geoffrey of Monmouth's treatment of the Moravians as a separate people with distinct origins has been enlarged to emphasise the lawlessness of Moray. He has also pointed to the renaming of Geoffrey's Sodric as Rodoric, and suggested that this might be a reference to Ruaidrí, who appears along with Meic Uilleim in the last known rising in 1230.[86] Finally, it has been suggested that the arrangements described in relation to Cumbria in the tenth century are reminiscent of what was agreed in the Treaty of Paris in 1259, except that in the Treaty Henry III did homage to the king of France for Gascony (which was held by Edward as heir), whereas in Fordun's chronicle homage was performed by the designated heir himself to the king of England for Cumbria.[87] This adaptation would be natural, though, given Vairement's concern for Scottish freedom. It is possible, then, that Vairement's history was written in the 1260s towards the end of his life, and that the specific allusions to Moray and the north of England were not because these were current issues (it will be recalled that claims to northern England had been surrendered in 1237), but because they would still have been remembered, and as such would have added verisimilitude to his narrative (if, indeed, his intention was not to provide some kind of background to help explain why these issues had been so contentious in living memory). One fiction that must have been particularly close to his heart is the account of the alliance between Charlemagne and 'Achaius' king of Scots, inaugurating a friendship between the Scots and France which Vairement himself embodied.[88]

(ii) Proto-Fordun: the work of the synthesist

The synthesist seems to have set himself the task of consolidating Vairement's narrative by making it a more complete record of the Scottish past. He approached this in two ways. First, he attached passages from alternative accounts (particularly relating to the remote past, such as the 'Partholón' account of Scottish origins) without substantially rewriting them, and seems to have done this in such a way that they were (as far as possible) integrated within the existing narrative, rather than opposed to it. This was achieved by skilful use of the Latinate version of the royal genealogy as a chronological backbone. The genealogy was also used to create the episode of Eochaid 'Rothai', a space-filling figure in the pedigree whose epithet was latched onto as an eponym for Rothesay, allowing the synthesist to create a Scottish settlement on the Hebrides 500 years before Fergus son of Ferchar, the first king on the mainland. His use of this in *GAI* as an assertion of Scottish sovereignty over the Hebrides is notable,[89] as is his interest in Bute, whose name he etymologises as Gaelic *both*, referring in the process to Gaelic as 'our language'.[90]

He seems also to have been keen to preserve the idea, probably in Vairement's narrative, that Picts and Scots arrived in Scotland at about the same time, and to negate the challenge of a king-list like **o** in which Scots would have preceded Picts. It is not clear whether he or Fordun would have been responsible for passages from well-known works such as those by Bede, Geoffrey of Monmouth or William of Malmesbury (some of which could, of course, have been included by Vairement himself). This also appears to have involved him in tidying up chronological problems in Vairement's narrative. For example, the uncertainty about whether 'Hurgust' or 'Durst' was king when St Andrew's relics arrived in Scotland was evidently cured, maybe in part by resort to another version of the Pictish king-list. The second way he sought to make Vairement's narrative more complete was to extend it to the present day. *GAI* as it stands is a history of St Margaret's ancestors and descendants up to 2 February 1285. It is difficult to know how far his exemplar of *GAI* extended, and how much he has added from different sources or (towards the end) written himself. Professor Duncan has noted textual correspondences with material in the Chronicle of Melrose as far as the death of Alexander II.[91] It will be recalled that an account of the inauguration of Alexander III was also used (possibly from the same source).[92] Uncertainty about this is especially unfortunate, because if it could be shown that he wrote (rather than copied) the item which points to April 1285 as the latest date for the work, then that would give it more weight. As it is, there are other indications that the work dates from before the end of 1290 and before 1296.[93]

(iii) Additions (the dossier of documents and GAII)

The first item to be added was the dossier of documents beginning with the Declaration of Arbroath (1320) and consisting otherwise of material relating to the defence of Scottish independence by Baldred Bisset and his team of procurators at the curia in 1301. This was followed by a variety of texts which are likely to have been added piecemeal: the last of these was Aelred's eulogy of David I. Finally *GAII* was tacked on at the end, derived from a putative St Andrews source which ceased at 1363. A number of interpolations into *GAI* have been noted (some making reference to the period of the wars of independence): one appears to refer to information in *GAII*, in which case if the interpolations were made on one occasion (and the fact that a number of them share the feature of a closing stanza would support this), then it would have occurred after 1363.

(iv) John of Fordun's chronicle (1384×7)

Fordun's main contribution appears to have been to bring *GAI* and Vairement's text together into a coherent unit as far as the death of David I, including a copy of Aelred's eulogy of David (presumably taken from the additional texts between the dossier and *GA*II). He also added a copy of the Latinate version of the royal genealogy, headed by David I, which he acquired from Walter Wardlaw, bishop of Glasgow. The critical passage for dating his activity is his reference to Wardlaw as 'cardinal of Scotland'. He became cardinal on 23 December 1383 and died probably on 21 or 23 August 1387.[94] It is difficult to know if Fordun contributed much else to the chronicle that has gone by his name. It will be recalled that he was decidedly uncertain about its chronology. Given the level of inaccuracy in Boece's information on Vairement, it would be unwise to assume that points of detail cited by him (or Chalmers, who inspires even less confidence) as from Veremundus that are not present in Fordun should be regarded as evidence that Fordun made changes to the text.[95]

Serious consideration must now be given to the possibility that the main narrative as far as Mael Coluim III's accession is almost entirely Vairement's work. Given that some of the passages on the theme of Scottish freedom can be attributed to Vairement, there is no reason why they cannot all be. The forty (or forty-five)[96] kings between the two Ferguses could have been omitted by Fordun, but they might equally have been removed by the synthesist. This would have been easy if they were simply listed by Vairement.

VAIREMENT AS CREATOR OF A NATIONAL HISTORY

The revelation that Richard Vairement was the creator of Scotland's first 'national' history, providing the Scots with an account of their origins and a narrative of their freedom under their kings from ancient times, makes it possible to set much of what has hitherto been regarded as Fordun's work in a new context. Its author was very well connected. He was a member of Queen Marie's household while she was in Scotland (1239–50), and he was a member of the ecclesiastical establishment of the kingdom's most important bishopric. He therefore operated within the circles of those who devised and performed the statement of the kingship's sovereignty at Alexander III's inauguration. In his work, the idea of Scottish independence was given its fullest and most evocative expression until the wars of independence.

There were limits, however. The Declaration of Arbroath's pithy summary of Scottish history sketched the essentials of an unambiguous portrayal of the Scots as a sovereign kingdom in which there was room for identifying only with Scots, not Picts, and with Scotland as the homeland, not Ireland. This was easy to achieve in the genre of a letter to the pope, of course; it could only be sustained in a full-scale history, however, by resorting almost entirely to fiction. Vairement and (especially) the synthesist made effective use of their meagre resources, rather than ignoring them. Their creative response to this material, however, suggests that they were not slaves to their sources, either. It will be recalled that proto-Fordun served to perpetuate the significance of the long-established image of Scotland north of the Forth, the umbilical tie with Ireland and the dynastic link with English kingship. We must assume that he did so because he approved of these elements – although, in the case of the synthesist, this cannot be distinguished from the deep respect for existing writings which is the hallmark of his work. Vairement was evidently a freer spirit who was prepared to create narrative and rewrite his sources as necessary. It is all the more significant, therefore, that he also was prepared to deploy his talents to give new life both to the idea of Ireland as the homeland of the Scots, and to a vision of the ancient kingdom as shared by Picts and Scots and confined to north of the Forth.[97] It may also be inferred from his decision to stop with Mael Coluim III that he approved of the existing dynastic history of Margaret's descendants with its emphasis on English royal ancestry. All this suggests that the legacy of identifying the kingship with the islands of Britain and Ireland, and with the landmass north of the Forth, remained powerful. Vairement's achievement was to add to these ideas a vision of the Scots as an ancient and free people, and to sustain this in his narrative within the established geographical frame of reference. This was, nonetheless, a radical departure. The incontestable reality of geography was no longer the chief resource for legitimising ultimate secular power. The focus had now begun to move decisively to the people, and to a definition of the kingdom. This is the fundamental development identified by Susan Reynolds when she observed that 'kingdoms and peoples came to seem identical'. It was only in this context that an idea of the Scots as a sovereign entity took shape in a way that we can begin to recognise today. The core idea, however, was also fundamentally different from that of a modern nation. It was of the Scots as a people obedient to the inherited authority of their king, free from the control of another king. The doctrine was that sovereign kingdoms constituted peoples, not that ethnic communities should be politically independent; nations were communities of submission, not people bound together equally by a common culture; they were justified by extended king-lists and long narratives about the deeds of kings, not fat dictionaries or vernacular epics. Vairement's idea of kingdom and people can, nonetheless, be seen as an important stage in its own right, one that could lead directly to the sentiments expressed in the Declaration of Arbroath.[98]

NOTES

1. Broun, *Irish Identity*, chs 2–6: see esp. 72–8, 91–5, 109, 115–17, 128–32.
2. The evidence is discussed in Nicola Royan, 'Hector Boece and the question of Veremund', *IR* 52 (2001), 42–62.
3. Before Royan the least negative comment by a modern scholar was that 'there does not seem to be any evidence to decide the point': Barrow, *Kingdom of the Scots*, 2nd edn, 195 n. 46 (in an article first published in 1952).
4. Royan, 'Hector Boece and the question of Veremund'; N. R. Royan, 'The *Scotorum Historia* of Hector Boece: a Study', unpublished D.Phil. dissertation (Oxford University, 1996), 197–215.
5. *Chron. Fordun*, i. xxxviii n. 1. Skene knew only of Vairement's activities in 1267. For a full discussion of the evidence for Vairement's career, see Barrow, *Kingdom of the Scots*, 2nd edn, 192–3 and D. E. R. Watt, *A Biographical Dictionary of Scottish Graduates to AD. 1410* (Oxford, 1977), 559–60.
6. Broun, *Irish Identity*, 109 (summarising ch. 5).
7. For what follows, see Broun, *Irish Identity*, 69 and 115–17.
8. See above, 166–70.
9. *Chron. Fordun*, i. 30, ii. 28–9, where he gives a figure of 'two hundred years at least': this king-list would have given 265 years (Broun, *Irish Identity*, 125–6).
10. There is no trace in Fordun of a copy of the royal genealogy akin to Wyntoun's which was derived from a text different from the Latinate version used by the synthesist. On Wyntoun's text, see Broun, *Irish Identity*, 181–2.
11. Broun, *Irish Identity*, 76–8.
12. John and Winifred MacQueen (eds), *Scotichronicon by Walter Bower in Latin and English*, gen. ed. D. E. R. Watt, vol. i (Edinburgh, 1993), xxviii–xxix.
13. *Ibid.*, i. xxvi.
14. Anderson, *Kings and Kingship*, 186–9; Broun, *Irish Identity*, 87, 90; and 91–5, 104–9, 112–15, 128 for discussion.
15. Broun with Scott (eds), '*Liber Extravagans*'; Broun, *Irish Identity*, 121–32.
16. As far as the king-list included in α is concerned, versions of texts ancestral to α were still being updated (probably) in Scotland *ca* 1290 (king-list I: Anderson, *Kings and Kingship*, 2nd edn, 279–85) and 1296×1306 (the principal king-list source of the Scottish poem in *Liber Extravagans*).
17. List N could be derived from ς: see Broun, *Irish Identity*, 126 n. 74.
18. See above, 169–70.
19. See below, 252–4.
20. See below, 247–8.
21. These are given in the middle of book III chapter 2 of Fordun's chronicle: *Chron. Fordun*, i. 88, ii.79.

22. See below, 000.

23. Broun, *Irish Identity*, 116–17.

24. Cruithne (the first king) *clemens iudex accepit monarchiam*: Anderson, *Kings and Kingship*, 265, 271; see also 279. See also *Chron. Fordun*, i. 152; John and Winifred MacQueen (eds), *Scotichronicon by Walter Bower in Latin and English*, gen. ed. D. E. R. Watt, vol. ii (Aberdeen, 1989), 298.

25. *Chron. Fordun*, i. 25–7, 29, ii. 25–8; Broun, *Irish Identity*, 56–60.

26. *Chron. Fordun*, i. 66–7, ii. 59: *Scotorum conregnantibus pacifice gentibus et Pictorum iunctisque uiribus suas ubique regiones protegentibus*.

27. *Chron. Fordun*, i. 145–48, 151, ii. 136–9.

28. See above, 262; Brown, 'Birth of Scottish History', 21 n. 71.

29. Broun, *Irish Identity*, 78–81, 117–19.

30. *Ibid.*, 187–93.

31. See above, 237.

32. *Chron. Fordun*, i. 40–1, ii. 36–7.

33. This could be linked to Fulgentius, referred to as 'leader of the Britons of *Albania*' in the Scottish Monmouth, and whose patrimony extended to the Humber. Fulgentius's significance has been brought to light recently by Steve Boardman: see below, 254–5.

34. *Chron. Fordun*, i. 41–2, ii. 37–8.

35. This is put most graphically in Barrow, *Kingdom of the Scots*, 2nd edn, 332.

36. This issue is discussed in the introduction to Dauvit Broun and Martin MacGregor (eds), *Mìorun Mór nan Gall: the Great Ill-will of the Lowlander? Lowland Perceptions of the Highlands* (forthcoming).

37. *Chron. Fordun*, i. 262, ii. 257–8; see above, 177–8. A comparison with the source for the passage relating to 1173 shows that *montani* and *bruti* have been added, possibly by the synthesist, but possibly by his main source, which probably reached as far as Alexander III's inauguration where *montanus* appears again (see below, 261). For the comparison, see Duncan, 'Sources and uses of the Chronicle of Melrose', 177.

38. . . . *conjuratione facta, se a regno Scocie eodem anno diuidentes . . . Ochtredus itaque filius Fergusii quia uerus extiterat Scotu, nec flecti potuit*: *Chron. Fordun* i. 266, ii. 261; also Corner, Scott, Scott and Watt (eds), *Scotichronicon*, iv. 322–3, from where the translation has been taken.

39. Note also **ꞅ**, except that the decision there to make Stainmore the southern limit may have been inspired more by a textual problem as much as anything else. See 168–9, above.

40. Broun, *Irish Identity*, 156–66.

41. In the eleventh century they could be presented as successors to either, but not in the same regnal-list: see above, 55–8.

42. Dauvit Broun, 'The Picts' place in the kingship's past before John of Fordun', in Edward J. Cowan and Richard J. Finlay (eds), *Scottish History: the Power of the Past* (Edinburgh, 2002), 11–28.

43. Broun, *Irish Identity*, 80.

44. *Ibid.*, 49 (XX.2.d).

45. *Ibid.*, 115–18.

46. *Ibid.*, 116, referring to 57–8 (XXXI).

47. *Ibid.*, 117. The alternative possibility of presenting the Picts as Scotland's original inhabitants would not, of course, have been acceptable within this framework. In Fordun's chronicle it is stated (presumably in a passage derived from 'proto-Fordun') that the joint arrival of Scots and Picts was found in 'various ancient histories' (*Chron. Fordun*, i. 28, ii. 30). No such 'history' survives; but then neither does the Éber account, except through the synthesist's work.

48. MacQueen and MacQueen (eds), *Scotichronicon*, i. xxviii–xxix.

49. *Chron. Fordun*, i. 46–9, ii. 43–6; MacQueen and MacQueen (eds), *Scotichronicon*, i. 198–205.

50. *Ibid.*, i. 354, 355.

51. Wright (ed.), *Historia Regum Britannie*, i. §55; Lewis Thorpe (trans.), *Geoffrey of Monmouth. The History of the Kings of Britain* (Harmondsworth, 1966), 107–8. Book and chapter numbers correspond to those used by Thorpe.

52. Bk III, ch. 12; Wright (ed.), *Historia Regum Britannie*, i. §46.

53. Wright (ed.), *Historia Regum Britannie*, i. §8.

54. Such as the tower of Brigantia (i.e., Bregon's tower: see, e.g., Carey in Koch (ed.), *Celtic Heroic Age*, 257.

55. Wright (ed.), *Historia Regum Britannie*, i. §16.

56. *Ibid.*, i. §20.

57. Broun, *Irish Identity*, 116.

58. *Pace* Bruce Webster, 'John of Fordun and the independent identity of the Scots', in Alfred P. Smyth (ed.), *Medieval Europeans: Studies in Ethnic Identity and National Perspectives in Medieval Europe* (Basingstoke, 1998), 85–102, at 93–4, cites the passage just discussed and the one below on this basis.

59. . . . *nobilis et liberi degere poteritis, cum sit hominum summa nobilitas et cordis cuiusque generosi desideratissima rerum iocunditas immo gemma cunctis mundi merito preferenda iocalibus nullius alienegene dominantis imperium pati sed successiue solummodo proprie nacionis uti spontaliter potestate*: Broun, *Irish Identity*, 45 (XVI.i–l).

60. E.g., Bruce Webster, *Medieval Scotland: the Making of an Identity* (Basingstoke, 1997), 100.

61. The first part of what follows was first discussed in Broun, 'Birth of Scottish History', 15–22.

62. Shead, Stevenson and Watt (eds), *Scotichronicon*, vi. 170–1.

63. Broun, 'Birth of Scottish History', 22.

64. Royan, 'Hector Boece and the question of Veremund', 49–50.

65. MacQueen and MacQueen (eds), *Scotichronicon*, i. xxviii, 381; Wright (ed.), *Historia Regum Britannie*, i. §72 (=Bk. IV, ch. 19).

66. On the basis that (i) Bisset and his team referred to Columba as first of a series of Scottish missionaries to England (Shead, Stevenson and Watt (eds), *Scotichronicon*, vi. 149, Skene (ed.), *Chronicles*, 249–50), and that (ii) it would have been relatively straightforward to find out that the Pictish king, Bridei, was particularly associated with Columba (in king-lists and Bede's *Ecclesiastical History*), and that in Adomnán's *Life of Columba* Aedán mac Gabráin (who appears as a king of Scots in the king-lists) was ordained king by Columba. Starting with these kings would also have made sense, no doubt, if the conversion of the English were reckoned from St Augustine's mission (which began the same year as Columba died).

67. Broun, 'Birth of Scottish History', 16–17, 22.

68. The identity of this and other drafts is explained by Donald Watt in Shead, Stevenson and Watt (eds), *Scotichronicon*, vi. 260–3. See also Broun, 'Birth of Scottish History', 16.

69. Skene (ed.), *Chronicles*, 248.

70. *Chron. Fordun*, i. 77, ii. 72.

71. This is as far as the argument got in Broun, 'Birth of Scottish History', 15–22, beyond noting also that the mention of 'Erth', 'Echadius' and his brother 'Eugenius' (see below) shows that Bisset and his team had a source used by Fordun, which was assumed to be the synthesist's work (as also in Broun, *Irish Identity*, 72–3).

72. Skene (ed.), *Chronicles*, 248.

73. Steve Boardman, 'Late medieval Scotland and the Matter of Britain', in Edward J. Cowan and Richard J. Finlay (eds), *Scottish History: the Power of the Past* (Edinburgh, 2002), 47–72, at 56–8.

74. *Chron. Fordun*, i. 90–1, ii. 81–2.

75. The appearance of Eochaid (rather than Grim) in the MacQueens' translation at book III chapter 5 line 5 is clearly a slip. (Their rendering of *Eugenius* as Eochaid is unfortunate in the light of the discussion of this name at the end of the previous chapter: see below, 230.) MacQueen and MacQueen (eds), *Scotichronicon*, ii. 13.

76. Broun, *Irish Identity*, 72.

77. See further Broun, 'Welsh identity', 30–4.

78. Royan, 'Hector Boece and the question of Veremund', 47.

79. It has been shown that the epithet was originally applied to Mael Coluim IV, but was misapplied to Mael Coluim III, probably by the late thirteenth century: Duncan, *Kingship of the Scots*, 51–2, 74–5.

80. Royan, 'Hector Boece and the question of Veremund', 45.

81. See references above, n. 5, and Barrow, *Robert Bruce*, 4th edn, 18.

82. See above, 227–8.

83. Royan, 'Hector Boece and the question of Veremund', 49–50.

84. Boece's negative portrayal includes kings portrayed positively in Fordun: see *ibid.*, 52.

85. Boardman, 'Late medieval Scotland and the Matter of Britain', 58.

86. Alasdair Ross, 'The Province of Moray c.1000–1350', 2 vols, unpublished Ph.D. dissertation (University of Aberdeen, 2003), i. 234–40.

87. Broun, 'Welsh identity', 131 n. 84.

88. David Chambers refers to Vairement as containing an account of this episode: Royan, 'Hector Boece and the question of Veremund', 59.

89. The issue was settled formally in the Treaty of Perth (1266), of course, but that would not mean that Scottish sovereignty no longer need to be justified historically.

90. See further Broun, *Irish Identity*, 129–30, where attention is drawn to a possible contrast between the author of the Éber account (who we can now recognise as Vairement), who seems to betray himself as not a Gaelic speaker, and to approve of Gaelic's decline, and the synthesist, who identified with Gaelic (although he would not have been literate to the extent of knowing elementary Irish pseudo-history).

91. Duncan, 'Sources and uses of the Chronicle of Melrose', 172–3.

92. See n. 37 above for *montanus* used in relation to events in 1173 as well as 1249, which might suggest they came from the same source if this usage is regarded as rare in this period.

93. See above, 219.

94. Watt and Murray (eds), *Fasti*, 191.

95. The evidence is discussed in Royan, 'Hector Boece and the question of Veremund', 49–53 (and 59 for Chalmers), and key parts quoted in *Chron. Fordun*, i. xxxviii n. 1.

96. The evidence is discussed in Broun, 'Birth of Scottish History', 21 n. 71.

97. All this follows from the identification of the Éber account and the Scottish Monmouth as one work, so that Vairement's authorship of the latter applies also to the former.

98. See further, Broun, 'The Declaration of Arbroath'.

Conclusion

10

Conclusion:
From British Identity to Scottish Nation

Susan Reynolds has discussed the convergence of kingdoms and peoples in the mental landscape of Europeans in the period 900–1300 with regard to law and custom, government and consent, and ideas of common descent and language.[1] At the core of ideas of kingdoms and peoples in Britain and Ireland, however, was the incontestable fact that each was an island. It was this reality which shaped the way the highest secular authority relating to each people was defined, and which gave the very idea of being English, Irish and Welsh its enduring power over other identities. When, in the eleventh and twelfth centuries, it came to conjuring up visions of long successions of kings and accounts of their deeds stretching back into the primordial past, it was natural that these should be conceived in terms of kingships of Britain or Ireland, even though each narrative was written specifically with the English, Irish or Welsh in mind. Once these histories took root in the historical consciousness – made easier by their telling in the vernacular – they became a key part of the infrastructure of English, Irish and Welsh identity for centuries to come, and helped to sustain the intimate bond between people and island, even though, in the case of Britain, two peoples claimed it as their own. It was inevitable, moreover, that the English, as the dominant force, would find it especially difficult, not to say impossible, to make a clear distinction between their country, England, and the island, Britain.

FROM PICTISH IDENTITY TO SCOTTISH NATION

How did the Scots fit into this pattern? There is no suggestion that they made a claim to Britain as their own in the same way as did the English or Welsh. Nonetheless, the underlying significance of Britain is forever enshrined in the Gaelic name for their country, *Alba*, originally denoting the island. This, it is suggested, can best be explained ultimately as the Pictish name for themselves. The implication is that the Picts (like the

Welsh) found in the island of Britain a way of identifying themselves as a people which transcended local and regional affiliations. That such a wider sense of being a people was a meaningful concept is amply attested by the distinctive style and repertoire of symbols carved on upright stones from Fife in the south-east (with one example in Midlothian) to Shetland in the north and North Uist and Skye in the west. The distinctiveness of these carefully crafted monuments, whose message must have been intelligible within their own society, is also a vivid indication of how this people of Britain marked itself off from the Romanised Britons further south. Before the Romans there was, perhaps, only one basic notion of Britishness held by those with the mobility to know the simple fact of inhabiting the island. Be this as it may, when it came to casting a supreme kingship for this Pictish inflection of Britishness, it was not defined directly in relation to a people. It was, like all others in Britain and Ireland, conceived in terms of geography: not the island of Britain, however, but the landmass north of the Forth where Britain is effectively separated in two. It is true that the area known in Welsh as *Manaw* appears (from place-names like Clackmannan and Slamannan that preserve its memory) to have stretched across this divide. The significance of this feature was not dependent on whether it was an actual barrier to local communication, however. It was because it was a vivid geographical limit which would have been obvious to any king and his entourage who wished to cross it (which, before a bridge was built at Stirling, would only have been easy at the Fords of Frew for anyone wishing to travel far from north to south).

In the reign of Causantín son of Cinaed, king of the Picts 862–76, if not earlier, the division of Britain at the Forth was imagined as the southern bounds of the primordial Pictish kingdom. It was sufficiently vivid to ensure that for centuries to come it remained the border of *Alba* (or *Albania/Scotia* in Latin) whenever *Alba* or *Scotia* was called to mind. It was perfectly understandable, therefore, that Mael Coluim III (1058–93), for all the Irish ancestry that may have been duly proclaimed (we may guess) at his inauguration, could be portrayed as the latest in a prodigiously long succession of Pictish kings. It was this identification with the mainland from the Forth to Caithness, in particular, that endowed the kingship of *Alba* with the expectation of an innate precedence over other rulers in north Britain. Mael Coluim's long pedigree was, of course, important, but its deeper layers would not on its own have marked him out as inherently a cut or two above (say) his contemporary, Mael Snechta king of Moray (d.1085), who would have boasted the same ancestry as Mael Coluim below Erc mac Echdach, the agreed progenitor of all major kindreds of Dál Riata.[2] It is striking that the most successful rulers of Moray in the eleventh century all sought to become kings of *Alba* rather than move to break with the south, even though there are indications that, on the ground, Moray came to be regarded as separate from 'Scotland'.[3] And it is no surprise that, after becoming king of *Alba*, the most successful Moravian ruler, Mac Bethad (Macbeth) (1040–57), should have been presented as a successor of Picts, even when an ancient precedent for close ties with a fellow Gael, the Leinster king Domnall mac Maíl na mBó, may have been intended.[4]

The kingship of *Alba* was understood by all as the highest prize north of the Forth. Yet the inescapable fact was that, although it had a clear geographical identity, the islands of Britain and Ireland are much larger and more compelling. How much more would the idea of the kingship as the highest secular authority of the Scots be legitimised if it could claim an intimate connection with the ultimate idea of kingdoms of Ireland or Britain? It was in this context that the remoter parts of the royal genealogy would have come into their own, showing the king as a direct descendant of ancient kings of Ireland. This Irish dimension can only have been boosted when Flann Mainistrech and Gilla Coemáin developed a complete and continuous history of Ireland as a kingdom of deepest antiquity. In the poem known as *Duan Albanach*, written when Mael Coluim III was king (1058–93), *Alba* was provided with a history modelled in miniature on the latest construction of Ireland's past, with a series of prehistoric settlements followed by a king-list.[5] The most influential Scottish application of this Irish style of kingship-historiography, however, was the king-list of summarised death-tales from Cinaed mac Ailpín (d.858), which probably existed soon after David I came to the throne in 1124. This may have had more narrative interest than the rather mechanical *Duan Albanach*, but it was chronologically remarkably shallow. It has been suggested that this reflected a greater dependence for the kingship's authenticating antiquity on the association with the (by now) magnificent structure of Ireland's royal past.[6]

By this time the kings of Scots had gained a much more impressive profile in Britain through St Margaret which enabled them to be advertised as representing the lineage of pre-Conquest kings of England. This was signalled at once by the names given to Margaret's first four sons (each called after a generation in Margaret's pedigree). The increased prestige that came with this can have done them no harm, and may have been one of the factors behind the recognition of the eldest of Margaret's sons, Edward, as Mael Coluim III's heir, ahead of other members of the royal kindred. Margaret was not only the definitive ancestor of the ruling dynasty in the twelfth and thirteenth centuries, however, but was soon regarded as a saint – a saint, moreover, who was represented in her *Life* as an exemplar of Christian queenship, rather than as gaining her holiness by withdrawing from her exalted position or by martyrdom. There was more to Margaret than simply being a genealogical trapdoor allowing privileged access to the crypt of English kings of old, of whom the greatest were adorned by twelfth-century history-writing with striking literary personalities as rulers of Britain. But the importance of this to her royal descendants cannot be denied, and the fame of such ancestors as individuals and their significance as kings of England outshone any prestige that a bare (if nonetheless impressively long) list of Pictish kings could offer. When a continuous regnal history was created for England in the 1120s and 1130s, it was natural that Margaret's offspring would identify with it as their history. It made perfect sense for William of Malmesbury to offer his work first of all to David I as well as Matilda, Henry I's heir. It was also appropriate for David I to imagine that Edinburgh was the Castle of the Maidens mentioned by Geoffrey of Monmouth as being founded by Ebraucus, ruler of Britain for thirty-nine years and eponymous founder of York. (Perhaps David could not resist this connection because, according to Geoffrey, Ebraucus reigned when David was king of Judea.) Once the patterns of looking predominantly to both Irish and English pasts had been established in the early twelfth century as ways of explaining the kingship's position as the ultimate secular authority within its realm, it would not have been necessary to develop a continuous history of the Scottish kingship on its own by following the outline of Pictish kings deep into antiquity. *Alba* continued to be understood as a distinct geographical entity, and the Forth as its border in defiance of cultural or political reality, even to the extent of regarding the Firth of Forth as dividing the kingdoms of the Scots and the English – as revealed in a passing remark in *De Situ Albanie*, written during the reign of William I (1165–1214). Its decline in importance in the way the kingdom was imagined historically was only because the kingship now had intimate access to stronger and more powerful symbols, not simply in the mere fact that Ireland and Britain were islands, but because each island had now been furnished with impressive histories as kingdoms – impressive histories which kings of Scots could call their own through their descent from Mael Coluim III and Margaret. It was this link with the most obvious geographical entities, not a particular association with a distinct people – the Scots – which was regarded as most pertinent to Scottish kings in the twelfth century.

Scotland is significant, however, not only because it provides a stark example of how the conception of a chronologically deep regnal past was focused primarily on the islands of Britain and Ireland. It is also remarkable because, by the late thirteenth century, a new sense of kingdom, country and people emerged which, of necessity, was based on something other than the logic of geography. At the end of the twelfth century the kingdom was seen by contemporaries as comprising several countries, with the Scots identified as the inhabitants north of the Forth. If we take evidence from the Chronicle of Melrose as our guide, this had begun to change by *ca* 1220 when 'Scotland' appears to have meant the kingdom as a whole. By the early 1280s at the latest, not only had kingdom and country become one, but all its inhabitants were now Scots.[7] The English, Welsh and Irish, by contrast, never lost their identification with the islands of Britain and Ireland, whatever else may also in time have contributed to their sense of being peoples and countries.

King-list **ξ** (the archetype of Marjorie Anderson's X-group which is found in a greater proportion of Scottish manuscripts than her Y-group) may be seen as a crude attempt in the reign of Alexander II (1214–49) to express this sense of the Scottish kingship as corresponding to an ancient territory, using the Pictish past alongside Dál Riata rather than on its own. In this, we can detect the landmass north of the Forth beginning to return to centre stage as emblematic of the highest secular authority. A tiny modification in a subsequent version of the king-list produced a more impressive effect. Instead of seeing the Pictish and Dál Riatan sections as chronologically parallel, these kings were presented as belonging to a single series, so that Pictish kings were preceded by the 'Scottish' kings of Dál Riata, who were thus propelled back by a millennium. This allowed the number of kings to jump from over fifty to over a hundred (as seen in two different reckonings during the reign of King John, 1292–1304). Only a gradual attempt was made to describe the kingdom's primordial limits as an approximation to its thirteenth-century bounds, however (and the boldest statement, far from being a brazen piece of fancy, was prompted initially by a response to the puzzle of 'Stuaginnuer' in an inherited account of the original kingdom's bounds).

The precursor to Fordun's chronicle, completed by 1285, was a much more sophisticated attempt to project this image of kingdom and country as one into the primordial past and furnish it with a continuous regnal narrative up to the present. But its vision of a self-contained Scottish past was not sufficiently compelling to meet the straightened circumstances of enforced English overlordship in 1291 and subsequent conquest and war from 1296. The work which I have dubbed 'proto-Fordun' was problematic chiefly because it did not give a clear account of Scotland as homeland exclusively of the Scots. Not only had its author copied without comment origin-legend material in which Ireland was portrayed as the Scottish homeland, but the image of Scotland's ancient territorial integrity had been achieved (following the simple pattern of king-list ξ) by bringing Scots together with Picts. This approach had no doubt been adopted from proto-Fordun's principal source, the lost narrative of Scottish history which may be attributed to 'Veremundus', identified as Richard Vairement, *céle Dé* of St Andrews and chancellor of Marie de Coucy, queen of Scots, whose career in Scotland spanned the mid-thirteenth century. Although his work is only dimly discernible, it can be recognised as a lively account beginning with a fresh telling of Scottish origins and continuing with material adapted from Geoffrey of Monmouth, including a defiant letter extolling freedom despatched by both the king of the Picts and the Scottish king to Julius Caesar. The failure to portray Scotland as exclusively Scottish in its formative years was 'solved' by the Scottish procurators at the Curia in 1301 and most famously in the Declaration of Arbroath (1320) by insisting that the Scots, when they first arrived in Scotland in the deep past, took over the entire country and destroyed the Picts. The fact that the Picts were now seen as an historical nuisance is striking testimony to how the idea of kingdom, country and people had crystallised in the heat of war into a seamless unity without any consideration of geographical reality.

THE GROWTH OF SCOTTISH INDEPENDENCE

Proto-Fordun and Veremundus may have failed to meet the needs of lawyers and politicians who required more brutal weapons in their defence of Scottish independence before the pope than either text could provide. They did, however, create with some flair and skill the continuous narrative of a distinctive past for the Scottish kingdom which it had lacked. It is not difficult to see this as the result of new expectations about the relative standing of the Scottish kingship with other kingdoms. As long as kings of Scots did not regard themselves as of equal status, it must have seemed appropriate for them to look to the glorious and deep-rooted past of kings of England/Britain and Ireland as their own, and see this as sufficient for the legitimation of Scottish kingship through history. And as long as the Scottish king remained in undisputed control of affairs within his own kingdom, there is no reason to doubt that submissions to kings of England, attendance at his court or occasional service in his armies would have been regarded as irksome. Good relations with a superior power could be enjoyed for its own sake, but might also be urgently required if life-threatening challenges were being faced at home. But this began to change when Henry II in the Treaty of Falaise (1174) transformed this relationship: although it was formally rescinded, the precedent it set of intrusive lordship could not be forgotten. It has been suggested by Archie Duncan that the experience of this humiliation contributed to the emergence of a 'distinct political culture' in Scotland, so much so that, when William was again in a vulnerable position in 1209, Professor Duncan doubted that Scottish barons would have tolerated a repeat of the subjection their fathers had meekly endured.[8] At this stage, however, it seems that no-one could conceive of resistance on the basis that the Scottish kingship was of equal standing with the king of England. They could not yet think beyond the political reality that the king of England was the predominant force in Britain, nor confront the compelling idea that the English kingship was the successor to an ancient line of kings of Britain.

Yet within the experience of Falaise lay the seeds of a major change that would alter the mental landscape of kingship for ever. By trying to define the submission in writing, Henry II crossed the threshold into a new more legalistic approach conducted in a medium which promised clarity of detail and permanence instead of ambiguity and contingency. Instead of seeing relations between kings as defined chiefly by politics, kingship from Henry II to Edward I (1272–1307) was seen within an increasingly tight jurisdictional framework. Within this context, the subordination of one king to another, each representing the highest secular authority within their realms, inevitably began to seem incongruous. It was not enough for the dominant king to be chief king of Britain: if he was king of Britain in any meaningful sense, then this would have to mean lordship over the land, including the kingdom of Scotland, and ultimately, in Edward I's day, the unambiguous assertion of suzerainty. For kings of England this was a particularly acute dilemma, given how difficult it was for them to make a clear distinction between England and Britain. This change can readily be seen as a reflection of the growing power and efficacy of royal authority in the safeguarding of property-rights and in the administration of justice, a development that becomes particularly visible in England in the reign of Henry II and in Scotland in the reign of Alexander II. Once these patterns were established it was inevitable that the authority of a kingship over its people would be seen more in terms of jurisdiction rather than simply power and prestige. A king who recognised a higher authority in temporal matters would cease to have jurisdiction over his people. It was axiomatic, therefore, that to be a king was to have equal status with other kings. At the same time, the kingship's pre-eminence within Scottish society would no longer benefit from the reflected glory of the English and Irish regnal past, but would require a deep continuous history that was exclusively its own.

In the case of the Scottish kingship this process can be traced back to the very first challenge to its authority over Scottish society in the first surviving papal document addressed to Scots dated December 1100. This, an instruction to show obedience to the new archbishop of York, elicited the first declaration of an independent Scottish realm, albeit in a purely ecclesiastical context. When this issue was finally resolved, however, there was still no generally agreed sense of the kingdom as a single country. What was enshrined in *Cum universi* (1189/1192) as the definitive settlement of the kingdom's ecclesiastical status was not Scottish independence pure and simple, but the independence of each diocese within the framework of a Scottish church. In the face of English opposition this may have been as much as could be expected. It can, however, also be recognised as the successful outcome of Bishop Jocelin's campaign to preserve Glasgow's independence, a campaign that went as far as to encourage a sense of Glasgow's Welsh identity as a way of emphasising the diocese's distinctiveness from 'Scotland' and from the 'bishop of the Scots' at St Andrews. In the thirteenth century the spotlight turned directly on the kingship itself. From the way the prose of royal charters was recalibrated, it can be seen how the idea of the king as being of equal status to other kings was first hatched in the 1220s and gradually became established during Alexander II's reign, culminating in the enactment of the king's sovereign status at the inauguration of the boy king Alexander III in 1249 and depiction of him with crown and sceptre on the seal of his minority. This may not seem so obviously to be linked to wider European developments as the struggle for ecclesiastical independence obviously was, but it can nonetheless be recognised as part of a more general redefinition of secular authority. Sovereign kingship was espoused by Alexander II's counterpart in Norway, while in Britain, a greater emphasis in the thirteenth century on law as a way of defining Wales has been identified by Rees Davies,[9] an idea with a clear resonance with the idea of kingdoms as jurisdictional entities. This may also be reflected in the creation of more than one extension of Geoffrey of Monmouth's British history with an account of events in Wales, although the archetype of *Brut y Tywysogion* should no doubt be seen more directly as a response to the conquest of Wales by Edward I in 1282–3.

What made the works of Veremundus and proto-Fordun so remarkable was that they created and consolidated a distinctively Scottish continuous history where none had existed before, making clever and careful use of some very unpromising material. Although the result, insofar as this can be recovered from Fordun's chronicle, would appear to have been successful in providing both a compelling narrative and an impressively coherent chronological framework, there is nonetheless something altogether less certain about the Scots' subsequent profile as an ancient kingdom with a continuous history compared with that which was espoused by the English, Irish and Welsh. No narrative was composed to give substance to the Declaration of Arbroath's unambiguous statement of Scotland as homeland of the Scots, so in a sense the account drawn up in 1285 might be said to have endured by default, for all that it had been found wanting during the wars of independence. Another contrast between the Scottish regnal narrative and its English, Irish and Welsh equivalents is that it was not, like the others, given a full treatment in the vernacular until much later – not until the sixteenth century.[10] Unlike them, it cannot be said to have entered the historical bloodstream of medieval elites except in the most attenuated form. The principal vernacular celebration of Scottish independence was Barbour's *Bruce* (1375/6) and, later, Blin Harry's *Wallace* (composed a century later). The grand narrative of Scotland's past which, in chapter 9, was identified as the work of Richard Vairement (possibly in the 1260s), and which was probably augmented in 1285, seems only to have caught the imagination, and then chiefly of scholars, in the late fourteenth and fifteenth centuries when it was edited by Fordun and successively copied, continued and refashioned.[11] Not until towards the end of the fifteenth century is there any evidence of a vernacular version, and even this is a drastic abridgement.[12] Wyntoun's chronicle, written in Scots sometime between 1408 and 1424, hardly assumes a specifically Scottish focus until it reaches the eleventh century. He appears to have been entirely ignorant of Fordun's work. In some ways, then, the narrative of an ancient and independent Scottish nation only took off during the Renaissance after it was refashioned and elaborated by Hector Boece in 1527 and Boece's work was translated into Scots and adapted by John Bellenden in 1536.[13] The lure of Britain, moreover, retained its vitality, as Stephen Boardman has emphasised, citing for example how the Stewart dynasty of kings, who ruled from 1371 celebrated their ancestry from British kings in a lost work by Barbour written for Robert II (1371–90).[14]

NATIONAL ORIGINS

Although few can agree on how to define national identity, it is not difficult to recognise one of its core ingredients in the concept of ultimate secular authority in relation to peoples. Susan Reynolds's observations on how medieval ideas about kingdoms and peoples were very like modern ideas about nations immediately come to mind. What, then, can be learned about the origins of Scottish nationhood in the period before the wars of independence? The traditional approach is to describe how Scots, Picts, Britons and Angles were inexorably united to form a single country (typically by a series of conquests or dynastic unions). The main elements, as found in almost all reputable textbooks, are now contested by scholars of Scottish history before 1100 as unsupported by evidence that meets basic criteria of acceptability. It has been argued, in fact, that it is sustained not by a simple consideration of sources as much as by what is expected in the narrative of a nation's origins, and of Scotland's early history.[15] There is both a general predisposition towards types of story-line, and a particular legacy of how key moments have been constructed in previous tellings of Scotland's story, some of which go back to Richard Vairement and beyond.

Even if these problems were not so stark in Scotland's case, the traditional account would, in any event, cut no ice with most scholars of national identity. At the risk of misrepresenting a bewilderingly complex field, these fall broadly into two tendencies. One emphasises continuity, and therefore allows a place in the room, if not necessarily at the dining table, for medieval historians. (A standard label for those of this persuasion is 'perennialists'.) The other emphasises nations as modern phenomena that have become part of the identity of societies at large, typically after being constructed and sustained by intellectuals in the nineteenth and early twentieth centuries. The medievalist can expect to knock in vain at the door of the well-endowed buildings occupied by these scholars, whose standard designation is 'modernists' or 'constructivists'. When perennialists dine with medieval historians the conversation naturally turns to those elements of the modern understanding of national identity which is shared. A notable example is Adrian Hastings' emphasis on written vernacular literatures and 'pressures of the state', which are brought together with a perceptive appreciation of the role of the Old Testament in providing an authoritative model of a people and their king.[16]

This is still, of course, vulnerable to a constructivist's insistence on the nation as essentially something which is real only in the mind, not in terms of any objective historical criteria. A classic summary of this view is Benedict Anderson's celebrated definition of a nation as an 'imagined community'.[17] It is clear, though, that if constructivists were to bring medieval historians into their lecture halls, they might recognise some of the issues that they might hear. The espousal of a Welsh identity by the cathedral establishment of Glasgow in the twelfth century, when none would have spoken Welsh themselves or had any meaningful contact with Welsh culture, is a striking example of how identity could be contingent, that is to say, directly related to a group's aspirations in a particular set of circumstances. Much more impressive still, however, would be the realisation that national history itself, in its classic form as a continuous regnal and territorial narrative reaching deep into the past, originated in some instances in the Middle Ages. English, Irish and Welsh histories constructed in the eleventh and twelfth centuries were reformulated and retold for centuries, and are still visible (particularly in the case of English history) in the foundations of how national history was taught at schools and universities until recently. Rather than look for objective aspects of modern nationhood in the Middle Ages, the nation as essentially imagined can be seen to derive directly from these pioneering visions of Irish, English and Welsh history. Instead of peopling national pantheons with kings, poets and freedom fighters, a constructivist alternative could give pride of place to Flann Mainistrech and Gilla Coemáin, Gaimar and Wace, and Geoffrey of Monmouth and the anonymous first translators of his work into Welsh.

What would happen, though, if perennialists and constructivists sought out the medievial historian in his or her own abode among strange and impenetrable manuscripts and documents? A premium here is placed on trying to understand the past through an appreciation of how it was lived at the time. And what emerges from considering the assumptions that governed the way national histories were first constructed is how, before notions of territorial sovereignty or statehood were ever imagined, it was possible to sustain a compelling vision of ultimate secular power for a people by focusing on incontestable geographical entities, rather than on peoples as such or the actual bounds of kingdoms. It was the power of geography, particularly apparent for Britain and Ireland, that allowed those for whom kingship mattered among the Irish, English and Welsh to develop a strong sense of belonging to distinct societies that were, or aspired to be, under the authority of their own supreme king.

What, then, of the Scots? On one level their independence only began as a conscious aspiration when it was first threatened at the start of the twelfth century: a reaction to external pressures which inspired them to articulate claims to freedom for the first time. On another level it only became fully formed as an idea of territorial sovereignty in the mid-thirteenth century. At the same time, something recognisable to us as related to modern assumptions about nations can be found in Richard Vairement's vision of the Scots as free under their own kings from the beginning. In the end, however, the origins of independence can be seen to lie in the sense of secular authority bestowed by the geographical reality of the near division of Britain by the Forth. This can be traced back to the Picts in the ninth century, and beyond that to what was possibly an identification with the island of Britain. Scottish leaders and men of letters had to work harder than their counterparts elsewhere in Britain and Ireland to maintain this conceptually as well as politically, and showed much ingenuity and skill in the process. As a result, it is possible to see more clearly in the case of Scotland than elsewhere both the continuity of the concept of ultimate secular authority, and the way its components changed over time quite radically. There is not only deep continuity with the lived experience of our forbears, but a strong impression of contingency as each generation maintained this image of ultimate secular power as applying particularly to them. By the mid-thirteenth century this was not so much a matter of geography as of the efficacy of royal authority as guarantor of property and possessions. In the late middle ages war with England and its aftermath became the definitive experience, and Bruce and Wallace replaced Vairement and proto-Fordun in giving life to Scottish sovereignty in terms of the past.

The importance of continuity and change in understanding nations has been recognised by scholars of identity before, of course, notably Anthony Smith, albeit that it is formulated differently.[18] So far, though, discussions tend to be dominated by assumptions about nations that are rooted in modern ways of thinking in which national identity and ethnicity are intimately associated with each other. This is perfectly natural: we live today, and our mental landscape is conditioned accordingly. We can be modern in another way, though. If more emphasis is placed on the up-to-date critical insights into sources that have been developed by medievalists, then there is a real chance that hitherto unexpected vistas will be revealed through engaging with the aspirations and assumptions of our forbears. At the very least this will yield new questions. It might even give us an opportunity to think the unthinkable.

NOTES

1. Reynolds, *Kingdoms and Communities*, ch. 8.
2. M. A. O'Brien (ed.), *Corpus Genealogiarum Hiberniae*, vol. i, with intro. by J. V. Kelleher (Dublin, 1976), 329. The pedigree headed by Mael Snechta (d.1085) and Mac Bethad (d.1057) advertised Moray's ruling kindred as descendants of Loarn, brother of Fergus son of Erc. The middle section has been concocted, probably on the understanding that the kindred were regarded as Cenél Loairn.
3. See above, 8.
4. See above, 57–8.
5. See above, 59–60. In this Scottish example the series of settlements was followed by a list of Christian kings, not pre-Christian kings as in the Irish examples.
6. Broun, *Irish Identity*, ch. 8, esp. 189–93.
7. This is discussed in the light of the new edition of the Chronicle of Melrose in D. Broun, 'Melrose abbey and its world', in Dauvit Broun and Julian Harrison (eds), *The Chronicle of Melrose: a Stratigraphic Edition*, vol. i (forthcoming).
8. A. A. M. Duncan, 'John king of England and the kings of Scots', in S. D. Church (ed.), *King John: New Interpretations* (Woodbridge, 1999), 247–71, esp. 259–61, 263–4, and 270.
9. R. R. Davies, 'Law and national identity in thirteenth-century Wales', in R. R. Davies and others (eds), *Welsh Society and Nationhood* (Cardiff, 1984), 51–69.
10. The version of Fordun's chronicle known as the Book of Pluscarden was translated into French in 1519 for John, duke of Albany: see N. Royan with D. Broun, 'Versions of Scottish nationhood', in Ian Brown and others (eds), *Edinburgh History of Scottish Literature* (forthcoming).
11. A nearly full account of the manuscripts of Fordun, Bower and their derivatives (but not the Book of Pluscarden) is given in Watt (ed.), *Scotichronicon*, ix. 186–203 (with Bower's ideograph discussed at 148–85).
12. W. A. Craigie (ed.), *The Asloan Manuscript*, vol. i (Edinburgh, 1923), 245–70.
13. R. W. Chambers, Edith C. Batho and H. Winifred Husbands (eds), *The Chronicles of Scotland, compiled by Hector Boece. Translated into Scots by John Bellenden, 1531*, 2 vols (Edinburgh, 1938, 1941). Boece's work was also translated soon after its publication in George Watson (ed.), *The Mar Lodge Translation of the History of Scotland*, vol. i (Edinburgh, 1946). It was also translated into Scots verse at about the same time by David Stewart. See Royan with Broun, 'Versions of Scottish nationhood', in Ian Brown and others (eds), *Edinburgh History of Scottish Literature* (forthcoming).
14. Boardman, 'Late medieval Scotland and the Matter of Britain', 51–6.
15. Dauvit Broun, 'Scotland before 1100: writing Scotland's origins', in Bob Harris and Alan R. MacDonald (eds), *Scotland: the Making and Unmaking of the Nation, c. 1100–1707* (Dundee, 2006), 1–16, at 5–6.

16. Adrian Hastings, *The Construction of Nationhood: Ethnicity, Religion, and Nationalism* (Cambridge, 1997).

17. Benedict Anderson, *Imagined Communities: Reflections on the Origin and Spread of Nationalism* (London, 1983); 2nd edn (London, 1991).

18. For example Anthony D. Smith, *The Nation in History. Historiographical Debates about Ethnicity and Nationalism* (Oxford, 2000).

Bibliography of Works Cited

Aird, W. M., 'Northern England or Southern Scotland? The Anglo-Scottish border in the eleventh and twelfth centuries and the problem of perspective', in John C. Appleby and Paul Dalton (eds), *Government, Religion and Society in Northern England 1000–1700* (Stroud, 1997), 27–39

Amours, F. J. (ed.), *The Original Chronicle of Andrew of Wyntoun*, 6 vols (Scottish Text Society, 1903–14)

Anderson, A. O., 'Anglo-Scottish relations from Constantine II to William', *SHR* 42 (1963) 1–20

Anderson, Alan Orr, *Early Sources of Scottish History,* A.D. *500–1286*, 2 vols (Edinburgh, 1922)

Anderson, Alan Orr, *Scottish Annals from English Chroniclers,* A.D. *500 to 1286* (London, 1908)

Anderson A. O. and Anderson, M. O. (eds), *The Chronicle of Melrose from the Cottonian Manuscript, Faustina B. IX in the British Museum*, with an index by W. Croft Dickinson (London, 1936)

Anderson, Benedict, *Imagined Communities: Reflections on the Origin and Spread of Nationalism* (London, 1983); 2nd edn (London, 1991)

Anderson, M. O., 'Dalriada and the creation of the kingdom of the Scots' in Whitelock, McKitterick and Dumville (eds), *Ireland in Early Mediaeval Europe*, 106–32

Anderson, M. O., *Kings and Kingship in Early Scotland*, 2nd edn (Edinburgh, 1980)

Anderson, M. O., 'St Andrews before Alexander I', in G. W. S. Barrow (ed.), *The Scottish Tradition* (Edinburgh, 1974), 1–13

Arnold, Ivor (ed.), Wace, *Le Roman de Brut*, La Société des Anciens Textes Français, 2 vols (Paris, 1938–40)

Arnold, Thomas (ed.), *Symeonis Monachi Opera Omnia*, vol. ii (London, 1885)

Bagge, Sverre, *From Gang Leader to the Lord's Anointed: Kingship in* Sverris saga *and* Hákonar saga Hákonarsonar (Odense, 1996)

Bain, Joseph (ed.), *Calendar of Documents relating to Scotland*, vol. i, *1108–1272* (London, 1881)

Bannerman, John, *Studies in the History of Dal Riata* (Edinburgh, 1974)

Bannerman, John, 'The king's poet and the inauguration of Alexander III', *SHR* 68 (1989) 120–49

Bannerman, John, 'The Scottish takeover of Pictland and the relics of Columba', in D. Broun and T. O. Clancy (eds), *Spes Scotorum, Hope of Scots. Saint Columba, Iona and Scotland* (Edinburgh, 1999), 71–94

Banton, Nicholas, 'Monastic reform and the unification of tenth-century England', in Stuart Mews (ed.), *Religion and National Identity*, Studies in Church History, no. 18 (Oxford, 1982), 71–85

Barlow, Frank, *Durham Jurisdictional Peculiars* (London, 1950)

Barlow, Frank, *Edward the Confessor* (London, 1970)

Barlow, Frank, *William Rufus* (London, 1983)

Barrell, A. D. M., *Medieval Scotland* (Cambridge, 2000)

Barrell, A. D. M., 'Scotland and the papacy in the reign of Alexander II', in Oram (ed.), *The Reign of Alexander II*, 157–77

Barrell, A. D. M., 'The background to *Cum universi*: Scoto-papal relations, 1159–1192', *IR* 46 (1995) 116–38

Barrow, G. W. S., 'A writ of Henry II for Dunfermline Abbey', *SHR* 36 (1957) 138–43

Barrow, G. W. S., *David I of Scotland (1124–1153). The Balance of New and Old*. The Stenton Lecture 1984 (Reading, 1985)

Barrow, G. W. S., 'King David I and the Honour of Lancaster', *EHR* 70 (1955) 85–9

Barrow, G. W. S., *Kingship and Unity: Scotland 1000–1306*, 2nd edn (Edinburgh, 2003); 1st edn (London, 1981)

Barrow, G. W. S., 'Observations on the Coronation stone of Scotland', *SHR* 76 (1997) 115–21

Barrow, G. W. S. (ed.), *Regesta Regum Scottorum*, vol. i, *The Acts of Malcolm IV King of Scots 1153–1165, together with Scottish Royal Acts prior to 1153 not included in Sir Archibald Lawrie's 'Early Scottish Charters'* (Edinburgh, 1960)

Barrow, G. W. S. (ed.), with the collaboration of W. W. Scott, *Regesta Regum Scottorum*, vol. ii, *The Acts of William I, King of Scots 1165–1214* (Edinburgh, 1971)

Barrow, G. W. S., review of Somerville, *Pope Alexander III*, *SHR* 58 (1979)

Barrow, G. W. S., *Robert Bruce and the Community of the Realm of Scotland*, 3rd edn (Edinburgh, 1988)

Barrow, G. W. S., *Scotland and its Neighbours in the Middle Ages* (London, 1992)

Barrow, G. W. S., 'Scotland's experience of feudalism in the twelfth century', *History Teaching Review Year Book* 14 (2000) 5–9

Barrow, G. W. S., *The Anglo-Norman Era in Scottish History* (Oxford, 1980)

Barrow, G. W. S. (ed.), *The Charters of King David I. The Written Acts of David I King of Scots, 1124–53 and of his son Henry Earl of Northumberland, 1139–52* (Woodbridge, 1999)

Barrow, G. W. S., 'The idea of freedom in late medieval Scotland', *IR* 30 (1979) 16–34

Barrow, G. W. S., *The Kingdom of the Scots*, 2nd edn (Edinburgh, 2003)

Barrow, G. W. S., 'Wales and Scotland in the middle ages', *Welsh Historical Review*, 10 (1980–1), 302–19

Bartlett, Robert, *England under the Norman and Angevin Kings 1075–1225* (Oxford, 2000)

Bartlett, Robert, *The Making of Europe. Conquest, Colonization and Cultural Change 950–1350* (London, 1993; repr. 1994)

Bartlett, Robert (ed.), *The Miracles of St Æbbe of Coldingham and Saint Margaret of Scotland* (Oxford, 2003)

Barton, Simon and Fletcher, Richard, *The World of El Cid: Chronicles of the Spanish Reconquest* (Manchester, 2000)

Bartrum, P. C. (ed.), *Early Welsh Genealogical Tracts* (Cardiff, 1966)

Bartrum, Peter C., 'Was there a British "Book of Conquests"?', *BBCS* 23 (1968–70) 1–6

Bates, David (ed.), *Regesta Regum Anglo-Normannorum. The Acta of William I (1066–1087)* (Oxford, 1998)

Bell, Alexander (ed.), *L'Estoire des Engleis by Geffrei Gaimar*, Anglo-Norman Text Society (Oxford, 1960)

Best, R. I. and O'Brien, M. A. (eds), *The Book of Leinster, formerly known as Lebar na Núachongbála*, vol. iii (Dublin, 1957)

Bethell, Denis, 'English monks and Irish reform in the eleventh and twelfth centuries', in T. D. Williams (ed.), *Historical Studies: papers read before the Irish Conference of Historians, VIII Dublin 27–30 May 1969* (Dublin, 1971), 111–35

Birch, W. de Gray, *History of Scottish Seals*, vol. i (Stirling and London, 1905)

Bjørn, Claus, Grant, Alexander and Stringer, Keith J. (eds), *Nations, Nationalism and Patriotism in the European Past* (Copenhagen, 1994)

Blanchard, Ian, 'Lothian and beyond: the economy of the "English empire" of David I', in Richard Britnell and John Hatcher (eds), *Progress and Problems in Medieval England. Essays in Honour of Edward Miller* (Cambridge, 1996), 23–43

Bliss, W. H. (ed.), *Calendar of Entries in the Papal Registers relating to Great Britain and Ireland: Papal Letters*, vol. i, *1198–1304* (London, 1893)

Bloch, M., 'An unknown testimony on the history of coronation in Scotland', *SHR* 23 (1925–6) 105–6

Boardman, Stephen, 'Dunfermline as a royal mausoleum', in Richard Fawcett (ed.), *Royal Dunfermline* (Edinburgh, 2005), 139–53

Boardman, Steve, 'Late medieval Scotland and the Matter of Britain', in Cowan and Finlay (eds), *Scottish History: the Power of the Past*, 47–72

Brett, Caroline, 'The prefaces of two late thirteenth-century Welsh Latin chronicles', *BBCS* 35 (1988) 63–72

Brett, Martin, *The English Church under Henry I* (Oxford, 1975)

Bromwich, Rachel (ed.), *Trioedd Ynys Prydein. The Welsh Triads*, 2nd edn (Cardiff, 1978)

Bromwich, Rachel and Evans, D. Simon (eds), *Culhwch and Olwen. An Edition and Study of the Oldest Arthurian Tale* (Cardiff, 1992)

Brooke, Christopher, 'The archbishops of St David's, Llandaff and Caerleon-on-Usk', in [Nora K. Chadwick (ed.)], *Studies in the Early British Church* (Cambridge, 1958), 201–33

Broun, Dauvit, '*Alba*: Pictish homeland or Irish offshoot?', in Pamela O'Neill (ed.), *Exile and Homecoming. Papers from the Fifth Australian Conference of Celtic Studies, University of Sydney, July 2004* (Sydney, 2005), 234–75

Broun, Dauvit, 'A new look at *Gesta Annalia* attributed to John of Fordun', in Crawford (ed.), *Church, Chronicle and Learning*, 9–30

Broun, Dauvit, 'Contemporary perspectives on Alexander II's succession: the evidence of king-lists', in Oram (ed.), *The Reign of Alexander II, 1214–49*, 79–98

Broun, Dauvit, 'Defining Scotland and the Scots before the wars of independence', in Dauvit Broun, Richard J. Finlay and Michael Lynch (eds), *Image and Identity: the Making and Remaking of Scotland through the Ages* (Edinburgh, 1998), 4–17

Broun, Dauvit, 'Gaelic literacy in eastern Scotland, 1124–1249', in Huw Pryce (ed.), *Literacy in Medieval Celtic Societies* (Cambridge, 1998), 183–201

Broun, Dauvit, 'Scotland before 1100: writing Scotland's origins', in Bob Harris and Alan R. MacDonald (eds), *Scotland: the Making and Unmaking of the Nation, c. 1100–1707* (Dundee, 2006), 1–16

Broun, Dauvit, 'The absence of regnal years from the dating clause of charters of kings of Scots', in Gillingham (ed.), *Anglo-Norman Studies XXV*, 47–63

Broun, Dauvit, 'The adoption of brieves in Scotland', in Marie-Thérèse Flanagan and Judith A. Green (eds), *Charters and Charter Scholarship in Britain and Ireland* (London, 2005), 164–83

Broun, Dauvit, 'The birth of Scottish History', *SHR* 76 (1997) 4–22

Broun, Dauvit, 'The church and the origins of Scottish independence in the twelfth century', *RSCHS* 31 (2002) 1–36

Broun, Dauvit, 'The church of St Andrews and its foundation-legend in the early twelfth century: recovering the full text of Version A of the foundation legend', in Taylor (ed.), *Kings, Clerics and Chronicles in Scotland*, 108–14

Broun, Dauvit, 'The Declaration of Arbroath: pedigree of a nation?', in Geoffrey Barrow (ed.), *The Declaration of Arbroath: History, Significance, Setting* (Edinburgh, 2003), 1–12

Broun, Dauvit, *The Irish Identity of the Kingdom of the Scots in the Twelfth and Thirteenth Centuries* (Woodbridge, 1999)

Broun, Dauvit, 'The origin of Scottish identity', in Bjørn, Grant and Stringer (eds), *Nations, Nationalism and Patriotism in the European Past*, 35–55

Broun, Dauvit, 'The origin of Scottish identity in its European context', in B. E. Crawford (ed.), *Scotland in Dark Age Europe* (St Andrews, 1994), 21–31

Broun, Dauvit, 'The origin of the Stone of Scone as a national icon', in Welander, Breeze and Clancy (eds), *The Stone of Destiny: Artefact and Icon*, 183–97

Broun, Dauvit, 'The Picts' place in the kingship's past before John of Fordun', in Cowan and Finlay (eds), *Scottish History: the Power of the Past*, 11–28

Broun, Dauvit, 'The seven kingdoms in *De situ Albanie*: a record of Pictish political geography or an imaginary map of Alba?', in Cowan and McDonald (eds), *Alba: Celtic Scotland in the Middle Ages*, 24–42

Broun, Dauvit, 'The Welsh identity of the kingdom of Strathclyde, *ca* 900–*ca* 1200', *Innes Review* 85 (2004) 111–80

Broun, Dauvit and Harrison, Julian (eds), *The Chronicle of Melrose Abbey: a Stratographic Edition*, vol. i (forthcoming)

Broun Dauvit, with Scott, A. B. (eds), '*Liber Extravagans*', in D. E. R. Watt (ed.), *Scotichronicon by Walter Bower in Latin and English*, vol. ix (Edinburgh, 1998), 54–127

Brown, David E., 'The Scottish Origin-legend before Fordun', unpublished Ph.D. dissertation (Edinburgh University, 1988)

Byrne, Francis John, *Irish Kings and High-kings* (London, 1973)

Byrne, F. J., '*Clann Ollaman Uaisle Emna*', *Studia Hibernica* 4 (1964) 54–94

Calise, J. M. P., *Pictish Sourcebook: Documents of Medieval Legend and Dark Age History* (Westport, CT, 2002)

Cambridge, E., 'The early building-history of St Andrews Cathedral, Fife, and its context in northern transitional architecture', *Antiquaries Journal* 57 (1977) 277–88

Campbell, A. (ed.), *Chronicle of Æthelweard* (London, 1962)

Carey, John, *A New Introduction to Lebor Gabála Érenn. The Book of the Taking of Ireland* (London, 1993)

Carey, John, '*Lebor Gabála* and the legendary history of Ireland', in Helen Fulton (ed.), *Medieval Celtic Literature and Society* (Dublin, 2005), 32–48

Carey, John, '*Lebor Gabála Érenn*, The Book of Invasions', in John T. Koch (ed.), in collaboration with John Carey, *The Celtic Heroic Age: Literary Sources for Ancient Celtic Europe and Early Medieval Ireland and Wales* (Malden, Mass., 1995), 213–66

Carey, John, *The Irish National Origin-Legend: Synthetic Pseudohistory*, Quiggin pamphlet no. 1 (Cambridge, 1994)

Carpenter, David, *The Struggle for Mastery: Britain 1066–1284* (London, 2003)

Chadwick, Nora, 'The colonisation of Brittany from Celtic Britain', *PBA* 51 (1965) 235–99

Chambers, R. W., Batho, Edith C. and Husbands, H. Winifred (eds), *The Chronicles of Scotland, compiled by Hector Boece. Translated into Scots by John Bellenden, 1531*, 2 vols (Edinburgh, 1938, 1941)

Chaplais, Pierre, *English Royal Documents King John–King Henry VI, 1199–1461* (Oxford, 1971)

Charles-Edwards, Thomas, *Early Christian Ireland* (Cambridge, 2000)

Cheney, C. R., *English Bishops' Chanceries 1100–1250* (Manchester, 1950)

Clancy, Thomas Owen, 'A Gaelic polemic quatrain from the reign of Alexander I, ca. 1113', *Scottish Gaelic Studies*, 20 (2000) 88–96

Clancy, T. O., 'Kingmaking and images of kingship in medieval Gaelic literature', in Welander, Breeze and Clancy (eds), *The Stone of Destiny: Artefact and Icon*, 85–105

Clancy, Thomas Owen, 'Scotland, the "Nennian" recension of the *Historia Brittonum*, and the *Lebor Bretnach*', in Taylor (ed.), *Kings, Clerics and Chronicles*, 87–107

Clancy, Thomas Owen (ed.), *The Triumph Tree. Scotland's Earliest Poetry* A.D. *550–1350* (Edinburgh, 1998)

Clancy, T. O. and Crawford, B. E., 'The formation of the Scottish kingdom', in R. A. Houston and W. W. J. Knox (eds), *The New Penguin History of Scotland from the Earliest Times to the Present Day* (London, 2001), 28–95

Close Rolls of the Reign of Henry III, A.D. *1256–1259* [ed. K. H. Ledward] (London, 1932)

Colgrave, Bertram and Mynors, R. A. B. (eds), *Bede's Ecclesiastical History of the English People*, reprinted with corrections (Oxford, 1991)

Cooper, James, *Four Scottish Coronations*, special issue of the Aberdeen Ecclesiological Society and the Glasgow Ecclesiological Society (Aberdeen, 1902)

Corner, D. J., Scott, A. B., Scott, W. W. and Watt, D. E. R. (eds), *Scotichronicon by Walter Bower in Latin and English*, gen. ed. D. E. R. Watt, vol. iv (Edinburgh, 1994)

Cowan, Edward J., 'Destruction of a Celtic people: the Viking impact upon Pictland', *Celtic Collections, Acta* 16 (1989) 99–112

Cowan, E. J., 'Norwegian sunset, Scottish dawn', in Reid (ed.), *Scotland in the Reign of Alexander III*, 103–31

Cowan, Edward J., 'The Scottish chronicle in the Poppleton manuscript', *IR* 32 (1981) 3–21

Cowan, Edward J. and McDonald, R. Andrew (eds), *Alba: Celtic Scotland in the Middle Ages* (East Linton, 2000)

Cowan, Edward J. and Finlay, Richard J. (eds), *Scottish History: the Power of the Past* (Edinburgh, 2002)

Craigie, W. A. (ed.), *The Asloan Manuscript*, vol. i (Edinburgh, 1923)

Crawford, B. E. (ed.), *Church, Chronicle and Learning in Medieval and Early Renaissance Scotland: Essays presented to Donald Watt on the completion of the publication of Bower's Scotichronicon* (Edinburgh, 1999)

Crawford, Barbara E., 'The earldom of Caithness and the kingdom of Scotland, 1150–1266', in Stringer (ed.), *Essays on the Nobility of Medieval Scotland*, 25–43

Crick, Julia C., *The Historia Regum Britannie of Geoffrey of Monmouth*, vol. iii, *Summary Catalogue of Manuscripts* (Cambridge, 1989)

Crick, Julia C., *The Historia Regum Britannie of Geoffrey of Monmouth*, vol. iv, *Dissemination and Reception in the Later Middle Ages* (Cambridge, 1991)

Crick, Julia, 'Two newly located manuscripts of Geoffrey of Monmouth's *Historia Regum Britannie*', in James P. Carley and Felicity Riddy (ed.), *Arthurian Literature XIII* (Cambridge, 1995), 151–6

Crone, G. R., *Early Maps of the British Isles* A.D. *1000*–A.D. *1579* (London, 1961)

Damian-Grint, P., 'A 12th-century Anglo-Norman Brut fragment (MS BL Harley 4733, f.128)', in Ian Short (ed.), *Anglo-Norman Anniversary Essays*, Anglo-Norman Text Society (London, 1993), 87–104

Damian-Grint, Peter, *The New Historians of the Twelfth-Century Renaissance: Inventing Vernacular Authority* (Woodbridge, 1999)

David, Pierre, *La Pologne et l'Évangélisation de la Poméranie aux XIᵉ et XIIᵉ siècle*, Études Historiques et Littéraires sur la Pologne Médiévale (Paris, 1928)

Davidson, Hilda Ellis (ed.) and Fisher, Peter (trans.), Saxo Grammaticus, *The History of the Danes*, vol. i (Cambridge, 1979); vol. ii, commentary (Cambridge, 1980)

Davidson, Michael Raymond, 'Submission and Imperium in the Early Medieval Insular World', unpublished Ph.D. dissertation (Edinburgh, 2003)

Davies, John Reuben, *The Book of Llandaf and the Norman Church in Wales* (Woodbridge, 2003)

Davies, R. R., *Beth Yw'r Ots Gennyf i am – Brydain? Darlith Goffa Syr Thomas Parry-Williams 1998* (Aberystwyth, 1998)

Davies, R. R., *Domination and Conquest: the Experience of Ireland, Scotland and Wales 1100–1300* (Cambridge, 1990)

Davies, Rees, ' "Keeping the natives in order": the English king and the "Celtic" rulers 1066–1216', *Peritia* 10 (1996) 212–24

Davies, R. R., 'Law and national identity in thirteenth-century Wales', in R. R. Davies and others (eds), *Welsh Society and Nationhood* (Cardiff, 1984), 51–69

Davies, R. R., *The Age of Conquest: Wales 1063–1415* (Oxford, 1991)

Davies, R. R., *The First English Empire: Power and Identities in the British Isles, 1093–1343* (Oxford, 2000)

Davies, Rees, *The Matter of Britain and the Matter of England. An Inaugural Lecture delivered before the University of Oxford on 29 February 1996* (Oxford, 1996)

Davies, R. R., 'The peoples of Britain and Ireland 1100–1400. 1. Identities', *TRHS* 6th series 4 (1994) 1–20

Davies, R. R., 'The peoples of Britain and Ireland 1100–1400. 4. Language and historical mythology', *TRHS* 6th series 7 (1997) 1–24

Davies, W. S. (ed.), 'The Book of Invectives of Giraldus Cambrensis', *Y Cymmrodor: the Magazine of the Honourable Society of Cymmrodorion* 30 (1920) 1–248

de Fougerolles, Paula, 'Pope Gregory VII, the archbishopric of Dol and the Normans', in Christopher Harper-Bill (ed.), *Anglo-Norman Studies XXI, Proceedings of the Battle Conference 1998* (Woodbridge, 1999), 47–66

Delisle, Leopold (ed.), *Recueil des Actes de Henri II, Roi d'Angleterre et Duc de Normandie*, vol. i (Paris, 1909)

Deyermond, A. D., *Epic Poetry and the Clergy: Studies on the "Mocedades de Rodrigo"* (London, 1968)

Dickinson, W. Croft, rev. A. A. M. Duncan, *Scotland from the Earliest Times to 1603* (Oxford, 1977)

Dobbs, M. E., 'The pedigree of the family of Flann Mainistrech', *Journal of the County of Louth Archaeological Society* 5 (1923) 149–53

Dobosz, Józef, *Monarchia i Możni wobec Kosciola w Polsce do początku XIII wieku* (Poznań, 2002)

Donaldson, Gordon, *Scottish Historical Documents* (Edinburgh, 1974)

Donaldson, Gordon, *Scotland: the Shaping of a Nation* (London, 1974), 3rd edn (Nairn, 1993)

Donnelly, J., 'The earliest Scottish charters?', *SHR* 68 (1989) 1–22

Driscoll, S. T., with contributions by Susan Bain and others, *Excavations at Glasgow Cathedral 1988–1997* (London, 2002)

Driscoll, Stephen T., 'The archaeology of state formation in Scotland', in W. S. Hanson and E. A. Slater (eds), *Scottish Archaeology: New Perceptions* (Aberdeen, 1991), 81–111

Duchesne, L. and Fabre, P. (eds), *Le Liber Censuum de l'Église Romaine*, 3 vols in 2 (Paris 1889–1952)

Duffy, Seán, 'Ireland and the Irish Sea Region, 1014–1318', unpublished Ph.D. dissertation (Trinity College Dublin, 1993)

Dumville, David N., 'Britain and Ireland in *Táin Bó Fraích*', *Études Celtiques* 32 (1996) 175–87

Dumville, David N., '*Cethri Prímchenéla Dáil Riata*', *Scottish Gaelic Studies* 20 (2000) 170–91

Dumville, David N., '*Historia Britonum*: an insular history from the Carolingian age', in A. Scharer and G. Scheibelreiter (eds), *Historiographie im frühen Mittelalter* (Munich, 1994), 406–34

Dumville, David N., 'Ireland and North Britain in the Earlier Middle Ages: contexts for *Míniugud Senchusa Fher nAlban*', in Colm Ó Baoill and Nancy R. McGuire (eds), *Rannsachadh na Gàidhlig 2000* (Aberdeen, 2002), 185–212

Dumville, D. N., 'Kingship, genealogies and regnal lists', in P. H. Sawyer and I. N. Wood (eds), *Early Medieval Kingship* (Leeds, 1977), 72–104

Dumville, David N., 'Latin and Irish in the Annals of Ulster, A.D. 431–1050', in Whitelock, McKitterick and Dumville (eds), *Ireland in Early Mediaeval Europe*, 320–41

Dumville, David N., 'The Chronicle of the Kings of Alba', in Taylor (ed.), *Kings, Clerics and Chronicles*, 73–86

Dumville, David N., *The Churches of North Britain in the First Viking-Age. The Fifth Whithorn Lecture, 14th September 1996* (Whithorn, 1997)

Dumville, D. N., 'The Corpus Christi "Nennius"', *BBCS* 25 (1974) 369–80

Dumville, David N. (ed.), *The Historia Brittonum*, vol. iii, The 'Vatican' Recension (Cambridge, 1985)

Dumville, D. N., 'The textual history of "Lebor Bretnach": a preliminary study', *Éigse* 16 (1975–6) 255–73

Dumville, David N., *Wessex and England from Alfred to Edgar* (Woodbridge, 1992)

Duncan, A. A. M., 'Before coronation: making a king at Scone in the thirteenth century', in Welander, Breeze and Clancy (eds), *The Stone of Destiny. Artefact and Icon*, 139–67

Duncan, A. A. M., 'John king of England and the kings of Scots', in S. D. Church (ed.), *King John: New Interpretations* (Woodbridge, 1999), 247–71

Duncan, A. A. M., 'Roger of Howden and Scotland, 1187–1201', in Crawford (ed.), *Church, Chronicle and Learning*, 135–59

Duncan, A. A. M., *Scotland: the Making of the Kingdom* (Edinburgh, 1975)

Duncan, A. A. M., 'Sources and uses of the Chronicle of Melrose', in Taylor (ed.), *Kings, Clerics and Chronicles in Scotland*, 146–85

Duncan, A. A. M., 'St Kentigern at Glasgow Cathedral in the twelfth century', in Richard Fawcett (ed.), *Medieval Art and Architecture in the Diocese of Glasgow* (Leeds, 1998), 9–24

Duncan, A. A. M., 'The earliest Scottish charters', *SHR* 37 (1958) 103–35

Duncan, A. A. M., *The Nation of the Scots and the Declaration of Arbroath (1320)*, Historical Association Pamphlet (London, 1970)

Duncan, A. A. M., *The Kingship of the Scots, 842–1292: Succession and Independence* (Edinburgh, 2002)

Duncan, A. A. M., 'Yes, the earliest Scottish charters', *SHR* 78 (1999) 1–38

Durkan, John, 'Glasgow diocese and the claims of York', *IR* 50 (1999) 89–101

Engel, Josef (ed.), *Grosser Historischer Weltatlas*, vol. ii, Mittelalter (München, 1970)

Evans, Nicholas J., 'The Textual Development of the Principal Irish Chronicles in the Tenth and Eleventh Centuries', unpublished Ph.D. dissertation (University of Glasgow, 2003)

Ferguson, Paul C., *Medieval Papal Representatives in Scotland: Legates, Nuncios, and Judges-Delegate*, Stair Society (Edinburgh, 1997)

FitzPatrick, Elizabeth, *Royal Inauguration in Gaelic Ireland c.1100–1600: a Cultural Landscape Study* (Woodbridge, 2004)

FitzPatrick, Elizabeth, 'The Practice and Siting of Royal Inauguration in Medieval Ireland', 2 vols, unpublished Ph.D. dissertation (Trinity College, Dublin, 1997)

Flanagan, Marie-Thérèse, *Irish Society, Anglo-Norman Settlers, and Angevin Kingship: Interactions in Ireland in the Late Twelfth Century* (Oxford, 1989)

Fletcher, R. A., *St James's Catapult. The Life and Times of Diego Gelmírez of Santiago de Compostela* (Oxford, 1984)

Fletcher, R. A., *The Episcopate in the Kingdom of León in the Twelfth Century* (Oxford, 1978)

Flórez, Ferrer, 'Mallorca y la teocracia pontificia', *Analecta Sacra Tarraconensia. Revista de Ciencias Histórico-Eclasiásticas* 23 (1950) 15–30

Foot, Sarah, 'The making of *Angelcynn*: English identity before the Norman Conquest', *TRHS* 6th series 6 (1996) 25–49

Forbes, Alexander Penrose (ed.), *Lives of S. Ninian and S. Kentigern compiled in the Twelfth Century* (Edinburgh, 1874)

Foreville, Raymonde, *L'Eglise et la Royauté en Angleterre sous Henri II Plantagenet (1154–1189)* ([Paris], 1943)

Forsyth, Katherine, 'Evidence of a lost Pictish source in the *Historia Regum Anglorum* of Simeon of Durham', in Taylor (ed.), *Kings, Clerics and Chronicles*, 19–32

Forsyth, Katherine, *Language in Pictland. The Case against 'non-Indo-European Pictish'* (Utrecht, 1997)

Foster, Sally M., *Picts, Gaels and Scots*, 1st edn (London, 1996); 2nd edn (London, 2004)

Frame, Robin, *The Political Development of the British Isles, 1100–1400* (Oxford, 1990)

Fraser, Ian A., 'The place-names of Argyll: an historical perspective', *TGSI* 54 (1984–6)

Fulton, Helen, 'Tenth-century Wales and *Armes Prydein*', *THSC* n.s. 7 (2001) 5–18

Galbraith, V. H., 'Seven charters of Henry II at Lincoln Cathedral', *Antiquaries Journal* 12 (1932) 269–78

Gieysztor, A., 'Medieval Poland', trans. K. Cękalska, in Stefan Kieniewicz, *History of Poland* (Warsaw, 1968), 29–165

Gillingham, John (ed.), *Anglo-Norman Studies XXV: Proceedings of the Battle Conference 2002* (Woodbridge, 2003)

Gillingham, John, 'The beginnings of English imperialism', *Journal of Historical Sociology*, 5 (1992) 392–409

Gillingham, John, 'The context and purposes of Geoffrey of Monmouth's History of the Kings of Britain', in Marjorie Chibnall (ed.), *Anglo-Norman Studies XIII. Proceedings of the Battle Conference 1991* (Woodbridge, 1990) 99–118

Gillingham, John, *The English in the Twelfth Century: Imperialism, National Identity and Political Values* (Woodbridge, 2000)

Gillingham, John, 'The English invasion of Ireland', in Brendan Bradshaw and others (eds), *Representing Ireland: Literature and the Origins of Conflict, 1534–1660* (Cambridge, 1993), 24–42

Gillingham, John, 'The foundations of a disunited kingdom', in Alexander Grant and Keith J. Stringer (eds), *Uniting the Kingdom? The Making of British History* (London, 1995), 48–64

Giry, A., *Manuel de Diplomatique* (Paris, 1894)

Goodall, W. (ed.), *Joannis de Fordun Scotichronicon cum Supplementis et Continuatione Walteri Boweri*, 2 vols (Edinburgh, 1759)

Gransden, Antonia, *Historical Writing in England*, vol. i, *c.500–c.1307* (London, 1974)

Grant, Alexander, 'Aspects of National Consciousness in Medieval Scotland', in Bjørn, Grant and Stringer (eds), *Nations, Nationalism and Patriotism in the European Past*, 68–95

Grant, Alexander and Stringer, Keith J. (eds), *Medieval Scotland. Crown, Lordship and Community: Essays Presented to G. W. S. Barrow* (Edinburgh, 1993)

Green, Judith, 'Anglo-Scottish relations, 1066–1174', in Michael Jones and Malcolm Vale (eds), *England and her Neighbours 1066–1453. Essays in Honour of Pierre Chaplais* (London, 1989), 53–72

Green, Judith A., 'David I and Henry I', *SHR* 75 (1996) 1–19

Greenway, Diana (ed.), *Henry, Archdeacon of Huntingdon, Historia Anglorum, The History of the English People* (Oxford, 1996)

Haddan, A. W. and Stubbs, W. (eds), *Councils and Ecclesiastical Documents Relating to Great Britian and Ireland*, vol. ii, part i (Oxford, 1873)

Hair, Greta-Mary and Knott, Betty I. (eds), *Vespers, Matins and Lauds for St Kentigern, Patron Saint of Glasgow* (Glasgow, forthcoming)

Hasselbach, Carl Friedrich Wilhelm, Kosegarten, Johann Gottfried Ludwig and von Medem, Baron Friedrich Ludwig Carl (eds), *Codex Pomeraniae diplomaticus oder Sammlung der die Geschichte Pommerus und Rugens* (Greifswald, 1843/1862)

Hastings, Adrian, *The Construction of Nationhood: Ethnicity, Religion, and Nationalism* (Cambridge, 1997)

Hearne, Thomas (ed.), Alfred of Beverley, *Annales, siue Historia de Gestis Regum Britannie* (Oxford, 1716)

Helle, Knut, 'The Norwegian kingdom: succession disputes and consolidation', in Knut Helle (ed.), *The Cambridge History of Scandinavia*, vol. i, *Prehistory to 1520* (Cambridge, 2003), 369–91

Hennessey, W. M. (ed.), *Chronicum Scotorum. A Chronicle of Irish Affairs from the Earliest Times to* A.D. *1135, with a supplement, containing the events from 1141 to 1150* (London, 1866)

Herbert, Máire, *Iona, Kells and Derry: the History and Historiography of the Monastic* familia *of Columba* (Oxford; repr. Dublin, 1996)

Herbert, Máire, '*Rí Éirenn, Rí Alban*: kingship and identity in the ninth and tenth centuries', in Taylor (ed.), *Kings, Clerics and Chroniclers*, 62–72

Herbert, Máire, 'Sea-divided Gaels? Constructing relationships between Irish and Scots *c.* 800–1169', in Brendan Smith (ed.), *Britain and Ireland 900–1300* (Cambridge, 1999), 87–97

Hewlett, Henry G. (ed.), *The Flowers of History by Roger de Wendover*, 3 vols, Rolls (London, 1886–9)

Higgitt, John, 'Bower's working text: Corpus MS. Decoration and illustration', in Watt (ed.), *Scotichronicon*, ix. 157–85

Howlett, David, 'The structure of *De Situ Albanie*', in Taylor (ed.), *Kings, Clerics and Chronicles*, 124–45

Howlett, Richard (ed.), *Chronicles of the Reigns of Stephen, Henry II, and Richard I*, vol. iii (London, 1886)

Hudson, Benjamin T., *Kings of Celtic Scotland* (Westport, CT, 1994)

Hudson, Benjamin T., *The Prophecy of Berchán: Irish and Scottish High-Kings of the Early Middle Ages* (Westport, Conn., 1996)

Hudson, Benjamin T., 'The Scottish Chronicle', *SHR* 77 (1998) 129–61

Hudson, John, 'Legal aspects of Scottish charter diplomatic in the twelfth century: a comparative approach', in Gillingham (ed.), *Anglo-Norman Studies XXV*, 121–38

Huneycutt, Lois L., 'The idea of the perfect princess: the Life of St Margaret in the reign of Matilda II (1100–1118)', in Marjorie Chibnall (ed.), *Anglo-Norman Studies XII Proceedings of the Battle Conference 1989* (Woodbridge, 1990), 81–97

Huneycutt, Lois L., *Matilda of Scotland* (Woodbridge, 2003)

Innes, Cosmo (ed.), *Facsimiles of the National Manuscripts of Scotland*, 3 parts (Southampton, 1867–71)

Innes, Cosmo (ed.), *Liber S. Marie de Calchou*, Bannatyne Club (Edinburgh, 1846)

Innes, Cosmo (ed.), *Liber Sancte Marie de Melros. Munimenta Vetustiora Monasterii Cisterciensis de Melros*, 2 vols, Bannatyne Club (Edinburgh, 1837)

Innes, Cosmo (ed.), *Liber S. Thome de Aberbrothoc*, Bannatyne Club, 2 vols (Edinburgh, 1848–56)

Innes, Cosmo (ed.), *Registrum Episcopatus Glasguensis*, Maitland and Bannatyne Clubs, 2 vols (Glasgow and Edinburgh, 1843)

Innes, Cosmo (ed.), *Registrum Episcopatus Moraviensis*, Bannatyne Club (Edinburgh, 1837)

Innes, Cosmo (ed.), *Registrum Monasterii de Passelet*, Maitland Club (Edinburgh, 1832)

Innes, Thomas, *A Critical Essay on the Ancient Inhabitants of the Northern Parts of Britain, or Scotland* (1729; repr. Edinburgh, 1879)

Insley, Charles, 'Fact and fiction in thirteenth-century Gwynedd: the Aberconwy charters', *Studia Celtica* 33 (1999) 235–50

Irvine, Susan (ed.), *The Anglo-Saxon Chronicle. A Collaborative Edition*, gen. ed. David Dumville and Simon Keynes, vol. vii, *MS E* (Cambridge, 2004)

Jackson, K. H., 'The Duan Albanach', *SHR* 36 (1957) 125–37

Jackson, Kenneth H., *The Gaelic Notes in the Book of Deer* (Cambridge, 1982)

Jackson, K. H., 'The Pictish language', in F. T. Wainwright (ed.), *The Problem of the Picts* (Edinburgh, 1955), 129–66

Jackson, K. H., 'The poem *A eolcha Alban uile*', *Celtica* 3 (1955) 149–67

Jackson, K. H., 'Two early Scottish names', *SHR* 33 (1954) 14–18

Jaffé, Ph., rev. Löwenfeld, Samuel, and others, *Regesta Pontificum Romanorum*, 2 vols (Leipzig, 1885–8)

James, Edward, *Britain in the First Millennium* (London, 2001)

James, M. R. (ed.), revised C. N. L. Brooke and R. A. B. Mynors, *Walter Map, De Nugis Curialium: Courtiers' Trifles* (Oxford, 1983)

John, Eric, *Orbis Britannie and Other Studies* (Leicester, 1966)

Johnson, Charles (ed.), revised M. Brett, C. N. L. Brooke and M. Winterbottom, *Hugh the Chanter, The History of the Church of York 1066–1127* (Oxford, 1990)

Johnston, Dafydd (ed.), *Iolo Goch, Poems* (Llandysul, 1993)

Jones, Dafydd Glyn, *Agoriad yr Oes* (Tal-y-bont, 2002)

Jones, Dafydd Glyn, *Gwlad y Brutiau, Darlith Goffa Henry Lewis 1990* (Abertawe, 1991)

Jones, Thomas (ed.), *Brenhinedd y Saesson or The Kings of the Saxons* (Cardiff, 1971)

Jones, Thomas (trans.), *Brut y Tywysogion or The Chronicle of the Princes. Peniarth MS. 20 Version* (Cardiff, 1952)

Jones, Thomas (ed.), *Brut y Tywysogion or The Chronicle of the Princes. Red Book of Hergest Version* (Cardiff, 1955)

Jones, Thomas (gol.), *Brut y Tywysogion Peniarth MS. 20* (Caerdydd, 1941)

Jones, Thomas, 'Historical writing in medieval Welsh', *Scottish Studies* 12 (1968) 15–27

Jones, Thomas, 'Teir ynys Prydein a'e their rac ynys', *BBCS* 17 (1958) 268–9

Kapelle, William E., *The Norman Conquest of the North. The Region and its Transformation 1000–1135* (London, 1979)

Ker, N. R., *Medieval Libraries of Great Britain. A List of Surviving Books*, 2nd edn (London, 1964)

Kirby, D. P., 'Strathclyde and Cumbria: a survey of historical development to 1092', *TCWAAS* 62 (1962) 71–94

Koch, John T. (ed.), *The Gododdin of Aneirin. Text and Context from Dark-Age North Britain* (Cardiff, 1997)

Koch, J. T., 'The loss of final syllables and loss of declension in Brittonic', *BBCS* 30 (1983) 201–30

Kroman, E. (ed.), *Danmarks Middelalderlige Annaler* (Copenhagen, 1980)

Labuda, Gerard, *Wielkie Pomorze w Dziejach Polski* [Greater Pomerania in Polish History] (Poznań, 1947)

Laing, David (ed.), *The Orygynale Cronykil of Scotland by Androw of Wyntoun*, 3 vols (Edinburgh, 1872–9)

Landon, Lionel (ed.), *The Cartæ Antiquæ, Rolls 1–10, Printed from the Original MSS*, Publications of the Pipe Roll Society vol. lv (new series, vol. xvii) (London, 1939)

Leckie, R. William jnr, *The Passage of Dominion: Geoffrey of Monmouth and the Periodization of Insular History in the Twelfth Century* (Toronto, 1981)

Legge, M. D., 'The inauguration of Alexander III', *PSAS* 80 (1948) 73–82

Lewis, Henry (gol.), *Brut Dingestow* (Llandysul, 1942)

Lindsay, William Alexander, Dowden, John and Thomson, J. Maitland (eds), *Charters, Bulls and Other Documents relating to the Abbey of Inchaffray*, Scottish History Society (Edinburgh, 1908)

Linehan, Peter, *The Spanish Church and the Papacy in the Thirteenth Century* (Cambridge, 1971)

Lomax, Derek W., *The Reconquest of Spain* (London, 1978)

Luard, H. R. (ed.), *Annales Monastici*, 4 vols (1864–9)

Lustig, R. I., 'The Treaty of Perth: a re-examination', *SHR* 58 (1979) 35–57

Mac Airt, S. and Mac Niocaill, G. (eds), *The Annals of Ulster (to A.D. 1131). Part I: Text and Translation* (Dublin, 1983)

Macalister, R. A. S. (ed.), *Lebor Gabála Érenn, The Book of the Taking of Ireland*, 5 vols, Irish Texts Society (London, 1938–56)

Mac Eoin, Gearóid, 'On the Irish legend of the origin of the Picts', *Studia Hibernica* 4 (1964) 138–54

Mackay, Angus and Ditchburn, David (eds), *Atlas of Medieval Europe* (London, 1997)

Macquarrie, Alan, *Medieval Scotland: Kingship and Nation* (Stroud, 2004)

MacQueen, Hector L., 'Canon law, custom, and legislation', in Oram (ed.), *The Reign of Alexander II, 1214–49*, 221–51

MacQueen, Hector L., '*Regiam Majestatem*, Scots law and national identity', *SHR* 74 (1995) 1–25

MacQueen, Hector L., 'Sheriffdoms', in *Atlas of Scottish History to 1707*, ed. Peter G. B. McNeill and Hector L. MacQueen (Edinburgh, 1996), 192–4

MacQueen, Hector L., 'Tears of a legal historian: Scottish feudalism and the *ius commune*', *Juridical Review* (2003) 1–28

MacQueen, John and MacQueen, Winifred (eds), *Scotichronicon by Walter Bower in Latin and English*, gen. ed. D. E. R. Watt, vol. i (Edinburgh, 1993)

MacQueen, John and MacQueen, Winifred (eds), *Scotichronicon by Walter Bower in Latin and English*, gen. ed. D. E. R. Watt, vol. ii (Aberdeen, 1989)

MacQueen, John, MacQueen, Winifred and Watt, D. E. R. (eds), *Scotichronicon by Walter Bower in Latin and English*, vol. iii (Edinburgh, 1995)

Matthew, Donald, *The Norman Kingdom of Sicily* (Cambridge, 1992)

McDonald, R. Andrew, *Outlaws of Medieval Scotland: Challenges to the Canmore Kings 1058–1266* (East Linton, 2003)

McFadden, George, 'The *Life of Waldef* and its author, Jocelin of Furness', *IR* 6 (1955) 5–13

McGurk, P. (ed.), *The Chronicle of John of Worcester*, vol. iii (Oxford, 1998)

Migne J.-P. (ed.), *Patrologiæ cursus completes . . . series Latina*, 221 vols (Paris, 1844–64)

Miller, Karen, 'Ecclesiastical Structural Reform in Ireland and Scotland in the Eleventh and Twelfth Centuries', unpublished Ph.D. dissertation (University of Aberdeen, 2004)

Miller, Molly, 'Geoffrey's early royal synchronisms', *BBCS* 28 (1978–80) 373–89

Miller, Molly, 'Matriliny by treaty: the Pictish foundation-legend', in Whitelock, McKitterick and Dumville (eds), *Ireland in Early Mediaeval Europe*, 133–61

Miller, Molly, 'The last century of Pictish succession', *Scottish Studies* 23 (1979) 39–67

Mortimer, Richard, *Angevin England 1154–1258* (Oxford, 1994)

Munch, P. A. (ed.), *Chronica Regum Manniæ et Insvlarvm* (Christiana, 1860)

Murphy, Denis (ed.), *The Annals of Clonmacnoise* (Dublin, 1896)

Murphy, Gerard, *Early Irish Metrics* (Dublin, 1961)

Musset, Lucien, 'Les évêques normands envisagés dans le cadre Européen (Xᵉ–XIIᵉ siècles)', in Pierre Bouet and François Neveux (eds), *Les évêques normands du XIᵉ siècle* (Caen, 1995), 53–65

Mynors R. A. B., with Thomson, R. M. and Winterbottom, M. (eds), *William of Malmesbury, Gesta Regvm Anglorvm*, vol. i (Oxford, 1998)

Nelson, Janet L., *Politics and Ritual in Early Medieval Europe* (London, 1986)

Nicholl, Donald, *Thurstan, Archbishop of York (1114–1140)* (York, 1964)

O'Brien, M. A. (ed.), *Corpus Genealogiarum Hiberniae*, vol. i, with intro. by J. V. Kelleher (Dublin, 1976)

Ó Corráin, Donncha, *Ireland before the Normans* (Dublin, 1972)

Ó Corráin, Donnchadh, 'Irish origin-legends and genealogy: recurrent aetiologies', in Tore Nyberg and others (eds), *History and Heroic Tale: a Symposium* (Odense, 1985), 51–96

Ó Fiaich, Tomás, 'The church of Armagh under lay control', *Seanchas Ardmhacha* 5 (1969) 75–127

Oram, R. D., 'David I and the conquest and colonisation of Moray', *Northern Scotland* 19 (1999) 1–19

Oram, Richard, *David I: the King who made Scotland* (Stroud, 2004)

Oram, Richard D., 'In obedience and reverence: Whithorn and York *c*.1128-*c*.1250', *IR* 42 (1991) 83–100

Oram, Richard D., 'Introduction: an overview of the reign of Alexander II', in Oram (ed.), *The Reign of Alexander II*, 1–47

Oram, Richard, *The Lordship of Galloway* (Edinburgh, 2000)

Oram, Richard D. (ed.), *The Reign of Alexander II, 1214–49* (Leiden, 2005)

Owen, D. R. R., *William the Lion 1143–1214: Kingship and Culture* (East Linton, 1997)

Paden, William D., jr., Tilde Sankovitch and Patricia H. Stäblein (eds), *The Poems of the Troubadour Bertran de Born* (Berkeley/Los Angeles, 1986)

Parsons, E. J. S., *The Map of Great Britain circa A.D. 1360 known as the Gough Map* (Oxford, 1958)

Penman, Michael, *David II, 1329–71* (East Linton, 2004)

Pennington, Kenneth, *Pope and Bishops: the Papal Monarchy in the Twelfth and Thirteenth Centuries* (Philadelphia, 1984)

Phythian-Adams, Charles, *Land of Cumbrians. A Study in British Provincial Origins, A.D. 400–1200* (Aldershot, 1996)

Potthast, Augustus, *Regesta Pontificum Romanorum*, 2 vols (Berlin, 1874–5)

Pryce, Huw, 'British or Welsh? National identity in twelfth-century Wales', *English Historical Review* 116 (2001) 775–801

Pryce, Huw (ed.), with the assistance of Charles Insley, *The Acts of Welsh Rulers 1120–1283* (Cardiff, 2005)

Raine, James (ed.), *The Historians of the Church of York and its Archbishops*, 3 vols, ii (London, 1886)

Raine, James (ed.), *The History and Antiquities of North Durham* (London, 1852)

RCAHMS *Stirlingshire*, vol. i (Edinburgh, 1963)

Reid, Norman H. (ed.), *Scotland in the Reign of Alexander III, 1249–1286* (Edinburgh, 1990)

Reuter, Timothy, 'A list of bishops attending the Council of Tours (1163)', *Annuarium Historiae Conciliorum* 8 (1976) 116–25

Reynolds, Susan, 'Fiefs and vassals in Scotland: a view from outside', *SHR* 82 (2003) 176–93

Reynolds, Susan, *Fiefs and Vassals: the Medieval Evidence Reinterpreted* (Oxford, 1994)

Reynolds, Susan, *Kingdoms and Communities in Western Europe 900–1300*, 2nd edn (Oxford, 1997)

Reynolds, Susan, 'Medieval *origines gentium* and the community of the realm', *History* 68 (1983) 375–90

Richter, Michael (ed.), *Canterbury Professions*, The Canterbury and York Society vol. 67 (1973)

Richter, M., 'Canterbury's primacy in Wales and the first stage of Bishop Bernard's opposition', *Journal of Ecclesiastical History* 22 (1971) 177–89

Richter, Michael, *Giraldus Cambrensis: the Growth of the Welsh Nation*, rev. edn (Aberystwyth, 1976)

Roberts, Brynley F. (ed.), *Brut y Brenhinedd Llanstephan MS. 1 Version* (Dublin, 1971)

Roberts, Brynley F., 'Geoffrey of Monmouth and Welsh historical tradition', *Nottingham Mediaeval Studies* 20 (1976) 29–40

Roberts, Brynley F., 'Testunau hanes Cymraeg canol', in Geraint Bowen (gol.), *Y Traddodiad Rhyddiaith yn yr Oesau Canol* (Llandysul, 1974), 274–302

Roberts, Brynley F., 'The Red Book of Hergest version of *Brut y Brenhinedd*', *Studia Celtica* 12/13 (1977/8) 147–86

Robertson, Joseph (ed.), *Concilia Scoticana*, 2 vols (Edinburgh, 1866)

Robertson, Joseph (ed.), *Liber Collegii Nostre Domini . . . Accedunt Munimenta Fratrum Predicatorum de Glasgu* (Edinburgh, 1846)

Robinson, I. S., *The Papacy 1073–1198: Continuity and Innovation* (Cambridge, 1990)

Ross, Alasdair, 'The Province of Moray c.1000–1350', 2 vols, unpublished Ph.D. dissertation (University of Aberdeen, 2003)

Royan, Nicola, 'Hector Boece and the question of Veremund', *IR* 52 (2001) 42–62

Royan, N. R., 'The *Scotorum Historia* of Hector Boece: a Study', unpublished D.Phil. dissertation (Oxford University, 1996)

Royan, Nicola with Broun, Dauvit, 'Versions of Scottish nationhood', in Ian Brown and others (eds), *Edinburgh History of Scottish Literature* (forthcoming)

Rule, Martin (ed.), *Eadmeri Historia Novorum in Anglia* (London, 1884)

Rymer, Thomas (ed.), *Foedera, Conventiones, Literæ et cujuscunque generis Acta Publica inter Reges Anglie et Alios. . .*, vol. i (London, 1704)

Sachsse, Carl, 'Tiara und Mitra der Päpste', *Zeitschrift für Kirchengeschichte* 35 (1914) 481–501

Sawyer, Peter H., *Anglo-Saxon Charters: an Annotated List and Bibliography*, web edition: http://www.trin.cam.ac.uk/charterwww/eSawyer.99/eSawyer2. html: The Electronic Sawyer: an on-line version of the revised edition of Sawyer's *Anglo-Saxon Charters* section one [S 1–1602] prepared under the auspices of the British Academy/Royal Historical Society Joint Committee on Anglo-Saxon Charters by S. E. Kelly and adapted for the WWW by S. M. Miller

Scott, J. G., 'The partition of a kingdom: Strathclyde 1092–1153', *TDGNHAS* 3rd series 72 (1997) 11–40

Scott, W. W., 'Fordun's description of the inauguration of Alexander II', *SHR* 50 (1971) 198–200

Scott, W. W., 'The March Laws reconsidered', in Grant and Stringer (eds), *Medieval Scotland. Crown, Lordship and Community*, 114–30

Scoular, James, *Handlist of the Acts of Alexander II, 1214–1249* (Edinburgh, 1959)

Scowcroft, R. Mark, '*Leabhar Gabhála*, part I: the growth of the text', *Ériu* 38 (1987) 79–140

Sellar, W. D. H., 'Hebridean sea kings: the successors of Somerled, 1164–1316', in Cowan and McDonald (eds), *Alba: Celtic Scotland in the Middle Ages*, 187–218

Shead, N. F., 'Jocelin, abbot of Melrose (1170–1174) and bishop of Glasgow (1175–1199)', *IR* 54 (2003) 1–22

Shead, N. F., review of Barrow, *David I and the Church of Glasgow*, in *SHR* 76 (1997) 264–5

Shead, N. F., 'The origins of the medieval diocese of Glasgow', *SHR* 48 (1969) 220–5

Shead, Norman F., Stevenson, Wendy B. and Watt, D. E. R. and others (eds), *Scotichronicon by Walter Bower in Latin and English*, vol. vi (Aberdeen, 1991)

Simms, Katharine, *From Kings to Warlords* (Woodbridge, 1987)

Simpson, Grant G., 'Kingship in minature: a seal of minority of Alexander III, 1249–1257', in Grant and Stringer (eds), *Medieval Scotland: Crown, Lordship and Community*, 131–9

Skene, Felix J. H. (trans.), *John of Fordun's Chronicle of the Scottish Nation*, ed. W. F. Skene (Edinburgh, 1872)

Skene, W. F., *Celtic Scotland*, vol. i, *History and Ethnology* (Edinburgh, 1876)

Skene, W. F. (ed.), *Chronicles of the Picts, Chronicles of the Scots* (Edinburgh, 1867), 378–90

Skene, W. F. (ed.), *Johannis de Fordun Chronica Gentis Scotorum* (Edinburgh, 1871)

Skene, W. F., 'The coronation stone', *PSAS* 8 (1869) 68–99

Smith, Anthony D., *The Nation in History. Historiographical Debates about Ethnicity and Nationalism* (Oxford, 2000)

Smith, Peter J., 'Early Irish historical verse: the evolution of a genre', in Próinséas Ní Chatháin and Michael Richter (eds), *Ireland and Europe in the Early Middle Ages: Texts and Transmission* (Dublin, 2002), 326–41

Smyth, Alfred P., *Warlords and Holy Men: Scotland* A.D. *80–1000* (London, 1984; repr. Edinburgh 1992)

Somerville, R., 'The Council of Clermont (1095) and Latin Christian society', *Archivum Historiae Pontificae* 12 (1974) 55–90

Somerville, R., *Pope Alexander III and the Council of Tours 1163* (Berkeley, California, 1977)

Somerville, Robert, *Scotia Pontificia. Papal Letters to Scotland before the Pontificate of Innocent III* (Oxford, 1982)

Southern, R. W., *St Anselm and his Biographer. A Study of Monastic Life and Thought 1059–c.1130* (Cambridge, 1966)

Stevenson, Joseph (ed.), *Chronica de Mailros* (Edinburgh, 1835)

Stevenson, Joseph (ed.), *Chronicon de Lanercost. MCCI–MCCCXLVI*, Bannatyne Club (Edinburgh, 1839)

Stevenson, J. H. and Wood, M., *Scottish Heraldic Seals*, 3 vols (Glasgow, 1940)

Stevenson, W. H. (ed.), *Asser's Life of King Alfred*, with article by Dorothy Whitelock (Oxford, 1959)

Stocking, Rachel L., *Bishops, Councils and Consensus in the Visigothic Kingdom, 589–633* (Ann Arbor, Michigan, 2000)

Stokes, Kaele, 'The delineation of a medieval "nation": *Brittones, Cymru* and *Wealas* before the Norman conquest', in Pamela O'Neill (ed.), *Nation and Federation in the Celtic World: Papers from the Fourth Australian Conference of Celtic Studies* (Sydney, 2003), 304–16

Stokes, Whitley, 'The Annals of Tigernach. Third fragment A.D. 489–766'. *Revue celtique* 17 (1896) 119–263; 'The Annals of Tigernach. The fourth fragment A.D. 973–A.D. 1088', *Revue celtique* 17 (1896) 337–420; 'The Annals of Tigernach. The continuation A.D. 1088–1178', *Revue celtique* 18 (1897) 9–59, 150–97, 268–303

Stokes, Whitley (ed.), *The Tripartite Life of Patrick with Other Documents Relating to that Saint*, vol. ii (London, 1887)

Stones, E. L. G. (ed.), *Anglo-Scottish Relations 1174–1328: Some Selected Documents*, 2nd edn (Oxford, 1970)

Strickland, Matthew, *War and Chivalry. The Conduct and Perception of War in England and Normandy 1066–1217* (Cambridge, 1996)

Stringer, Keith J., 'Acts of lordship: the records of the lords of Galloway to 1234', in T. Brotherstone and David Ditchburn (eds), *Freedom and Authority: Scotland c.1050–c.1650: Historical and Historiographical Essays presented to Grant G. Simpson* (East Linton, 2000), 203–34

Stringer, Keith J. (ed.), *Essays on the Nobility of Medieval Scotland* (Edinburgh, 1985)

Stringer, Keith J., 'Kingship, conflict and state-making in the reign of Alexander II: the war of 1215–17 and its context', in Oram (ed.), *The Reign of Alexander II, 1214–49*, 99–156

Stringer, Keith J., 'The charters of David, earl of Huntingdon and lord of Garioch: a study of Anglo-Scottish diplomatic', in Stringer (ed.), *Essays on the Nobility of Medieval Scotland*, 72–101

Stringer, Keith J., *The Reign of Stephen: Kingship, Warfare and Government in Twelfth-Century England* (London, 1993)

Stuart, John with Burnett, George (eds), *The Exchequer Rolls of Scotland*, vol. i, A.D. *1264–1359* (Edinburgh, 1878)

Stubbs, William (ed.), *Chronica Magistri Rogeri de Houedene*, 4 vols (London, 1868–71)

Stubbs, William (ed.), *Gesta Regis Henrici Secundis Benedicti Abbatis*, 2 vols (London, 1867)

Stubbs, William (ed.), *Radulfi de Diceto Opera Omnia*, 2 vols (London, 1876)

Sułkowska-Kuraś, I. and Kuraś, S. (eds), *Bullarium Poloniae* (Rzym, 1982)

Taylor, Simon (ed.), *Kings, Clerics and Chronicles in Scotland, 500–1297. Essays in honour of Marjorie Ogilvie Anderson on the occasion of her ninetieth birthday* (Dublin, 2000)

Taylor, Simon and Watt, D. E. R., with Scott, Brian (eds), *Scotichronicon by Walter Bower in Latin and English*, vol. v (Aberdeen, 1990)

Tellenbach, Gerd (trans. Timothy Reuter), *The Church in Western Europe from the Tenth to the Early Twelfth Century* (Cambridge, 1993)

Thompson, E. A., *The Goths in Spain* (Oxford, 1969)

Thomson, R. M., with collaboration of Michael Winterbottom, *William of Malmesbury Gesta Regum Anglorum, the History of the English Kings*, vol. ii, General Introduction and Commentary (Oxford, 1999)

Thomson, Thomas (ed.), *Liber Cartarum Prioratus Sancti Andree in Scotia. E registro ipso in archivis baronum de Panmure hodie asservato*, Bannatyne Club (Edinburgh, 1841)

Thomson, Thomas and Innes, Cosmo (eds), *Acts of the Parliament of Scotland*, vol. i, A.D. *MCXXIV–*A.D. *MCCCCXXIII* (Edinburgh, 1844)

Thorpe, Lewis (trans.), *Geoffrey of Monmouth. The History of the Kings of Britain* (Harmondsworth, 1966)

Thurlby, Malcolm, 'St Andrews Cathedral-Priory and the beginnings of Gothic architecture in northern Britain', in John Higgitt (ed.), *Medieval Art and Architecture in the Diocese of St Andrews* (Leeds, 1994), 47–60

Todd, J. M., *Syllabus of Scottish Cartularies: North Berwick* [1996]

Tyson, Diana B., 'Handlist of manuscripts containing the French prose Brut chronicle', *Scriptorium* 48 (1994) 333–44

Ullmann, Walter, *A Short History of the Papacy in the Middle Ages* (London, 1972)

Ullmann, Walter, *Law and Jurisdiction in the Middle Ages*, ed. George Garnett (London, 1988)

Ussher, James, *Britannicarum Ecclesiarum Antiquitates* (Dublin, 1639)

Van Hamel, A. G. (ed.), *Lebor Bretnach: The Irish Version of the Historia Britonum ascribed to Nennius* (Dublin, [1932])

Vaughn, Sally N., 'Eadmer's *Historia Novorum*: a reinterpretation', in R. Allen Brown (ed.), *Anglo-Norman Studies X: Proceedings of the Battle Conference, 1987* (Woodbridge, 1988), 259–89

Vigfusson, Gudbrand (ed.), *Icelandic Sagas*, vol. ii, *Hakonar Saga and a fragment of Magnus Saga, with appendices* (London, 1887)

Wade-Evans, A.W. (ed.), *Vitae Sanctorum Britanniae et Genelogiae* (Cardiff, 1944)

Walsh, P. G. and Kennedy, M. J. (trans.), *William of Newburgh, The History of English Affairs*, book I (Warminster, 1988)

Watson, George (ed.), *The Mar Lodge Translation of the History of Scotland*, vol. i (Edinburgh, 1946)

Watson, W. J., *The History of the Celtic Place-Names of Scotland* (Edinburgh, 1926)

Watt, D. E. R., *A Biographical Dictionary of Scottish Graduates to* A.D. *1410* (Oxford, 1977)

Watt, D. E. R., *Medieval Church Councils in Scotland* (Edinburgh, 2000)

Watt, D. E. R., 'The provincial council of the Scottish church, 1225–1472', in Grant and Stringer (eds), *Medieval Scotland: Crown, Lordship and Community*, 140–55

Watt, D. E. R. (ed), *Scotichronicon by Walter Bower in Latin and English*, vol. ix (Edinburgh, 1998)

Watt, D. E. R. and Murray, A. L., *Fasti Ecclesiae Scoticanae Medii Aevi Ad Annum 1638* (Edinburgh, 2003)

Watt, D. E. R. and Shead, N. F., *The Heads of Religious Houses in Scotland from the Twelfth to Sixteenth Centuries* (Edinburgh, 2001)

Webster, Bruce, 'John of Fordun and the independent identity of the Scots', in Alfred P. Smyth (ed), *Medieval Europeans: Studies in Ethnic Identity and National Perspectives in Medieval Europe* (Basingstoke, 1998), 85–102

Webster, Bruce, *Medieval Scotland. The Making of an Identity* (Basingstoke, 1997)

Weiss, Anzelm, *Biskupstwa bezpośrednio zależne od Stolicy Apostolskiej w średniowiecznej Europie* [The Exempted Bishoprics Subject to the Papacy in Medieval Europe] (Lublin, 1992)

Welander, Richard, Breeze, David J. and Clancy, Thomas Owen (eds), *The Stone of Destiny: Artefact and Icon* (Edinburgh, 2003)

Whitelock, Dorothy, Brett, Martin and Brooke, C. N. L. (eds), *Councils and Synods, with other documents relating to the English Church, 1:* A.D. *871–1204* (Oxford, 1981)

Whitelock, Dorothy, McKitterick, R. and Dumville, D. N. (eds), *Ireland in Early Mediaeval Europe. Studies in Memory of Kathleen Hughes* (Cambridge, 1982)

Williams, Ifor (gol.), *Armes Prydein o Lyfr Taliesin* (Caerdydd, 1955)

Williams, Ifor (ed.), *Armes Prydein. The Prophecy of Britain from the Book of Taliesin*, trans. R. Bromwich (Dublin, 1972)

Williams, Ifor (ed.), *Canu Aneirin*, 2nd edn (Caerdydd, 1961)

Wilson, C., 'The Cistercians as "missionaries of Gothic" in northern England', in C. Norton and D. Park (eds), *Cistercian Art and Architecture in the British Isles* (Cambridge, 1986), 86–116

Woolf, Alex, 'Birth of a nation', in Gordon Menzies (ed.), *In Search of Scotland* (Edinburgh, 2001), 24–45

Woolf, Alex, 'Dún Nechtain, Fortriu and the geography of the Picts', *SHR* 85 (2006) 182–201

Woolf, Alex, 'History or propaganda? Norway's claim to the Isles', unpublished lecture delivered at the Largs Viking festival in 2005

Woolf, Alex, 'The "Moray Question" and the kingship of Alba', *SHR* 79 (2000) 145–64

Wormald, Patrick, 'The emergence of the *regnum Scottorum*: a Carolingian hegemony?', in B. E. Crawford (ed.), *Scotland in Dark Age Britain* (St Andrews, 1996), 131–60

Wright, Neil (ed.), *The Historia Regum Britannie of Geoffrey of Monmouth*, vol. i, *Bern, Burgerbibliothek, MS. 568* (Cambridge, 1985)

Wright, Neil (ed.), *The Historia Regum Britannie of Geoffrey of Monmouth*, vol. ii, *The First Variant Version* (Cambridge, 1989)

Young, Simon, 'The bishops of the early medieval diocese of Britonia', *Cambrian Medieval Celtic Studies* 45 (Summer 2003) 1–19

Index